To dearest H[...]

with much love,

Jane — Neville

9/ix/89

WORDS
ABOUT
MUSIC

also by John Amis

AMISCELLANY

WORDS ABOUT MUSIC

An Anthology by

**John Amis
and
Michael Rose**

faber and faber

LONDON · BOSTON

First published in 1989
by Faber and Faber Limited
3 Queen Square London WC1N 3AU

Phototypeset by Wilmaset Birkenhead Wirral
Printed in Great Britain by
Richard Clay Ltd Bungay Suffolk

A CIP record for this book is available from the British Library
ISBN 0–571–14748–8

Contents

Taking therefore those precepts which being a childe I learned, and laying them together in order, I began to compare them with some other of the same kinde set downe by some late writers: But then was I in a worse case then before. For I found such diversitie betwixt them, that I knew not which part said truest, or whome I might best beleeve. Then was I forced to runne to the workes of manie, both strangers and Englishmen . . . But what labour it was to tomble, tosse, & search so manie bookes, & with what toyle & wearinesse I was enforced to compare the parts . . . I leave to thy discretion to consider: and none can fully understande, but he who hath had or shall have occasion to do the like . . .

THOMAS MORLEY *A Plaine and Easie Introduction to Practicall Musicke* 1597

Foreword

You could say that this anthology has been in preparation for a hundred years. For fifty years each of us has been immersed in music: playing it, listening to it, composing it, singing it, talking about it, writing about it – and reading about it. Reading biography, criticism, analysis, history, gossip, fiction, poetry: all the kinds of words about music that we could lay our hands on.

The original idea was a book of musical anecdotes. But the more we thought about that, the more difficult it seemed until, happily, the matter was decided for us by Norman Lebrecht, whose *Book of Musical Anecdotes* would certainly have put anything we produced straight out of the market. In any case, we had already begun to feel that there might be more satisfaction in something wider in scope, mainly drawn from our own memories (with the necessary prompting and verification): a sort of ragbag of prose, poetry, criticism, letters, humour and anything else that tumbled out of the residue of the years.

Of course, it's been done before – but perhaps not quite in this form, and not recently. Eric Blom's *Music Lover's Miscellany* is over fifty years old, and Arthur Jacobs's *Music Lover's Anthology* over forty. Others have been more specific in intention: Jacques Barzun's *Pleasures of Music* was essentially literary; Sam Morgenstern's *Composers on Music* limits itself as its title suggests; Hans Gal's *The Musician's World* concentrates entirely on letters. Our aim was more general: we deliberately cast the net as wide as possible, to include whatever we had enjoyed or been struck by for no better reason than that we had enjoyed or been struck by it, and were guided by no worthier purpose than a wish to share good things with other people.

Above all, it is a completely random selection. And that really is where our difficulties began: what sort of shape to give the random. Chronological? Not interesting enough – all those early mifspellings in one bunch, constant arguments about which came before what, modern stuff all together at the end. Alphabetical? Dull. Categorical? Better, except that it could be tedious to get, say, all the criticism in one fell swoop and, given the variousness of the material we wanted to include, it might often be difficult to decide on one category rather than another. All the same, variety seemed to be the clue, and the idea emerged of a sort of snake form, in which the pieces simply led on through categories which act, however, as general signposts to the reader and do not unduly fetter the authors.

Of course, there were problems: the snake tended to coil round on itself and pass by the same place twice. Is Liszt playing the piano a portrait or a performer? Or Ailred of Rievaulx a churchman or a critic? And where would you put the following note, which John Christie printed on the front of the 1935 Glyndebourne programme:

> Patrons are earnestly requested not to flash TORCHES during the Performances. It is aggravating to the rest of the audience but intolerable to the Artists. It is much worse than 'walking behind the bowler's arm' at cricket.

In the end, some pieces resisting classification, or at least organization, were included in a final section as a sort of ragbag within a ragbag. As a result, although we realize that this is a book for dipping into rather than for continuous reading, we hope that there is generally some sense of leading the reader on, and when there isn't – well, that the change of key is an acceptable one.

We have derived inspiration (and pinched a few ideas) from fellow anthologists like Frank Muir and John Julius Norwich, and many other friends and readers have helped to identify vague memories. We thank them all, and we hope that they, and you, will enjoy meandering through the result as much as we have enjoyed chopping it up and piecing it together on our kitchen tables.

JOHN AMIS, MICHAEL ROSE

Editors' Note

Minimal source information is given at the end of each extract – enough to lead the curious reader to the full details given in the main source list at the end of the book. The dates at the end of each extract are generally those of the publication from which it is taken. However, where they *precede* the title they refer to the date of the incident quoted.

Music is the eye of the ear

THOMAS DRAXE 1616

Music is a secret and unconscious mathematical problem of the soul

GOTTFRIED WILHELM VON LEIBNIZ 1714

Music is that which cannot be said but upon which it is impossible to be silent

ANON. attributed to Victor Hugo

[Music] is a method of employing the mind, without the labour of thinking at all, and with some applause from a man's self

SAMUEL JOHNSON quoted by Boswell 1785

Musick is the thing of the world that I love most

SAMUEL PEPYS *Diary* 30 July 1666

The Nature of Music

In all the twenty volumes of the latest edition of Grove's *Dictionary of Music and Musicians* (as Charles Rosen pointed out in his review of the *New Grove* in the *New York Review of Books*) there is no entry for 'Music'. Perhaps with reason: attempts to define music have invariably raised twice the number of questions that they have answered, and bear about as much relation to a Beethoven symphony as a lobster quadrille. Vaughan Williams's 'Music's a rum go!' is fine because VW was fine, but it gets us no further than Santayana's 'Music is essentially useless, as life is' – though it must be admitted it's a good deal less depressing. Shakespeare, being a poet, got round the problem very cleverly:

> Preposterous ass! that never read so far
> To know the cause why music was ordained!

But the first English music critic met it head on:

And grant that a man read all ye books of musick that ever were wrote, I shall not allow that musick is or can be understood out of them, no more than the tast of meats out of cookish receipt books.

And one has to say that, of the two, one's sympathies are with Roger North.

Nor is the purpose of music, or its effect, any easier to pin down. We all know that it soothes a savage breast, and Bacon tells us that, generally, it 'feedeth the disposition of spirit which it findeth' which is probably true but isn't necessarily a recommendation. Jane Austen considered it 'a very innocent diversion, and perfectly compatible with the profession of a clergyman', but then Jeremy Collier, only a little over a century earlier, felt so differently that it is hard to believe that they are talking about the same subject:

Musick is almost as dangerous as Gunpowder; and it may be requires looking after no less than the *Press* or the *Mint*. 'Tis possible a publick Regulation might not be amiss.

It doesn't help the Galway fan to be told by Theophrastus that 'the sound of the flute will cure epilepsy, and a sciatic gout' – nor a promenader listening to Mahler Eight that 'Musick helps not the tooth-ach' (George Herbert).

Is Auden's summing up, in the end, the only one that can't be questioned:

'Music can be made anywhere, is invisible, and does not smell'?*

It is a subject on which there is little unanimity.

*Yet, see page 207.

Now, what is music? This question occupied me for hours before I fell asleep last night. Music is a strange thing. I would almost say it is a miracle. For it stands halfway between thought and phenomenon, between spirit and matter, a sort of nebulous mediator, like and unlike each of the things it mediates – spirit that requires manifestation in time, and matter that can do without space.

We do not know what music is. But what good music is we know well enough; and even better, we know what music is bad. For of the latter our ears receive a larger quantity. Musical criticism must accordingly base itself on experience, not on *a priori* judgments; it must classify musical compositions only by their similarities, and take as standard only the impression that they create upon the majority.

Nothing is more futile than theorizing about music. No doubt there are laws, mathematically strict laws, but these laws are not music; they are only its conditions – just as the art of drawing and the theory of colours, or even the brush and palette, are not painting, but only its necessary means. The essence of music is revelation; it does not admit of exact reckoning, and the true criticism of music remains an empirical art.

HEINRICH HEINE *Letters on the French Stage* 1837

Though this is not in Hesiod,
Music was stolen from a God:

Not fire but notes the primal giver
Paid for with helpings of his liver

And virtuosi of the earth
Outsang the Gods who gave them birth.

When Orpheus plays we meet Apollo,
When there's theology to swallow

We set it to music, our greatest art,
One that's both intellect *and* heart,

There war and peace alike depict us
(Drums and trumpets in the Benedictus) –

It sang beneath the Grecian boat,
It kept Pythagoras afloat,

It suffered poets, critics, chat
And will no doubt survive Darmstadt;

This brandy of the damned of course*
To some is just a bottled sauce,

Its treasons, spoils and stratagems
Aleatory as women's hems

Yet beauty who indulged the swan
At death completes her with a song

And Paradise till we are there
Is in these measured lengths of air.

PETER PORTER 'Poems for Music' 1969

*See page 144.

I used to be much more fascinated by the pleasures of sound than the pleasures of smell. I was enthralled by them, but you broke my bonds and set me free. I admit that I still find some enjoyment in the music of hymns, which are alive with your praises, when I hear them sung by well-trained, melodious voices. But I do not enjoy it so much that I cannot tear myself away. I can leave it when I wish. But if I am not to turn a deaf ear to music, which is the setting for the words which give it life, I must allow it a position of some honour in my heart, and I find it difficult to assign it to its proper place. For sometimes I feel that I treat it with more honour than it deserves. I realize that when they are sung these sacred words stir my mind to greater religious fervour and kindle in me a more ardent flame of piety than they would if they were not sung; and I also know that there are particular modes in song and in the voice, corresponding to my various emotions and able to stimulate them because of some mysterious relationship between the two. But I ought not to allow my mind to be paralysed by the gratification of my senses, which often leads it astray. For the senses are not content to take second place. Simply because I allow them their due, as adjuncts to reason, they attempt to take precedence and forge ahead of it, with the result that I sometimes sin in this way but am not aware of it until later.

Sometimes, too, from over-anxiety to avoid this particular trap I make the mistake of being too strict . . . But when I remember the tears that I shed on hearing the songs of the Church in the early days, soon after I had recovered my faith, and when I realize that nowadays it is not the singing that moves me but the meaning of the words when they are sung in a clear voice to the most appropriate tune, I again acknowledge the great value of this practice. So I waver between the danger that lies in gratifying the senses and the benefits which, as I know from experience, can accrue from singing. Without committing myself to an irrevocable opinion, I am inclined to approve of the custom of singing in church, in order that by indulging the ears weaker spirits may be inspired with feelings of devotion. Yet when I find the singing itself more moving than the truth which it conveys, I confess that this is a grievous sin, and at those times I would prefer not to hear the singer.

This, then, is my present state. Let those of my readers whose hearts are filled with charity, from which good actions spring, weep with me and weep for me. Those who feel no charity in themselves will not be moved by my words. But I beg you, O Lord my God, to look upon me and listen to me. Have pity on me and heal me, for you see that I have become a problem to myself, and this is the ailment from which I suffer.

ST AUGUSTINE *Confessions c.* 400

St Augustine's view is a profoundly personal one, and strictly Christian at that. The principle of Harmony as the foundation of the Universe is very much older, and originates with Pythagoras who,

having ascertained that the pitch of notes depends on the rapidity of vibrations, and also that the planets move at different rates of motion, concluded that the planets must make sounds in their motion according to their different rates; and that, as all things in nature are harmoniously made, the different sounds must harmonize; whence the old theory of the 'harmony of the spheres'.

Brewer's Dictionary of Phrase and Fable 1870

It is proportion that beautifies every thing, this whole Universe consists of it, and Musicke is measured by it.

ORLANDO GIBBONS *The First Set of Madrigals* 1612

For I shall enter in a large sea of the praise of Musicke, and call to rehearsall how much it hath alwaies beene renowmed among them of olde time, and counted a holy matter: and how it hath beene the opinion of most wise Philosophers, that the worlde is made of musike, and the heavens in their moving make a melodie, and our soule is framed after the verie same sort and therefore lifteth up it selfe, and (as it were) reviveth the vertues and force of it selfe with Musicke. . . .

Doe ye not then deprive our Courtier of Musicke, which doth not onely make sweete the mindes of men, but also many times wilde beastes tame: and who so savoureth it not, a man may assuredly thinke him not to be well in his wits.

Behold I pray you what force it hath, that in times past allured a fish to suffer a man to ride upon it through the tempestuous sea.

We may see it used in the holy temples, to render laud and thankes unto God, and it is a credible matter that it is acceptable unto him, and that he hath given it unto us for a most sweete lightning of our travailes and vexations.

So that many times the boysterous labours in the fields, in the heat of the sun, beguile their paine with rude and carterly singing.

With this the unmannerly countrie woman, that ariseth before day out of her sleepe to spinne and carde, defendeth her selfe and maketh her labour pleasant.

This is the most sweete pastime after raine, winde and tempest, unto the miserable marriners.

With this doe the verie Pilgrimes comfort themselves in their troublesome and long voyages. And oftentimes prisoners, in adversitie, fetters and in stockes.

In like manner for a greater proofe, that the tunablenesse of musick (though it be but rude) is a verie great refreshing of all worldlye paines and griefes, a man woulde judge that nature hath taught it unto nurses for a speciall remedie to the continuall waylings of sucking babes, which at the sound of their voice fall into a quiet and sweete sleepe, forgetting the teares that are so proper to them, and given us of nature in that age, for a gesse of the rest of our life to come.

BALDASSARE CASTIGLIONE *The Book of the Courtier* 1561

> *Water* and *Air* he for the *Tenor* chose,
> *Earth* made the *Base*, the *Treble Flame* arose,
> To th'active *Moon* a quick brisk stroke he gave,
> To *Saturns string* a touch more soft and grave.
> The *motions Strait*, and *Round*, and *Swift*, and *Slow*,
> And *Short* and *Long*, were mixt and woven so,
> Did in such artful *Figures* smoothly fall,
> As made this decent measur'd *Dance* of *All*.
> And this is *Musick*.

ABRAHAM COWLEY 'Davideis' 1656

Music is what unifies

SEU-MA-TSEN 145–87 BC quoted by Stravinsky in *The Poetics of Music*

It is my temper, and I like it the better, to affect all harmony; and sure there is musick even in the beauty, and the silent note which *Cupid* strikes, far sweeter than the sound of an Instrument. For there is a Musick where ever there is a Harmony, order or proportion; and thus far we may maintain the Musick of the Spheres: for those well ordered motions and regular paces, though they give no sound unto the Ear, yet to the understanding they strike a note most full of harmony. Whatsoever is harmonically composed, delights in harmony; which makes me much distrust the symmetry of those heads which declaim against all Church-Musick. For my self, not only from my obedience, but my particular genius, I do embrace it: for even that vulgar and Tavern-Musick, which makes one man merry, another mad, strikes in me a deep fit of Devotion, and a profound contemplation of the first Composer; there is something in it of Divinity more than the Ear discovers: it is an Hieroglyphical and shadowed Lesson of the whole world, and Creatures of God, such a melody to the Ear, as the whole world well understood, would afford the understanding. In brief, it is a sensible fit of that harmony, which intellectually sounds in the Ears of God.

SIR THOMAS BROWNE *Religio Medici* 1643

From Harmony, from heav'nly Harmony
   This universal Frame began:
  When Nature underneath a heap
    Of jarring Atomes lay;
  And could not heave her Head,
The tuneful Voice was heard from high
   'Arise, ye more than dead!'
Then cold, and hot, and moist, and dry,
In order to their Stations leap,
   And MUSICK's pow'r obey.
From Harmony, from heavenly Harmony
   This universal Frame began:
   From Harmony to Harmony
Through all the Compass of the Notes it ran,
The Diapason closing full in Man. . . .

GRAND CHORUS

As from the pow'r of Sacred Lays
  The Spheres began to move,
And sung the great Creator's praise
  To all the blest above;
So when the last and dreadful Hour
This crumbling Pageant shall devour,
The TRUMPET shall be heard on high,
The dead shall live, the living die,
And MUSICK shall untune the Sky!

JOHN DRYDEN 'A Song for St Cecilia's Day' 22 November 1687

Later ages modified all this into a more acceptably romantic form (for nothing could, actually, be much *more* romantic than the music of the spheres). Here is a view from the father of German Romanticism: writer, music critic, composer and conductor – and, posthumously, the hero of Offenbach's last opera – E. T. A. Hoffmann was a source of inspiration to many nineteenth-century composers. (His fictional Kapellmeister Kreisler was the source of one of Schumann's most personal piano works.)

Our realm is not of this world. Where could we find, like the painters and sculptors, models of our art in nature? Sound is everywhere, but tones – that is, melodies speaking the higher language of the world of spirits – rest only in the breast of man . . . The musician – that is, he who develops music to clear, distinct consciousness – is everywhere surrounded by melody and harmony. It is not an empty simile and not an allegory when musicians say that colors, scents, and beams appear to them as tones, and that musicians are aware of their intermingling as in a wonderful concert. In the same sense in which . . . hearing is a seeing from within, so the musician may call seeing a hearing from within . . . Thus the sudden inspirations of musicians and the formation of melodies within the soul would be the conscious apperception and understanding of the secret music of nature as the principle of life and its activities. The sounds of nature, the rushing of wind, the bubbling of springs, and so on, are first of all sustained chords to the musician, and later melodies with the accompaniment of harmonies.

E. T. A. HOFFMANN Kreisleriana 1814

A greater Romantic tackled it like this:

Which of the two powers, love or music, is able to lift man to the sublimest heights? It is a great question, but it seems to me that one might answer it thus: love cannot express the idea of music, while music may give an idea of love. Why separate the one from the other? They are the two wings of the soul.

HECTOR BERLIOZ Memoirs 1870

History doesn't tell us whether Berlioz's copious reading extended to St Thomas Aquinas, but he might have appreciated the Angelic Doctor's definition of music:

The exaltation of the mind derived from things eternal bursting forth in sound.

The poets have always been great propounders of the 'romantic' view of music, 'moody food of us that trade in love'

To Musick

Begin to charme, and as thou stroak'st mine eares
With thy enchantment, melt me into tears.
Then let thy active hand scu'd o're thy Lyre:
And make my spirits frantick with the fire.
That done, sink down into a silv'rie straine;
And make me smooth as Balme, and Oile againe.

ROBERT HERRICK *Hesperides* 1648

It is a view that has been encapsulated for ever by Shakespeare:

If music be the food of love, play on;
Give me excess of it, that, surfeiting,
The appetite may sicken, and so die. –
That strain again! – it had a dying fall:
O, it came o'er my ear like the sweet sound,
That breathes upon a bank of violets,
Stealing and giving odour! – Enough; no more;
'Tis not so sweet now as it was before . . .

Twelfth Night 1623

Though the best of all Shakespeare's 'musical' poetry has surely to be Lorenzo's speech in the last act of *The Merchant of Venice*: often quoted – too often quoted, perhaps – but we don't see how a book like this can be without it

How sweet the moonlight sleeps upon this bank!
Here will we sit, and let the sounds of music
Creep in our ears: soft stillness and the night
Becomes the touches of sweet harmony.
Sit, Jessica. Look, how the floor of heaven
Is thick inlaid with patines of bright gold:
There's not the smallest orb which thou behold'st
But in his motion like an angel sings,
Still quiring to the young-eyed cherubins, –
Such harmony is in immortal souls;
But whilst this muddy vesture of decay
Doth grossly close it in, we cannot hear it.
(*Enter* MUSICIANS.)
Come, ho, and wake Diana with a hymn!
With sweetest touches pierce your mistress' ear,
And draw her home with music.   (*Music plays.*)
JESSICA: I am never merry when I hear sweet music.
LORENZO: The reason is, your spirits are attentive:
For do but note a wild and wanton herd,
Or race of youthful and unhandled colts,
Fetching mad bounds, bellowing, and neighing loud,
Which is the hot condition of their blood;
If they but hear perchance a trumpet sound,
Or any air of music touch their ears,
You shall perceive them make a mutual stand,
Their savage eyes turn'd to a modest gaze
By the sweet power of music: therefore the poet
Did feign that Orpheus drew trees, stones, and floods;
Since naught so stockish, hard, and full of rage,
But music for the time doth change his nature.
The man that hath no music in himself,
Nor is not mov'd with concord of sweet sounds,
Is fit for treasons, stratagems, and spoils;
The motions of his spirit are dull as night,
And his affections dark as Erebus:
Let no such man be trusted. – Mark the music.

The Merchant of Venice 1600

Three hundred years on, the poetic preoccupation continues

To Music
(The property of Frau Hanna Wolff)

Music: breathing of statues. Perhaps:
stillness of pictures. You speech, where speeches
end. You time,
vertically poised on the courses of vanishing hearts.

Feelings for what? Oh, you transformation
of feelings into . . . audible landscape!
You stranger: Music. Space that's outgrown us,
heart-space. Innermost ours,
that, passing our limits, outsurges, –
holiest parting:
where what is within surrounds us
as practised horizon, as other
side of the air,
pure,
gigantic,
no longer lived in.

RAINER MARIA RILKE *Poems 1906 to 1926*

Back to prose for a twentieth-century statement from a writer, now unfashion-
able, perhaps, who helped to shape the musical sensibilities of a generation

. . . Art is a somewhat trivial mystery. It is a mystery because the
pleasure we indisputably get from a work of art cannot easily be
related to our biological needs. Especially is this the case with music. It
is difficult to understand why, in the struggle for existence, a peculiar
sensibility to certain sequences of non-natural sounds should ever
have been developed. And the mystery is trivial because nothing but
an accidental and non-essential appetite appears to be involved. On
the basis of this estimate of art the theory of 'the aesthetic emotion' has
been proposed. This theory supposes that amongst the emotions
proper to a human being is one particular emotion which is excited by
works of art or, more generally, by all 'manifestations of the beautiful',
and which is excited by nothing else. The emotion appears to be
capable of degrees, but also of a maximum. Some works of art are
better than others, but it is also possible for a work of art to be 'perfect'.
The perfect work of art excites the aesthetic emotion to its maximum.

The nearest analogy to this state would seem to be provided by the sexual orgasm. The classification of works of art proper on this theory, therefore, is the classification into perfect and imperfect, those that produce orgasm and those that do not. Amongst perfect works of art may be a symphony, a line of melody, an epic poem or a Serbian mat. The same value must naturally be attributed to all these works, since they are all completely successful in the function of a work of art, which is to excite the aesthetic emotion to its maximum. The objection to this theory is that it entirely fails to take into account the most important of our reactions to a work of art. It is not true that works of art excite in us one specific emotion, and works of art are not adequately classified as perfect and imperfect. The difference in our responses to a late quartet by Beethoven and an early quartet by Haydn, for instance, is not described by saying that a specific emotion is more or less excited. The one is not a more perfect form of the other. It may be replied that both compositions possess the quality of *beauty*, and that our only relevant reaction, from the point of view of aesthetic theory, is our reaction to this quality, a reaction which is susceptible of degrees, but which is always of the same kind. Such a reply derives all its plausibility merely from the poverty of language. Language, as an historical accident, is poor in names for subjective states, and consequently in names for the imputed properties of objects that produce those states. Even such words as love and hate, dealing with emotions to which mankind has always paid great attention, are merely portmanteau words. Within their meanings are not only differences of degree, but differences of kind. To conclude, because the word 'beauty' exists almost in isolation, that it refers to some definite quality of objects, or that it is descriptive of some one subjective state, is to mistake a deficiency in language for a key to truth.

J. W. N. SULLIVAN *Beethoven: his Spiritual Development* 1927

And now, an altogether more robust twentieth-century view from the New World. Virgil Thomson, probably most famous as a composer for his collaboration with Gertrude Stein in the opera *Four Saints in Three Acts*, was also a controversial and influential music critic. The following paragraphs come from an article on the Expressive Content of Music. Two more related articles will be found later in this book: together they are as clear-headed as anything we know from this century on the aesthetics of music

Expressivity in music is its power of communication. All the music that is any good says something . . . For the passive listener it may be sufficient that a Beethoven or Tchaikovsky symphony seems pregnant with meaning in general, the imprecision of that meaning being part, indeed, of its power. The interpreter can afford no such vagueness. He must make a guess at the music's specific meaning. Otherwise he has no test for determining tempos, rhythmic inflections, and climactic emphases beyond the notes and markings of the score. And these are never enough, musical notation being as inefficient as it is.

Nor can the composer avoid deciding about the character of his work. He may have created it in a fine fury or in a semi-euphoric state of automatism; but if he wants anybody to use his creation he has to provide some clues to its meaning. He must indicate the speed, the loudness, the kind of lilt he wants. If he wishes orchestral performance he must clothe his creation in unalterable colors and accents. No composer can orchestrate a piece without deciding on the expression that he wishes given to every phrase. A theme conceived for flute has quite another character when played in unison by thirty-two violins. Though both versions may appear in the same composition, only the composer can determine which appears first; and that determination involves a decision about the kind of feeling that he wishes his music to communicate, both as a whole and in detail.

Any performance is correctly called an interpretation. The creator creates and then adds, somewhat later, as many aids as he can think of toward a clear interpretation. The final, or public, interpreter thereupon translates the whole into sound, making his own decisions in every measure about the exact inflection that will best transmit what he esteems to be the composer's meaning. If he thinks the composer's specific indication requires violation in order to attain what he believes to be the work's larger sense, he makes that violation and takes responsibility for it before the musical world. He is right to do so, though he should not do so without reflection. The composer's specific indications are themselves not always a part of his original creation but rather one musician's message to another about it, a hint about how to secure in performance a convincing transmission of the

work's feeling content without destroying its emotional and intellectual continuity. The latter continuity, of course, is not an end in itself;
it is merely the composer's means of achieving, of not interrupting,
emotional continuity.

. . . The creation of meaning by the use of musical lines and
formulas, familiar and unfamiliar, is the art of composition. Nothing
else is involved. Classical and structural observances have no other
value, nor has novelty. In themselves they are without significance,
and no employment of them in composition has any value beyond the
immediate context. Nor are they capable of acquiring any value in a
specific context other than that which the meaning of the whole lends
to them for that occasion.

A composer's education involves acquiring a vocabulary of useful
turns and formulas. The employment of these and the invention of
others in musical works with a unique expressive content is the
operation that determines a composer's quality as an artist. The
techniques of musical composition are many. The purpose of it is
single. That purpose is the creation of art. Art is an infinitive
multiplicity of unique objects known as works of art. Their materials
are limited; consequently they bear to one another a great material
resemblance. Where they differ notably is in meaning, or expressivity;
and their survival is determined by that meaning, provided their
structure is not just too stupid to bear repetition. If that meaning is
unique it can be remembered, and reconsulting it is a pleasure. If not,
remembering it is scarcely worth while. The original of which it is an
imitation is good enough for us.

. . . The determination of music's sense is the privilege, in any
group, of the leader, though there is always some communal contribution to this. The definition of this expressivity in words is the hardest
thing any critic or historian ever has to undertake, though the
recognition of its presence, and even the degree of its presence, in any
composer's work is not difficult. Most musicians and most habitual
concertgoers are able to recognize strength when they encounter it.
Sometimes their recognition takes the form of anger, sometimes not.
But it is likely to be fairly dependable. Audiences are easily bored by
nonentities but not easily angered by them. Active audience resistance
to anything is one of the clinical signs by which we recognize quality.
Because it is not the direction of an audience reaction that is critical;
what is significant is its strength. And that strength, believe me, is not
determined by the mere sounds made. It comes from the character,

the individuality of the music's expressive content. Audiences have always complained about what they call dissonance in one piece, while accepting the exact same tonal relations in another. Here is proof aplenty, if more is needed, that what they really mind is something in the expression.

13 April 1947

VIRGIL THOMSON *The Art of Judging Music* 1948

Bartók said:

I cannot conceive of music that expresses absolutely nothing.

It is a view that goes back at least as far as Chopin . . .

Nothing is more odious than music without hidden meaning.

. . . and was given a particular slant by Richard Strauss:

There is no such thing as Abstract Music; there is good music and bad music. If it is good, it means something – and then it is Programme Music.

The classic statement of the opposite point of view is Eduard Hanslick's, in *The Beautiful in Music*:

Music means itself.

But by far its strongest apologist in the twentieth century was Igor Stravinsky. 'A nose is not manufactured; a nose just *is*. Thus, too, my art.'

For I consider that music is, by its very nature, essentially powerless to *express* anything at all, whether a feeling, an attitude of mind, a psychological mood, a phenomenon of nature, etc. . . . *Expression* has never been an inherent property of music. That is by no means the purpose of its existence. If, as is nearly always the case, music appears to express something, this is only an illusion and not a reality. It is simply an additional attribute which, by tacit and inveterate agreement, we have lent it, thrust upon it, as a label, a convention – in short, an aspect [which], unconsciously or by force of habit, we have come to confuse with its essential being.

Music is the sole domain in which man realizes the present. By the imperfection of his nature, man is doomed to submit to the passage of time – to its categories of past and future – without ever being able to give substance, and therefore stability, to the category of the present.

The phenomenon of music is given to us with the sole purpose of establishing an order in things, including, and particularly, the coordination between *man* and *time*. To be put into practice, its indispensable and single requirement is construction. Construction once completed, this order has been attained, and there is nothing more to be said. It would be futile to look for, or expect anything else from it. It is precisely this construction, this achieved order, which produces in us a unique emotion having nothing in common with our ordinary sensations and our responses to the impressions of daily life. One could not better define the sensation produced by music than by saying that it is identical with that evoked by contemplation of the interplay of architectural forms. Goethe thoroughly understood that when he called architecture petrified music.

IGOR STRAVINSKY *An Autobiography* 1936

As a matter of fact, Goethe was far too cautious to commit himself so recklessly. What Eckermann reports him as saying is:

I have found among my papers a sheet . . . in which I call architecture frozen music.

And while we are about it we might as well have the full version of another famous pronouncement on the subject:

All art constantly aspires towards the condition of music, because, in its ideal, consummate moments, the end is not distinct from the means, the form from the matter, the subject from the expression; and to it, therefore, to the condition of its perfect moments, all the arts may be supposed constantly to tend and aspire.

WALTER PATER *The Renaissance* 1873

The common man's point of view comes, as so often and so lucidly, from the American composer, Aaron Copland

The whole problem can be stated quite simply by asking, 'Is there a meaning to music?' My answer to that would be, 'Yes'. And 'Can you state in so many words what the meaning is?' My answer to that would be, 'No'.

AARON COPLAND What to Listen for in Music 1939

An attempt to resolve the dilemma in terms that take account of the listener's intimate, personal reaction, comes not from a musician but from an architect in a letter to his cellist future wife

Take any work of art – which kind is unimportant – that you feel to be such from your own experience, and ask yourself why this is so. Then you will see that it is neither the content – that is, the idea – nor the external technique of the treatment which gives you this opinion of it. It is only the amount of all-embracing rhythm – that is to say, the way in which every single element, each note with the next, each line, each spot of colour, blends with, and is subordinated to, the whole – which coaxes from us this lofty impression, this silent and reverent sympathy . . . A work of art can only be created when its author is completely filled with the vision, when he is no longer himself but the mouthpiece and hand of the spirit which drives him. Purity and greatness of form in art correspond to pure greatness in the artist's spiritual passion, in his creative power . . . Bach knows no chaos. With him is structure, planning, proportions – architectonic order. And even the most sublime architecture must still have the ordering sense and the bonds afforded by the artist's conscious purpose, the idea. There is no point at which reason can be completely subordinated by feeling.

ERIC MENDELSOHN Letters of an Architect 1967

In the end, this brings us back very close to Stravinsky – and indeed, to Stravinsky's own personal experience as a composer

I was guided by no system whatever in *Le Sacre du printemps*. When I think of the other composers of that time who interest me – Berg, who is synthetic (in the best sense), Webern, who is analytic, and Schoenberg, who is both – how much more *theoretical* their music seems than *Le Sacre*; and these composers were supported by a great tradition,

whereas very little immediate tradition lies behind *Le Sacre du printemps*. I had only my ear to help me. I heard and I wrote what I heard. I
am the vessel through which *Le Sacre* passed.

IGOR STRAVINSKY *Expositions and Developments* 1962

Not all Stravinsky's predecessors, perhaps, would have regarded themselves
as vessels. Nevertheless, for most of us the composer is where music starts, so
here are a few random glimpses that happen to have stuck in our minds.

Composers

It seemed obvious to begin with Bach, but neither of us could remember any very graphic description of him as he was in life except that old story about the herrings – and Forkel wags a finger at that sort of thing

The many, sometimes adventurous pranks that are related of him, as, for example, that occasionally, dressed like a poor village school-master, he went into a church and begged the organist to let him play a chorale, in order to enjoy the general astonishment excited in the persons present by his performance, or to hear the organist say he must be either Bach or the devil, are mere fables. He himself would never hear of anything of the sort. Besides, he had too much respect for the art thus to make a plaything of it. An artist like Bach does not throw himself away.

J. N. FORKEL Life of Bach 1802

Perhaps the most vivid glimpse of this most unremittingly musical of all musicians is a purely musical one, seated at the organ in the Thomasschule,

not only . . . singing with one voice and playing his own parts, but watching over everything and bringing back to the rhythm and the beat, out of thirty or even forty musicians, the one with a nod, another by tapping with his foot, the third with a warning finger, giving the right note to one from the top of his voice, to another from the bottom, and to a third from the middle of it – all alone, in the midst of the greatest din made by all the participants, and, although he is executing the most difficult parts himself, noticing at once whenever and wherever a mistake occurs, holding everyone together, taking pre-cautions everywhere, and repairing any unsteadiness, full of rhythm in every part of his body – this one man taking in all these harmonies with his keen ear and emitting with his voice alone the tone of all the voices.

JOHANN MATTHIAS GESNER 1738

With Handel it is a different story – or rather, a whole lot of different stories.
One or two of those that we have remembered with particular pleasure will be
found later in this book; meanwhile, here is the classic description of Handel
as Dr Burney remembered him

The figure of Handel was large and he was somewhat corpulent and
unwieldy in his motions; but his countenance, which I remember as
perfectly as that of any man I saw but yesterday, was full of fire and
dignity, and such as impressed ideas of superiority and genius. He
was impetuous, rough and peremptory in his manners and conversation, but totally devoid of ill-nature or malevolence; indeed, there
was an original humor and pleasantry in his most lively sallies of anger
or impatience, which, with his broken English, were extremely risible.
His natural propensity to wit and humor and happy manner of
relating common occurrences in an uncommon way enabled him to
throw persons and things into very ridiculous attitudes. Had he been
as great a master of the English language as Swift, his *bons mots* would
have been as frequent and somewhat of the same kind.

Handel, with many virtues, was addicted to no vice that was
injurious to society. Nature, indeed, required a great supply of
sustenance to support so huge a mass, and he was rather epicurean in
the choice of it; but this seems to have been the only appetite he
allowed himself to gratify.

The late Mr. Brown, leader of His Majesty's band, used to tell me
several stories of Handel's love of good cheer, liquid and solid, as well
as of his impatience. Of the former he gave an instance which was
accidentally discovered at his own house in Brook Street, where
Brown, in the oratorio season, among other principal performers, was
at dinner. During the repast Handel often cried out – 'Oh – I have de
taught'; when the company, unwilling that, out of civility to them, the
public should be robbed of anything so valuable as his musical ideas,
begged he would retire and write them down; with which request,
however, he so frequently complied that at last one of the most
suspicious had the ill-bred curiosity to peep through the keyhole into
the adjoining room; where he perceived that *dese taughts* were only
bestowed on a fresh hamper of Burgundy, which, as was afterward
discovered, he had received as a present from his friend, the late Lord
Radnor, while his company was regaled with more generous and
spirited port.

CHARLES BURNEY . . . *in Commemoration of Handel* 1785

There is always something larger than life about Handel, and here is a powerful instance recorded by Mainwaring, his first biographer. In April 1737 the composer had been partially paralysed by a stroke

In this melancholic state, it was in vain for him to think of any fresh projects for retrieving his affairs. His first concern was how to repair his constitution. But tho' he had the best advice, and tho' the necessity of following it was urged to him in the most friendly manner, it was with the utmost difficulty that he was prevailed on to do what was proper, when it was any way disagreeable. For this reason it was thought best for him to have recourse to the vapor-baths of Aix la Chapelle, over which he sat near three times as long as hath ever been the practice. Whoever knows any thing of the nature of those baths, will, from this instance, form some idea of his surprising constitution. His sweats were profuse beyond what can well be imagined. His cure, from the manner as well as from the quickness, with which it was wrought, passed with the Nuns for a miracle. When, but a few hours from the time of his quitting the bath, they heard him at the organ in the principal church as well as convent, playing in a manner so much beyond any they had ever been used to, such a conclusion in such persons was natural enough. Tho' his business was so soon dispatched, and his cure judged to be thoroughly effected, he thought it prudent to continue at Aix about six weeks, which is the shortest period usually allotted for bad cases.

JOHN MAINWARING *Life of Handel* 1760

A rather less tempestuous eighteenth-century composer, Francesco Durante, was the subject of a touching account by Frank Walker in the 5th edition of Grove's *Dictionary of Music and Musicians*

Durante seems to have been a man of the utmost integrity, at once simple and profoundly wise. We find him, in the records of the Neapolitan conservatories, called in to compose the differences between his more excitable colleagues. He was a great 'character', who bore the sorrows and afflictions of his life with a positively super-human equanimity. He was thrice married, the first time to a real termagant, who lived for nothing but the lottery. She tried his patience sorely, and he was obliged to work extremely hard, and even deprive himself of sleep at nights, in order to earn enough to enable her to satisfy her passion for gambling. He returned one day from a journey to find she had sold all his compositions in manuscript. He sat down calmly and began the long task of writing them out again from

memory. At length death relieved him of this encumbrance, and after
a short time he married his servant, a young girl *di bellissime forme*,
whom he tenderly loved and with whom he was very happy until she
too died. The strength of character he exhibited at this time was
extraordinary. He arranged and himself conducted the music for the
funeral ceremony in his home, after which, with tranquil resignation
and without displaying any sign of emotion, he lifted the body from
the bed where it lay and deposited it in the coffin. Then, having
embraced his dead wife for the last time, he covered her face with a
piece of fine linen and himself nailed down the coffin lid. He later
married another of his servants.

His simple manners were endearing. Always rather slovenly
dressed, he nevertheless attached considerable importance to his wig,
on which a good deal of his dignity depended. In order not to
disarrange it he would carry his three-cornered hat under his right arm
and would often be seen to stop in the streets and purchase some fresh
figs, which he put in his hat and consumed on the way to the
conservatory. He seems to have been fond of fruit: Paisiello records
that he died 'of a diarrhoea brought on by a feed of melons'.

Grove's Dictionary 1954

Sad that the march of musicology should have banished so human and stylish
a piece of writing from the latest edition of Grove

Haydn must be one of the most sympathetic characters in the history of music.
This description, written by a friend in the year after the composer's death,
mentions one of his less attractive physical characteristics – which of course
never appeared in portraits of the time, especially if the painter wanted to get
his fee. (Photographs are less kind, and sixty years later there was no hiding
Liszt's warts.)

In stature, Haydn was of less than middle size. It is a commonly-noted
feature of small people of both sexes that the lower half of the body
does not seem big enough for the upper: but with Haydn this was
more than usually noticeable, owing to his adherence to the old
fashion of wearing trousers which came up only to the hips instead of
as far as the chest. His features were regular; his gaze was expressive
and ardent, but none the less temperate, kindly, and attractive. When
he was disposed to seriousness his features and his gaze combined to
give the impression of great dignity; but at other times his countenance during conversation was cheerful and smiling – though I never

heard him laugh aloud. His bone-structure was of average strength, but his muscles were weak. His hooked nose was swollen beyond its natural size through a polypus, which caused him much suffering; and, like his other features, it was covered with pock-marks. Indeed, the seams of these pock-marks so disfigured his nose as to give each nostril a different shape.

Haydn considered himself ugly, and mentioned to me a certain Count and his wife who simply could not stand him, 'because I was too ugly for them'. This presumed ugliness was not by any means in his figure, but solely in the brownness of his colour and in the way his skin had been eaten away by small-pox . . .

Love of order seemed to be an innate quality of his, as was industriousness. It was the first thing one noticed about him, together with that neatness which he applied both to his person and to his household. For instance he would never receive visits unless he had got properly dressed beforehand. Even if a friend paid a surprise visit, he would try to give himself at least time enough to put on his wig . . .

Cheerfulness and jollity were a part of his make-up, and he had a musical wit which was subtle in spite of making a broad appeal, and which was original to the highest degree. As has been recognized, it was this humour that gave rise to Haydn's leaning toward jesting in music.

He had a grateful heart, and those who did him kindness in his youth he repaid, by stealth, as soon as he was able. Nor did he forget his numerous relatives.

Honour and fame were the two considerations that influenced him most; but I know of no case in which he was corrupted through this seeking after honour – his natural modesty prevented that.

He never found fault with other composers.

In his young days he must have been very susceptible to the charms of the fair sex. I have not talked about it in these pages, but I may say that I noticed even in his old age how attentive he was to women, and how he used to make a habit of kissing their hands.

A. C. DIES *Joseph Haydn* 1810

The Irish tenor, Michael Kelly, who spent four years in Vienna between 1783 and 1787, has left us some of the most vivid pictures we have of Mozart. He first met him at a concert of Kozeluch's, after which he found himself seated at supper between Mozart and his wife

After supper the young branches of our host had a dance, and Mozart joined them. Madame Mozart told me, that great as his genius was, he was an enthusiast in dancing, and often said that his taste lay in that art, rather than in music.

He was a remarkably small man, very thin and pale, with a profusion of fine fair hair, of which he was rather vain. He gave me a cordial invitation to his house, of which I availed myself, and passed a great part of my time there. He always received me with kindness and hospitality. – He was remarkably fond of punch, of which beverage I have seen him take copious drafts. He was also fond of billiards, and had an excellent billiard table in his house. Many and many a game have I played with him, but always came off second best. He gave Sunday concerts, at which I never was missing. He was kind-hearted, and always ready to oblige, but so very particular, when he played, that, if the slightest noise were made, he instantly left off. He one day made me sit down to the piano, and gave credit to my first master, who had taught me to place my hand well on the instrument . . .

Kelly was the first Don Curzio (see pages 251–2) and has left a memorable glimpse of Mozart at a rehearsal for the first performance of *Figaro*

All the original performers had the advantage of the instruction of the composer, who transfused into their minds his inspired meaning. I never shall forget his little animated countenance, when lighted up with the glowing rays of genius; – it is as impossible to describe it, as it would be to paint sun-beams.

I called on him one evening, he said to me, 'I have just finished a little duet for my opera, you shall hear it.' He sat down to the piano, and we sang it. I was delighted with it, and the musical world will give me credit for being so, when I mention the duet, sung by Count Almaviva and Susan, 'Crudel perchè finora farmi languire così.' A more delicious morceau never was penned by man, and it has often been a source of pleasure to me, to have been the first who heard it, and to have sung it with its greatly gifted composer. I remember at the first rehearsal of the full band, Mozart was on the stage with his crimson pelisse and gold-laced cocked hat, giving the time of the music to the orchestra. Figaro's song, 'Non più andrai, farfallone amoroso', Bennuci gave, with the greatest animation, and power of voice.

I was standing close to Mozart, who, *sotto voce*, was repeating, Bravo! Bravo! Bennuci; and when Bennuci came to the fine passage 'Cherubino, alla vittoria, alla gloria militar,' which he gave out with stentorian lungs, the effect was electricity itself, for the whole of the performers on the stage, and those in the orchestra, as if actuated by one feeling of delight, vociferated Bravo! Bravo! Maestro. Viva, viva, grande Mozart. Those in the orchestra I thought would never have ceased applauding, by beating the bows of their violins against the music desks. The little man acknowledged, by repeated obeisances, his thanks for the distinguished mark of enthusiastic applause bestowed upon him . . .

MICHAEL KELLY 1785–6 *Reminiscences*

Most accounts of Beethoven are too reverent or too idealized to be accepted at their face value. Here are a couple, one near the beginning, the other towards the end of his career, that seem to escape both perils. The first is by Carl Czerny, who was only ten years old when he was taken to meet the composer – then just turned thirty

It was a winter's day when my father, Krumpholz, and I took our way from Leopoldstadt (where we still were living) to Vienna proper, to a street called *der tiefe Graben* (the Deep Ditch), and climbed endless flights to the fifth and sixth story, where a rather untidy-looking servant announced us to Beethoven and then admitted us. The room presented a most disorderly appearance; papers and articles of clothing were scattered everywhere, some trunks, bare walls, hardly a chair, save the wobbly one at the Walter fortepiano (then the best), and in this room was gathered a company of from six to eight persons, among them the two Wranitzky brothers, Süssmayr, Schuppanzigh and one of Beethoven's brothers.

Beethoven himself wore a morning-coat of some long-haired, dark-gray material and trousers to match, so that he at once recalled to me the picture in Campe's 'Robinson Crusoe', which I was reading at the time. His coal-black hair, cut *à la Titus*, bristled shaggily about his head. His beard – he had not been shaved for several days – made the lower part of his already brown face still darker. I also noticed with that visual quickness peculiar to children that he had cotton which seemed to have been steeped in a yellowish liquid, in his ears.

At that time, however, he did not give the least evidence of deafness. I was at once told to play something, and since I did not dare begin with one of his own compositions, played Mozart's great C major Concerto, the one beginning with chords. Beethoven soon gave me his attention, drew near my chair, and in those places where I had only accompanying passages played the orchestral melody with me, using his left hand. His hands were overgrown with hair and his fingers, especially at the ends, were very broad. The satisfaction he expressed gave me the courage to play his *Sonata pathétique*, which had just appeared, and, finally, his 'Adelaïde', which my father sang in his very passable tenor. When he had ended Beethoven turned to him and said: 'The boy has talent. I will teach him myself and accept him as my pupil. Send him to me several times a week . . .'

CARL CZERNY *c.* 1800 *Memoirs*

The other comes from within about two years of Beethoven's death

His papers and possessions were dusty and lay about higgledy-piggledy; and in spite of the dazzling whiteness and cleanliness of his linen and his repeated bodily ablutions, his clothes remained unbrushed. This inordinate bathing may, perhaps, in some past time have been the primary incidental cause and origin of his deafness – perhaps owing to a rheumatic inflammation – rather than his 'predisposition for intestinal complaints,' as so often has been taken for granted. He always had been in the habit, after he had sat for a long time at the table composing and this had heated his head, of rushing to the wash-stand, pouring pitchersful of water over his overheated head and, after having thus cooled himself off and only slightly dried himself, of returning to his work or, even, in the meanwhile, hastening out into the open for a brief walk. All this was done in the greatest hurry, so that he might not be snatched out of his imaginative flight. How little he thought at the time of the need of drying his thick hair, sopping wet, is proven by the fact that, without his noticing it, the water he had poured over his head would flood the floor in quantities, leak through it, and appear on the room-ceiling of the lodgers living beneath him. This, on occasion, led to annoyances on the part of his fellow-lodgers, the janitor and, finally, the owner of the house, and even was responsible for his being given notice.

He liked to have us invite him to dinner, and would often send us a portion of fish, if he had ordered some bought for himself in the market; for fish was one of his favorite dishes and when he himself liked something he liked to share it with his friends.

Beethoven's outward appearance, owing to that indifference to dress peculiar to him, made him uncommonly noticeable on the street. Usually lost in thought and grumbling to himself, he not infrequently gesticulated with his arms as well when walking alone. When he was in company, he spoke very loudly and with great animation and, since whoever accompanied him was obliged to write down his answers in the conversation note-book, the promenade was interrupted by frequent stops, something which in itself attracted attention and was made more conspicuous by the replies he made in pantomime . . .

The felt hat then worn, upon Beethoven's homecoming, though it might be dripping wet with rain, after merely giving it a slight shake (a habit he always observed in our house, without concern for what was in the room) he would clap on the very top of the hat-rack. In consequence it had lost its even top and was vaulted in an upward bulge. Brushed infrequently or not at all, before and after it had rained, and then again allowed to grow dusty, the hat acquired a permanently matted appearance. In addition he wore it, so far as possible, back from his face in order to leave his forehead free; while on either side his gray, disordered hair, as Rellstab so characteristically says, 'neither curly nor stiff, but a mixture of all,' stood out. Owing to his putting on and wearing his hat away from his face and back on his head, which he held high, the hat's hinder brim came into collision with his coat-collar, which at that time shot up high against the back of the head; and gave the brim in question a cocked-up shape; while the coat-collar itself, from its continual contact with the hat brim, seemed to have been worn away. The two unbuttoned coat-fronts, especially those of the blue frock coat with brass buttons, turned outward and flapped about his arms, especially when he was walking against the wind. In the same manner the two long ends of the white neckerchief knotted about his broad, turned-down shirt-collar streamed out. The double lorgnette which he wore because of his near-sightedness, hung loosely down. His coat-tails, however, were rather heavily burdened; for in addition to his watch, which often hung out on the one side, in the pocket of the other he had a folded quarto note-book, anything but thin, besides a conversation note-book in octavo format and a thick carpenter's pencil, for communication with friends and acquaintances whom he might meet; and also, in earlier days, while it still aided him, his ear-trumpet. The weight of the note-books considerably extended the length of the coat-tail containing them and, in addition, the pocket itself because of its own frequent pulling out and that of the note-books, hung down visibly on the same side, turned outward.

GERHARD VON BREUNING *c.* 1825 *Aus dem Schwarzspanierhause*

A vivid impression of the domestic problems that plagued the last years of Beethoven's life can be had from the notes he made about housekeeping matters on the blank pages of the calendar

Diaries of this kind have been found completely covering the years 1819, 1820 and 1823. The first (1819) contains only the following notations:

On January 31 gave the housekeeper notice.
February 15 the kitchen-maid entered upon her duties.
March 8 the kitchen-maid gave two weeks' notice.
March 22 the new housekeeper entered upon her duties.
May 12 arrived in Mödling.
Miser et pauper sum (I am poor and wretched).
May 14 the waitress entered service at 6 *Gulden* monthly.
July 20 gave the housekeeper notice.

The year 1820, however, already is richer in notices regarding household affairs, for example:

On April 17 the kitchen-maid entered upon her duties.
April 19 a poor day (i.e., nothing palatable apppeared on the Master's table because owing to his protracted sitting over his work the food already had been over-cooked or altogether spoiled).
May 16 gave notice to the kitchen-maid.
May 19 the kitchen-maid left.
May 30 the woman entered upon her duties.
July 1 the kitchen-maid entered upon her duties.
July 28 the kitchen-maid ran away in the evening.
July 30 the woman from Lower Döbling entered service. During the four evil days, August 10, 11, 12 and 13, I ate in Lerchenfeld (a suburb outside the city limits).
August 28 the woman's month up (i.e., she had only agreed to stay a month).
September 9 the girl entered service.
October 22 the girl left.
December 12 the kitchen-maid entered service.
December 18 the kitchen-maid gave notice.
December the new chamber-maid entered service.

ANTON SCHINDLER 1819–20 *Life of Beethoven*

Then there was Cherubini. Beethoven admired him, Berlioz pilloried him, and certainly he could be awfully dry. Does this anecdote suggest one of the reasons why?

How to keep one's umbrella has been presented to most people as a serious problem for a thoughtful mind. One of the best solutions propounded is due to Cherubini, and may be briefly summed up in a few words: 'Never lend your umbrella'. One day Cherubini was walking along a *boulevard* in Paris when it began to rain. A gentleman passing by in his carriage recognised the *maestro*, and alighting, begged that Cherubini would take the reins and drive home. The gentleman, who was going in a different direction, said, 'Will you, M. Cherubini, lend me your umbrella?' 'No; I never lend my umbrella,' was Cherubini's reply, as he drove off; and whatever we may think of his courtesy, there cannot be two opinions about his prudence.

F. J. CROWEST *Musicians' Wit* 1902

The delicately Victorian form of that anecdote recalls the way in which Mainwaring improves a famous Handel story. (And see also page 154.)

Having one day some words with Cuzzoni on her refusing to sing 'Falsa imagine' in *Ottone*; Oh! Madame, (said he) je sçais bien que Vous êtes une veritable Diablesse: mais je Vous ferai sçavoir, moi, que je suis Beelzebub le *Chéf* des Diables. With this he took her up by the waist, and, if she made any more words, swore that he would fling her out of the window.

It is to be noted, that this was formerly one of the methods of executing criminals in some parts of Germany; a process not unlike that of the Tarpeian rock, and probably derived from it.

JOHN MAINWARING *Life of Handel* 1760

Later generations have not always shared Beethoven's respect for Cherubini as a composer. Indeed, for many, his personality has been most sharply kept alive (if a little distorted) in the pages of Berlioz's *Memoirs*

The moment Cherubini took over the Conservatoire on the death of his predecessor, Perne, he determined to mark his accession by introducing revolutionary restrictions in the internal régime of the school, which had not been run on exactly puritan principles. In order that the two sexes should not mix except under the supervision of a teacher, he decreed that the men must use the door in the rue du Faubourg Poissonnière and the women the door in the rue Bergère, the two entrances being at opposite ends of the building.

One morning, knowing nothing of this moral edict, which had only just been promulgated, I proceeded to the Conservatoire and entered by the usual door in the rue Bergère – the *female* door. I was half-way to the library when a porter stopped me in the middle of the courtyard and tried to make me go back and return by the other entrance. I thought this so absurd that I sent the liveried Argus about his business and went on. The rogue, wishing to get in well with his new employer by showing that he could be just as strict, refused to admit defeat, and hurried off to report the matter to the director. I had been absorbed in *Alceste* for a quarter of an hour and had thought no more of the incident, when Cherubini, with my accuser behind him, stumped into the reading-room, his face more cadaverous and basilisk-eyed, his hair bristling more angrily, than ever. They made the rounds of the table, where several students were reading. The porter scrutinized each in turn, then came to a halt in front of me.

'That's him,' he said. Cherubini was so angry that for a moment he could not speak.

'Eh! Eh! So it is you,' he cried at last, with a strong Italian accent made more grotesque by his fury, 'it is you who come een by the door that I weel not 'ave you use?'

'Sir, I was not aware of the new regulation. Another time I will conform to it.'

'Anothair time! Anothair time! What – what – what are you doeeng 'ere?'

'As you see, sir, I am studying Gluck's scores.'

'And what – what – what are Gluck's scores to you? Where deed you get pairmission to come to the library?'

'Sir' (I was beginning to lose my self-possession), 'Gluck's scores are the finest examples of dramatic music I know and I need no one's permission to come here and study them. The Conservatoire library is open to the public from ten till three and I have the right to use it.'

'The – the – the right?'

'Yes, sir.'

'I weel not allow you to return.'

'I shall return none the less.'

'What – what – what ees your name?' he yelled, shaking with rage.

'Sir,' I answered, growing pale in my turn, 'my name will perhaps be familiar to you one day – but you will not have it now.'

'S-s-seize 'eem, Hottin,' he cried to the porter, 'I'll 'ave 'eem in preeson.'

Thereupon, to the stupefaction of the onlookers, the two of them, master and servant, began pursuing me round the table, knocking over stools and reading-desks in a vain attempt to catch me. In the end I made my escape, calling out with a laugh as I fled, 'You shan't have me or my name, and I shall soon be back here to study Gluck's scores.'

HECTOR BERLIOZ 1822 *Memoirs*

David Cairns's translation of the *Memoirs* is unquestionably the best now available, but for some of us (as for himself) our first memories of that wonderful book go back to the old Everyman edition, translated by Katharine Boult, mother of Sir Adrian, whose handling in English of Berlioz's impression of Cherubini's italianized French had a charm all of its own

My chief difficulty was the hall; it always is in Paris. For the only suitable one – the Conservatoire – I must have a permit from M. de Larochefoucauld and also the consent of Cherubini.

The first was easily obtained; not so the second.

At the first mention of my design Cherubini flew in a rage.

'Vant to gif a conchert?' he said, with his usual suavity.

'Yes, monsieur.'

'Must 'ave permission of Fine Arts Director first.'

'I have it.'

'M. de Larossefoucauld, 'e consent?'

'Yes, monsieur.'

'But me, I not consent. I vill oppose zat you get ze 'all.'

'But, monsieur, you can have no reasonable objection, since the hall is not engaged for the next fortnight.'

'But I tell you zat I vill not 'ave zat you gif zis conchert. Everyone is avay and no profit vill be to you.'

'I expect none. I merely wish to become known.'

'Zere is no necessity zat you become known. And zen for expense you vill want monee. Vhat 'ave you of monee?'

'Sufficient, monsieur.'

'A-a-ah! But vhat vill you make 'ear at zis conchert?'

'Two overtures, some excerpts from an opera and the *Death of Orpheus*.'

'Zat competition cantata? I vill not 'ave zat! She is bad – bad; she is impossible to play.'

'You say so, monsieur; I judge differently. That a bad pianist could not play it is no reason that a good orchestra should not.'

'Zen it is for insult of ze Académie zat you play zis?'

'No, monsieur; it is simply as an experiment. If, as is possible, the Academy was right in saying my score could not be played, then certainly the orchestra will not play it. If the Academy was wrong, people will only say that I made good use of its judgment and have corrected my score.'

'You can only 'ave your conchert on ze Sunday.'

'Very well, I will take Sunday.'

'But zose poor *employés* – ze doorkeepers – zey 'ave but ze Sunday for repose zem. Vould you take zeir only rest-day? Zey vill die – zose poor folks – zey vill die of fatigue.'

'On the contrary, monsieur. These poor folks are delighted at the chance of earning a few extra francs, and they will not thank you for depriving them of it.'

'I vill not 'ave it; I vill not! And I write to ze Director zat he vizdraw permission.'

'Most hearty thanks, monsieur, but M. de Larochefoucauld never breaks his word. I also shall write and retail our conversation exactly. Then he will be able to weigh the arguments on both sides.'

I did so, and was afterwards told by one of his secretaries that my dialogue-letter made the Director laugh till he cried. He was, above all, touched at Cherubini's tender consideration for those poor devils of *employés* whom I was going to kill with fatigue.

He replied, as any man blessed with commonsense would, repeating his authorisation and adding:

'You will kindly show this letter to M. Cherubini, who has already received the necessary *orders*.'

Of course I posted off to the Conservatoire and handed in my letter; Cherubini read it, turned pale, then yellow, and finally green, then handed it back without a word.

This was my first Roland for the Oliver he gave me in turning me out of the library. It was not to be my last.

HECTOR BERLIOZ 1828 Memoirs

I do not believe anyone could meet Berlioz without being struck with surprise at the utter originality and singularity of his features. His high brow, sharply cut over the deep-set eyes, his strongly aquiline hawk nose, the narrow, finely chiselled lips, the rather short chin, all crowned by an extraordinary abundance of light-brown curls whose fantastic waywardness yielded not even to the constraining iron of the hairdresser – once you had seen that head you could not forget it. And then the uncommon mobility of his face: the glance, one moment flashing, actually burning, and the next moment dull, lustreless, almost dying – the expression of his mouth, alternating between energy and withering contempt, between friendly smiling and scornful laughter! His figure was of middle size – slender but not elegant –

his bearing extremely careless. His speaking voice was rather weak but of course reflected the constant shifting of his emotions and his moods. His singing voice too was agreeable and had his excitement been less intense he could have brought out the full meaning and beauty of many of his own vocal compositions. But the overflowing emotion interfered with the listener's understanding of the music; if the performing artist wishes to move others, he must not be too deeply moved himself.

FERDINAND HILLER *Hector Berlioz* 1879

Heine is good on Berlioz too

Even the dullest minds were carried along by the force of the genius that is manifest in all the great master's works. Here is a wing-beat that reveals no ordinary songbird, it is a colossal nightingale, a lark as big as an eagle, such as must have existed in the primeval world. Yes, for me Berlioz's music in general has something primeval about it, if not something antediluvian; it reminds me of extinct species of animals, of fabulous kingdoms and fabulous sins, of sky-storming impossibilities, of the hanging gardens of Semiramis, of Nineveh, of the wonderful constructions of Mizraim. . . . His bent is the fantastic, not connected with feeling but with sentimentality; he bears a strong resemblance to Callot, Gozzi, and Hoffmann. To this, even his outward appearance points. It is a shame that he let his huge, antediluvian locks, the bristling hairs that rose from his forehead like a forest from a steep cliff, be cut. So, six years ago, I saw him for the first time; and so he will forever remain in my memory. It was at the Conservatory of Music; a great symphony of his was being performed, a fantastic night-piece, which is only occasionally lighted up by the sentimental white of a woman's dress, which now and again flutters through it, or by a sulphur-yellow flash of irony. The best thing in it is a Witches' Sabbath, where the Devil says Mass and Catholic church music is parodied with the utmost in ghastly and bloody ludicrousness.

HEINRICH HEINE *Letters on the French Stage* 1837

Heine also spoke of Mendelssohn's fine 'lizard-ear', and of 'Donizetti's fertility – not inferior to a rabbit's', and he left a vivid portrait of Spontini:

a terrifying, wasted figure with pale face and coal-black hair . . . whose appearance always foretells musical disasters, torn by envy and hatred of Meyerbeer; a withered spectre . . . offended by the life of the living.

HEINRICH HEINE *Letters on the French Stage* 1837

Nothing could be a greater contrast to Spontini than his compatriot Rossini, everybody's favourite guest in the ideal dinner party game. Here the young Mendelssohn describes one of Rossini's rare visits to Germany

. . . Early yesterday I went to see [Hiller], and whom should I find sitting there but Rossini, as large as life, in his best and most amiable mood. I really know few men who can be so amusing and witty as he, when he chooses; he kept us laughing incessantly the whole time. I promised that the St. Cecilia Association should sing for him the B minor Mass, and some other things of Sebastian Bach's. It will be quite too charming to see Rossini obliged to admire Sebastian Bach; he thinks, however, 'different countries, different customs', and is resolved to howl with the wolves. He says he is enchanted with Germany, and when he once gets the list of wines at the Rhine Hotel in the evening, the waiter is obliged to show him his room, or he could never manage to find it. He relates the most laughable and amusing things about Paris and all the musicians there, as well as of himself and his compositions, and entertains the most profound respect for all the men of the present day, – so that you might really believe him, if you had no eyes to see his sarcastic face. Intellect, and animation, and wit, sparkle in all his features and in every word, and those who do not consider him a genius, ought to hear him expatiating in this way, and they would change their opinion.

FELIX MENDELSSOHN Letter 14 July 1836

In person Mendelssohn was short, not so much as 5 ft. 7 ins. high, and slight of build; in figure lithe, and very light and mercurial. His look was dark and very Jewish; the face unusually mobile, and ever varying in expression, full of brightness and animation and with a most unmistakable look of genius. After a breakfast with him at B. Hawes's, Thackeray told Richard Doyle (who told the writer), 'His face is the most beautiful face I ever saw, like what I imagine Our Saviour's to have been.' His complexion was fresh, and showed a great deal of colour. His hair was black, thick and abundant, with a natural wave in it, and was kept back from his forehead, which was high and much developed. By the end of his life, however, it showed a good deal of grey, and he began to be bald. His mouth was unusually delicate and expressive, and had generally a pleasant smile at the corners. His whiskers were very dark, and his closely shaven chin and upper lip were blue from the strength of his beard. His teeth were beautifully white and regular; but the most striking part of his face were the large dark-brown eyes. When at rest he often lowered the eyelids as if he were slightly short-sighted – which indeed he was; but when animated they gave an extraordinary brightness and fire to his face and 'were as expressive a pair of eyes as were ever set in a human being's head'. They could also sparkle with rage like a tiger's. When he was playing extempore, or was otherwise much excited, they would dilate and become nearly twice their ordinary size, the brown pupil changing to a vivid black.

His laugh was hearty and frequent; and when specially amused he would quite double up with laughter and shake his hand from the wrist to emphasize his merriment. He would nod his head violently when thoroughly agreeing, so that the hair came down over his face. In fact his body was almost as expressive as his face. His hands were small, with taper fingers. On the keys they behaved almost like 'living and intelligent creatures, full of life and sympathy'. His action at the piano was as free from affectation as everything else that he did, and very interesting. At times, especially at the organ, he leant very much over the keys, as if watching for the strains which came out of his finger-tips. He sometimes swayed from side to side, but usually his whole performance was quiet and absorbed. . . .

Not less remarkable than his face was his way and manner. It is described by those who knew him as peculiarly winning and engaging; to those whom he loved, coaxing. The slight lisp or drawl which remained with him to the end made the endearing words and pet expressions, which he was fond of applying to his own immediate circle, all the more affectionate. . . .

We may mention the neatness and order with which he registered and kept everything. The forty-four volumes of MS music, in which he did for himself what Mozart's father so carefully did for his son, have been mentioned. But it is not generally known that he preserved all letters that he received, and stuck them with his own hands into books. Twenty-three large thick green volumes exist, containing apparently all the letters and memorandums, business and private, which he received from 29 October 1821, to 29 October 1847, together with the drafts of his oratorio books, and of the long official communications which, during his latter life, cost him so many unprofitable hours. . . . He had a passion for neatness, and a repugnance to anything clumsy. Perhaps this may have been one reason why he appears so rarely to have sketched his music. He made it in his head, and had settled the minutest points there before he put it on paper, thus avoiding the litter and disorder of a sketch.

SIR GEORGE GROVE in *Grove's Dictionary* 1878

When Mendelssohn visited Italy in 1831, he had an introduction to the wife of the military commandant at Milan, Dorothea von Ertmann, the intimate friend of Beethoven. Her name is immortalized on the title page of the Sonata, Op. 101. Mendelssohn was invited to her house, and had played her own special sonata and a great deal of Beethoven besides, when a little modest Austrian official who had been sitting in the corner came up and said timidly, 'Ach! Wollen sie nicht etwas vom lieben Vater spielen?' (Won't you play something of my dear father's?)

Mendelssohn: 'Who was your father?'

Austrian Official: 'Ach! Mozart.'

'And', said Mendelssohn, 'I *did* play Mozart for him, and for the rest of the evening.' This little touch of filial jealousy moved him deeply.

C. V. STANFORD *Unwritten Diary* 1914

Heine again, on Donizetti's last days

While his magical tunes bring joy to the world, while everyone sings them and trills them, he himself sits, a terrible picture of insanity, in a lunatic asylum near Paris. Until some time ago, he had kept a childish consciousness of clothes: he had to be attired carefully every day in full dress, his tail coat decorated with all his orders; and so, from early in the morning until late at night, he sat motionless, his hat in his hand. But even that is over with; he now recognizes no one. Such is the destiny of man.

HEINRICH HEINE *Letters on the French Stage* 1837

Chopin, by his mistress

He was a man of the world in the truest sense; not of the official big world, to wit, but of an intimate type of company, a drawing-room of twenty persons, at the time when the crowd has dispersed and only those of the closest circle have stayed, grouped round the great artist, set upon drawing from him the purest of his inspiration by gentle persuasion. There only would he pour out all his talent, all his genius. On such an occasion he was able to plunge his audience into profound bliss or into an abyss of sadness, as his music gripped one's soul with a sharp pang of hopeless despair, especially when he improvised. And then, to remove that impression and that memory of suffering from the others as well as from himself, he would turn surreptitiously to a mirror, arrange his hair and his cravat and instantly become a phlegmatic Englishman, or a sentimental, ridiculous lady, an imperti-nent old beggar, a sordid Jew. They were always sorry types, however comic; yet perfectly realized and so delicately reproduced that one could not help admiring them over and over again.

All those sublime, charming or eccentric features made him the life and soul of a chosen circle, and one would literally fight for his company. The nobility of his character, his indifference to mercenary rewards, his pride and justifiable self-esteem as a sworn enemy of everything pertaining to vanity, bad taste or insolent advertisement, the charm of his conversation, the exquisite delicacy of his manner made him an interesting and delightful companion.

To snatch him away from such flattery, to convert him to a simple, regular, studious way of living – him who had been brought up, as it were, on the knees of princesses – meant to deprive him of all that constituted his life; a fictitious kind of life, to be sure. Because, back home at night, like a woman who takes off her make-up, he would put off all his animation and seductive power and submit to a night of fever and insomnia. . . .

Chopin, this extreme type of artist, was not made for a long life in this world. He was consumed by a dream of an ideal that was never tempered by any philosophical tolerance or by any charity with respect to the practical limitations of the world of everyday. Never willing to compromise with human nature, he did not acknowledge reality. Intolerant of the smallest blemish, he had an unlimited enthusiasm for any semblance of light, which his imagination would try to see as a sun. . . . He was a compound of magnificent inconsistencies such as only God can create and which have their own particular logic. He was modest on principle and gentle by habit, but imperious by instinct and full of a legitimate pride of which he was hardly conscious. From this came sufferings for which he was unable to account, as they had no concrete source.

GEORGE SAND *Histoire de ma vie* 1854

Chopin, by Liszt

In his relations with others, he seemed interested only in *their* affairs; he kept the conversation within the sphere of their personalities lest it should turn to that of his own. If he devoted little of his time to mixing with others, yet that little was given without reserve. But as for his own feelings – his dreams and his hopes, his desires and triumphs, whether his thin white hand could strike a harmony between the brazen strings of life and the golden chords of his art – such questions no one ever asked him, because in his presence they were not allowed the leisure to think of them. . . .

His personality as a whole was harmonious and seemed not to call for any commentary to explain it. His blue eyes suggested a man of the spirit rather than a dreamer; he had a gentle, delicate smile which never turned to bitterness. His delicately pale complexion was very attractive; he had silky fair hair, a bent and expressively firm nose, and frail limbs, and was of only moderate stature. His gestures, which were many, were all graceful; his voice was rather lifeless, and often seemed stifled. His bearing was so distinctive and his manners so suggestive of the highest breeding that one could not help treating him like a prince. Everything about him brought to mind the convolvulus, which on its incredibly thin stalk supports a cup of heavenly colour, but which is of so fragile a tissue that the slightest touch destroys it.

When in company he displayed an evenness of temper usually associated with those whom nothing can worry since nothing interests them. It was normal for him to be gay; his caustic spirit was quick to seize on the ridiculous, and he caught it well below the superficial level at which it is commonly appreciated. In mimicry he displayed a lively and tireless sense of drollery. He would amuse himself by giving comic improvisations in which the musical formulas and tricks of particular virtuosos would be reproduced; he would imitate their gestures and movements, and impersonate their faces, with such skill that he seemed to express in a flash the personality of his victim. In doing so he worked such strange changes on his own features that they became unrecognizable. But even when imitating the boorish and grotesque he never lost his own grace; not even the grimaces he put on could make him appear gross. His fun, in fact, was the more piquant because he never took it beyond the limits of good taste. . . .

Anyone arriving [in Paris] from Poland was made welcome by him. Whether they had letters of recommendation or not, they were received with open arms as though they were members of his own family. To people from his own country (even though they were often quite unknown to him) he permitted a privilege which the rest of us never had – the right to disturb his routine. He put himself out for them, took them round, went twenty times over to the same place in order to show them the sights of Paris – and all this without any sign of being bored at having to stroll around and act the cicerone. Then he would take these dear fellow-countrymen (of whose very existence he had been unaware the previous evening) to dinner. He would prevent them from digging into their small change; he would lend them money – and moreover, one could see he was happy in doing these things: it was a real pleasure for him to speak his own language and to be in the company of his countrymen, for at their side he seemed to breathe again his native air. One saw how often he was content to listen to their tales of woe, to soothe their griefs, to soften their tearful memories, and to console them in the depths of their sorrow by holding out to them infinite promises and eloquent hopes. . . .

Chopin wrote regularly to his own people – but only to them. One of his most curious characteristics was to refrain from all exchange of letters, all sending of notes; one might have thought he had taken a vow never to write except to his own countrymen. It was strange to see the expedients to which he would resort in order to avoid writing even a few lines. Often he would prefer to go right across Paris from one end to the other in order to notify his refusal of an invitation to dinner, or in order to pass on some trifling information, rather than spare himself this trouble by means of a little sheet of paper. His very signature remained unknown to most of his friends.

FRANZ LISZT Chopin 1852

And Liszt by Grieg

After playing the minuet I felt that if it were possible to get Liszt to play for me now was the time; he was visibly inspired. I asked him, and he shrugged his shoulders a little; but when I said that it could not be his intention that I should leave the South without having heard a single tone by him, he made a turn and then muttered, 'Very well, I'll play whatever you like, I'm not like that,' and forthwith he seized a score he had lately finished, a kind of funeral procession to the grave of Tasso, a supplement to his famous symphonic poem for the orchestra, *Tasso: Lamento e Trionfo.*

Then he sat down and put the keys in motion. Yes, I assure you, he discharged, if I may use so inelegant an expression, one volley after another of heat and flame and vivid thoughts. It sounded as if he had evoked the *manes* of Tasso. He made the colours glaring, but such a subject is just the thing for him; the expression of tragic grandeur is his strong point. I did not know what to admire most in him, the composer or the pianist, for he played superbly. No, he does not really play – one forgets he is a musician, he becomes a prophet proclaiming the Last Judgement till all the spirits of the universe vibrate under his fingers. He enters into the most secret recesses of the mind and stirs one's inmost soul with demonic power.

When this was done Liszt said jauntily, 'Now let us go on with [your] sonata,' to which I naturally retorted: 'No, thank you, after this I do not want to.' But now comes the best part of the story. Liszt exclaimed: 'Why not? Then give it to me, I'll do it.' Now you must bear in mind, in the first place, that he had never seen or heard the sonata, and in the second place that it was a sonata with a violin part, now above, now below, independent of the pianoforte part. And what does Liszt do? He plays the whole thing, root and branch, violin and piano, nay, more, for he played fuller, more broadly. The violin got its due right in the middle of the piano part. He was literally over the whole piano at once, without missing a note, and how he did play! With grandeur, beauty, genius, unique comprehension. I think I laughed – laughed like an idiot. And when I stammered a few complimentary words, he muttered: 'Surely you must expect me to play a thing at sight, for I am an old experienced musician.'

EDVARD GRIEG quoted by H. T. Finck in Grieg and His Music

Most descriptions of Liszt centre on his virtuoso piano playing, and tend to emphasize its more demonic qualities. Charles Stanford, after hearing him at a semi-private gathering at Leipzig in 1875, left a different impression

He was only present as a listener, but everyone so markedly refused to leave the room after various young people had tremblingly performed, that he happily took the hint and sat down at the piano. The moment his fingers touched the keys, I realized the immense gap between him and all other pianists. He was the very reverse of all my anticipations, which inclined me, perhaps from the caricatures familiar to me in my boyhood, to expect to see an inspired acrobat, with high-action arms, and wild locks falling on the keys. I saw instead a dignified composed figure, who sat like a rock, never indulging in a theatrical gesture, or helping out his amazingly full tone with the splashes and crashes of a charlatan, producing all his effects with the simplest means, and giving the impression of such ease that the most difficult passages sounded like child's play. It was the very reverse of the style of the young lady to whom von Bülow, after hearing her performance, went up with a deep bow and said 'I congratulate you, Mademoiselle, upon playing the easiest possible passages with the greatest possible difficulty.' I and my companion, a very punctilious person, were so overwhelmed by the performance and the personality, that we could not but 'cap' him as he stalked out into the street. He had a magnetism and a charm which was all-compelling. We understood how he could meet Kings and Emperors on an equality, and fascinate with all the wiles of the serpent. He had two smiles: the one angelical, for artists, the other diabolical, for the satellite Countesses. How innately kind he could be was proved by a little incident which occurred in Berlin shortly after his visit to Leipzig. A young lady pianist had announced a recital, advertising herself (in the hope of attracting a larger audience) as a 'pupil of Liszt'. As she had never laid eyes upon him in her life, she was horrified to read in the papers on the morning of her concert that the Abbé had arrived in the city. The only thing to be done was to make a clean breast of it; she went to his hotel and asked for an interview. When she was shown in she confessed with many tears, and asked for absolution. Liszt asked her the name of the pieces she was going to play, chose one and made her sit down at the piano and play it. Then he gave her some hints about her performance, and dismissed her with a pat on the cheek, and the remark 'Now, my dear, you can call yourself a pupil of Liszt.'

C. V. STANFORD Unwritten Diary 1914

Wagner is a peculiarly difficult figure to visualize: the magnetic charm, which he clearly possessed, doesn't transmit well in written descriptions. What does come across is the compelling urgency, the eccentricity of behaviour, the theatricality mixed with intellectual pretension . . .

I still see him sitting in the chair near my window, I see him as he sat then, listening impatiently one evening while I spoke to him of the splendor of the future that surely lay before him. The sun had just gone down in glory, earth and heaven were radiant.

Wagner said: 'Why are you talking about the future when my manuscripts are lying locked up in the cupboard! Who is going to perform the work of art that I, only *I* can create with the help of happy demons – who is going to perform it so that all the world says yes, that's it, that's the way the Master saw his work and wanted it?'

He walked up and down the room excitedly. Stopping before me suddenly, he said, 'I'm organized differently, I have sensitive nerves –

I must have beauty, brilliance and light! The world owes me what I need! I can't live on a miserable organist's salary, like your Master Bach! Is it an unheard of presumption if I think I'm entitled to the bit of luxury I like? I who give pleasure to the world, to thousands!'

So speaking, he raised his head as if in defiance. Then he sat down in the chair at the window again and stared in front of him. What did he care about the magnificence of the view or the peace of nature?

ELIZA WILLE 1864 Recollections of Wagner

At the early rehearsals of *Tristan*:

He would listen with closed eyes to the artists singing to Bülow's pianoforte accompaniment. If a difficult passage went particularly well, he would spring up, embrace or kiss the singer warmly, or out of pure joy stand on his head on the sofa, creep under the piano, jump up on to it, run into the garden and scramble joyously up a tree, or make caricatures, or recite, with improvised disfigurements, a poem that had been dedicated to him. . . .

SEBASTIAN RÖCKL 1865 Ludwig II und Richard Wagner

At his villa near Lake Lucerne, with Friedrich Nietzsche and his sister

Triebschen was furnished according to the taste of a Parisian fournisseur who had been lavish with pink atlas silk and amourettes, so that the interior of this pleasant old house impressed me as rather unattractive. But the inhabitants and the landscape reconciled one to the curious interior decor, and even made it appear picturesque.

I remember the last evening I spent there. At sunset the four of us went for a walk along the so-called Robbers' Way close to the lake. Frau Cosima with my brother in front, in a red cashmere dress with broad facings of real lace which reached right down to the hem, and a big Florentine hat with a wreath of pink roses hanging over her arm. Behind her, with ponderous dignity, came the huge coal black Newfoundland dog Russ; then followed Wagner and I: Wagner in the costume of a Dutch painter: a coat of black velvet, knee breeches of black atlas silk, black silk stockings, a light blue richly folded atlas cravat, with fine linen and lace in between, and an artist's beret on his luxuriant brown hair. I can still see us walking silently through the trees in the fading light and looking out over the silvery lake. . . .

Gradually the silence was broken: Wagner, Cosima and my brother began to talk of the tragedy of human life, of the Greeks, of the Germans, of plans and hopes.

ELIZABETH FÖRSTER-NIETZSCHE c. 1867 The Nietzsche–Wagner Correspondence

Verdi was never an easy character to know, partly at least because most writers have treated him with such adulation. Here, then, is an honest if unflattering description, in a rebuttal of a previous article by Verdi's French publisher, Marie Escudier, along with some interesting comments on Verdi's Italian colleagues

As copyright holder of the latter's music, [Escudier] naturally praises him to the skies. He then reports with great affection that Verdi is a *handsome young man* (?) of *twenty-eight or twenty-nine*; who has *blue eyes with an expression that is at once gentle and bright* (?); and that the *Ave Maria* from *I Lombardi*, which M. Escudier requested the composer to play, is the finest number from that opera (it is certainly the worst of Ave Marias). M. Escudier then proceeds: *I need few words to describe this young maestro's appearance and character: he has a generous nature* (how galant!) *and an exceptional constitution* (what an eye Escudier has for anatomical-physiological-psychological detail!); *he resembles Donizetti in features and stature* (like a raven resembles a dove), *and Bellini in modesty of speech* (neither of them possessed this virtue – Bellini was lovably conceited, Verdi is solemnly so). Would my readers care for a short description of the best-known modern Italian operatic composers? . . . Your correspondent has often enjoyed their company during the past 30 years in Italy. About the characters of *Mercadante* and *Ricci* there is nothing in particular to relate. Grandfather *Rossini*: a handsome, interesting face, in his younger days a witty and jovial companion quite without pride but the king of all hoaxers. – *Donizetti*: handsome man (a faint similarity to our Spohr); his character resembles that of an honest German – pleasant and friendly, he sometimes makes witty remarks, and has no trace of pride. – *Pacini*: a somewhat small and thin man, educated, polite and modest; in society you could call him the Italian *Meyerbeer*. – *Bellini*: medium build, a handsome, somewhat pale and languishing face, blue eyes; although secretly he has a high opinion of himself, his whole personality could be termed kind. – *Verdi*: medium build, not ugly but far from handsome; earnest and self-important.

PETER LICHTENTAL [?] *Allgemeine Musikalische Zeitung* 1845

Perhaps (as with Bach) the best way to see Verdi is at work. This is a very famous description, but a vivid one, of a moment of great importance in Verdi's life

I recall that every morning and evening, in the foyer or on stage (according to whether the rehearsals were with piano or orchestra) we gazed anxiously at him as soon as he appeared and tried to guess from his eyes or from the way he greeted the artists whether there was some novelty in store for us that day. If he approached me almost smiling, and uttered a phrase that resembled a compliment, I was certain that he had some innovation to spring on me during the day's rehearsals. I bowed my head in resignation, but little by little I too conceived a great passion for this *Macbeth* which was turning out so differently from everything that had been previously written and performed.

I remember that for Verdi there were two high-points in the opera: the sleepwalking scene and my duet with the baritone. You will find it difficult to understand, but the sleepwalking scene took me three months to study: for three months, morning and evening, I tried to imitate those people who talk in their sleep, who utter words (as Verdi assured me) almost without moving their lips, and keeping other parts of their face, eyes included, motionless. It was enough to drive you insane.

And the duet with the baritone which begins: *Fatal mia donna, un murmure* – you might think that I exaggerate, but it was rehearsed more than 150 times: to ensure, the Maestro said, that it was more *said* than *sung*. Now listen to this. On the evening of the dress-rehearsal, with the theatre already full, Verdi insisted that the cast wear their costumes, and when he dug his heels in, woe betide you if you contradicted! And so there we were, ready, in costume, the orchestra in the pit, the chorus on stage – when Verdi beckoned to Varesi and me, called us into the wings and asked us, as a favour, to follow him to the foyer for another piano rehearsal of that accursed duet.

'But Maestro,' I said, terrified, 'we are already in our Scottish costumes: how can we?'

'Put a cloak over them.'

And Varesi, the baritone, exasperated at the unusual request, ventured to raise his voice a little, and said:

'But we've rehearsed it 150 times, for goodness' sake!'

'In half an hour, it'll be 151.'

Whether one wanted to or not, one had to obey the tyrant. I still remember the threatening looks Varesi shot at him, as he headed for the foyer; clenching the hilt of his sword, he seemed about to murder Verdi, just as later he would murder Duncan. Even he complied, however, and resigned himself to his fate. The 151st rehearsal took place, while the audience clamoured impatiently in the theatre.

And that duet – to say that it aroused enthusiasm and fanaticism would be a great understatement. It was something unbelievable, new, unheard of. Wherever I have sung *Macbeth* (and during the season at the Pergola it was every evening) the duet had to be repeated three or even four times – and once we had to give a fifth encore.

I shall never forget how, on the evening of the first performance, before the sleepwalking scene, which is one of the last in the opera, Verdi turned to me anxiously without saying a word: it was quite clear that the success, already great, would for him only be complete after that scene. And so I made the sign of the cross (a custom maintained even today on stage during difficult moments) and I made my entrance. The newspapers of the time will tell you if I interpreted rightly the dramatic and musical thought of the great maestro in that sleepwalking scene. This much I do know: the storm of applause had scarcely died down when I returned to my dressing-room, greatly moved, trembling and exhausted. The door was thrown open (I was already half undressed) and Verdi entered, waving his hands and moving his lips, as if wishing to make a great speech; he failed, however, to utter a single word. I smiled and wept and said nothing either; but as I looked at the Maestro, I noticed that he too had red eyes. We clasped hands tightly, whereupon he rushed out without a word. That violent scene of emotion more than compensated for the many months of hard work and constant agitation.

MARIANNA BARBIERI NINI 1847 quoted in EUGENIO CHECCHI *Giuseppe Verdi*

And this gives a more than usually convincing impression of Verdi's old age: he was eighty-three when Giordano, whose *Andrea Chénier* was still not to be performed for another two years, took his young wife to visit the Maestro on their honeymoon

The other day Olga and I were at Genoa and, in an attempt to be received by Verdi, we brought our visiting cards and asked the concierge when we might be received. The concierge returned and said 'At once!' Nothing was like what I had imagined. The Palazzo is the famous Palazzo Doria, which has a wonderful courtyard; but beneath an arcade there are several small doorways which open on to stone (not even marble!) staircases, and hung on these doors are brass plaques which bear the names of various companies. To my great surprise the concierge led us through one of these little doorways where there is, among the many residences, a small staircase hardly lit by the sun. On the first floor we found ourselves opposite an ordinary door, bearing a small white sign: *G. Verdi*. To one side of the door there hung a gas-torch for the evenings (without even a shade!). . . . There was no electric bell. We pulled the cord, the servant opened the door and led us through an antechamber and into the drawing-room.

Nothing special or luxurious was to be seen . . . nothing to reveal that a composer resided here except a small clay statue of Falstaff. Nothing else! A door soon opened and Verdi entered, still young and fresh. He paid us many compliments and then sat down to converse. He enquired about Nervi and its climate. After a while his wife entered, an old lady with a pink complexion and an auburn wig; she is short, plump and seems scarcely able to sustain herself on her legs. He was most affectionate with his wife, went to meet her, helped her to sit down and stayed near her. Having discussed the pleasant warmth of the drawing-room, she wished us to experience the warmth of her own room. We left the drawing-room and passed through Verdi's bedroom. What a *shrine*! It was like entering a church. Here too, there was nothing special to be seen: a grand piano, manuscript paper on the music-stand that showed he was working, many books in various little book-cases without glass fronts, a large writing desk and his bed. His wife's room was a beautiful lady's bedroom, hung with photographs of Verdi at several different ages, one of Manzoni and one of Princess Elena. And that is all I saw! No portraits of artists, no crowns, not a single sign of *greatness*. I was dumbfounded. Do you understand? And we, when we have written a single opera, consider we have to keep a carriage and horses and live in a palace. You see the modesty of the great? Superfluous to say that they were both delightful. We never spoke of music. He accompanied us to the door – and yet they say he is uncivil! Lies! He is only uncivil to those bores who wish to show off by mentioning his name.

UMBERTO GIORDANO Letter 1896

Stanford again, on Brahms

He opened the door of his little flat himself, clad in a jersey and trousers, and led us through a bare outer room, and his bedroom, scarcely less bare save for a drawing of 'Anselmo's Tomb' over his very short and stumpy bed, into his study, a double room crammed with books, music, and literature of all sorts. He greeted Richter warmly, and when I was introduced gave me a most distant and suspicious bow. . . . I was quite sure he was aware of who I was, but was going to measure my capacity for lion-hunting. His chance came; he offered Richter a cigar, and was then handing the box to me, when he snatched it back with a curt, 'You are English, you don't smoke!' To which I replied, with an impertinence which it required some courage to assume, 'I beg pardon, the English not only smoke, but they even compose music sometimes,' making a simultaneous dash after the retreating cigar-box. For one moment he looked at me like a dangerous mastiff, and then burst out laughing. The ice was broken and never froze again. I caught sight of some fine engravings, and he spent the best part of the morning showing me his complete collection of Piranesi engravings, and other treasures which he had picked up in Italy during the previous summer. He only mentioned music once. . . .

When I next visited Vienna I went to see him without an appointment, thinking that I should surely find him at home at eleven o'clock. But his housekeeper told me that he had just gone to dinner. I was so astonished that I said to her, 'In Heaven's name, what time does Brahms eat his breakfast?' 'At five,' said the dame; 'he does all his work before eleven, and is out the rest of the day.' However, I fell in with him later, and sat with him through a rehearsal of Gluck's *Alceste* at the Opera House, over which he waxed enthusiastic. His two favourite haunts in Vienna were Strauss's band and the Opera. While there I heard of a tremendous verbal castigation which he had given at a restaurant to a young man who thought he would gain his favour by sneering at Wagner. . . .

A most remarkable and extraordinary personality was Brahms. Humorous, fearless, far-seeing, sometimes over-rough to his contemporaries, but a worshipper of and worshipped by young children; with a very noble, generous, and ideal side to his character, and a curiously warped and sensual side as well. He could look like Jupiter Olympus at one moment, and like Falstaff the next.

C. V. STANFORD 1877 Studies and Memories

In 1876 George Henschel, then a young singer, visited Brahms and spent a holiday with him on the Baltic island of Rügen. The composer, still unbearded, was then forty-three, the singer twenty-six

Sunday, July 9

Early yesterday morning Brahms came up to go bathing with me. There was a fine surf on, and the temperature of the water being rather high, we stayed in it for nearly half an hour, enjoying ourselves hugely. I greatly admired Brahms's burly, well-knit, muscular body, which is only rather too much inclined to stoutness, I fear.

In the water he drew my attention to the possibility of keeping one's eyes open wide when diving. It is not only possible, he said, but also very agreeable and strengthening for the eyes. I at once followed his advice to try, succeeding immediately, and we greatly amused ourselves by throwing littler copper coins into the water and diving for them. . . .

Brahms is looking splendid. His solid frame, the healthy, dark-brown colour of his face, the full hair, just a little sprinkled with grey, all make him appear the very image of strength and vigour. He walks about here just as he pleases, generally with his waistcoat unbuttoned and his hat in his hand, always with clean linen, but without collar or tie. These he dons at table d'hôte only. His whole appearance vividly recalls some of the portraits of Beethoven. His appetite is excellent. He eats with great gusto and, in the evening, drinks his three glasses of beer, never omitting, however, to finish off with his beloved Kaffee.

July 11

We stretched ourselves out in the low grass – it was a very warm evening – lit cigarettes and lay listening in deepest silence, not a breath of wind stirring, for fully half an hour. Then we leaned over the pond, caught tiny little baby frogs and let them jump into the water again from a stone, which greatly amused Brahms, especially when the sweet little creatures, happy to be in their element once more, hurriedly swam away, using their nimble little legs most gracefully and according to all the rules of the natatory art. When they thought themselves quite safe, Brahms would tenderly catch one up again in his hand, and heartily laugh with pleasure on giving it back its freedom. . . .

July 15

Today I read out, from a Berlin paper, the news of the death, at Bayreuth, where *The Ring* was being performed for the first time, of a member of the Wagner orchestra. '*The first corpse*', said Brahms, dryly. . . .

July 17

'I sometimes regret,' he said to me after some moments of silence, 'that I did not marry. I ought to have a boy of ten now; that *would* be nice. But when I was of the right age for marrying, I lacked the position to do so, and now it is too late. . . .'

July 18

Yesterday, when, after our usual swim, we leisurely strolled to the Fahrnberg for dinner, a button on Brahms's shirt suddenly came off. As it was the one which served to hold the collar in its place, Brahms was greatly embarrassed. I proposed to help him out, and we went to my room, where I took out of my valise a little box containing sewing materials which my mother had given me to carry with me when travelling. The amusing situation of my sewing the button on to Brahms's shirt while he had it on, again recalled memories of his youth. 'When *I* went on my first journey,' he said, laughingly, 'my mother also put such a little box into my bag, and showed me how to use its contents. But I remember quite well, when I tore a hole in my trousers, I repaired it with sealing wax! It didn't last long, though. . . .'

           In the train to Berlin July 19
This morning, at five o'clock, I left Sassnitz. Strangely enough, it again poured in torrents, as on the night of my arrival. A horrid, chilly morning. Brahms was up at the Fahrnberg a little before five, and, to my delight, accompanied me in the diligence as far as Lancken, some three miles from Sassnitz. There he got out, we shook hands, and parted. For a long time I looked after him out of the carriage window in spite of the wind and the still pouring rain. It was a picture never to be forgotten. As far as the eye could reach, nothing but moor, and clouds, and – Brahms.

GEORGE HENSCHEL 1876 *Personal Recollections of Johannes Brahms*

It is a nice change to find that Brahms could be so pleasant. Perhaps it was the famous beard that made him prickly: incidentally, that growth only sprouted between the Violin Concerto and the B Flat Piano Concerto, a couple of years after the holiday with Henschel. But Henschel always seems to have brought out what was most bonhomous in Brahms. When they shared a bedroom together at a music festival they were both visiting, Brahms's snoring was so loud that the singer crept out to find another room. When he returned in the morning Brahms, knowing why Henschel had left, said cheerfully: 'Ah, there you are. I thought perhaps you'd gone and hung yourself. If I was snoring, why didn't you throw a boot at me?' Henschel adds (reverentially): 'The idea of throwing a boot at Brahms!'

Gounod was one of the most curious characters among composers. One of these days some Peter Shaffer or Ken Russell is going to make something fascinating out of his life, and particularly out of his strange relationship with the English Weldon family: Harry, the husband, and his extraordinary wife Georgina, who counted Thackeray and the artist Watts among her admirers and Arthur Sullivan among her conquests. She added Gounod to the list with romantic abandon and annotated the affair in diaries and reminiscences that read like scenes from a French farce rather than pages from the life of a rather solemn, middle-aged composer.

    A typical incident. A row had blown up with Georgina early in the morning

Gounod went to dress. He put on his winter coat, my sealskin cap, his strongest boots; he rummaged the things on my table for a bit, hoping it would give me the chance of saying something which would enable him to recommence his 'row'. But I held my head down, my eyes fixed on my books. I was nearly crying. He went off without another word. I heard him go downstairs; I heard the front door shut.

Later that afternoon he reappeared, bathed in sweat

In vain I tried to calm him. I tried to take him in my arms and coax him; he pushed me brutally away, almost with blows. 'Don't touch me,' he shrieked, 'it is *you* who have invited your husband to insult me, to outrage me, to defy me. I will die,' he shrieked, 'and all shall perish with me!' I was terrified. The thought struck me that he meant to set the place on fire but I followed him with my eyes, hoping that my looks might subdue him. He rushed like a madman to the cupboard where the orchestral score of 'Polyeucte' was carefully stored away. He seized hold of it, crying out, 'Polyeucte first; Polyeucte shall burn!' It was his custom, at the least contrariety, to burn the manuscript he was composing. It was his best way of getting anything he wanted out of me. It made me wretched to see him destroy his work.

    With strength lent me by the horror of despair, I threw myself on Gounod with all my weight; I knocked him down; I rolled on him; we tussled violently for possession of the treasure. I tore it from him; I flung it on the sofa; I suddenly picked myself off the floor; I sat upon it and screamed: 'You shall kill me first, but you shall not burn Polyeucte!' My strength then gave way, I burst into sobs, I stretched out my arms to him – 'My old man! My old treasure! why are you so wicked to me?' . . .

    Gounod, to whom the fight had done good, had calmed down, thank God: the score of 'Polyeucte' was saved.

After this, Gounod always kept a small bag packed and ready for any sudden departure (containing, among other things, a loaded pistol). Soon enough another scene blew up, and Gounod was off upstairs to get his bag

Twenty minutes after this Gounod returned. He had completely dressed himself anew. He had put on his best trousers, his new waistcoat, his black frock coat, his neatest shoes, his red socks, a clean white shirt, a black neckerchief (the bows most carefully tied), and he had on his head his Algerian fez. Under his arm he carried some music paper. He entered ceremoniously. He approached the table; he stood opposite my husband . . . took off his fez and made a profound salaam.

'Sir,' he said deliberately, 'I have reflected that it must be as disagreeable for you to have a humbug in your house as it is for me to remain in it. I have the honour of wishing you a very good morning.'

He replaced his fez on his head; he walked slowly with inexpressible dignity towards the door. My tears began to flow; I joined my hands together and I looked at my husband in the most imploring manner. My husband understood; he flew towards the door; he turned towards Gounod, with his back to the door, and, fixing his bright eyes on him, he said, 'You shall not go out.'

GOUNOD: To-day I am a prisoner; the other day I was brought back by you by the arm before all London; another time I was a *glutton*; another day I am a *liar*, now, to-day I am a *humbug*. Open the door, if you please.

MY HUSBAND: Come, my dear old man, what has come over you this morning?

Gounod burst into tears and fainted in Harry's arms. When they asked him what the music paper had been for, he said that he had meant to spend the day 'in the underground railway and note down on the way musical ideas, which I think would have occurred to me'. . . .

Later in the year, Gounod's son Jean joined the party and inevitably a new incident was precipitated, this time over the card table. Gounod ran for his bag, as usual, and after a little while Georgina followed him to his bedroom

He had pulled my sealskin cap over his ears; he had on his thick winter overcoat (the weather was very fine and hot – 16th August 1873), he had his little travelling bag, which contained his loaded pistol, in his hands, his warm trousers, his thick shoes; he was sitting on his bed with his legs hanging down. He took no notice of Jean, who was sitting crying on the portmanteau. Never were seen two beings so profoundly miserable.

paraphrased from EDWARD GRIERSON Storm Bird 1959

George Moore on Gounod:

A base soul who poured a sort of bath-water melody down the back of every woman he met. Margaret or Madeleine, it was all the same.

GEORGE MOORE Memoirs of My Dead Life 1906

In 1878 Massenet and Saint-Saëns were rival candidates for election to the
Institut de France

During the Byzantine intrigues which took place on election day,
Gounod emerged as Saint-Saëns' champion and Ambroise Thomas as
Massenet's. After two votes had been taken Massenet was duly
elected by an absolute majority. He always tried to avoid making an
enemy and therefore sent a polite telegram to Saint-Saëns. It read: 'My
dear colleague, the Institut has just committed a grave injustice.'
Immediately there came the furious reply: 'I entirely agree with you.
C. Saint-Saëns.'

JAMES HARDING *Saint-Saëns and his Circle* 1965

In November, 1875, Camille Saint-Saëns came to conduct and play
some of his works in Moscow. The short, lively man, with his Jewish
type of features, attracted Tchaikovsky and fascinated him not only by
his wit and original ideas, but also by his masterly knowledge of his
art. Tchaikovsky used to say that Saint-Saëns knew how to combine
the grace and charm of the French school with the depth and
earnestness of the great German masters. Tchaikovsky became very
friendly with him, and hoped this friendship would prove very useful
in the future. It had no results, however. Long afterwards they met
again as comparative strangers, and always remained so.

During Saint-Saëns' short visit to Moscow a very amusing episode
took place. One day the friends discovered they had a great many likes
and dislikes in common, not merely in the world of music, but in other
respects. In their youth both had been enthusiastic admirers of the
ballet, and had often tried to imitate the art of the dancers. This
suggested the idea of dancing together, and they brought out a little
ballet, *Pygmalion and Galatea*, on the stage of the Conservatoire. Saint-
Saëns, aged forty, played the part of Galatea most conscientiously,
while Tchaikovsky, aged thirty-five, appeared as Pygmalion. N.
Rubinstein formed the orchestra. Unfortunately, besides the three
performers, no spectators witnessed this singular entertainment.

MODESTE TCHAIKOVSKY *Life of Tchaikovsky* 1906

Not all meetings between composers are quite on this level, but here is an
account of an unusually starry one left to us by the wife of the violinist Adolph
Brodsky (who had given the first performance of Tchaikovsky's 'unperform-
able' Violin Concerto five years earlier)

In the summer of 1887 the Gewandhaus Committee invited Tschaikovsky to conduct some of his own compositions, and as he had

received similar invitations from other towns in Germany, he decided to accept them and so, for the first time, came abroad to conduct his own works. He arrived in Leipzig on Christmas Eve, it was a cold frosty evening, and the snow lay thick on the ground. My husband went to the station to meet Tschaikovsky, and my sister Olga and her little son who were our guests at that time helped me to prepare our Christmas tree. We wished it to be quite ready before Tschaikovsky arrived, and to look as bright as possible as a welcome for him. As we were lighting the candles we heard the sound of a sledge, and soon after Tschaikovsky entered the room followed by Siloti and my husband.

I had never seen him before. Either the sight of the Christmas tree or our Russian welcome pleased him greatly, for his face was illuminated by a delightful smile, and he greeted us as if he had known us for years. There was nothing striking or artistic in his appearance, but everything about him – the expression of his blue eyes, his voice, especially his smile, spoke of great kindliness of nature. I never knew a man who brought with him such a warm atmosphere as Tschaikovsky. He had not been an hour in our house before we quite forgot that he was a great composer. We spoke to him of very intimate matters without any reserve, and felt that he enjoyed our confidence.

The supper passed in animated conversation, and, notwithstanding the fatigues of his journey, Tschaikovsky remained very late before returning to his hotel. He promised to come to us whenever he felt inclined, and kept his word.

Among his many visits one remains especially memorable. It was on New Year's Day. We invited Tschaikovsky to dinner, but, knowing his shyness with strangers, did not tell him there would be other guests. Brahms was having a rehearsal of his trio in our house that morning with Klengel and A. B. – a concert being fixed for the next day. Brahms was staying after the rehearsal for early dinner. In the midst of the rehearsal I heard a ring at the bell, and expecting it would be Tschaikovsky, rushed to open the door. He was quite perplexed by the sound of music, asked who was there, and what they were playing. I took him into the room adjoining and tried to break, gently, the news of Brahms' presence. As we spoke there was a pause in the music; I begged him to enter, but he felt too nervous, so I opened the door softly and called my husband. He took Tschaikovsky with him and I followed.

Tschaikovsky and Brahms had never met before. It would be difficult to find two men more unlike. Tschaikovsky, a nobleman by birth, had something elegant and refined in his whole bearing and the greatest courtesy of manner. Brahms with his short, rather square figure and powerful head, was an image of strength and energy; he was an avowed foe to all so-called 'good manners'. His expression was often slightly sarcastic. When A. B. introduced them, Tschaikovsky said, in his soft melodious voice: 'Do I not disturb you?'

'Not in the least,' was Brahms' reply, with his peculiar hoarseness. 'But why are you going to hear this? It is not at all interesting.'

Tschaikovsky sat down and listened attentively. The personality of Brahms, as he told us later, impressed him very favourably, but he was not pleased with the music. When the trio was over I noticed that Tschaikovsky seemed uneasy. It would have been natural that he should say something, but he was not at all the man to pay unmeaning compliments. The situation might have become difficult, but at that moment the door was flung open and in came our dear friends – Grieg and his wife, bringing, as they always did, a kind of sunshine with them. They knew Brahms, but had never met Tschaikovsky before. The latter loved Grieg's music, and was instantly attracted by these two charming people, full as they were of liveliness, enthusiasm and unconventionality, and yet with a simplicity about them that made everyone feel at home. Tschaikovsky with his sensitive nervous nature understood them at once. After the introductions and greetings were over we passed to the dining-room. Nina Grieg was seated between Brahms and Tschaikovsky, but we had only been a few moments at the table when she started from her seat exclaiming: 'I cannot sit between these two. It makes me feel so nervous.'

Grieg sprang up, saying, 'But I have the courage'; and exchanged places with her. So the three composers sat together, all in good spirits. I can see Brahms now taking hold of a dish of strawberry jam, and saying he would have it all for himself and no one else should get any. It was more like a children's party than a gathering of great composers. My husband had this feeling so strongly that, when dinner was over and our guests still remained around the table smoking cigars and drinking coffee, he brought a conjurer's chest – a Christmas present to my little nephew – and began to perform tricks. All our guests were amused, and Brahms especially, who demanded from A. B. the explanation of each trick as soon as it was performed. . . .

We were sorry when our guests had to go. Tschaikovsky remained till the last. As we accompanied him part of the way home A. B. asked how he liked Brahms' trio.

'Don't be angry with me, my dear friend,' was Tschaikovsky's reply, 'But I did not like it.'

ANNA LVOVNA BRODSKY *Recollections of a Russian Home* 1904

Stravinsky has left a vivid glimpse of Tchaikovsky, just two weeks before his death, at the fiftieth anniversary performance of Glinka's *Russlan and Ludmilla* in St Petersburg

It was the most exciting night of my life, and completely unexpected because I had no hopes of attending the opera at all; eleven-year-olds were rarely seen at grand, late-night social events. The *Russlan* semi-centennial had been declared a national holiday, and my father must have considered the occasion important for my education. Just before theatre time Bertha burst into my room saying: 'Hurry, hurry, we are going, too.' I dressed quickly and climbed into the carriage by the side of my mother. I remember that the Mariinsky was lavishly decorated that night, and pleasantly perfumed, and I could find my seat even now – indeed, the eye of my memory leaps to it like filings to a magnet. A ceremony and a parade had preceded the performance; poor Glinka, who was only a kind of Russian Rossini, had been Beethovenized and nationally-monumented. I watched the performance through my mother's mother-of-pearl lorgnette binoculars. In the first interval we stepped from our loge into the small foyer behind. A few people were already walking there. Suddenly my mother said to me: 'Igor, look, there is Tchaikovsky.' I looked and saw a man with white hair, large shoulders, a corpulent back, and this image has remained in the retina of my memory all my life.

IGOR STRAVINSKY 1893 *Expositions and Developments*

A Norwegian genius in the 1890s

Do you desire a portrait?
   Grieg is small, thin, and slightly built. His is a child's body, always in movement; his motions are short and quick, strangely jerky and angular, and with every step he takes his whole body shakes as though from a limp. He is all nervous sensibility; his energy is striking. His head, which seems too large for his body, is intelligent and very fine, with its long grey hair brushed backwards; his face is lean, his chin clean-shaven, his nose short and arched. And his eyes – what eyes! They are grey-green: one can imagine in them a corner of his native Norway, with its sad fjords and its light mists. His look is serious, and infinitely gentle; he has a particular expression which seems at once morbid, uneasy, and childishly naïve. The total impression his countenance gives is one of kindness, gentleness, uprightness, sincerity and modesty. He has a sort of horror at the

flattering inquisitiveness which the crowd shows towards a celebrity. There is not the least pose about him, and his behaviour is that of an ordinary person; he never thinks of himself as being the object of people's gaze (which is a very rare thing in an artist) and never seems to be proclaiming: 'Here I am: take a good look at me!'

ERNEST CLOSSON *Edvard Grieg* 1892

From the New World

As spring approached Dvořák wanted more than ever to escape from the noisy city. He was anxious to work on some new music that he had in mind. One day Josef Kovarik (son of the Spillville schoolmaster, and assistant and secretary to Dvořák) suggested that Dvořák accompany him on a visit to Iowa. Apparently his master did not hear, for he paid no attention to the remark and made no comment. A few days later, however, he quite unexpectedly asked Kovarik about Spillville. Kovarik explained that Spillville was a little Bohemian settlement, where his native language was spoken in the street; that it was peaceful and quiet, as well as beautiful; and most important of all, there were no railroads in Spillville. Several days passed. Then Dvořák asked his assistant to draw a map of Spillville, indicating every house, every street, every person who lived in each house, and what they did. That was all; Dvořák made no comments. But when some friends of his from South Carolina tried to persuade him to go there for his rest he said, 'No, I am going to Spillville.' So it was that a lovely day in June saw Antonin Dvořák, his wife, their six children, a sister, a maid, and his assistant, alight from the train at the little station of Calmar, eleven miles from Spillville. Kovarik sent the family on to the village while he remained to look after the baggage. Upon his arrival he found Dvořák strolling around, smoking his pipe, quite at home, and apparently very much pleased with his surroundings. . . .

'Dr. Dvořák liked nothing better than to get a few of our Spillville "old settlers" together every afternoon and listen to the narration of their struggles and experiences in the Middle West,' says one of these friends. 'They so allured him that he would ply the speaker with question after question. He, in turn, would tell stories of mutual friends in the Old World, or of the New Yorkers whom he could not entirely fathom. . . . At our house Mother was the first to rise. When, the morning following the Dvořák arrival, she saw the master strolling before the school building she thought something had gone wrong. When she ran out to ask what had happened, not knowing he was an early riser, he said, 'Why, nothing has happened. And yet – a great deal. I have been rambling in the wood, along the brook, and for the first time in eight months I hear the birds sing. But I must go home now to breakfast. Afterwards I shall come again.' Sometimes he would sit for hours at his second-storey window as though again in an Old World village, gazing down silently at passers-by and listening to the sounds of nature. Sometimes, the neighbours say, he would sit that way all evening, then, late at night, they would hear him playing his violin, songs of the far-off homeland, or melodies which had come to him as he pondered.

And so the Spillville friends humbly and lovingly recall 'neighbour Dvořák', and the vivid and extraordinary personality of 'that modest artist' and 'God-fearing gentleman'.

H. G. KINSCELLA 1893 *Musical America*

The sailor of 'the Mighty Handful' describes the chemist of the group

I became a frequent visitor at Borodin's; often staying overnight as well. We discussed music a great deal; he played his projected works and showed me the sketches of the symphony. He was better informed than I on the practical side of orchestration, as he played the cello, oboe and flute. Borodin was an exceedingly cordial and cultured man, pleasant and oddly witty to talk with. On visiting him I often found him working in the laboratory which adjoined his apartment. When he sat over his retorts filled with some colourless gas and distilled it by means of a tube from one vessel into another, – I used to tell him that he was 'transfusing emptiness into vacancy'. Having finished his work, he would go with me to his apartment, where we began musical operations or conversations, in the midst of which he used to jump up, run back to the laboratory to see whether something had not burned out or boiled over; meanwhile he filled the corridor with incredible sequences from successions of ninths or sevenths. Then he would come back, and we proceeded with the music or the interrupted conversation. . . .

Borodin, who had always given but little of his time to music and who often said (when reproached for it) that he loved chemistry and music equally well, began to devote still less time to music than before. Yet it was not science that enticed him. He had become one of the prominent workers in establishing medical courses for women and had begun to participate in various societies for the aid and support of student-youth, especially women. The meetings of these societies, the office of treasurer, which he filled in one of them, the bustling, the solicitations in their behalf, came to take up all of his time. . . .

His inconvenient apartment, so like a corridor, never allowed him to lock himself in or pretend he was not at home to anybody. Anybody entered his house at any time whatsoever and took him away from his dinner or his tea. Dear old Borodin would get up with his meal or his drink half-tasted, would listen to all kinds of requests and complaints and would promise to 'look into it'. People would hang on him with unintelligible explanations of their business, gabble and chatter by the hour, while he himself constantly wore a hurried look, having this or that still to do. My heart broke at seeing his life completely filled with self-denial *owing to his own inertia.*

To this must be added also that Yekatyerina Sergeyevna [his wife] continually suffered from her asthma, passed sleepless nights, and always got up at 11 or 12 a.m. [Borodin] had a difficult time with her at night, rose early, and got along with insufficient sleep. Their whole home life was one unending disorder. Dinner-time and other meal-times were most indefinite. Once I came to their house at 11 in the evening and found them at dinner. Leaving out of account the girls, their *protégées*, of whom their house had never any lack, their apartment was often used as shelter or a night's lodging by various poor (or 'visiting') relations, who picked that place to fall ill or even lose their minds. Borodin had his hands full of them, doctored them, took them to hospitals, and then visited them there. In the four rooms of his apartment there often slept several strange persons of this sort; sofas and floors were turned into beds. Frequently it proved impossible to play the piano, because someone lay asleep in the adjoining room. At dinner and at tea, too, great disorder prevailed. Several tom-cats that found a home in Borodin's apartment paraded across the dinner-table sticking their noses into plates, unceremoniously leaping to the diners' backs. . . .

Owing to his infinite kindliness and his entire lack of self-love, these surroundings made it extremely inconvenient for him to work at composition. One might come again and again and keep demanding how much he had written. New result – a page or two of score, or else – nothing at all. To the query: 'Alyeksandr Porfiryevich, have you done the writing?' he would reply: 'I have.' And then it would turn out that the writing he had done was on a batch of letters! 'Alyeksandr Porfiryevich, have – you – finally – transposed such and such a number of the opera score?' – 'Yes, I have,' – he replies earnestly. 'Well, thank the Lord! at last!' – 'I transposed it from the piano to the table' – he would continue with the same earnestness and composure!

RIMSKY-KORSAKOV *c.* 1877 *My Musical Life*

Here is Stravinsky again, with memories of another Russian colleague. (He has just been speaking of Maeterlinck's *Life of the Bee*)

This bee-ology reminds me of Rachmaninov, of all people, for the last time I saw that awesome man he had come to my house in Hollywood bearing me the gift of a pail of honey. I was not especially friendly with Rachmaninov at the time, nor, I think, was anyone else: social relations with a man of Rachmaninov's temperament require more perseverance than I can afford: he was merely bringing me honey. It is curious, however, that I should meet him not in Russia, though I often heard him perform there in my youth, nor later when we were neighbours in Switzerland, but in Hollywood.

Some people achieve a kind of immortality just by the totality with which they do or do not possess some quality or characteristic. Rachmaninov's immortalizing totality was his scowl. He was a six-and-a-half-foot-tall scowl.

I suppose my conversations with him, or rather, with his wife, for he was always silent, were typical:

MME RACHMANINOV: What is the first thing you do when you rise in the morning? [This could have been indiscreet, but not if you had seen how it was asked.]

MYSELF: For fifteen minutes I do exercises taught me by a Hungarian gymnast and Kneipp Kur maniac, or, rather, I did them until I learned that the Hungarian had died very young and very suddenly, then I stand on my head, then I take a shower.

MME RACHMANINOV: You see, Serge, *Stravinsky* takes showers. How extraordinary. Do you still say you are afraid of them? And you heard Stravinsky say that he exercises? What do you think of that? Shame on you who will hardly take a walk.

RACHMANINOV: (Silence.)

I remember Rachmaninov's earliest compositions. They were 'water-colours', songs and piano pieces freshly influenced by Tchaikovsky. Then at twenty-five he turned to 'oils' and became a very old composer indeed. Do not expect me to spit on him for that, however: he was, as I have said, an awesome man, and besides, there are too many others to be spat upon before him. As I think about him, his silence looms as a noble contrast to the self-approbations which are the only conversation of all performing and most other musicians. And, he was the only pianist I have ever seen who did not grimace. That is a great deal.

IGOR STRAVINSKY *Conversations* 1959

Stravinsky (or anyhow, Stravinsky in collaboration with Craft) had a real gift
for sharp instant description

[Franz] Werfel was an attractive person, with large, lucid, magnetic
eyes – indeed, his eyes were the most beautiful I have ever seen, as his
teeth were the most horrible. We were regular guests in each other's
homes during the war. I recall seeing him for the last time in his house
one evening when we were together with Thomas Mann. Soon after I
stood in a 'mortuary' grieving for him, an occasion that confronted me
for the first time in thirty-three years with the angry, tortured, burning
face of Arnold Schoenberg.

IGOR STRAVINSKY 1943 ibid.

And here is Stravinsky himself, caught by two observers at the time of the
composition of *The Soldier's Tale*

One day in Geneva Stravinsky called, asked if we had a piano, then
said that he would visit us and play something very beautiful. In the
afternoon our housekeeper announced that a man whose like she had
never seen was at the door. And he did look strange, since, attached to
his belt, were cases and boxes of several sizes, containing various
percussion instruments. Soon after he had arranged these around the
piano, Stravinsky arrived, saying, 'It is the Soldier's Tale, the popular
story known to all Russian children. You, Georges, will be the stage
director and take the part of the Devil. Liudmilla will be the Princess.
Now I will play it for you,' Stravinsky said, and with this he pounced
on the piano and percussion, while imitating other instruments with
his voice. Fireworks seemed to be exploding in our little salon, and
Stravinsky reminded me of a devil in a Byzantine icon, so red, so black,
so resonant. A doleful melody . . . and the percussion growled,
purred, crackled. The fracas at the end tore the atmosphere to shreds
. . . We were ecstatic, happy, shocked. . . .

We went to Lausanne and lived there during the rehearsals. . . . We
were dancing mutes. Georges, as the Devil, fluttered and threw
himself about, and I was the melancholy, unsmiling Princess,
charmed out of her apathy by the soldier's violin. How fascinating
were the interminable discussions with Stravinsky, Ramuz, Auberjo-
nois, though the three men were so different that they could never
understand each other. . . . Stravinsky is captivating. . . . His curiosity is so great that he awakens this quality in all those around him
and leads them into unknown kingdoms.

LIUDMILLA PITOËFF 1918 Souvenirs Intimes

Stravinsky and Ramuz were in charge of daily rehearsals – the former always in a frenzy of enthusiasm, inventiveness, joy, indignation, headache; leaping on the piano as if it were a dangerous foe that had to be subdued by a bout of fisticuffs, then bounding on to the stage, swallowing glasses of kirsch whose after-effects had to be combated with the aid of aspirin: the latter, calm, attentive, friendly, rather bashful when giving advice, seeing things from our point of view, trying (like us) to find the right answers, showing an indomitable patience, and following with malicious enjoyment the genial capers of his collaborator.

JEAN VILLARD-GILLES 1918 *Souvenirs du Diable*

In 1947 Beecham organized a festival of the music of Richard Strauss, by then eighty-three years old, a legendary figure whom people were almost surprised to find still living. Norman Del Mar describes the tense expectancy with which he was awaited in London; finally . . .

He came. Sir Thomas gave two concerts at Drury Lane in which three of the Tone Poems were played . . . excerpts from *Feuersnot* and *Ariadne auf Naxos*, and the new Symphonic Fantasia from *Die Frau ohne Schatten*. Strauss attended both concerts with their rehearsals. During my own rehearsal of the *Frau ohne Schatten* Fantasia (Sir Thomas had generously assigned the work to me as part of my London début) he came up to the podium, glumly regarded the score for a few moments, muttered 'All my own fault', and went away. Throughout the entire visit he was very terse and uncommunicative, and only twice do I remember him being roused to any liveliness. The first occasion was when the fireman at Drury Lane Theatre had inadvertently locked the communicating door between house and stage, thus blocking Strauss's way when he wanted to come round to see Sir Thomas. I can still see him stamping and shouting about the 'Gott-verdammte Tür'. The second occasion was after the concert performance of *Elektra* which Sir Thomas gave in conjunction with the BBC. At the end the overjoyed Strauss came forward and embraced Beecham. This was an occasion I shall never forget. Nor shall I forget the embrace; I had not realized that Beecham was so small or that Strauss was so large.

It was at a rehearsal for the concert that he conducted himself on this occasion that Strauss made the most memorable remark of this visit. Something was not as he liked it, and he was overheard saying

No, I know what I want, and I know what I meant when I wrote this. After all, I may not be a first-rate composer, but I *am* a first-class second-rate composer!

NORMAN DEL MAR 1947 *Richard Strauss*

Britten, remembered by Ronald Duncan, an early collaborator and later librettist of *The Rape of Lucretia*, who knew the composer for forty years: it is a picture that provides a welcome contrast to the melancholy photographs we too often see nowadays of Britten in premature old age, a wheel chair and ill-fitting dentures

I saw him as a very ordinary looking young man similar to hundreds I'd seen at my school and university. His only conspicuous feature was that he could have passed anywhere unnoticed. He had short mouse-coloured curly hair, a receding chin and a nose which, like mine, was not quite straight on his face. He had a boyish manner and dressed casually like any student. . . .

Britten remained essentially a young man in his physical appearance, manner and dress, until he was sixty. He was wiry and athletic – walking with him, I found it difficult to keep pace with his stride. On the tennis court, he made me feel a rabbit; on the beach, I used to shiver watching him while he took his daily dip. He always dressed in the casual manner of an undergraduate; ate like a schoolboy, not in quantity, but in his preference for simple sweet foods. His manner was always relaxed except when he was composing, when his whole facial expression changed and he appeared stern with concentration, taut and utterly ruthless. I often noticed that when he composed, a muscle beneath one of his eyes used to twitch. His concentration then was such that nobody dared interrupt him, nor would they have succeeded even if they had attempted it. But while scoring a composition he was completely relaxed; he did not hesitate to converse at the same time. This chore, as he called it, appeared to be effortless, I never knew him go to a piano to check a passage. . . .

He ignored the fashion and wore his hair short. He did not stoop nor slouch with his hands in his pockets but seemed always ready for a game of tennis. His features were unremarkable: his chin was weak and belied his determination; his eyes were not penetrating or undipped such as are depicted in the romantic busts of Beethoven. There was no sign of the fanatic in Britten's eyes, they were seldom fully open as though lidded by diffidence. He never gesticulated, seldom lost his temper. With orchestral players and singers he was patient and tactful, though he had no time for journalists or hangers-on. He was essentially shy except with his closest friends. Though he enjoyed the company of ordinary people – like Billy who had a small boat at Aldeburgh and used to take us out herring fishing or to empty his lobster pots – with his close friends, Ben was altogether another person. He never smoked; he enjoyed driving fast cars, loved the countryside and loathed the cities.

Ben had a schoolboy's sense of humour. Of his party tricks one was to wind up an invisible handle by his ear then stick his tongue out imitating a cash register; another was to turn his head right round opening and shutting his eyes pretending to be a lighthouse. Children loved him and he loved children. Indeed, he always remained a child.

RONALD DUNCAN *Working with Britten* 1981

Britten himself remembered the obstacles he encountered in breaking with his own childhood background

During the summer holidays, he was at a tennis party in Lowestoft and was asked by another guest what career he would take up. 'I'm going to be a composer,' he replied. 'Yes,' said his questioner, 'but what else?' More ominous was the *sotto voce* remark which [John] Ireland said was made by one of the other two adjudicators at Britten's college scholarship examination: 'What is an English public schoolboy doing writing music of this kind?'

MICHAEL KENNEDY 1930 *Britten*

English public schoolboys had a hard time of it. Gwen Raverat, born in Darwin and later a collaborator in Vaughan Williams's *Job*, remembered as a child overhearing scraps of conversation about her young cousin

. . . 'that foolish young man, Ralph Vaughan Williams', who *would* go on working at music when 'he was so hopelessly bad at it'. This memory is confirmed by a letter of Aunt Etty's: 'He has been playing all his life, and for six months *hard*, and yet he can't play the simplest thing decently. They say it will simply break his heart if he is told that he is too bad to hope to make anything of it.' She held much the same opinion of the early writings of E. M. Forster, a family friend: 'His novel is really *not* good; and it's too unpleasant for the girls to read. I very much hope he will turn to something else, though I am sure I don't know what.'

GWEN RAVERAT *Period Piece* 1952

The whole question of the relationship between the creative artist and society is a vast one which we really can't embark on in this book. Here are a couple of Wagner letters, however, which might fuel discussion

12 December 1861

Dear Hornstein,

I hear that you have become rich. In what a wretched state I myself am you can easily guess from my failures. I am trying to retrieve myself by seclusion and a new work. In order to make possible this way of my preservation – that is to say, to lift me above the most distressing obligations, cares and needs that rob me of all freedom of mind – I require an immediate loan of ten thousand francs. With this I can again put my life in order, and again do productive work.

It will be rather hard for you to provide me with this sum; but it will be possible if you *wish* it, and do not shrink from a sacrifice. This, however, I desire, and I ask it of you against my promise to endeavour to repay you in three years out of my receipts.

Now let me see whether you are the right sort of man!

If you prove to be such for me, – and why should not this be expected of someone some day? – the assistance you give me will bring you into very close touch with me, and next summer you must be pleased to let me come to you for three months at one of your estates, preferably in the Rhine district. . . .

27 December 1861

Dear Herr von Hornstein,

It would be wrong of me to pass over without censure an answer such as you have given me. Though it will probably not happen again that a man like me will apply to you, yet a perception of the impropriety of your letter ought itself to be a good thing for you.

You should not have presumed to advise me in any way, even as to who is really rich; and you should have left it to myself to decide why I do not apply to the patrons and patronesses to whom you refer.

If you are not prepared to have me at one of your estates, you could have seized the signal opportunity I offered you of making the necessary arrangements for receiving me in some place of my choice. It is consequently offensive of you to say that you will let me know when you will be prepared to have me.

You should have omitted the wish you express with regard to my *Tristan*; your answer could only pass muster on the assumption that you are totally ignorant of my works.

Let this end the matter. I reckon on your discretion, as you can on mine.

Yours obediently,
RICHARD WAGNER

Rebecca West has defined genius as 'outrageous behaviour justifying itself in the production of masterpieces'. This sounds like Wagner all right, but what about Beethoven, what about Verdi, what about Brahms? Perhaps this might be the place to include a couple of contrasting pieces about the attitude of composers to women – seen realistically, rather than sentimentally imagined, as they so often are.

The first, curiously enough, is from the hand of one of the few women to have made any real mark as a composer. If there was ever a human being who defied society it was Ethel Smyth, a nineteenth-century general's daughter who actually managed to get unchaperoned to Leipzig to study composition. Michael Hurd, in *Grove*, remarks that 'she was larger than life as a character, and there is nothing shrinking about her music'; she was a friend of Brahms, Grieg and Tchaikovsky, and ended up by falling in love with Virginia Woolf.

The Brahms connection came through his great friend Elisabeth von Herzogenberg (Lisl), the wife of one of her teachers at Leipzig

From the very first I had worshipped Brahms's music, as I do some of it now; hence I was predisposed to admire the man. But without exactly disliking him, his personality neither impressed nor attracted me, and I could never understand why the faithful had such an exalted opinion of his intellect. Rather taciturn and jerky as a rule, and notoriously difficult to carry on a conversation with, after meals his mind and tongue unstiffened; and then, under the stimulus of countless cups of very strong black coffee, he was ready to discuss literature, arts, politics, morals, or anything under the sun. On such occasions, though he never said anything stupid, I cannot recall hearing him say anything very striking, and when his latest pronouncement on Bismarck, poetry, or even music was ecstatically handed round, it generally seemed to me what anyone might have said. . . .

I think what chiefly angered me was his views on women, which after all were the views prevalent in Germany. . . . Brahms, as artist and bachelor, was free to adopt what may be called the poetical variant of the *Kinder, Kirche, Küche* axiom, namely that women are playthings. He made one or two exceptions, as such men will, and chief among these was Lisl, to whom his attitude was perfect . . . reverential, admiring, and affectionate, without a tinge of amorousness. Being, like most artists, greedy, it specially melted him that she was such a splendid *Hausfrau*; indeed as often as not, from love of the best, she would do her own marketing. During Brahms's visits she was never happier than when concocting some exquisite dish to set before the king; . . . she would come in, flushed with stooping over the range, her golden hair wavier than ever from the heat, and cry: 'Begin that movement again; that much you owe me!' and Brahms's worship would flame up in unison with the blaze in the kitchen. In short he was adorable with Lisl . . .

To see him with Lili Wach, Frau Schumann and her daughters, or other links with his great predecessors, was to see him at his best, so gentle and respectful was his bearing; in fact to Frau Schumann he behaved as might a particularly delightful old-world son. I remember a most funny conversation between them as to why the theme of his D major Piano Variations had what she called 'an unnecessary bar tacked on', this being one of the supreme touches in that wonderful, soaring tune. She argued the point lovingly, but as ever with some heat, and I thought him divinely patient.

His ways with other women-folk – or to use the detestable word for ever on his lips, *Weibsbilder* – were less admirable. If they did not appeal to him he was incredibly awkward and ungracious; if they were pretty he had an unpleasant way of leaning back in his chair, pouting out his lips, stroking his moustache, and staring at them as a greedy boy stares at jam-tartlets. People used to think this rather delightful, specially hailing it, too, as a sign that the great man was in high good-humour, but it angered me, as did also his jokes about women, and his everlasting gibes at any, excepting Lisl of course, who possessed brains or indeed ideas of any kind. . . .

I am bound to say his taste in jokes sometimes left much to be desired, and can give an instance on the subject of my own name, which all foreigners find difficult, and which, as I innocently told him, my washerwoman pronounced *Schmeiss*. Now the verb *schmeissen*, to throw violently, is vulgar but quite harmless; there is however an antique noun, *Schmeiss*, which means something quite unmentionable, and a certain horrible fly which frequents horrible places is called *Schmeiss-Fliege*. As Brahms was for ever commenting on the extreme rapidity of my movements he found the play upon words irresistible and nicknamed me *die Schmeiss-Fliege*, but Lisl was so scandalized at this joke that he had to drop it. . . .

To me personally he was very kind and fatherly in his awkward way, chiefly, no doubt, because of the place I held in his friend's heart; but after a very slight acquaintance I guessed he would never take a woman-writer seriously, and had no desire, though kindly urged by him to do so, to show him my work. At last one day, without asking my leave, Lisl showed him a little fugue of mine, and when I came in and found them looking at it he began analysing it, simply, gravely, and appreciatively, saying this development was good, that modulation curious, and so on. Carried away by surprise and delight I lost my head, and pointing out a constructive detail that had greatly fussed Herzogenberg – the sort of thing that made him call me a bad pupil – asked eagerly: 'Don't you think if I feel it that way I have a right to end on the dominant?' Suddenly the scene changed, back came the ironic smile, and stroking his moustache he said in a voice charged with kindly contempt: 'I am quite sure, dear child, you may end when and where you please!' . . . There it was! he had suddenly remembered I was a girl, to take whom seriously was beneath a man's dignity, and the quality of the work, which had I been an obscure male he would have upheld against anyone, simply passed from his mind.

ETHEL SMYTH *c.* 1878 *Impressions that Remained*

Here, from Verdi, is a characteristic statement of independence, coupled with a demand for its respect, in a marvellous letter to his patron and erstwhile father-in-law, Antonio Barezzi

I don't believe that of your own accord you would have written me a letter which you know was bound to distress me. But you live in a town where people have the bad habit of prying into other people's affairs and of disapproving of everything that does not conform to their own ideas. It is my custom never to interfere, unless I am asked, in other people's business and I expect others not to interfere in mine. All this gossip, grumbling and disapprobation arises from that. I have the right to expect in my own country the liberty of action that is respected even in less civilized places. Judge for yourself, severely if you will, but coolly and dispassionately: What harm is there if I live in isolation? If I choose not to pay calls on titled people? If I take no part in the festivities and rejoicings of others? If I administer my farmlands because I like to do so and because it amuses me? I ask again: What harm is there in this? In any case, no one is any the worse for it. . . .

There, I've laid bare to you my opinions, my actions, my wishes, my public life, I would almost say, and since we are by way of making revelations, I have no objection to raising the curtain that veils the mysteries contained within four walls, and telling you about my private life. I have nothing to hide. In my house there lives a lady, free, independent, a lover like myself of solitude, possessing a fortune that shelters her from all need. Neither I nor she owes to anyone at all an account of our actions. On the other hand, who knows what relationship exists between us? What affairs? What ties? What claims I have on her, and she on me? Who knows whether she is or is not my wife? And if she is, who knows what the particular reasons are for not making the fact public? Who knows whether that is a good thing or a bad one? Why should it not be a good thing? And even if it is a bad thing, who has the right to ostracize us? I will say this, however: in my house she is entitled to as much respect as myself – more even; and no one is allowed to forget that on any account. And finally she has every right, both on account of her conduct and her character, to the consideration she never fails to show to others.

GIUSEPPE VERDI 21 January 1852

What neither Brahms nor Verdi, in their different ways, possessed was the urbanity and sophistication to treat the complexities of modern society as they deserve. There is a story of that extraordinary man, Hans von Bülow, pianist, conductor and ardent supporter of Wagner, whose wife, Cosima Liszt, left him for Wagner thus precipitating the most notorious divorce in nineteenth-century music. Bülow was the guest of honour at a party given by Edward Dannreuther at his London house. . . .

A lady asked her host to introduce her to the great man, and began her conversation with the question, 'Oh! Monsieur von Bülow, vous connaissez Monsieur Wagner, n'est ce pas?' While the drops of perspiration were bursting out on Dannreuther's forehead, Bülow made a low bow and answered without a sign of surprise, 'Mais oui, Madame, c'est le mari de ma femme.'

C. V. STANFORD *Unwritten Diary* 1914

Composition

The Composer

All the others translate: the painter sketches
A visible world to love or reject;
Rummaging into his living, the poet fetches
The images out that hurt and connect,

From Life to Art by painstaking adaption,
Relying on us to cover the rift;
Only your notes are pure contraption,
Only your song is an absolute gift.

Pour out your presence, a delight cascading
The falls of the knee and the weirs of the spine,
Our climate of silence and doubt invading;

You alone, alone, imaginary song,
Are unable to say an existence is wrong,
And pour out your forgiveness like a wine.

W. H. AUDEN 1938

Never compose anything unless the not composing of it becomes a positive nuisance to you.

GUSTAV HOLST

I don't choose what I compose. It chooses me.

GUSTAV MAHLER

In music there is no form without logic, there is no logic without unity.

ARNOLD SCHOENBERG

There are only twelve tones. You must treat them carefully.

PAUL HINDEMITH

When asked how he composed, Tchaikovsky used to answer: 'Sitting down'.

For some, composition appears to have been easy

[Dvořák] is one of the phenomena of the nineteenth century, – a child of nature, who did not stop to think, and said on paper anything which came into his head. I once asked him whether he wrote as fast as his music suggested. He answered that he generally completed six pages of full score in a morning, that if six was multiplied by 365 the result was 2,190 pages, 'which is far more music than anyone wants to listen to.'

C. V. STANFORD *Unwritten Diary* 1914

Perhaps too easy

Mascagni worked with a precision, an exactness and a regularity that was astonishing in a man so exuberant and volcanic. In the evening, after dinner, a few friends from Livorno would come in, there would be a couple of hands of *scopone* which usually gave rise to a fairly lively – well, let's say highly lively – discussion, after which the maestro would go into his studio to compose.

Sometimes, however, the game would be interrupted; on some

evenings the maestro would make mistakes, play his cards badly –
you could see that his mind was elsewhere. And suddenly he would
get up and say: 'Forgive me, let's stop there for this evening'. He
would go into his studio, re-read the section of libretto that he had to
set, and then sit down at the piano. From those first chords, little by
little, grew tentative melodies and recitatives; he sketched them with
his voice, then started again and modified them until they blossomed,
exact, precise and complete, as he wanted them.

The piano was his orchestra. Often I stood outside the door of his
studio, listening: mostly the melody, the musical commentary on the
action, were beautiful and I would say to myself, 'Tonight we've got
it'. Occasionally on some evenings I would hear a passage less happy
in its effect, generally on an evening when the *scopone* party had not
been interrupted – and alas I knew that, after he had written a piece,
very, very rarely did Mascagni change it. . . .

GIOVACCHINO FORZANO Come li ho conosciuti 1957

Verdi's comment to Gino Monaldi about *Cavalleria Rusticana* was brief but
acute: 'Ah, a fine moment of sincerity, my word!' But a few years later:

'What a pity! What a pity! He is a young man, whose feeling for music
exceeds his knowledge of it . . . He could achieve much . . . but . . . I
think he has now lost his way'.

G. MONALDI 1891 and 1896 Verdi

Compare his advice to Mascagni's younger colleague, Umberto Giordano

. . . never correct what you wrote on the previous day – you will not
like it any more and you will mistakenly destroy all that you have
done. Compose the first act, without pausing, without corrections;
when you have done this, put the sheets of music to one side and start
the second act. Proceed with the second act in exactly the same way,
and then continue with the third and fourth acts. Then rest. When you
have recovered your strength, revise and correct everything; you can
be sure that this is the only way of avoiding error. . . . Work every day,
at any work to hand – without such daily exercise the hand . . . grows
stiff . . . Never read newspaper reviews after a première and never
pay homage to journalists with your visiting-card.

VERDI in D. Cellamare Umberto Giordano 1949

For others, composing was profoundly hard. Everyone who has ever tried to write anything knows what it is like to sit down in front of a blank page and start. Imagine Berlioz, sitting down to the five acts and nine tableaux of the full score of *Les Troyens*

When I am back in Paris I shall try to shake off all other business and begin my musical task. It will be hard: may all Virgil's gods come to my aid, or I am lost. What is so terribly difficult is to find the musical *form* – that form without which music does not exist, or at most exists only as the humble slave of the words. There is Wagner's crime; he wants to dethrone music, to reduce it to *expressive accents*, thus going even further than Gluck (who most fortunately did not succeed in following his own ungodly theory). I am for the kind of music which you yourself call *free*. Yes, free and proud and sovereign and conquering. I want it to grasp everything, to assimilate everything. . . . How to find the way to be *expressive, true*, without ceasing to be a musician; how to provide music, instead, with new means of action – that is the problem. . . . And there's another rock in my way: the feelings that must be expressed move me too deeply. That's no good. One must try to do coolly things that are fiery. It was this that held me up so long in the adagio of *Romeo and Juliet* and the finale of reconciliation; I thought I would never see my way.

Time! . . . Time! . . . He is the great master! Unfortunately, like Ugolino, he eats his children. . . .

HECTOR BERLIOZ Letter 12 August 1856

It must be wonderful to be able to write in the presence of grand scenery! . . . Alas! such a joy is denied me! Beautiful country, towering peaks, a turbulent sea absorb me completely, instead of exciting me to thought. I feel but cannot express myself. I am only able to paint the moon when seeing its image at the bottom of a well.

HECTOR BERLIOZ Letter to Wagner 10 September 1855

How much one must first find, and then suppress, to reach the bare flesh of emotion.

CLAUDE DEBUSSY

In spite of romantic notions to the contrary, most composers find a regular domestic life essential to work

. . . In the warmer parts of the year Haydn rose at 6.30, and straightway shaved himself – no one else ever shaved him until his seventy-third year. Then he would get fully dressed. Sometimes a pupil would be present while he was dressing. The pupil would have to play on the piano the lesson he had been set, after which Haydn would point out his mistakes and inform him of the rules he had infringed: and then a new exercise would be set for the pupil to prepare for the next lesson.

At eight Haydn had breakfast. Immediately afterwards he sat down at the piano and improvised until he had lighted upon ideas which served the purposes he had in mind: and these ideas he straightway committed to paper. In this way the initial drafts of his works were begun.

At 11.30 he received visits, or else went for a walk and paid visits himself.

The hour from two to three was given up to the midday meal.

After the meal Haydn looked into the business of his household, or went to his library and took a book to read.

At four he returned to his musical work, taking the sketches he had made in the morning and putting them into score. Over this he spent three or four hours.

At eight in the evening he usually went out, returning about nine. Then he either sat down to further writing of scores or took his book again and read. This went on till ten, at which time he had supper. He made a rule never to take anything more than bread and wine in the evening, and he broke that rule only when he was invited out somewhere to supper.

He loved joking, and merry talk generally, at the table.

At 11.30 he went to bed – when he was old, even earlier. The only difference which winter made to his routine was that he rose half an hour later; everything else went on as in summer.

A. C. DIES *Joseph Haydn* 1810

There is a widely held belief among musicians that it is somehow cheating to use a piano when composing: as a matter of fact a great many composers have made use of the keyboard – though it is somehow surprising to find Haydn one of their number

I would sit down [at the piano], and begin to improvise, whether my spirits were sad or happy, serious or playful. Once I had captured an idea, I strove with all my might to develop and sustain it in conformity with the rules of art. In this way I tried to help myself, and this is where so many of our newer composers fall short: they string one little piece onto another and break off when they have scarcely started.

Nothing remains in one's heart after one has listened to such compositions.

I was never a quick writer and always composed with care and diligence. However, such works are lasting, and the connoisseur knows this immediately from the score. When Cherubini would look over some of my manuscripts, he would always recognize those passages which deserved special marks of distinction.

G. A. GRIESINGER *Biographische Notizen*, 1809

'Musical ideas pursue me to the point of torture. I cannot get rid of them, they stand before me like a wall. If it is an *allegro* that pursues me, my pulse beats faster, I cannot sleep; if an *adagio*, I find my pulse beating slowly. My imagination plays upon me as if I were a keyboard.'

Then Haydn smiled, the blood suddenly flamed in his cheeks as he said 'I really am a living keyboard.'

A. C. DIES *Joseph Haydn* 1810

With Chopin it could hardly have been otherwise

His creation was spontaneous and miraculous. He found it without seeking it, without foreseeing it. It came on his piano suddenly, complete, sublime, or it sang in his head during a walk, and he was impatient to play it to himself. But then began the most heart-rending labour I ever saw. It was a series of efforts, of irresolutions and of frettings to seize again certain details of the theme he had heard; what he had conceived as a whole he analysed too much when wishing to write it, and his regret at not finding it again, in his opinion, clearly defined, threw him into a kind of despair. He shut himself up in his room for whole days, weeping, walking, breaking his pens, repeating a bar a hundred times, writing and effacing it as many times, and recommencing the next day with a minute and desperate persever-ance. He spent six weeks over a single page to write it at last as he had noted it down at the very first.

GEORGE SAND *Histoire de ma vie* 1854

César Franck was another confirmed keyboard man. Vincent d'Indy describes him thrashing away at the *Meistersinger* Overture, or some piece by Bach, Beethoven or Schumann

After a while, sooner or later as the situation developed, the deafening clatter would die down gradually to a murmur, to near silence, and at last to nothing at all . . . The Master had found what he was looking for.

VINCENT D'INDY *César Franck* 1906

'At such moments', says Charles Bordes, 'Franck was positively orgiastic . . . bellowing like a stag at his piano and heating up his inspiration by playing through his own scores, to key himself up for the business of writing some more.' Curious behaviour for so saintly a figure. Little wonder, perhaps, that Mme Franck, on first hearing the composer play though his Piano Quintet at their apartment on the Boulevard Saint Michel exclaimed 'What is that music you are playing? I emphatically dislike it!'

Compare Elgar's experience in the autumn of 1898

One evening, after a long and tiresome day's teaching, aided by a cigar, I musingly played on the piano the theme as it now stands. The voice of C. A. E. [Elgar's wife] asked with a sound of approval,
'What is that?'
I answered
'Nothing – but something might be made of it.'

BASIL MAINE *Elgar: his life and works* 1933

'Something', in this case, was the *Enigma Variations*. And after all, seated one day at the organ, it was the same procedure that discovered 'The Lost Chord'. Though . . .

It should be 'The Lost Progression', for the young lady was mistaken in supposing she had ever heard any single chord 'like the sound of a great Amen.' Unless we are to suppose that she had already found the chord of C major for the final syllable of the word and was seeking the chord for the first syllable; and there she is on the walls of a Milanese restaurant arpeggioing experimental harmonies in a transport of delight to advertise Somebody and Someone's pianos and holding the loud pedal solidly down all the time. Her family had always been unsympathetic about her music. They said it was like a loose bundle of firewood which you never can get across the room without dropping sticks; they said she would have been so much better employed doing anything else.

Fancy being in the room with her while she was strumming about and hunting after her chord! Fancy being in heaven with her when she had found it!

SAMUEL BUTLER *Note-Books* 1912

The concept of inspiration, that Haydn, Chopin, César Franck and the young lady were so sedulously courting, is considered, with his usual practicality, by Richard Strauss

What is an inspiration? In general, a musical inspiration is known as a motive, a melody with which I am suddenly 'inspired', unbidden by the intelligence, particularly in the morning immediately on awakening, or in a dream – Sachs in the *Meistersinger*: 'Glaubt mir, des Menschen wahrster Wahn wird ihm im Träume aufgetan.' Did my imagination work independently at night, without my consciousness, without being bound to 'recollection' (Plato)?

My own experience: when at night I am stuck at a certain point in my composition, and in spite of all my digging no further profitable work seems possible, I shut the piano or my sketchbook, go to bed, and when I wake up in the morning, the continuation is there. By means of which mental or physical process?

Or shall we, following current colloquial usage, term inspiration that which is so new, so thrilling, so compelling and which penetrates 'into the very depths of the heart' (Leonore), that it can not be compared with anything that preceded it. Quality? Whence stem the indescribable melodies of our classicists (Haydn, Mozart, Beethoven, Schubert), for which no models exist? Even in Johann Sebastian Bach's Adagios and in the works of his son, Philipp Emanuel, we hardly find themes which can be compared with the soaring, endless melodies of Mozart – not only in the arias of his dramatic works, but also in his instrumental works (I am thinking particularly of his G minor String Quintet). What then is direct inspiration, primary invention, and what is the work of the intelligence in these divine forms? Where is the boundary between intellectual activity and imagination?

The question is especially difficult to decide among our classicists; the wealth of their melodies is so enormous, the melody itself so new, so original and at the same time so individually varied, that it is difficult to determine the line between the first immediate inspiration and its continuation, its extension to the finished, expanded singing phrase. Particularly in Mozart and Schubert who died so young, and at the same time created a lifework of such colossal scope! (My father always said: 'What Mozart did, that is, composed up to his thirty-sixth year, the best copyist of today could not write down in the same amount of time.') It must have been prompted – as in the lovely concluding tableau in the first act of Pfitzner's *Palestrina* – by the flying pen of angels. For the kind of work which is to be seen in Beethoven's sketchbooks can hardly exist here. Here everything seems immediate inspiration.

It has been my own experience in creative activity that a motive or a two to four measure melodic phrase occurs to me suddenly. I put it down on paper and immediately extend it to an eight, sixteen, or thirty-two bar phrase, which naturally does not remain unaltered, but after a shorter or longer 'maturing' is gradually worked out into its definitive form which holds its own against even the most severe, blasé self-criticism. This work now proceeds at a rate which depends primarily on my awaiting the moment at which my imagination is capable and ready to serve me further. But this readiness is mostly evoked and promoted by considerable leisure, after lengthy reflection, also through inner excitement (also anger and indignation). These mental processes pertain not only to innate talent, but to self-criticism and self-development. 'Genie ist Fleiss' [Genius is industry], Goethe is supposed to have said. But industry and the desire to work are inborn, not merely acquired.

RICHARD STRAUSS *On Inspiration in Music c.* 1940

Strauss's own inspiration functioned with an extraordinary facility. 'A poem will jolt me,' he remarked, 'and a musical idea for it will come to me, often before I've finished reading it properly: I sit down; the whole song is done in ten minutes.' There are stories of Schubert writing songs on the backs of dinner menus and failing to recognize them a couple of days later.

Sometimes Strauss's facility led him onto dangerous ground. One can understand so well the *cri de coeur* in one of Hofmannsthal's letters when Strauss was at grips with the last act of *Die Frau ohne Schatten*

. . . Even so, are we really to have yet another spinning out of the original passage? More and more! Must that be? My dear Dr Strauss! However grand and beautiful this melody in E flat major is sure to be, do think about it twice!

HUGO VON HOFMANNSTHAL Letter 24 July 1916

In the end, both for Strauss and the young lady seeking her mislaid chord, it is a question of intellectual control over an instinctive musical gift. Here, then, is a second instalment of Virgil Thomson, this time on the Intellectual Content of Music (for the two companion pieces see pages 13–15 and 408–10).

Music, a creation of the human mind, has its appeal for all the faculties of the mind. Its message, its direct communication, is to the feelings, of course. But the methods by which continuity is sustained and interest held are a result of thought taken. And though it is desirable that this thought be not too evident, that it not interfere with the transmission of feeling that is music's both immediate and final aim, it does have a listener interest over and above its functional efficiency, because any construction of the human mind is fascinating to the human mind. This is the workmanship aspect of music, the quality that adds beauty to expression. . . .

The intellectual content of anything – of music, painting, poetry, oratory, or acting – consists of references to tradition, to the history of its own technique as an art, of a wealth of allusions, indeed, to many things under the sun. Expressive content is personal, individual, specific, unique. It cannot be borrowed. If it is not spontaneous it is not sincere, hence not, in the long run, convincing. But intellectual content is all borrowed; it is only the choice and the appropriate usage of allusions and devices that give them validity in any work. . . .

The richness of music's intellectual substance varies from composer to composer. It is greater in Bach, for instance, than in Handel, though the latter, predominantly a man of the theater, has a plainer and more direct emotional appeal. Mozart's frame of reference, likewise, is more ample than that of Haydn. It is characteristic of both Bach and Mozart to use dance meters without the idea of dancing being the only thought communicated. Bach writes between an organ toccata and its fugue a siciliana which is at the same time a religious meditation. And Mozart writes in a piano sonata (O, how often) a slow movement which is both a minuet and a love duet, as well as a piano solo. . . . It is Beethoven's gift for working opposites in together that gives to his concert music its phenomenal power of suggesting drama, which is struggle. Beethoven has for this reason intellectual content to a high degree. He did not refer much, except in his later works, where he employed constantly the deliberate archaism of fugal style, to the history of composing techniques; but he did manage by careful handling of the contemporary techniques, to make one thing mean many things (as in the variation form) and to make many things one (as in the ten-theme symphony form). He holds attention to this day, in consequence. He keeps the listener occupied.

Wagner's operas have the highest intellectual content of any. I don't mean the philosophical tomfoolery of his librettos, either, though this was necessary to him as a pretext for elaborateness of musical texture and for the whole psychological refinement that was his chief legacy to the stage. Puccini's operas have probably the lowest intellectual content of any, though their plots are far from stupid. Their expressive content, which is chiefly self-pity, is powerful by its simplicity. But the emotional composition of this has little depth or perspective, and the musical textures employed are of small interest as workmanship.

Tchaikovsky, Sibelius, and Shostakovich are demagogic symphonists because the expressive power of their work is greater than its interest as music; it does not fully or long occupy an adult mind. Debussy and Stravinsky are fascinating to the adult mind. They stimulate feelings and provoke thought. Schoenberg and Hindemith are overrich of intellectual interest in proportion to their feeling content; they are a little dry, in consequence. Bartók, Milhaud, and Copland strike a sound balance between mental and emotional appeal, even though their intensity in both kinds is less than one could wish it were. Roy Harris oscillates between extreme intellectuality, for which he has little gift, and a banal, a borrowed emotionalism, which he cultivates out of a yearning for quick-and-easy success. At his best, however, he is both moving and interesting. Olivier Messiaen is a similar case, though his musical gift is greater and his mind more ingenious. . . .

What makes possible the writing of good music, beyond that talent for handling sound that is required for being a musician at all, is emotional sincerity and intellectual honesty. Both can be cultivated, of course; but no man can quite lift himself by his boot straps. Unless he has a good heart (the psychiatrists nowadays call this affectivity) and a strong, vigorous mind, he will not write any music capable at once of touching the human heart and interesting the human mind. Art that does not do both dies quickly. And longevity is the glory, perhaps even the definition, of civilization's major achievements.

20 April 1947
VIRGIL THOMSON *The Art of Judging Music* 1948

Some forms of intellectual control are fairly straightforward

Moreover you must have a care that when your matter signifieth ascending, high heaven and such like, you make your musicke ascend: and by the contrarie where your dittie speaketh of descending, lowenes, depth, hell and others such, you must make your musicke descend, for as it will be thought a great absurditie to talke of heaven and point downwarde to the earth: so will it be counted great incongruitie if a musician upon the wordes 'hee ascended into heaven' shoulde cause his musicke [to] descend. . . .

THOMAS MORLEY *A Plaine and Easie Introduction to Practicall Musicke* 1597

Others need more careful application

While composing music is not the time to recall the rules which might hold our genius in bondage. We must have recourse to the rules only when our genius and our ear seem to deny what we are seeking.

JEAN-PHILIPPE RAMEAU *Le nouveau système de musique théorique* 1726

There must be deviations from the rule in order to express almost everything. One must know how to describe the sane man who leaves by the door and the madman who jumps out of the window.

ANDRÉ-ERNEST-MODESTE GRÉTRY: *Mémoires, ou Essais sur la musique* 1789

The fact is, there are no rules, and there never were any rules, and there never will be any rules of musical composition except rules of thumb; and thumbs vary in length, like ears.

BERNARD SHAW *Music in London* 1890–94

The extent to which rules and conventions should be broken or changed has been argued fiercely since music began

Musical innovation is full of danger to the State, for when modes of music change, the laws of the State always change with them.

PLATO (428–347 BC) *The Republic*

Well, if that's modern music, I don't like it.

VAUGHAN WILLIAMS after conducting his own Fourth Symphony

Most critics of 'modern' music, at every stage in musical history, have complained above all of the increase of dissonance. It is therefore interesting to find a distinguished academic figure like Dr Burney coming down with great lucidity on the other side

No one will, I believe, at present deny the necessity of *discord* in the composition of music in parts; it seems to be as much the essence of music, as shade is of painting; not only as it improves and meliorates concord by opposition and comparison, but, still further, as it becomes a necessary stimulus to the attention, which would languish over a succession of pure concords. It occasions a momentary distress to the ear, which remains unsatisfied, and even uneasy, till it hears something better; for no musical phrase can end upon a discord; the ear must be satisfied at last. Now, as discord is allowable, and even necessarily opposed to concord, why may not *noise*, or a seeming jargon, be opposed to fixed sounds and harmonical proportion? Some of the discords in modern music, unknown till this century, are what the ear can but just bear, but have a very good effect as to contrast. The severe laws of preparing and resolving discord, may be too much adhered to for great effects; I am convinced that provided the ear be at length made amends, there are few dissonances too strong for it.

CHARLES BURNEY *The Present State of Music in France and Italy* 1771

What distinguishes dissonances from consonances is not a greater or lesser degree of beauty, but a greater or lesser degree of comprehensibility.

ARNOLD SCHOENBERG *Style and Idea* 1951

The fairest harmony springs from discord.

HERACLITUS (*c.* 540–480 BC)

Or, as Schoenberg says (perhaps rather more controversially) elsewhere

There is no such thing as dissonance: it is only an extreme form of consonance.

But Schoenberg's chief contribution to musical history has been less associated with dissonance than with the destruction of tonality – or key

Haydn has produced some of his most striking effects by the sudden change of key. Every practitioner in the art must have noticed the various complexions, so to speak, by which they are characterized. By *Key*, we mean any system of notes which regards a certain tone as its base or centre, to which all the adjacent harmonies gravitate, or tend. In the 15th century, Music was generally written in the key of F, and its relative D minor. This order of sounds was first adopted, probably on account of its being the most agreeable to the ear. And as some of the grandest sounds of the natural world – the rushing of the storm, the murmurs of the brook, and the roar of the sea, are to be referred to this harmony, it may be denominated the *Key of Nature*. As science improved, other notes were taken as the centres of systems, by which other keys were formed, and we have now not less than 24 keys, both major, and minor.

We shall endeavour to characterize some of them.

| F | This key is rich, mild, sober and contemplative. |
| its relative D Minor | Possesses the same qualities, but of a heavier and darker cast: more doleful, solemn and grand. |

C	Bold, vigorous, and commanding: suited to the expression of war and enterprise.
A Minor	Plaintive, but not feeble.
G	Gay and sprightly. Being the medium key, it is adapted to the greatest range of subjects.
E Minor	Persuasive, soft and tender.
D	Ample, grand, and noble. Having more fire than C, it is suited to the loftiest purposes. In choral music, it is the highest key, the treble having its cadence note on the 4th line.
B Minor	Bewailing, but in too high a tone to excite commiseration.
A F sharp Minor	Golden, warm, and sunny. Mournfully grand.
E in sharps	Bright and pellucid: adapted to brilliant subjects. In this key Haydn has written his most elegant thoughts. Handel mistook its properties when he used it in the chorus, 'The many rend the skies with loud applause.' Though higher than D, it is less loud, as it stretches the voice beyond its natural power.
B in sharps	Keen and piercing. Seldom used.
B flat	The least interesting of any. It has not sufficient fire to render it majestic, or grand, and is too dull for song.
G Minor	Meek and pensive. Replete with melancholy.
E flat Major	Full and mellow; sombre, soft and beautiful. It is a key in which all musicians delight. – Though less decided in its character than some of the others, the regularity of its beauty renders it a universal favorite.
C Minor	Complaining, having something of the whining cant of B minor.

A flat
Major
 	
F
Minor
	The most lovely of the tribe.
	    Unassuming, gentle, soft, delicate and tender, having none of the pertness of A in sharps. Every author has been sensible of the charm of this key, and has reserved it for the expression of his most refined sentiments.
	    Religious, penitential, and gloomy.

D flat Major	Awfully dark. In this remote key, Haydn and Beethoven have written their sublimest thoughts. They never enter it but for tragic purposes.

It is sufficient to have hinted at these effects. To account for them, is difficult; but every musician is sensible of their existence.

JOHN ROWE PARKER A Musical Biography 1824

Mozart was not given to theorizing about his music, and his many letters contain few references of any significance to composition in progress: among the operas the correspondence with his father about *Idomeneo* is exceptional, and there is one fascinating letter about the first act of *Entführung* – a rare instance of a composer trying to explain his expressive intentions and the technical means he has used to achieve them

In working out the aria I have . . . allowed Fischer's beautiful deep notes to glow. The passage 'Drum beim Barte des Propheten' is indeed in the same time, but with quick notes; but as Osmin's rage gradually increases, there comes (just when the aria seems to be at an end) the allegro assai, which is in a totally different tempo and in a different key; this is bound to be very effective. For just as a man in such a towering rage oversteps all the bounds of order, moderation and propriety and completely forgets himself, so must the music too forget itself. But since passions, whether violent or not, must never be expressed to the point of exciting disgust, and as music, even in the most terrible situations, must never offend the ear, but must please the listener, or in other words must never cease to be *music*, so I have not chosen a key remote from F (in which the aria is written), but one related to it – not the nearest, D minor, but the more remote A minor. Let me now turn to Belmonte's aria in A major, 'O wie ängstlich, o wie feurig'. Would you like to know how I have expressed it – and even indicated his throbbing heart? By the two violins playing octaves. This is the favourite aria of all those who have heard it, and it is mine also. I wrote it expressly to suit Adamberger's voice. You feel the trembling – the faltering – you see how his throbbing breast begins to swell; this I have expressed by a crescendo. You hear the whispering and the sighing – which I have indicated by the first violins with mutes and a flute playing in unison.

The Janissary chorus is, as such, all that can be desired, that is, short, lively and written to please the Viennese. I have sacrificed Constanze's aria a little to the flexible throat of Mlle Cavalieri, 'Trennung war mein banges Los und nun schwimmt mein Aug' in Tränen'. I have tried to express her feelings, as far as an Italian bravura aria will allow it. . . .

Now for the trio at the close of Act I. Pedrillo has passed off his master as an architect – to give him an opportunity of meeting his Constanze in the garden. Bassa Selim has taken him into his service. Osmin, the steward, knows nothing of this, and being a rude churl and a sworn foe to all strangers, is impertinent and refuses to let them into the garden. It opens quite abruptly – and because the words lend themselves to it, I have made it a fairly respectable piece of real three-part writing. Then the major key begins at once pianissimo – it must go very quickly – and wind up with a great deal of noise, which is always appropriate at the end of an act. The more noise the better, and the shorter the better, so that the audience may not have time to cool down with their applause.

MOZART Letter to his father 26 September 1781

And here is Rossini on the composition of operatic overtures: giving advice to a young colleague. This letter was apparently written at Ricordi's music shop in Milan 'while he was dictating and checking orchestral parts'

Wait till the evening before the opening night. Nothing primes inspiration like necessity, whether it takes the form of a copyist waiting for your work or the coercion of an exasperated impresario tearing his hair out in handfuls. In my day all the impresarios in Italy were bald at thirty.

I wrote the overture to *Otello* in a little room at the Barbaja Palace, in which the baldest and fiercest of these impresarios had locked me by force with nothing but a plate of *maccheroni* and the threat that I should not leave the room alive until I had written the last note. I wrote the overture to *La Gazza Ladra* on the day of the first performance in the theatre itself, where I was imprisoned by the director and watched over by four stage-hands, who had instructions to throw my manuscript out of the window page by page to the copyists who were waiting to transcribe it below. In the absence of pages, they were to throw me.

With the *Barber* I did better still. I didn't compose an overture, but simply took one which had been meant for an *opera semiseria* called *Elisabetta*. The public was delighted.

The overture to *Conte Ory* I wrote while fishing, with my feet in the water, in the company of Signor Aguado who was talking about Spanish finance. The one for *William Tell* was done under more or less similar circumstances. As for *Mosé*, I just didn't write one at all.

GIOACCHINO ROSSINI Letter undated

There are of course, a variety of different reasons for composing a piece of music

15 May 1899

My dear Claude,

Out of a love for rich rhyme which comes to her, no doubt, from her father, Mlle Louise de Hérédia is exchanging her name for that of Louise Louÿs, which is more symmetrical and balanced. So that's why I haven't seen you for so many days and nights.

The wedding will take place at Saint-Philippe in six weeks' time. Do you know the organist of this curious edifice? I have it in mind to suggest to him a little Sebastianbacchic programme, which might be preceded by the celebrated and unpublished *Hochzeitmarsch* of Debussy. Would you be disposed to pen two hundred bars for two keyboards and pedals, in the outlandish rhythm of a march in four time – something pompous, lustful and ejaculatory in style, as is suitable at nuptial processions? One of those little masterpieces that you turn out every day on a corner of the table, between the whiskey and the first bottle of wine. You can't refuse that to an old friend, can you?

Yours,
Pierre

PIERRE LOUÿS Letter to Debussy

Debussy replied that he did not 'have the honour of knowing the organist who dispenses harmony to the faithful at Saint-Philippe', but that he would certainly undertake to write the necessary bars. 'If they are not very beautiful, they will at least be very fraternal', but whichever they were, they do not appear to have survived in the catalogue of his works.

Prokofiev's seventh and last symphony, written at the height of the Stalinist musical repressions, has a quiet ending. But in a work to be entered for the Stalin Prize a quiet ending was not politically expedient. So the conductor Samosud, as a friend, telephoned Prokofiev

[He said that if he] did not make another ending, well, . . . Now, the Stalin Prize has three different awards: the first prize is 100,000 roubles, second prize 50,000 and the third prize 25,000. So Samosud said to Prokofiev: 'If you would like to have 25,000 instead of 100,000, you will leave the old ending: if you would like to have 100,000, you will compose a new one'. And Prokofiev said to me, 'Of course, I compose a new one for 100,000. But Slava, you will still live much longer than I, and you must take care that this new ending never exists after me'.

MSTISLAV ROSTROPOVICH Interview September 1986

More composers are interested in money than might be supposed. Arthur Rubinstein describes a dinner with Rachmaninov and Stravinsky around 1940

. . . Rachmaninoff called . . . 'We would like you and your wife to come for dinner tomorrow night. There will only be the Stravinskys.'

'What? The Stravinskys?' I couldn't believe it.

'Ah, my wife and Mrs Stravinsky became very friendly at the Farmers' Market.' Ah-ha, that is more like it. The two men had spoken with such disgust of each other's works that it was inconceivable to imagine them dining together.

We arrived a little late and here was the picture: Rachmaninoff, sitting on a low chair, complained about a stomachache, holding his hand on his tummy. Stravinsky walked around the room looking at the books on the shelves with apparent great interest.

'A-a-h, you read Hemingway, do you?' he asked the host.

'We rented this house, books and all,' our host grunted. The two ladies chattered happily in a corner.

After a while, we were called to the dining room. When we were seated, Rachmaninoff, in his best Russian manner, poured out vodka from a carafe. He raised his little glass and, nodding toward us, drank. We reciprocated with a few 'zakouski's'; he repeated the gesture and we all drank. After a little while, a third small glass was emptied by us. It was only at that moment that the conversation became alive and our voices rose. Swallowing a morsel of pressed caviar, Rachmaninoff addressed Stravinsky with a sardonic laugh. 'Ha-ha-ha, your *Petrushka*, your *Firebird*, ha-ha, never gave you a cent of royalties – eh?' Stravinsky's face was flushed and suddenly turned grey with anger. 'What about your C sharp Prelude and all those concertos of yours, all you published in Russia, eh? You had to play concerts to make a living, uh?'

The ladies and I were terrified that it might lead to a nasty scene between the two composers but, lo and behold, quite the contrary happened. Both great masters began to count out the sums they could have earned and became so involved in this important matter that when we got up they retired to a small table and continued happily daydreaming of the immense fortunes they might have earned. When we were leaving, they exchanged a hearty handshake at the door and promised each other to find more sums to think of.

ARTHUR RUBINSTEIN My Many Years 1980

*Instruments
and the
Orchestra*

The ability to imagine sounds in advance of their being heard in actuality is one factor that widely separates the professional from the layman. Professionals themselves are unevenly gifted in this respect. More than one celebrated composer has struggled to produce an adequate orchestral scoring of his own music. Certain performers, on the other hand, seem especially gifted in being able to call forth delicious sonorities from their instrument. The layman's capacity for imagining unheard sound images seems, by and large, to be rather poor. This does not apply on the lowest plane of sound apprehension where, of course, there is no difficulty. Laboratory tests have demonstrated that differences in tone color are the first differences apparent to the untrained ear. Any child is capable of distinguishing the sound of a human voice from the sound of a violin. The contrast between a voice and its echo is apparent to everyone. But it bespeaks a fair degree of musical sophistication to be able to distinguish the sound of an oboe from that of an English horn, and a marked degree to imagine a whole group of woodwinds sounding together. If you have ever had occasion, as I have, to perform an orchestral score on the piano to a group of non-professionals, you will have soon realized how little sense they have of how this music might be expected to sound in an orchestra.

It is surprising to note how little investigation has been devoted to this whole sphere of music. There are no textbooks solely designed to examine the sound stuff of music – the history of its past by comparison with its present; or its future; or its potential. Even so-called orchestration texts, written ostensibly to describe the science of combining orchestral instruments, are generally found to steer shy of their subject, concentrating instead on instrumentation, that is, on the examination of the technical and tonal possibilities of the individual instrument. The sonorous image appears to be a kind of aural mirage, not easily immobilized and analyzed. The case of the individual sound is rather different, since it is more comparable to that of the primary colors in painting. It is the full spectrum of the musician's 'color' palette that seems to lend itself much less well to discussion and consideration than that of the painter.

AARON COPLAND *Music and Imagination* 1952

A symphony that sleeps in a score for a hundred years is one of the most esoteric things ever devised: meaningless to all but trained specialists. (In which it widely differs from a play in MS – open, even if never performed, to the most fortuitous reader.) A score that awakens to potential life in the conductor's study is a challenge and an adventure, something paradoxically in progress between abstraction and reality. But a symphony performed is the most lively, palpable, and palpitating manifestation of music – a world of hard and mellow musical facts. Not of the deepest and purest: music's Parthenons and music's Leonardo and Rembrandt drawings are Josquin motets and Byrd masses *a cappella*, Mozart quintets and Beethoven quartets for strings, and Bach's never instrumented *Art of the Fugue*, and Beethoven's beyond-the-piano *Diabelli Variations*. But music's Breughels, Titians, Grecos, and Goyas, are symphony and opera.

Yet it must be owned that SCORING, in the technical sense of orchestrating, is very rarely an essential of music. Schumann, though not so poor an orchestrator as he is often called, cannot compete in this respect with Meyerbeer, now deservedly forgotten. Good four-hand players have their essential Haydn symphony at home, in black and white. Of works that exist in two versions, for piano and for orchestra – such as Liszt's *Mephisto Waltz* and Ravel's *Alborada del gracioso* – the keyboard alternative is as satisfactory as the orchestral, sometimes more so. And even the *Tannhäuser* Overture – an orchestral Rubens – was hardly ever better performed than when played by Busoni in Liszt's piano transcription.

There is, however, an incomparably glowing and intoxicating quality in orchestral sound and colour, something overwhelming, even crushing, now and then. Amphion's Thebes and Orpheus' wild beasts were built and tamed to a single player's chamber music; but the walls of Jericho were overthrown by an orchestra of trumpets and trombones. . . .

And as a whole, the full orchestra, with its new-old and old-new colours blended, is young – hardly older than the violin; and it has changed, during the few centuries of its existence, almost beyond recognition. The orchestra of a Haydn symphony is nearer in effect to any sextet for strings, oboe, and horn of the same period than to the orchestra of *Daphnis et Chloé*; and it is almost absurd to speak of Bach's scoring and of Debussy's as of two varieties of the same technique.

The romantic nineteenth century has been the classic age of the orchestra, and Weber, Berlioz, and Liszt were its classics – the romantic contemporaries of Goya, Delacroix, and Corot. In fact, in their approach to musical colour they were rather the spiritual 'contemporaries' of Titian and Tintoretto. And later, when music became more and more eager to learn its own history, the orchestra had its pre-Raphaelites, its Impressionists, and its Primitivists. Debussy was interested in and inspired by Javanese *gamelans*, and Stravinsky by other exoticisms. And at the 1925 Venice festival of modern music those who played and those who attended (with the exception of Professor Edward Dent, as usual aware of the real significance of musical events) seem to have been reminded (by a piece for six trumpets by Carl Ruggles) of the first orchestral experiments at Jericho, or of the promised last, in Josephat Valley.

FREDERICK GOLDBECK *The Perfect Conductor* 1960

Then an herald cried aloud, To you it is commanded, O people, nations and languages,
That at what time ye hear the sound of the cornet, flute, harp, sackbut, psaltery, dulcimer, and all kinds of musick, ye fall down and worship the golden image that Nebuchadnezzar the king hath set up.
And whoso falleth not down and worshippeth shall the same hour be cast into the midst of a burning fiery furnace.
Therefore at that time, when all the people heard the sound of the cornet, flute, harp, sackbut, psaltery, and all kinds of musick, all the people, the nations, and the languages, fell down and worshipped the golden image that Nebuchadnezzar the king had set up.

DANIEL III 4–7

(An amusing comparison, here, with Britten's orchestra for *The Burning Fiery Furnace*)

By the rivers of Babylon, there we sat down, yea, we wept, when we remembered Zion.
We hanged our harps upon the willows in the midst thereof.
For there they that carried us away captive required of us a song; and they that wasted us required of us mirth, saying, Sing us one of the songs of Zion.
How shall we sing the Lord's song in a strange land?
If I forget thee, O Jerusalem, let my right hand forget her cunning.
If I do not remember thee, let my tongue cleave to the roof of my mouth; if I prefer not Jerusalem above my chief joy.

PSALM 137

If only the Hebrews had waited until . . .

25 November 1947

A waterproof Irish harp, manufactured by Melville Clark of Syracuse, New York, strung with pre-shrunk nylon strings, is given its first public demonstration in New York by a mermaid-shaped harpist enclosed in a glass tank filled with water, in a fluvially fluent demonstration of marine arpeggios, underwater glissandos and aquatic passages of enharmonic liquidity.

NICOLAS SLONIMSKY *Music Since 1900*

Was Walter de la Mare's Musician a harpist?

The Song of Shadows

Sweep thy faint strings, Musician,
    With thy long lean hand;
Downward the starry tapers burn,
    Sinks soft the waning sand;
The old hound whimpers couched in sleep,
    The embers smoulder low;
Across the walls the shadows
    Come and go.

Sweep softly thy strings, Musician,
    The minutes mount to hours;
Frost on the windless casement weaves
    A labyrinth of flowers;
Ghosts linger in the darkening air,
    Hearken at the open door;
Music hath called them, dreaming,
    Home once more.

WALTER DE LA MARE *Peacock Pie* 1913

The orchestral harp was much in demand by oratorio composers in the nineteenth century; the precise number used was a matter for debate, as in this exchange between the sanctimonious Gounod and that old tough, Sir Michael Costa, at Birmingham in 1882

He was not at all so kindly to Gounod, who conducted the first performance of the 'Redemption' on the same occasion. He disliked the Frenchman's pose and resented the suggestion of 'The Assumption of Gounod' which his attitude pictured. I fully expected to see a miracle: the opening of the Town Hall ceiling and the ascent of the composer into a layer of Black Country fog. There was nearly an open breach about the number of harps. Gounod wanted six, Costa would only consent (with many grumbles) to four. The secretary came to Costa in despair saying that 'M. Gounod insists on six harps.'

COSTA: The old fool! he thinks that he will go to Heaven with six harps! He shall have four' (*banging the table*).

C. V. STANFORD 1882 Unwritten Diary

'The harp is ancient and universal', says Percy Scholes in *The Oxford Companion to Music*: 'there is record of it, in some form, in every age of human history and in every place inhabited by men or spirits – except Hell.'

He is equally good on the harpsichord, summarizing its tone as 'a sort of agreeable twang', and quotes an American description:

. . . a scratch with a sound at the end of it . . .

and a (still more unappreciative) English one:

. . . a performance on a bird-cage with a toasting-fork . . .

The Virginal was the earliest and simplest form of harpsichord. One of its kind proved an unsatisfactory example of export-import in the seventeenth century

Right Honorable

The Virginall I do pitch upon is an excellent peece, made by Johannes Rickarts att Antwerp. It is a dobbel staert stick as called, hath foure registers, the place to play on att the inde. The Virginal was made for the late Infante, hath a fair picture on the inne side of the Covering, representing the Infantas parke, and on the opening, att the part where played, a picture of Rubens, representing Cupid and Psiche, the partie asks £30 sterling. Those Virginals wch have noe pictures cost £15. – Y^r hon^r will have time enuf to consider on the sum, cause I can keepe the Virginal long enuf att my house.

I take my leave and rest,

Yo^r hon^{rs}, &c.

BALTHAZAR GERBIER

Letter to Sir Francis Windebank
Secretary of State, Brussels, January 1638

S^r:

The Virginall wch yo^u sent me, is com safe, and I wish it were as usefull as I know yo^u intended it. But the workman, that made it, was much mistaken in it, and it wantes 6 or 7 Keyes, so that it is utterly unserviceable. If either he could alter it, or wolde change it for another that may have more Keyes, it were well: but as it is, our musick is marr'd.

SIR FRANCIS WINDEBANK
Letter to Balthazar Gerbier,
Master of the Horse to the Duke of Buckingham, 1638

Might Sir Francis have preferred the keyboard instrument displayed at the Great Exhibition of 1851?

The piano, in place of being supported by legs in the ordinary manner, is supported by a frame which again rests upon a hollow base; inside such hollow base is placed a couch, which is mounted upon rollers and can be drawn out in front of the piano; the front surface of the couch when slid inside the base forming the front side thereof. . . . A hollow space is formed in the middle of the frame for rendering the pedals accessible to the performer's feet, and on one side of such space is formed a closet, having doors opening in front of the piano, and which is designed to contain the bed clothes. On the other side of the space so formed, firstly, a bureau with drawers, and second, another closet for containing a wash-hand basin, jug, towels and other articles of toilet. The bureau and second closet are made to open at the end of the frame, the front surface of that part of the latter being formed with false drawers to correspond in appearance with the doors of the before-mentioned closet on the other side of the space. . . .

　　Another part of the invention consists in constructing a music stool which is so arranged that in addition it contains a work-box, a looking glass, a writing desk or table, and a small set of drawers. (Eng. Pat. 1806)

Manufacturer's description 1851

READY TUNED AND INSURED

The scene is the forecourt of Sid's new and used pianos, a large repair and tuning depot just off the North Circular Road. The manager, who is wearing a sheepskin jacket and a badge reading 'Schubert's Unfinished and I'm Not Feeling Too Great Myself', is standing there wiping his dusty hands. A customer comes up to him, pushing an old upright.

CUSTOMER: Sid?

MANAGER: He's not here.

CUSTOMER: Do you know where he is?

MANAGER: No idea. He died in 1947. We kept the name for tax purposes.

CUSTOMER: Ah. Well, if you're in charge, I wonder if you could have a look at my piano. I'm having a bit of trouble with it at speed.

MANAGER: Sure. Just park it over by that yellow Bechstein and we'll give it the once over at the weekend.

CUSTOMER: I'd be grateful if you could have a look now. I need it this evening.

MANAGER: All right, squire. (*He opens the top and hits the keys once or twice.*) Blimey, I'm not surprised you've been having trouble. When did you last clean the return mechanism?

CUSTOMER: Well, I . . .

MANAGER: Got to keep the return mechanism clean. When it gets dirty, it starts to stick and then you can't get those repeated notes, know what I mean?

CUSTOMER: So it's just the return mechanism needs cleaning, is it? That's a relief.

MANAGER: And these hammers are worn. Oh dear, oh dear, oh dear. Worn? They're more like cotton wool on a stick than hammers. And look at these strings. Oh deary, deary me.

CUSTOMER: Is it bad then?

MANAGER: Bad? I'm not saying it's bad. I'm just saying that considering it's an old Carl Schumann piano, made in Dresden seventy years ago, you're lucky it's still going at all. What do you use it for?

CUSTOMER: Beethoven, mostly. Though I quite often relax with some boogie-woogie.

MANAGER: Well, there you are then. That stuff really punishes a piano.

CUSTOMER: It's very quiet boogie-woogie.

MANAGER: Boogie-woogie? I'm talking about your actual Beethoven. He's murder on a little old upright like this. Quite honestly, squire, it's hardly worth mending this lot. Know what I'd do? I'd put in a factory reconditioned frame and new set of strings and hammers. I could do it for £600, sir.

CUSTOMER: £600!

MANAGER: We'd reline the pedals and put in a new sustainer as well, of course. All in the price. And top up with new varnish.

CUSTOMER: It's almost like buying a new piano . . .

MANAGER: Now you're talking! By complete coincidence, I have here a wonderful upright, only one previous owner, a little lady who stuck to Mozart all her life and never went faster than moderato, straight up! Only just gone on sale. Bound to be snapped up by the weekend.

CUSTOMER: But I only came in to get a quick overhaul, not a whole new piano.

MANAGER: Suit yourself, mate. You want to push on with the old one, that's your privilege.

CUSTOMER: Well . . . how much are you asking?

MANAGER: £1,100.

CUSTOMER: £1,100, for this old thing?

MANAGER: It's got a beautiful response, this machine. Nice tuning, lovely action. Tell you what, I'll make it £1,050. Couldn't bring it lower without bankrupting myself.

MILES KINGTON Moreover, too . . . 1985

The Old Lute

Of cord and cassia-wood is the lute compounded;
Within it lie ancient melodies.
Ancient melodies – weak and savourless,
Not appealing to present men's taste.
Light and colour are faded from the jade stops;
Dust has covered the rose-red strings.
Decay and ruin came to it long ago,
But the sound that is left is still cold and clear.
I do not refuse to play it, if you want me to;
But even if I play, people will not listen.

How did it come to be neglected so?
Because of the Ch'iang flute and the zithern of Ch'in.

PO CHU-I (772–846) translated from the Chinese by Arthur Waley

In Heaven a spirit doth dwell
  'Whose heart-strings are a lute';
None sing so wildly well
  As the angel Israfel,

And the giddy Stars (so legends tell),
Ceasing their hymns, attend the spell
Of his voice, all mute.

EDGAR ALLAN POE Israfel 1836

The TRUMPET's loud Clangor
  Excites us to Arms,
With shrill Notes of Anger
  And mortal Alarms.
The double double double beat
  Of the thund'ring DRUM
  Cryes, Heark! the Foes come;
Charge, charge, 'tis too late to retreat!

JOHN DRYDEN 'A Song for St Cecilia's Day' 22 November 1687

The trumpeter's responsibility is a heavy one, however

For if the trumpet give an uncertain sound, who shall prepare himself to the battle?

I CORINTHIANS XIV 8

Mozart's ear was so sensitive that, when he was a child, he could not bear the sound of the solo trumpet

Until he was almost nine he was terribly afraid of the trumpet when it was sounded alone, without other instruments. Merely holding a trumpet towards him was like aiming a loaded pistol at his heart. Papa wanted to cure him of this childish fear and once asked me to blow my trumpet at him despite his entreaties, but my God! I ought never to have allowed myself to be persuaded; Wolfgang had scarcely heard the blaring sound, when he turned pale and began to collapse and, had I continued, would certainly have had a fit.

J. A. SCHACHTNER Letter 1792

Sidney Smith said of an acquaintance that '[his] idea of heaven is, eating *pâté de foie gras* to the sound of trumpets'.

For many of us the trumpet is the precursor of Heaven or Hell

Behold, I shew you a mystery: We shall not all sleep, but we shall all be changed, in a moment, in the twinkling of an eye, at the last trump: for the trumpet shall sound, and the dead shall be raised incorruptible, and we shall be changed.

I CORINTHIANS XV 51–2

But in the English language the greatest of all trumpets are those that greeted Mr Valiant-for-Truth

After this it was noised abroad that Mr *Valiant-for-Truth* was taken with a summons by the same post as the other; and had this for a token that the summons was true, *That his pitcher was broken at the fountain.* When he understood it, he called for his friends, and told them of it. Then, said he, I am going to my Father's; and though with great difficulty I am got hither, yet now I do not repent me of all the trouble I have been at to arrive where I am. My sword I give to him that shall succeed me in my pilgrimage, and my courage and skill to him that can get it. My marks and scars I carry with me, to be a witness for me that I have fought his battles who now will be my rewarder. When the day that he must go hence was come, many accompanied him to the river side, into which as he went he said, *Death, where is thy sting?* And as he went down deeper, he said, *Grave, where is thy victory?* So he passed over, and all the trumpets sounded for him on the other side.

JOHN BUNYAN *The Pilgrim's Progress* 1678–84

And when one of his companions demaunded him what kinde of Musicke did please him best of all that he had hearde there [Venice], hee saide: All were good, yet among the rest I saw one blow on a straunge Trumpet, which at every push thrust it into his throate more than two handfull, and then by and by drew it out againe, and thrust it in a fresh, that you never saw a greater wonder.

Then they all laughed, understanding the fond imagination of him that thought the blower thrust into his throat that part of ye Shagbut that is hid in putting it backe againe.

BALDASSARE CASTIGLIONE *The Book of the Courtier* 1561

There is no instrument the sound of which proclaims such vast internal satisfaction as the drum. I know not whether it be that the sense we have of the corpulency of this instrument predisposes us to imagine it supremely content: as when an alderman is heard snoring the world is assured that it listens to the voice of his own exceeding gratulation.

GEORGE MEREDITH Sandra Belloni 1886

> The soft complaining FLUTE
>   In dying Notes, discovers
>   The Woes of hopeless Lovers,
> Whose dirge is whisper'd by the warbling LUTE.
>
>   Sharp VIOLINS proclaim
> Their jealous Pangs and Desperation,
> Fury, frantick Indignation,
> Depth of Pains and Height of Passion.
>   For the fair, disdainful Dame.

JOHN DRYDEN 'A Song for St Cecilia's Day' 1687

I sat down to my brown loaf, my egg, and my rasher of bacon, with a basin of milk besides, and made a most delicious meal. While I was yet in the full enjoyment of it, the old woman of the house said to the Master –

'Have you got your flute with you?'

'Yes,' he returned.

'Have a blow at it,' said the old woman, coaxingly. 'Do!'

The Master, upon this, put his hand underneath the skirts of his coat, and brought out his flute in three pieces, which he screwed together, and began immediately to play. My impression is, after many years of consideration, that there never can have been anybody in the world who played worse. He made the most dismal sounds I have ever heard produced by any means, natural or artificial. I don't know what the tunes were – if there were such things in the performance at all, which I doubt – but the influence of the strain upon me was, first, to make me think of all my sorrows until I could hardly keep my tears back; then to take away my appetite; and lastly, to make me so sleepy that I couldn't keep my eyes open. They begin to close again, and I begin to nod, as the recollection rises fresh upon me. Once more the little room, with its open corner cupboard, and its square-backed chairs, and its angular little staircase leading to the room above, and its three peacock's feathers displayed over the mantelpiece – I remember wondering when I first went in, what that peacock would have thought if he had known what his finery was doomed to come to – fades from before me, and I nod, and sleep. The flute becomes inaudible, the wheels of the coach are heard instead, and I am on my journey. The coach jolts, I wake with a start, and the flute has come back again, and the Master at Salem House is sitting with his legs crossed, playing it dolefully, while the old woman of the house looks on delighted. She fades in her turn, and he fades, and all fades, and there is no flute, no Master, no Salem House, no David Copperfield, no anything but heavy sleep.

I dreamed, I thought, that once while he was blowing into this dismal flute, the old woman of the house, who had gone nearer and nearer to him in her ecstatic admiration, leaned over the back of his chair and gave him an affectionate squeeze round the neck, which stopped his playing for a moment. I was in the middle state between sleeping and waking, either then or immediately afterwards; for, as he resumed – it was a real fact that he had stopped playing – I saw and heard the same old woman ask Mrs. Fibbitson if it wasn't delicious (meaning the flute), to which Mrs. Fibbitson replied, 'Ay, ay! yes!' and nodded at the fire: to which, I am persuaded, she gave the credit of the whole performance.

CHARLES DICKENS David Copperfield 1850

Syrinx

Most surgical of instruments!
Aeolian tube with rods and keys
Poised in the balanced hands to squeeze
The slender soul through its precise space,
Like a rare serpent of the desert south
Worshipped in its narrow place,
Drawing the soul from the hovering mouth!

A trickle that defies gravity, creating
Pools of articulated notes that fly
From each prestidigitating hand,
A shining elevated wand
Whose buttons the fingers do up so quickly!

It is like a telescope for the wind's song
Extended from the lips and tongue
As from an eye to which horizons are strangely near.

Then the silver body is broken in three
And the music survives in the ear.

JOHN FULLER Waiting for the Music 1982

Here is Pepys, ravished by the sound of wind instruments

All the morning at my office, and at noon home to dinner; and thence with my wife and Deb to the King's House, to see *Virgin Martyr*, the first time it hath been acted a great while, and it is mighty pleasant; not that the play is worth much, but it is finely Acted by Becke Marshall; but what did please me beyond anything in the whole world was the wind-musique when the Angell comes down, which is so sweet that it ravished me; and endeed, in a word, did wrap up my soul so that it made me really sick, just as I have formerly been when in love with my wife; that neither then, nor all the evening going home and at home, I was able to think of anything, but remained all night transported, so as I could not believe that ever any music hath that real command over the soul of man as this did upon me; and it makes me resolve to practice wind-music and to make my wife do the like.

SAMUEL PEPYS Diary 27 February 1668

Which famous composer survived longest as teacher at a girls' school? Gustav Holst, with twenty-nine years at St Paul's in London, seems a contender, but is beaten by nine years by Antonio Vivaldi. The red-haired priest wins hands down, too, in the amount of music he wrote for his little charges at the Ospedale della Pietà in Venice: several hundred concertos between 1703 and his death in 1741 – not bad for a priest who couldn't even say Mass after two years because his chest was too weak

They sing like angels and play the violin, the flute, the organ, the cello, and the bassoon; in short, there is no instrument, however unwieldy, that can frighten them. They are cloistered like nuns. It is they alone who perform, and about forty girls take part in each concert. I vow to you that there is nothing so diverting as the sight of a young and pretty nun in a white habit, with a bunch of pomegranate blossoms over her ear, conducting the orchestra and beating time with all the grace and precision imaginable.

CHARLES DE BROSSES Letters from Italy 1739–40

The most famous orchestra of the eighteenth century, and the largest, was that which served the court of the Elector Palatine at Mannheim. Its influence on Haydn and, particularly, Mozart was profound ('You can imagine that I am looking forward with childish delight to hearing that excellent orchestra' wrote Leopold Mozart to his son before *Idomeneo*), and it produced a school of composers of its own of which the Stamitz family provided three members. Dr Burney heard it in 1772

I cannot quit this article, without doing justice to the orchestra of his electoral highness, so deservedly celebrated throughout Europe. I found it to be indeed all that its fame had made me expect: power will naturally arise from a great number of hands; but the judicious use of this power, on all occasions, must be the consequence of good discipline; indeed there are more solo players, and good composers in this, than perhaps in any other orchestra in Europe; it is an army of generals, equally fit to plan a battle, as to fight it.

But it has not been merely at the Elector's great opera that instrumental music has been so much cultivated and refined, but at his *concerts*, where this extraordinary band has 'ample room and verge enough,' to display all its powers, and to produce great effects without the impropriety of destroying the greater and more delicate beauties, peculiar to vocal music; it was here that Stamitz, stimulated by the productions of Jomelli, first surpassed the bounds of common opera overtures, which had hitherto only served in the theatre as a kind of court cryer, with an 'O Yes!' in order to awaken attention, and bespeak silence, at the entrance of the singers. Since the discovery which the genius of Stamitz first made, every effect has been tried which such an aggregate of sound can produce; it was here that the *Crescendo* and *Diminuendo* had birth; and the *Piano*, which was before chiefly used as an echo, with which it was generally synonimous, as well as the *Forte*, were found to be musical *colours* which had their *shades*, as much as red or blue in painting.

I found, however, an imperfection in this band, common to all others, that I have ever yet heard, but which I was in hopes would be removed by men so attentive and so able; the defect, I mean, is the want of truth in the wind instruments. I know it is natural to those instruments to be out of tune, but some of that art and diligence which these great performers have manifested in vanquishing difficulties of other kinds, would surely be well employed in correcting this leaven, which so much sours and corrupts all harmony. This was too plainly the case to-night, with the bassoons and hautbois, which were rather too sharp, at the beginning, and continued growing sharper to the end of the opera.

My ears were unable to discover any other imperfection in the orchestra, throughout the whole performance; and this imperfection is so common to orchestras, in general, that the censure will not be very severe upon this, or afford much matter for triumph to the performers of any other orchestra in Europe.

CHARLES BURNEY 1772 *The Present State of Music in Germany*

A hundred years after Mannheim, court orchestras had become rare, but the Meiningen band was an exception – and Hans von Bülow an exceptional Kapellmeister. (Later holders of the position were Richard Strauss and Max Reger.)

. . . In precision the orchestra is unsurpassed and hardly has an equal. There is probably not another orchestra which could duplicate its feat of playing the accompaniment for Brahms' D Minor Concerto – more a great symphony than an accompaniment – with Bülow at the piano but not conducting. An even more astounding feat is that of the whole string orchestra in playing flawlessly Beethoven's formidable Quartet Fugue, Opus 133 – a tonal wilderness in which the best string quartets are prone to lose their way. A stunt, to be sure, and thoroughly unenjoyable at that; but the orchestra which can bring it off securely can challenge the mightiest rival. Where the Meiningen Orchestra does not measure up to the Vienna Philharmonic is in sensuous beauty of tone, fullness of sound, warmth and temperament of interpretation, and, finally, in brilliance of total effect. One should not forget, of course, that it has only forty-eight men, as compared with the Vienna Philharmonic's ninety. And the fault may well be with the instruments rather than with the players. Bülow's violinists are excellent musicians, but without the compelling force of the Vienna violinists; the double basses and trombones are splendid, the oboes often sharp and shrill, the clarinets and horns good, but not equal to the Viennese. The connoisseur will readily appreciate the effects which Bülow achieves with this comparatively weak orchestra, some- times by prudent conservation, sometimes by the concentration of all his sources at a given point – as, for example, in the last movement of Beethoven's Symphony in C Minor and the Overture to *Der Freischütz*.

Of inventive spirit, and given to experimentation, Bülow has introduced several effective innovations. One of them is the five-stringed bass, which extends down to the low C; the usual four-stringed bass reaches only to E. Another is the Ritter alto viola. Of stronger construction than the common viola, it surpasses it in fullness of tone and reduces the all-too-great distance normally separating violas and violoncellos. And finally, the chromatic kettledrums, which can be retuned by pedals while being played. Another much-dis- cussed innovation – and one which strikes me as of doubtful value – is that of having the orchestra stand while playing. This is actually a reversion to an older custom, possibly attributable in former times to the limited space of the old concert halls and the etiquette of court orchestras. It was probably in Vienna that the fashion of playing while seated first took hold. Dittersdorf, at any rate, writes in his autobiography: 'I had long desks and benches made, for I introduced the Viennese custom of playing while seated, and arranged the orchestra in such a way that every player faced the audience.' Standing is a kind of insurance against carelessness and ease-taking on the part of the players; sitting conserves their strength. The first is more military, the latter more humane.

Bülow conducts the orchestra as if it were a little bell in his hand. The most admirable discipline has transformed it into an instrument upon which he plays with utter freedom and from which he produces nuances possible only with a discipline to which larger orchestras would not ordinarily submit. Since he can achieve these nuances securely, it is understandable that he applies them at those places where they would seem appropriate to him if he were playing the same piece on the piano. It would be unjust to call these tempo changes 'liberties', since conscientious adherence to the score is a primary and inviolable rule with Bülow. It is hard to draw the line. Opinion will vary according to individual taste and the character of specific passages. Metronomic evenness of tempo has, in any case, been disavowed by all modern conductors.

. . . In his treatise *On Conducting*, Richard Wagner gave expression to a number of dangerous theories, but when he himself conducted, one readily accepted many liberties – in this very Overture to *Der Freischütz*, for instance. Bülow is entitled to claim the same privileges, since his respect for the great masters is unquestioned and his artistic individuality always interesting. His personal physical mannerisms, however, can hardly be pleasing to anyone. If it were true that the best conductor is he who is least conspicuous, then we should have in Bülow the exact opposite. But Bülow would not be Bülow were he able to stand stock still while conducting. One must accept him as he is, with all his weaknesses and quirks; and indeed we are happy to do so in cordial acknowledgment of his brilliant virtues and accomplishments. Hans von Bülow, the inspired pianist, conductor, and writer, is a real individual, unduplicated in the musical present.

EDUARD HANSLICK Review December 1884

Conductors

'I think you might do something better with the time,' she said, 'than waste it asking riddles with no answers.'

'If you knew Time as well as I do,' said the Hatter, 'you wouldn't talk about wasting *it*. It's *him*.'

'I don't know what you mean,' said Alice.

'Of course you don't!' the Hatter said, tossing his head contemptuously. 'I dare say you never even spoke to Time!'

'Perhaps not,' Alice cautiously replied: 'but I know I have to beat time when I learn music.'

'Ah! that accounts for it,' said the Hatter. 'He won't stand beating.'

LEWIS CARROLL Alice's Adventures in Wonderland 1865

Talking of which, Michael Kelly mentions a performance of *Richard Coeur de Lion* at Drury Lane when, the singer who was to take the chief part having fallen ill at the last moment, the celebrated tragedian John Kemble stepped in

. . . when Kemble was rehearsing the romance, sung by Richard, Shaw, the leader of the band, called out from the orchestra, 'Mr. Kemble, my dear Mr. Kemble, you are murdering time.' Kemble calmly and coolly, taking a pinch of snuff, said, 'My dear Sir, it is better for me to murder time at once, than be continually beating him as you do.'

MICHAEL KELLY Reminiscences 1826

Louis Spohr, the German violinist, composer and conductor, is usually credited with the introduction of the baton and so, in a sense, the invention of conducting. If so, he certainly has a lot to answer for

It was still the custom in London at that time, when symphonies and overtures were performed, for the pianist to have the score before him, not exactly to conduct from it but rather to read after and to play in with the orchestra at pleasure, which often produced a very bad effect. The real conductor was the first violin, who gave the tempi and, every now and then when the orchestra began to falter, gave the beat with his bow. Thus a large orchestra, standing so far apart from each other as the members of the Philharmonic, could not possibly be exactly together, and despite the excellence of individual members, the ensemble was much worse than we are accustomed to in Germany. I had therefore resolved that, when my turn came to direct, I would try to remedy this defective system. Fortunately at the morning rehearsal on the day I was to conduct the concert, Mr Ries took his place at the piano and readily assented to relinquish the score and to remain wholly excluded from all participation in the performance. I then took my stand with the score at a separate music desk in front of the orchestra, drew my directing baton from my coat pocket and gave the signal to begin. Quite alarmed at such a novel procedure, some of the directors wished to protest against it, but when I besought them to grant me at least one trial, they quieted down. The symphonies and overtures that were to be rehearsed were well known to me, and I had already directed their performance in Germany. Therefore, I could not only give the tempi in a very decisive manner, but could indicate all their entries to the wind instruments and horns, which gave them a confidence they had not known hitherto. I also felt free to stop, when the execution did not satisfy me and, in a polite but earnest manner, to remark upon the manner of execution, which remarks Mr Ries interpreted at my request to the orchestra. Incited thereby to more than usual attention, and given assurance by the conductor's clearly visible manner of marking time, they played with a spirit and correctness such as they had never been heard to achieve until then. The orchestra, surprised and inspired by the result, immediately expressed its collective assent to the new mode of conducting after the first part of the symphony, and thereby overruled all further opposition on the part of the directors. In the vocal pieces also, of which I assumed the conducting at the request of Mr Ries, leading with the baton was completely successful particularly in the recitative, after I had explained the meaning of my movements, and the singers repeatedly expressed to me their satisfaction at the precision with which the orchestra now supported them.

The results that evening were more brilliant than I could have hoped. It is true, the audience was at first startled by the novelty and there was considerable whispered comment, but when the music began and the orchestra executed the well known symphony with unusual power and precision, general approbation was shown immediately on the conclusion of the first part by long-sustained applause. The triumph of the baton as a time-giver was decisive, and no conductor was seen seated at the piano any more during the performance of symphonies and overtures.

LOUIS SPOHR 1820 *Autobiography*

The solo violinist of the Vienna Philharmonic once called over to me at a rehearsal when, my baton not being at hand, I was about to take another: 'Not that one, Doctor – that one has no rhythm.'

RICHARD STRAUSS *Recollections and Reflections* 1949

Spohr had seen Beethoven conducting in Vienna. It was only with the increasing complexity of music from Beethoven onwards that conducting became necessary at all, and clearly something a little more generally applicable than Beethoven's method (even allowing for the deafness) was an urgent priority

Although I had heard much of his conducting, yet it surprised me greatly. Beethoven was wont to give the signs of expression to his orchestra by all manner of extraordinary motions of his body. Whenever a *sforzando* occurred, he flung his arms wide, previously crossed upon his breast. At a *piano*, he bent down, and all the lower in proportion to the softness of tone he wished to achieve. Then when a crescendo came, he would raise himself again by degrees, and upon the commencement of the *forte*, would spring bolt upright. To increase the *forte* yet more, he would sometimes shout at the orchestra, without being aware of it. . . .

It was easy to see that the poor deaf maestro could no longer hear the *pianos* of his own music. This was particularly remarkable in a passage in the second part of the first 'Allegro' of the symphony (No. 7). At that part there are two holds in quick succession, the second of which is *pianissimo*. This Beethoven had probably overlooked, for he again began to give the time before the orchestra had executed this second hold. Without knowing it, therefore, he was already from ten to twelve bars in advance of the orchestra when it began the *pianissimo*. Beethoven, to signify this in his own way, had crept completely under the desk. Upon the ensuing crescendo, he again made his appearance, raising himself continually and then springing up high at the moment when, according to his calculations, the *forte* should have begun. As this did not take place, he looked around him in dismay, stared with astonishment at the orchestra, which was still playing *pianissimo*, and only recovered himself when at length the long-expected *forte* began, and was finally audible to himself.

LOUIS SPOHR 1814 *Autobiography*

Berlioz was a real conductor, and one of the first to direct the orchestra from a full orchestral score.

The most famous of all the early conductor stories was told by Berlioz in his *Memoirs*. It concerns the first performance of the *Requiem* in December 1837 at an official ceremony at Les Invalides in commemoration of the death of General Damrémont. (François-Antoine Habeneck was then conductor of the Conservatoire concerts)

. . . I was about to begin rehearsals when X sent for me. 'You are aware,' he said, 'that Habeneck is officially in charge of all important state musical occasions.' (There we go, I thought, here comes another catch.) 'It is true that you are now in the habit of conducting your works yourself, but Habeneck is an old man' (look out!) 'and I happen to know that he would be deeply hurt if he did not direct the performance of your Requiem. How do you get on with him?'

'We're on bad terms, I have no idea why . . . However, as I can see that he feels he should figure at Marshal Damrémont's service, and as it would clearly gratify you, I agree to let him conduct; but I reserve the right to take one rehearsal myself.'

'No difficulty at all,' X replied; 'I shall tell him so.'

Both sectional and general rehearsals proceeded smoothly, great care being taken over them. Habeneck treated me as if relations had never been interrupted. All seemed likely to go well.

On the day of the performance, royalty, ministers, peers, deputies, the entire French Press, the correspondents of the foreign newspapers, and an immense crowd of people, thronged the chapel of the Invalides. A success was absolutely vital for me; a mediocre result would be fatal; by the same token a failure would destroy me utterly.

Now mark what follows.

My forces had been divided into several groups spread over a wide area; necessarily so because of the four brass bands which I use in the Tuba Mirum, and which have to be placed beyond the main body of performers, one at each corner. At the point where they enter, at the beginning of the Tuba Mirum – which follows the Dies Irae without a pause – the music broadens to a tempo twice as slow. First, all four groups break in simultaneously – at the new tempo – then successively, challenging and answering one another from a distance, the entries piling up, each a third higher than the one before. It is therefore of the utmost importance to indicate the four beats of the slower tempo very clearly the moment it is reached; otherwise the great cataclysm, a musical representation of the Last Judgment, prepared for with such deliberation and employing an exceptional combination of forces in a manner at the time unprecedented and not attempted since – a passage which will, I hope, endure as a landmark in music – is mere noise and pandemonium, a monstrosity.

With my habitual mistrust I had stayed just behind Habeneck. Standing with my back to him, I supervised the group of timpani (which he could not see), as the moment approached for them to join in the general tumult. There are perhaps a thousand bars in my Requiem. In the very bar I have been speaking of, the bar in which the tempo broadens and the brass proclaim their tremendous fanfare – the one bar, in fact, in which the conductor's direction is absolutely indispensable – Habeneck laid down his baton and, calmly producing his snuff-box, proceeded to take a pinch of snuff. I had been keeping my eye on him. In a flash I turned on my heel, sprang forward in front of him and, stretching out my arm, marked out the four great beats of the new tempo. The bands followed me and everything went off in order. I conducted the piece to the end. The effect I had dreamed of was attained. When, at the final words of the chorus, Habeneck saw that the Tuba Mirum was saved, he said, 'God! I was in a cold sweat. Without you we would have been lost.'

'I know,' I replied, looking him straight in the eye. I did not say another word. Had he done it deliberately? Was it possible that this man, in collusion with X (who hated me) and with Cherubini's friends, had actually planned and attempted to carry out an act of such base treachery? I would rather not think so. Yet I cannot doubt it. God forgive me if I am doing him an injustice!

HECTOR BERLIOZ 1837 *Memoirs*

The accuracy of this description has been debated, often with some vigour, for over a hundred years. At the end of his translation of the *Memoirs*, David Cairns has marshalled the arguments on both sides: they are inconclusive but, as he sagely observes, 'even allowing for the vast difference between modern and early 19th-century notions, the opening of the Tuba Mirum is of all places in the Requiem the most unlikely for snuff-taking if the conductor is merely negligent, the most likely if he is actuated by malice'

For the works of Beethoven, Berlioz, Wagner, etc. I see fewer advantages than elsewhere (and even elsewhere I would contest them) in the conductor's functioning like a windmill, sweating profusely, the better to communicate warmth to his personnel. In these works, above all, where it is a question of understanding and feeling, a question of addressing the intelligence and of firing hearts in a communion with the beautiful, the great and the true in art and in poetry, the capacity and the ancient routine of the average *maître de chapelle* are no longer *adequate*, indeed are contrary to the dignity and sublime freedom of art. Though it displease my complacent critics, I shall . . . never accommodate myself to the role of 'professor' of time-beating, for which my twenty-five years of experience, study and sincere passion for art have in no way prepared me.

Whatever esteem I profess for many of my colleagues, and no matter how freely I am pleased to acknowledge the good services they have performed and continue to perform for art, I do not feel obliged to follow their example in every instance, whether in the choice of works to be performed or the manner of conceiving and directing them. The real task of the conductor consists, in my opinion, in making himself ostensibly quasi-useless. We are pilots, not drill-masters. Even though this idea in particular will meet still more opposition, I can not change it, since I hold it to be just. Put into practice with the orchestra at Weimar, it has led to excellent results which my critics themselves have praised. I shall continue therefore, without discouragement or false modesty, to serve art in the best way I understand it, which I hope will be the *best* way.

FRANZ LISZT Letter 5 November 1853

Richard Strauss was another who was more pilot than drillmaster; his gestures were minimal – yet, as anyone present at his last Albert Hall concert in 1947 can testify, even at 83, when he raised his arm (as opposed to simply moving his hand and wrist) the roof nearly fell in with the strength of the sound.

He was best at Strauss and Mozart, and the Ten Golden Rules which he wrote for the album of a young conductor in about 1922 can best be read with these two composers in mind

1 Remember that you are making music not to amuse yourself but to delight your audience.
2 You should not perspire when conducting: only the audience should get warm.
3 Conduct *Salome* and *Elektra* as if they were by Mendelssohn: Fairy Music.

4 Never look encouragingly at the brass, except with a short glance to give an important cue.

5 But never let the horns and woodwind out of your sight: if you can hear them at all they are still too strong.

6 If you think that the brass is not blowing hard enough, tone it down another shade or two.

7 It is not enough that you yourself should hear every word the soloist sings – you know it off by heart anyway: the audience must be able to follow without effort. If they do not understand the words they will go to sleep.

8 Always accompany a singer in such a way that he can sing without effort.

9 When you think you have reached the limits of prestissimo, double the pace.*

10 If you follow these rules carefully you will, with your fine gifts and your great accomplishments, always be the darling of your listeners.

*Today (1948) I should like to amend this as follows: Go twice as slowly (addressed to conductors of Mozart!)

RICHARD STRAUSS *Betrachtungen und Erinnerungen* 1949

The left hand has nothing to do with conducting. Its proper place is the waistcoat pocket from which it should only emerge to restrain or to make some minor gesture for which in any case a scarcely perceptible glance would suffice.

It is better to conduct with the ear instead of with the arm: the rest follows automatically.

RICHARD STRAUSS *ibid.*

In many cases, however, it is the drillmaster who predominates

. . . 'conductor' means *Duce*, means *Führer*, *Caudillo* – there is no getting away from that. And worse: these connotations are not merely the dictionary's. A historian and sociologist comparing music and politics could without malevolence or paradox reason as follows: primitive or traditional orchestras, as gypsy bands, gamelans, and the like, are organic, unbroken, real communities with hieratic fiddler kings, etc.; Elizabethan or eighteenth-century chamber-music-minded orchestras with harpsichord-playing *Kapellmeisters* are liberal yet tradition-inspired republics; the modern orchestra, like modern society, is a pseudo-community in need of dictatorial forces to hold together scattered individualisms; and, *si parva licet*, in both cases, the musical and the political, the dictators do their bit by using the same sort of methods: a good deal of brutality and a good deal of 'pin-up glamour'. And worst of all; not a few conductors – some most remarkable – let themselves be tempted to see their calling in that light. To them conducting is primarily and essentially an exercise of will-power. They are sculptors of performance who are always hammering stone, never kneading clay. But as a philosopher has remarked, the hammer's work is always negative. It can free a beautiful statue, by ridding it of the material which hides it – it does executive work according to plan; but the creative work is better done by moulding and kneading. Only a Michelangelo can afford to do it all in imagination.

In the musical field, our previous disquisitions provide us with a broad hint at this question: measurable things (pitch, metre, relief of timbre) can be hammered in; rhythm, melody, tempo and *rubato* have to be moulded. And orchestras can be hammered into discipline but have to be moulded into unanimity and enthusiasm. . . .

FREDERICK GOLDBECK *The Perfect Conductor* 1960

The dictator image, however, was hard to eradicate

There were few soloists in the Philharmonic's concerts at this period, and only the very best got a chance to appear. Mahler engaged Busoni, for instance, to play Beethoven's Concerto in E Flat Major. Travelling down from Berlin on the night express, Busoni reached Vienna just after 9 a.m. to find a message awaiting him at his hotel. He was to report to the Opera House at once, where *Direktor* Mahler had something important to tell him. Without breakfasting, washing or shaving – a circumstance which he found highly distasteful – he rushed to the Opera House. Mahler kept him waiting for an hour, then burst out of the directorial office and extended his hand. 'Not too fast in the last movement, Herr Busoni – all right?' he said, whistling the main theme. Then, with an '*Auf Wiedersehen!*', he vanished again.

OTTO KLEMPERER *c.* 1905 *Memories of Gustav Mahler*

Though it certainly didn't preclude quality

Mahler was far and away the finest conductor I ever knew, with the most all-embracing musical instinct, and it is one of the small tragedies of my life that just when he was considering the question of producing my opera *The Wreckers* at Vienna they drove him from office. At the time I am speaking of in Leipzig I saw but little of him, and we didn't get on; I was too young and raw then to appreciate this grim personality, intercourse with whom was like handling a bomb cased in razor-edges.

ETHEL SMYTH 1888 *Impressions that Remained*

Mahler's most famous dictum as a conductor was 'Tradition ist Schlamperei' ('tradition is slovenliness' – though it sounds better in German), but there is another that is perhaps more interesting: 'What is best in music is not to be found in the notes.'

Furtwängler spoke of 'routine which, with its loveless mediocrity and its treacherous perfection, lies like hoar-frost on the performance of the world's most beautiful and best loved masterpieces'.

Toscanini's displays of temperament were hair-raising, but almost more so when cool and deliberate. Yehudi Menuhin remembers one such when he was in New York to do the Beethoven Concerto. This was the teenage Menuhin, at about the time he was first allowed to cross the road on his own; it was a life innocent of violence . . . so far

It was during the preparation for this performance that Toscanini showed me what it meant to be sure of oneself. In his apartment at the Hotel Astor on Times Square – which had an Italian proprietor and no doubt reliable pasta – we had reached the middle of the slow movement where, after the second tutti, the sound marked *perdendosi* hangs by a thread, when the telephone rang. Naturally I ignored it; so did my father in his unobtrusive corner; so fumbling at the piano (for he was not a great pianist), did Toscanini. There was a second ring. We went on playing, I at least tensely aware that the pressure in the room was boiling up to a reaction. At the third ring Toscanini stopped, rose from the piano stool, and with light quick determined steps walked not to the telephone, but to the installation in the wall and jerked the whole thing bodily out, wooden fitting, plaster, dust, severed dangling wires; then, without a word uttered, he came back to take up where we had stopped, in total serenity. When the third movement ended there was a timid knock at the door. Relaxed, unembarrassed, amiable, Toscanini gently called, '*Avanti!*' – his first word since the incident – and the door opened on an abject trio, his wife, the hotel proprietor and an electrician, all promising to do better another time.

YEHUDI MENUHIN *c.* 1930 *Unfinished Journey*

More often Toscanini's violence emerged . . . *strepitoso*!

The public performance of *La Bohème* was perfect until the final four bars of the opera. So great was the tension of the orchestra and the Maestro as the opera drew to a close that at the concluding chords the brasses entered a fraction of a second too soon. The error was so insignificant that only the nervous brasses and the Maestro could have noticed it. A moment later the opera was over and the audience broke into thunderous applause. The Maestro, with head bowed, left the stage and went swiftly to his dressing-room, leaving the singers to take their bows alone. Once in his room, the Maestro abandoned himself to an elemental rage more devastating than any I had ever witnessed. Screaming and roaring incomprehensible things, he tore at his clothing and upset every movable object that yielded to his inspired strength. His piano and a large desk resisted all his efforts at dislodgment, and in exasperation he kicked them repeatedly with such fury that I feared for his legs. After minutes of fulmination and wreakage he suddenly desisted and said: 'Send me the *porci* [the swine]. I wish to speak with them.' The erring players had not dared to leave the hall. There were nine of them, and I led them into the Maestro's room, where they took up an uneasy position in a line against a wall, their faces pale, their heads down. The Maestro walked up and down in front of them like a sergeant inspecting his squad, glaring at each one with hatred and contempt.

At length he said with bitter sincerity: 'I hide my head in shame. After what happen-ed tonight my life is finish-ed. For me it is impossible to look in the face of any*baw*dy. *I* can live no more. But *you –*' and he pointed straight at the man at the head of the dejected line – 'you will sleep with your wife tonight as if no*thing* happen-ed. I know you!' The Maestro turned away, and the men sadly filed out.

SAMUEL CHOTZINOFF *Toscanini, an Intimate Portrait* 1956

Toscanini was the greatest of all interpreters of Puccini – as the composer himself gratefully realized – but quarrels were not infrequent, and could break out at inconvenient moments. Now Puccini customarily sent his friends *panettones* as Christmas greetings. One year he found that Toscanini had been sent one of these confections just after they had had a row. So he telegraphed

PANETTONE SENT BY MISTAKE STOP PUCCINI

Toscanini replied

PANETTONE EATEN BY MISTAKE STOP TOSCANINI

A rare conductor who made himself felt off the podium as well as on it was Serge Koussevitsky, whose wife was rich enough to enable him to commission an impressive list of new works. One of them was Bartók's Concerto for Orchestra – a product of the composer's last years in the USA, when his health was deteriorating fast. The original idea came from Joseph Szigeti who, meeting Koussevitsky by chance in New York, suggested that something should be done for Bartók. Koussevitsky acted at once

The meeting of the elegant man of the world and the emaciated, giant-eyed Bartók in his hospital bed must have been an extraordinary sight. Koussevitsky made his gesture at the outset of their conversation, offering the composer a commission for an orchestral work of his choosing.

'But look at me, Mr Koussevitsky, I am hardly myself any longer – how could I write a new piece for you in this condition?'

'Never mind, Mr Bartók,' said Koussevitsky in his famous Russian-English. 'You write piece when you feeling better!'

Bartók, with a sigh, said that he would gladly do so.

'It is all settled, then,' said Koussevitsky, and took out his bank-book to write a cheque for the fee.

'Oh no,' Bartók raised a pale, skinny hand, 'you can pay me only after I have completed the piece.'

Whereupon Koussevitsky, with a quick look at Bartók and an even quicker flash of thought, answered: 'I am sorry, Mr Bartók, conditions commission oblige write cheque for half commission fee when commission is made.'

About the première many tales circulated. Members of the Boston Symphony Orchestra told me that when Bartók arrived for the last rehearsal, Koussevitsky told him: 'Mr Bartók, whenever you have a remark to make, please do not hesitate!'

Bartók thanked him.

Only four or five bars into the first movement he raised his hand and explained something to Koussy in a whispered conference.

Ten bars later – another interruption.

Two more bars – a third.

And so on.

After about twenty minutes this became very tiresome and Koussevitsky said: 'Mr Bartók, perhaps you could take paper and pencil and make your notes as we go. At the end you then will tell me all you want.'

This happened, and the orchestra members observed Bartók sitting in the stalls feverishly writing all the time. When the last movement ended, he went on scribbling for a while and then rose, armed with his notes, and, as my informant put it, 'full of pep'. The tired Koussy led him, with bent back and dragging step, to the conductor's dressing room, where they disappeared.

The intermission lasted an unusually long time. When they finally reappeared, the sight was different: Koussevitsky led the way with easy, springy gait, Bartók shuffled behind him listlessly.

Koussevitsky then mounted the rostrum and announced: 'Gentlemen, Mr Bartók agrees with everything.'

ANTAL DORATI 1943–4 *Notes of Seven Decades*

Some conductors are better over money than others

George Szell . . . had a notorious tongue and a reputation for eating alive anyone who crossed his path. With very few exceptions, orchestral musicians loathed him, although no musician worthy of the name could fault him artistically. On the podium he was incapable of generating warmth, although warmth and tenderness were evident in the results he produced . . . When he died in the nineteen-seventies almost all the obituaries could not resist the comment that he did not suffer fools gladly, but it would be nearer the truth to say that he did not suffer fools at all. His physical presence was austere: only very occasionally did he smile, let alone laugh, but his mind was sharp and uncluttered with inessentials. He was Hungarian, and almost impossible to outwit. Years later I was present in Zurich when he came to see Rosengarten to negotiate a new [recording] contract, and for once Rosengarten was slightly nervous. He needed Szell, and Szell knew as much. Rosengarten had his ammunition ready, and it was formidable when he chose to use it at full force; but Szell, taking his example from (I believe) an incident in the life of Berlioz, sailed into Rosengarten's office, bearing the last thing Rosengarten expected, which was a broad grin. 'Mr Rosengarten,' he said, 'we are here to discuss a contract, which you think is going to be difficult. Let us be clear about one thing immediately. I know that you are an artist, a man of great sensitivity and musical perception, which I would not dare to match. I, on the other hand, am a simple business man, whose only interest is money. I shall therefore put forward proposals which, needless to say, are not subject to alteration.' It was the only time in my life that I saw Rosengarten floored with one blow, for his standard technique was to spend ten minutes flattering an artist until he judged that the moment had come to announce the lowest possible terms. Szell, in turning the tables on him, left him speechless. The contract was signed, and on Szell's terms.

JOHN CULSHAW *Putting the Record Straight* 1981

Beecham was another conductor with money. He tended to lose it regularly, however, by forming opera companies – though he never *looked* as if he had lost it. His platform manner and conducting technique were, and still are, unforgettable, and when all the Beecham stories are over it is good to have the conductor evoked for us once again by someone who knew him well and worked with him for many years

What is conducting technique? It is the means by which any man gifted with authority and strong powers of communication conveys his musical intentions unmistakeably to a body of musical executants by movements of a baton, his fingers, hands, arms, facial expressions, and glances. Mutual understanding and detailed preparation must be achieved in rehearsals. Beecham was not an ostentatious time-beater but he got what he wanted. His technical mastery of orchestras began with his unfailing courtesy to his players. He often said: 'Get the best players, pay them well, then conducting is not *so* difficult.' He had a clear down-beat, usually slashed (from the audience's view) from northeast to southwest. He trusted, encouraged, and helped his wind principals and string players – when they had soli – to play freely and with more expression than they had imagined themselves capable of, and smiled to them his own delight at each beautifully shaped phrase.

For his first *Heldenleben* with the Hallé he had brass-band players as necessary reinforcements. Brass-band players are usually at sea with orchestral parts and this Strauss was for them mid-Atlantic. After an hour's patient rehearsal trying to get the bandsmen to play the right notes at the right time, he put down his baton: 'Gentlemen. Unfortunately I have no more time now but we shall meet again this evening at the concert. You will then keep in touch with me, won't you?'

Beecham had a soft spot for what orchestral players call 'the Kitchen'. One of the most typical gestures was a violent lunge as if he were chucking a cricket ball overarm at the noisiest section of the orchestra. He beamed at every loud cymbal-crash and at the tintinabulations of high percussion which gave extra sparkle to the general din. In later years his technique was extended to include his own noisy vocal urgings to the orchestra to play louder. He loved what he called 'grand tunes' and in his extravagantly generous heart he wanted the orchestra, the audience, and, last but not least, Thomas Beecham, to enjoy themselves. A good time must be had by all! After devoting the best part of his life to popularizing opera and concerts in Britain he ruefully remarked: 'The British don't like music – only the noise it makes.'

WALTER LEGGE in *On and Off the Record* 1982

Language can often be a problem with visiting foreign conductors. The classic 'In Chairmany ve make it other' is reputed to have come from Erich Kleiber, and the Swiss conductor, Ernest Ansermet, not having any tenses but the past, was responsible for the great outburst: 'Don't spoke! Don't spoke! If you didn't like it, you went!'

It was Ansermet again who, getting irritated by the continual atmosphere of levity at a rehearsal of the BBC Symphony Orchestra, was moved to cry out in exasperation: 'A joke then and now sometimes yes very but always by God never!'

In later years Ansermet's knowledge of the language improved;

. . . [he] said no more than needed to be said and in perfectly understandable English. *His* problem was that he prided himself on the use of idioms, which, more often than not, went wrong. In one altercation in Kingsway Hall he announced loudly, 'You think I know fuck nothing, but you are wrong, I know fuck all!'

JOHN CULSHAW *Putting the Record Straight* 1981

Conductors' foibles are not invariably well received by their players

. . . petty issues often distorted one's view of Karajan the musician. The orchestra, for example, never forgot his instruction that they should not stand up as he passed through the departure lounge to board the plane first when they were on tour. What irked them was two-fold: his assumption that they would stand up (which, in a public lounge, would have looked at the very least odd), and his reason for not wanting them to stand up – which was no more than his consciousness of his small stature. He simply could not bear to be in the presence of tall people unless they were sitting down, or unless he could find a high stool on which to perch himself.

JOHN CULSHAW *ibid.*

Perhaps orchestral conductors just aren't tough enough?

One icy day in winter 1943–44, a bandmaster gave me an invaluable lesson. The best bands had been summoned to Drury Lane Theatre to audition for long tours overseas. The intonation of all these bands even in the near-Arctic conditions of the unheated theatre was flawless. At the lunch-break I congratulated the assembled conductors on this extraordinary feat, which I had never been able to achieve with Europe's best orchestras under better conditions. One of them opened my eyes – 'You would have no intonation troubles if you had our authority to put any man who played out of tune on seven days latrine duty.' This is a luxury no great conductor has yet enjoyed.

WALTER LEGGE in *On and Off the Record* 1982

Maybe something on these lines is what is required?

The band at Heanton Punchardon Church (Devon) comprised a fiddle, cornet and trombone. On special occasions a clarionet player came over from Braunton, and now and then there was also a flute. The band sat in the western gallery of the Church, so did the choir of about twelve boys and girls with an adult leader named Richard Clarke. During the early part of the service band and choir sat in mystic seclusion behind two red curtains running on rods. When the time came for the hymn these curtains were noisily drawn back, and the congregation turned round in the pews, and with back to the Altar faced the performers.

From his box below the pulpit William Clogg, the parish clerk, gave out the hymn with the usual preface: 'Let us zeng, to the praäse and glary of Goad.' Then might be heard from the gallery the word 'pitch!' and the sound of a tuning-fork struck by the choir-leader, with the remark, 'Doänt 'ee zeng till I do zeng!' He marked the time of the hymn by stumping all through with his wooden leg. The artificial limb was also used as an instrument of correction on the boys of the choir, and the girls were rapped with the tuning-fork; sometimes the harmony was interrupted by the yell of a sufferer. Meanwhile the good Richard Clarke offered admonitions which could be heard all over the church. 'Zeng oop, zeng oop, or I'll whack 'ee I 'ull. Zeng oop, there's visitors in rectory pew.'

Devonshire and Cornwall Notes and Queries, vol. x.

Or even this?

> There is Hallelujah Hannah
>   Walking backwards down the lane,
> And I hear the loud Hosanna
>   Of regenerated Jane;
> And Lieutenant Isabella
>   In the centre of them comes,
> Dealing blows with her umbrella
>   On the trumpets and the drums.

A. E. HOUSMAN *c.* 1897 from a letter to his step-mother.

The lot of the conductor has never been an easy one

Sir Symphony: Come, pray, let's begin. O Gad: there's a flat note! there's art! how surprisingly the key changes! O law! there's a double relish! I swear, sir, you have the sweetest little finger in England! ha! that stroke's new; I tremble, every inch of me; now ladies, look to your hearts – softly, gentlemen – remember the echo – captain, you play the wrong tune – O law! my teeth! my teeth! for God's sake, captain, mind your cittern – Now the fuga, bases! again, again! lord! Mr. Humdrum, you come in three bars too soon. Come now, the song.

THOMAS SOUTHERNE The Maid's Last Prayer 1693

The rehearsal has started, and among the eighty-one musicians present, [the conductor] is both the happiest and the unhappiest.

The happiest: all his reading, meditating, and fancying done, he is at last going to hear live music. So are the others, and not without pleasure: for when it comes down to brass tacks even the most hardened fiddlers and pipers love to bow and to blow, and even in modern times there is something intoxicating in fiddling and piping together. Yet there is an enormous difference. No orchestral player plays the whole of the music. Every single one hears himself and his immediate neighbours (and even himself not always, if he happens to be a cellist and the trombone's neighbour); for him the rest is fragmentary and blurred.

Further: among all possible performers of music the conductor is the least tight-rope-walking and acrobatic. A quarter of a line's lapse means for a pianist a wrong note which will spoil, for a moment, the most perfect reading. A singer's velvety notes are at the mercy of a draught. Such petty dangers our hero is spared: nothing much will happen if one of his beats comes down an inch or two higher or lower than intended. And even if in the heat of the fight he omits to look at the second violins when playing the tenth bar of the Scherzo (as he had for good reasons intended to do) he will more often than not be the only one to notice the difference.

And third: the performance is his. He is the captain, and it cannot but prove more exciting to be in command of the sailing than to be even the smartest of midshipmen.

For these advantages, however, the conductor has to pay a high price. First of all he will be in the grip of lack of time, as permanent a fiend in the conductor's life as lack of cash is in ordinary life. Pianists can prepare their recitals by giving in their studios as many solitary recitals as they like. They may even rise in the middle of a sleepless night to test a few tricky passages: the neighbours will be miserable, but no pianist feels obliged to love his neighbour more than himself. The conductor has to do a major part of his work, here and now, in so many hours – or rather in so few. Habits vary in different countries; two rehearsals of three hours or two-and-a-half each are the artistic minimum not always granted. Time-nabobs in Brussels and in Boston have five rehearsals and still rightly feel that they would need more to bring a programme of two hours to maturity. Within these minutes hurrying by, everything must be done, said, settled. The choice between bettering one point and accepting another passage as it stands has to be made almost at every bar and will allow of no hesitation.

And then he has to do this in public, in front of, and with, eighty extremely competent critics. And the part of the work he has to do for himself – training to perform this particular music with this particular orchestra – has to be taken in the stride of the rehearsal with nobody noticing. For the fiction (perhaps a necessary fiction) is that rehearsal's work consists merely in training the orchestra under the guidance of the fully prepared and near-infallible conductor.

. . . Musicians, in orchestras even more than elsewhere, are fellows of amicable disposition; if they were not, they would have chosen rather to be policemen, dentists, or stockbrokers. But the first cellist and one of the flautists are conductors themselves, and the triangle man always dreamed of being one. The solo viola player, a RAM professor, is a composer who hates the *Variations* of 'that degenerate' modernist, to be presently rehearsed. Luckily the deputy-leader (a former member of the Pro Arte Quartet) is pleased with the choice of this work and twinkles most encouragingly. But on the whole the temper is on the phlegmatic side. The orchestra is determined to play in its most business-like manner, but it cannot help caring less than the conductor for 'the torrid or the frozen zone' of interpretation. . . .

To the conductor of the dictatorial type an orchestra's assumed superiority is red rag to the bull. At once he calls up the drill sergeant that never sleeps in the dictator's soul, and begins to rehearse the *Egmont* Overture as if it had to be a Schoenberg first performance, uprooting every stone, bowing down where others bowed up, and contrariwise, declaring openly or making felt (according to tact) that the 'grand tradition' is lousy routine. Orchestras infuriated by such challenges often play exceedingly well, and sparkling performances, hard as nails, are the result. In other cases the *coup d'état* fails, and the dictator is unlikely to come back very soon.

Our hero prefers a sort of jiu-jitsu technique. Either he will start with a work unknown to the orchestra, 'modern' and difficult. No traditions have in this case to be questioned, and the conductor – after an ingratiating remark about the orchestra's impeccable sight-reading – wins everybody by building up the *Variations*, shaped by now, out of a maze of queer sounds, into quite acceptable music. ('Not what *we* call good writing, of course', says the viola professor; 'not one real theme – but they all know how to make a show with their noises, these cunning modish fellows of nowadays.') Or – if he feels in good spirits, he just plays the *Egmont* Overture from beginning to end. The pleasure of playing reassures the orchestra: the performance will be up to accustomed standards; and the conductor's interpretation is brought in by means of which the orchestra is not clearly conscious.

FREDERICK GOLDBECK *The Perfect Conductor* 1960

That enchanting man, Frederick Goldbeck, was tall and extremely ugly, like a Dutch version of J. Worthington Foulfellow; terrible teeth of black and metal, thick spectacles, after every word a loud descending 'ER' that prevented his listener from cutting in, genial, brilliant and lovable. He once wrote his own life story as follows

Born at the Hague, 1902. Nevertheless, prefers to live in Paris. Writes about music; nevertheless, prefers to read scores, and books not about music. Goes to concerts; nevertheless, prefers not to go nine times out of ten. Conducts; nevertheless prefers to dispense with conducting rather than conduct without rehearsing. Partial to the harmless, necessary twelve-tone composer; nevertheless, prefers cats.

Imogen Holst must have been about as unlike Freddie Goldbeck in appearance as one person can be to another. Dressed in sensible, pre-Laura Ashley fashion, she looked like a true product of the folk-song and dance movement, but her rather fey charm was powered by a will of iron. Very much Gustav's daughter, she was a thoroughly practical musician, and the following notes bring back the flavour of many concerts in churches at which she was herself the central figure

Things that can go wrong on the day. You should arrive at least half an hour before the combined rehearsal is due to begin, bringing two or three helpers with you. (This may seem over-cautious, but you can never know what will go wrong at the last minute, and on more than one occasion I have been faced with having to move a heavy brass lectern without any assistance.) The unexpected set-backs could include any of the following: the key of the organ will have disappeared (it is wise to take a screw-driver to the rehearsal); a coach-load of sightseers from the next county will arrive to look at the chancel tombs just as you were hoping to get the music stands in position; members of the Guild of Church Workers will come armed with huge vases of evergreens which they will place in front of the pulpit just where you had intended the second violins to sit; a road-drill will begin digging up the pavement outside the church porch, or a traffic diversion will cut off the access to the church car-park. . . . The lorry bringing the hired chairs will not have appeared on time, and you will have to part with one of your assistants, so that he can find out what has happened. When the chairs arrive, you should see that there are strong, intelligent helpers to unload them and put them in position: give them copies of your seating plan, so that they know exactly what to do. (It is only incompetent organizers who insist on arranging chairs and carrying platforms while other people stand by and watch them: your job is to keep still so that you can answer the dozens of questions that everyone will want to ask you.) . . . There will be chaos during the five minutes before the rehearsal. The organist's A will be greeted with groans of protest from the orchestra. (The organ should have been tuned very recently, as close to the day of the performance as possible; and the temperature in the church during the tuning should be approximately the same as the temperature during the concert. It is important that the swell-boxes should have been left open: a modern organ has a gadget which automatically opens the boxes, but on an old organ the player has to remember to do it himself.) The orchestra will have several other difficulties to contend with. Cellists' spikes will squeak as they slither across the stone floor: someone should have reminded them to bring a small mat with them. The cellists will also be finding it uncomfortable to have to sit on the extreme edge of the sort of chair that slopes backwards because it has been shaped for stacking. But if you manage to discover one or two old-fashioned wooden chairs in the vestry they will probably be so rickety with age that they will collapse under the players' weight. The leading violinist may be asking for a cushion to make his chair the right height for playing, and the only available substitute will be a hassock, which will be much too high. The borrowed folding music-stands will have come apart during their journey in the boot of a car, and no one will have thought of tying a label to each half to make it easier to put them together. When the odd bits and pieces have at last been joined, enthusiastic helpers will seize a stand without waiting to see if it has been screwed up tightly enough; they will almost certainly hold it near the top instead of near the bottom, so that the metal joints will fall apart again, to the peril of anyone within reach. It is as well to be provided with sticking-plaster on these occasions. In fact, a conductor needs to bring a good deal of equipment in case of emergencies: the list includes spare conducting sticks; any available spare copies of the music; a tuning fork or pitch pipe; pencils and rubbers; several sheets of manuscript paper; scissors; adhesive tape; and a few medium-sized squares of cardboard which can be used either as a firm backing for flimsy orchestral parts or as tightly folded wedges to prevent a platform rocking to and fro on an uneven floor.

. . . At the very beginning of the rehearsal your time-schedule is likely to be upset by the arrival of a photographer from the local newspaper. It is no good losing your temper with him: he has to earn his living. Ask everyone to sing and play the first note of the first piece on a fortissimo-held pause, and bring them all in with a triumphant flourish of your stick. If the wretched man says that he also wants a close-up of the soloists, you must quickly gather them round you while you hold out your full score for them to look at: open it at random and point to a word at the top of a page as if you had only just noticed it for the first time. This never fails to satisfy a photographer, and with any luck he will clear off without having wasted more than three or four precious minutes.

IMOGEN HOLST Conducting a Choir – a Guide for Amateurs 1973

A choir rehearsal at the Royal Orphanage School, just before the outbreak of the Second World War

Apart from the air-raid drills there was no change in the school curriculum. . . . Preparations went ahead for Sports Day. . . . I was chosen for the choir which was to lead the entire school in a programme of songs conducted by Mr Gibbs. They included 'The Mermaid' (in which Mr Gibbs was the soloist), a Gilbert and Sullivan selection and '*Non Nobis Domine*'. We rehearsed every day, except Saturdays and Sundays, for a month. Our rehearsals were the only times we could be sure we would not be interrupted by air-raid drills. . . . Mr Gibbs conducted in his shirt sleeves. Perfectly round beads of sweat appeared on his forehead as if it had been squeezed like orange peel . . . music was the only subject which he seemed to take actual pleasure in teaching. He urged us to enjoy the exercise. 'To sing is to make a joyful noise', he declared. 'Let me hear joy in your voices.' To encourage us he laughed up and down the scale, guffawing into our faces as if to make us inhale his enthusiasm. Close up he looked drunk. A gold tooth gleamed in his open mouth. His thinning hair which had come ungummed in the heat of the rehearsal shook as if it was stirred by a fan. His eyes bulged. He placed our hands on his belly so that we could feel the notes vibrate. It was like standing on the edge of a railway platform which began to tremble as the train approached.

PHILIP OAKES 1939 From Middle England

Amateurs

The Village Choir

Half a bar, half a bar,
Half a bar onward!
Into an awful ditch
Choir and precentor hitch,
Into a mess of pitch,
    They led the Old Hundred.
Trebles to right of them,
Tenors to left of them,
Basses in front of them,
    Bellowed and thundered,
Oh, that precentor's look,
When the sopranos took
Their own time and hook
    From the Old Hundred!

Screeched all the trebles here,
Boggled the tenors there,
Raising the parson's hair,
    While his mind wandered;
Theirs not to reason why
This psalm was pitched too high:
Theirs but to gasp and cry
    Out the Old Hundred.
Trebles to right of them,
Tenors to left of them,
Basses in front of them,
    Bellowed and thundered.
Stormed they with shout and yell,
Not wise they sang nor well,
Drowning the sexton's bell,
    While all the Church wondered.

Dire the precentor's glare,
Flashed his pitchfork in air
Sounding fresh keys to bear
    Out the Old Hundred.

Swiftly he turned his back,
Reached he his hat from rack,
Then from the screaming pack,
    Himself he sundered.
Tenors to right of him,
Tenors to left of him
Discords behind him,
    Bellowed and thundered.
Oh, the wild howls they wrought:
Right to the end they fought!
Some tune they sang, but not,
    Not the Old Hundred.

ANON. after Tennyson

A village choir inevitably suggests Hardy and the whole scene of English amateur country music-making which crops up continually in everything he writes

Going the Rounds

Shortly after ten o'clock the singing-boys arrived at the tranter's house, which was invariably the place of meeting, and preparations were made for the start. The older men and musicians wore thick coats, with stiff perpendicular collars, and coloured handkerchiefs wound round and round the neck till the end came to hand, over all which they just showed their ears and noses, like people looking over a wall. The remainder, stalwart ruddy men and boys, were dressed mainly in snow-white smock-frocks, embroidered upon the shoulders and breasts, in ornamental forms of hearts, diamonds, and zig-zags. The cider-mug was emptied for the ninth time, the music-books were arranged, and the pieces finally decided upon. The boys in the meantime put the old horn-lanterns in order, cut candles into short lengths to fit the lanterns; and, a thin fleece of snow having fallen since the early part of the evening, those who had no leggings went to the stable and wound wisps of hay round their ankles to keep the insidious flakes from the interior of their boots.

Mellstock was a parish of considerable acreage, the hamlets composing it lying at a much greater distance from each other than is ordinarily the case. Hence several hours were consumed in playing and singing within hearing of every family, even if but a single air were bestowed on each. There was Lower Mellstock, the main village; half a mile from this were the church and vicarage, and a few other houses, the spot being rather lonely now, though in past centuries it had been the most thickly-populated quarter of the parish. A mile north-east lay the hamlet of Upper Mellstock, where the tranter lived; and at other points knots of cottages, besides solitary farmsteads and dairies.

Old William Dewy, with the violoncello, played the bass; his grandson Dick the treble violin; and Reuben and Michael Mail the tenor and second violins respectively. The singers consisted of four men and seven boys, upon whom devolved the task of carrying and attending to the lanterns, and holding the books open for the players. Directly music was the theme, old William ever and instinctively came to the front.

'Now mind, naibours,' he said, as they all went out one by one at the door, he himself holding it ajar and regarding them with a critical face as they passed, like a shepherd counting out his sheep. 'You two counter-boys, keep your ears open to Michael's fingering, and don't ye go straying into the treble part along o' Dick and his set, as ye did last year; and mind this especially when we be in "Arise, and hail". Billy Chimlen, don't you sing quite so raving mad as you fain would; and, all o' ye, whatever ye do, keep from making a great scuffle on the ground when we go in at people's gates; but go quietly, so as to strik' up all of a sudden, like spirits.'

'Farmer Ledlow's first?'

'Farmer Ledlow's first; the rest as usual.'

'And, Voss,' said the tranter terminatively, 'you keep house here till about half-past two; then heat the metheglin and cider in the warmer you'll find turned up upon the copper; and bring it wi' the victuals to church-hatch, as th'st know.'

Just before the clock struck twelve they lighted the lanterns and started. The moon, in her third quarter, had risen since the snow-storm; but the dense accumulation of snow-cloud weakened her power to faint twilight, which was rather pervasive of the landscape than traceable to the sky. The breeze had gone down, and the rustle of their feet and tones of their speech echoed with an alert rebound from every post, boundary-stone, and ancient wall they passed, even where the distance of the echo's origin was less than a few yards. Beyond their own slight noises nothing was to be heard, save the occasional bark of foxes in the direction of Yalbury Wood, or the brush of a rabbit among the grass now and then, as it scampered out of their way.

Most of the outlying homesteads and hamlets had been visited by about two o'clock; they then passed across the outskirts of a wooded park toward the main village, nobody being at home at the Manor.

Pursuing no recognized track, great care was necessary in walking lest their faces should come in contact with the low-hanging boughs of the old lime-trees, which in many spots formed dense overgrowths of interlaced branches.

'Times have changed from the times they used to be,' said Mail, regarding nobody can tell what interesting old panoramas with an inward eye, and letting his outward glance rest on the ground, because it was as convenient a position as any. 'People don't care much about us now! I've been thinking we must be almost the last left in the county of the old string players? Barrel-organs, and they things next door to 'em that you blow wi' your foot, have come in terribly of late years.'

'Ay!' said Bowman, shaking his head; and old William, on seeing him, did the same thing.

'More's the pity,' replied another. 'Time was – long and merry ago now! – when not one of the varmits was to be heard of; but it served some of the choirs right. They should have stuck to strings as we did, and keep out clar'nets, and done away with serpents. If you'd thrive in musical religion, stick to strings, says I.'

'Strings be safe soul-lifters, as fur as that do go,' said Mr Spinks.

'Yet there's worse things than serpents,' said Mr Penny. 'Old things pass away, 'tis true; but a serpent was a good old note: a deep rich note was the serpent.'

'Clar'nets, however, be bad at all times,' said Michael Mail. 'One Christmas – years agone now, years – I went the rounds wi' the Weatherbury choir. 'Twas a hard frosty night, and the keys of all the clar'nets froze – ah, they did freeze! – so that 'twas like drawing a cork every time a key was opened; the players o' 'em had to go into a hedger-and-ditcher's chimley-corner, and thaw their clar'nets every now and then. An icicle o' spet hung down from the end of every man's clar'net a span long; and as to fingers – well, there, if ye'll believe me, we had no fingers at all, to our knowing.'

'I can well bring back to to my mind,' said Mr Penny, 'what I said to poor Joseph Ryme (who took the tribble part in Chalk-Newton Church for two-and-forty year) when they thought of having clar'nets there. "Joseph," I said, says I, "depend upon't, if so be you have them tooting clar'nets you'll spoil the whole set-out. Clar'nets were not made for the service of the Lard; you can see it by looking at 'em," I said . . . And what cam o't? Why, souls, the parson set up a barrel-organ on his own account within two years o' the time I spoke, and the old choir went to nothing.'

'As far as look is concerned,' said the tranter, 'I don't for my part see that a fiddle is much nearer heaven than a clar'net. 'Tis further off. There's always a rakish, scampish twist about a fiddle's looks that seems to say the Wicked One had a hand in making o'en; while angels be supposed to play clar'nets in heaven, or som'at like 'em, if ye may believe picters.'

'Robert Penny, you was in the right,' broke in the eldest Dewy. 'They should ha' stuck to strings. Your brass-man is a rafting dog – well and good; your reed-man is a dab at stirring ye – well and good; your drum-man is a rare bowel-shaker – good again. But I don't care who hears me say it, nothing will spak to your heart wi' the sweetness o' the man of strings!'

'Strings for ever!' said little Jimmy.

'Strings alone would have held their ground against all the new comers in creation.' ('True, true!' said Bowman.) 'But clar'nets was death.' ('Death they was!' said Mr Penny.) 'And harmonions,' William continued in a louder voice, and getting excited by these signs of approval, 'harmonions and barrel-organs' ('Ah!' and groans from Spinks) 'be miserable – what shall I call 'em? – miserable –'

'Sinners,' suggested Jimmy, who made large strides like the men, and did not lag behind like the other little boys.

'Miserable dumbledores!'

'Right, William, and so they be – miserable dumbledores!' said the choir with unanimity.

By this time they were crossing to a gate in the direction of the school, which, standing on a slight eminence at the junction of three ways, now rose in unvarying and dark flatness against the sky. The instruments were retuned, and all the band entered the school enclosure, enjoined by old William to keep upon the grass.

'Number seventy-eight,' he softly gave out as they formed round in a semicircle, the boys opening the lanterns to get a clearer light, and directing their rays on the books.

Then passed forth into the quiet night an ancient and time-worn hymn, embodying Christianity in words orally transmitted from father to son through several generations down to the present characters, who sang them out right earnestly:

> Remember Adam's fall,
>   O thou Man:
> Remember Adam's fall
>   From Heaven to Hell.
> Remember Adam's fall;
> How he hath condemn'd all
> In Hell perpetual
>   There for to dwell.

Remember God's goodnesse,
    O thou Man:
Remember God's goodnesse,
    His promise made.
Remember God's goodnesse;
He sent His Son sinlesse
Our ails for to redress;
    Be not afraid!

In Bethlehem He was born,
    O thou Man:
In Bethlehem He was born,
    For mankind's sake.
In Bethlehem He was born,
Christmas-day i' the morn:
Our Saviour thought no scorn
    Our faults to take.

Give thanks to God alway,
    O thou Man:
Give thanks to God alway
    With heart-most joy.
Give thanks to God alway
On this our joyful-day:
Let all men sing and say,
    Holy, Holy!

Having concluded the last note, they listened for a minute or two, but found that no sound issued from the schoolhouse.

'Four breaths, and then, "O, what unbounded goodness!" number fifty-nine,' said William.

This was duly gone through, and no notice whatever seemed to be taken of the performance.

'Good guide us, surely 'tisn't a' empty house, as befell us in the year thirty-nine and forty-three!' said old Dewy.

'Perhaps she's jist come from some noble city, and sneers at our doings?' the tranter whispered.

''Od rabbit her!' said Mr Penny, with an annihilating look at a corner of the school chimney, 'I don't quite stomach her, if this is it. Your plain music well done is as worthy as your other sort done bad, a' b'lieve, souls, so say I.'

'Four breaths, and then the last,' said the leader authoritatively. '"Rejoice, ye Tenants of the Earth," number sixty-four.'

At the close, waiting yet another minute, he said in a clear loud voice, as he had said in the village at that hour and season for the previous forty years –

'A merry Christmas to ye!'

But the answer was silence. And worse was to come

'Now to Farmer Shiner's, and then replenish our insides, father?' said the tranter.

'Wi' all my heart,' said old William, shouldering his bass-viol.

Farmer Shiner's was a queer lump of a house, standing at the corner of a lane that ran into the principal thoroughfare. The upper windows were much wider than they were high, and this feature, together with a broad bay-window where the door might have been expected, gave it by day the aspect of a human countenance turned askance, and wearing a sly and wicked leer. To-night nothing was visible but the outline of the roof upon the sky.

The front of this building was reached, and the preliminaries arranged as usual.

'Four breaths, and number thirty-two, "Behold the Morning Star,"' said old William.

They had reached the end of the second verse, and the fiddlers were doing the up bow-stroke previously to pouring forth the opening chord of the third verse, when, without a light appearing or any signal being given, a roaring voice exclaimed –

'Shut up, woll 'ee! Don't make your blaring row here! A feller wi' a headache enough to split his skull likes a quiet night!'

Slam went the window.

'Hullo, that's a' ugly blow for we!' said the tranter, in a keenly appreciative voice, and turning to his companions.

'Finish the carrel, all who be friends of harmony!' said old William commandingly; and they continued to the end.

'Four breaths, and number nineteen!' said William firmly. 'Gi'e it him well; the choir can't be insulted in this manner!'

A light now flashed into existence; the window opened, and the farmer stood revealed as one in a terrific passion.

'Drown en! – drown en!' the tranter cried, fiddling frantically. 'Play fortissimy, and drown his spaking!'

'Fortissimy!' said Michael Mail, and the music and singing waxed so loud that it was impossible to know what Mr Shiner had said, was saying, or was about to say; but wildly flinging his arms and body about in the form of capital Xs and Ys, he appeared to utter enough invectives to consign the whole parish to perdition.

'Very onseemly – very!' said old William, as they retired. 'Never such a dreadful scene in the whole round o' my carrel practice – never! And he a churchwarden!'

THOMAS HARDY *Under the Greenwood Tree* 1872

The amateur in society, however, is a very different animal

Hell is full of musical amateurs: music is the brandy of the damned.

BERNARD SHAW

'Tis the common disease of all your musicians, that they know no mean, to be entreated either to begin or to end.

BEN JONSON

All singers have this fault: if asked to sing among friends they are never so inclined; if unasked, they never leave off.

HORACE

In the Elizabethan period it had become a matter for shame not to have some skill in music. Thomas Morley's *Plaine and Easie Introduction to Practicall Musick*, the first great English book on music, opens with a dialogue in which Polymathes asks Philomathes about a banquet he had attended on the previous night, at which the discourse was mainly of music

POLYMATHES: I trust you were contented to suffer others to speake of that matter.

PHILOMATHES: I would that had been the worst: for I was compelled to discover mine own ignorance, and confesse that I knewe nothing at all in it.

POLYMATHES: How so?

PHILOMATHES: Among the rest of the guestes, by chaunce, master *Aphron* came thether also, who falling to discourse of Musicke, was in an argument so quickely taken up & hotly pursued by *Eudoxus* and *Calergus*, two kinsmen of *Sophobulus*, as in his owne art he was overthrowne. But he still sticking in his opinion, the two gentlemen requested mee to examine his reasons and confute them; but I refusing & pretending ignorance, the whole companie condemned mee of discurtesie, being fully perswaded, that I had beene as skilfull in that art as they tooke mee to be learned in others. But supper being ended, and Musicke books, according to the custome being brought to the table: the mistresse of the house presented mee with a part, earnestly requesting mee to sing. But when after manie excuses, I protested unfainedly that I could not: everie one began to wonder. Yea, some whispered to others demaunding how I was brought up, so that upon shame of mine

ignorance I go nowe to seeke out mine olde friende Master
Gnorimus, to make my selfe his scholler.

THOMAS MORLEY *A Plaine and Easie Introduction to Practicall Musicke* 1597

Philomathes is clearly determined to put an end to his ignorance once and for
all (and indeed, there is the whole of Morley's book to tell us how he does it).
But his twentieth-century successor is inspired by no such desire for better-
ment

'Of course, this sort of music's not intended for an audience, you see,'
Welch said as he handed the copies round. 'The fun's all in the
singing. Everybody's got a real tune to sing – a real tune,' he repeated
violently. 'You could say, really, that polyphony got to its highest
point, its peak, at that period, and has been on the decline ever since.
You've only got to look at the part-writing in things like, well, *Onward,
Christian Soldiers,* the hymn, which is a typical . . . a typical . . .'

'We're all waiting, Ned,' Mrs Welch said from the piano. She played
a slow arpeggio, sustaining it with the pedal. 'All right, everybody?'

A soporific droning filled the air round Dixon as the singers
hummed their notes to one another. Mrs Welch rejoined them on the
low platform that had been built at one end of the music-room, taking
up her stand by Margaret, the other soprano. A small bullied-looking
woman with unabundant brown hair was the only contralto. Next to
Dixon was Cecil Goldsmith, a colleague of his in the College History
Department, whose tenor voice held enough savage power, especially
above middle C, to obliterate whatever noises Dixon might feel
himself impelled to make. Behind him and to one side were three
basses, one a local composer, another an amateur violinist occasionally summoned at need by the city orchestra, the third Evan Johns.

Dixon ran his eye along the lines of black dots, which seemed to go
up and down a good deal, and was able to assure himself that
everyone was going to have to sing all the time. He'd had a bad
setback twenty minutes ago in some Brahms rubbish which began
with ten seconds or so of unsupported tenor – more accurately, of
unsupported Goldsmith, who'd twice dried up in face of a tricky
interval and left him opening and shutting his mouth in silence. He
now cautiously reproduced the note Goldsmith was humming and
found the effect pleasing rather than the reverse. Why hadn't they had
the decency to ask him if he'd like to join in, instead of driving him up
on to this platform arrangement and forcing sheets of paper into his
hand?

The madrigal began at the bidding of Welch's arthritic forefinger.

Dixon kept his head down, moved his mouth as little as possible consistent with being unmistakably seen to move it, and looked through the words the others were singing. 'When from my love I looked for love, and kind affections due,' he read, 'too well I found her vows to prove most faithless and untrue. But when I did ask her why . . .' He looked over at Margaret, who was singing away happily enough – she turned out regularly during the winter with the choir of the local Conservative Association – and wondered what changes in their circumstances and temperaments would be necessary to make the words of the madrigal apply, however remotely, to himself and her. She'd made vows to him, or avowals anyway, which was perhaps all the writer had meant. But if he'd meant what he seemed to mean by 'kind affections due', then Dixon had never 'looked for' any of these from Margaret. Perhaps he should: after all, people were doing it all the time. It was a pity she wasn't a bit better-looking. One of these days, though, he would try, and see what happened.

'Yet by, and by, they'll arl, deny, arnd say 'twas *bart* in jast,' Goldsmith sang tremulously and very loudly. It was the last phrase; Dixon kept his mouth open while Welch's finger remained aloft, then shut it with a little flick of the head he'd seen singers use as the finger swept sideways. All seemed pleased with the performance and anxious for another of the same sort. 'Yes, well, this next one's what they called a ballet. Of course, they didn't mean what we mean by the similar . . . Rather a well-known one, this. It's called *Now is the Month of Maying*. Now if you'll all just . . .'

A bursting snuffle of laughter came from Dixon's left rear. He glanced round to see Johns's pallor rent by a grin. The large short-lashed eyes were fixed on him. 'What's the joke?' he asked. If Johns were laughing at Welch, Dixon was prepared to come in on Welch's side.

'You'll see,' Johns said. He went on looking at Dixon. 'You'll see,' he added, grinning.

In less than a minute Dixon did see, and clearly. Instead of the customary four parts, this piece employed five. The third and fourth lines of music from the top had *Tenor* i and *Tenor* ii written against them; moreover, there was some infantile fa-la-la-la stuff on the second page with numerous gaps in the individual parts. Even Welch's ear might be expected to record the complete absence of one of the parts in such circumstances. It was much too late now for Dixon to explain that he hadn't really meant it when he'd said, half an hour before, that he could read music 'after a fashion'; much too late to transfer allegiance to the basses. Nothing short of an epileptic fit could get him out of this.

'You'd better take first tenor, Jim,' Goldsmith said; 'the second's a bit tricky.'

Dixon nodded bemusedly, hardly hearing further laughter from Johns. Before he could cry out, they were past the piano-ritual and the droning and into the piece. He flapped his lips to: 'Each with his bonny lass, a-a-seated on the grass: fa-la-la la, fa-la-la-la-la-la la la-la . . .' but Welch had stopped waving his finger, was holding it stationary in the air. The singing died. 'Oh, tenors,' Welch began; 'I didn't seem to hear . . .'

Mercifully, there is an interruption; the plot thickens, and Dixon makes his escape in a very different frame of mind from that of his Elizabethan forebear

'Look here, Dixon, you're talking as if you want a bloody good punch on the nose, aren't you?'

Dixon, when moved, was bad at ordering his thoughts. 'If I did, you don't think you're the one to give me one, do you?'

Bertrand screwed up his face at this enigma. 'What?'

'Do you know what you look like in that beard?' Dixon's heart began to race as he switched to simplicity.

'All right; coming outside for a bit?'

The latest of this string of questions was drowned by a long rumbling shake in the bass of the piano. 'What?' Dixon asked.

Mrs Welch, Margaret, Johns, the Goldsmiths, and the contralto woman all seemed to turn round simultaneously. 'Ssshh,' they all said. It was like a railway engine blowing out steam under a glass roof. Dixon got up and tip-toed to the door. Bertrand half rose to follow, but his girl stopped him.

Before Dixon could reach the door, it opened and Welch entered. 'Oh, you've started, have you?' he asked without dropping his voice at all.

'Yes,' Dixon whispered. 'I think I'll just . . .'

'Pity you couldn't have waited a little longer. I've been on the phone, you see. It was that chap from the . . . from the . . .'

'See you later.' Dixon began edging past to the doorway.

'Aren't you going to stay for the P. Racine Fricker?' . . .

KINGSLEY AMIS *Lucky Jim* 1954

Domestic music making can take many different forms

'I like that one best of *all*,' she said, 'and *how* kind of you to have been able to spare us a moment tonight, and to have given us *all such* a treat, and to have sung *so* many songs. I do hope it hasn't *tired* you; you must take care of that precious throat. The Ambassador has so enjoyed it; we *all* have, and you must come to tea and sing another song very soon.' And as she talked she took Miss Sims's music from the pianoforte, and rolled it up neatly in a *rouleau*, and tied it with a little piece of pink ribbon, and presented it to her with a charming but completely final bow, and calling Herbert Napier she said to him, 'Mr Napier, will you take Miss Sims to have a cup of tea and some lemonade?' And so saying, she led the guests back to the drawing-room, and Napier conducted Miss Sims to a small buffet on the top of the staircase, where there were refreshments, whence she was ultimately shown out.

'She may do for concerts in England,' said Lady Lawless. 'One never knows what English people will like.'

MAURICE BARING 'C' 1924

This is from Izaak Walton's *Life of George Herbert*

His chiefest recreation was Musick, in which heavenly Art he was a most excellent Master, and did himself compose many *divine Hymns* and *Anthems*, which he set and sung to his *Lute* or *Viol*; and, though he was a lover of retiredness, yet his love to *Musick* was such, that he went usually twice every week on certain appointed days, to the *Cathedral Church* in *Salisbury*; and at his return would say, *That his time spent in Prayer, and Cathedral Musick, elevated his Soul, and was his Heaven upon Earth*: But before his return thence to *Bemerton*, he would usually sing and play his part, at an appointed private Musick-meeting. . . .

In [one of his walks] to *Salisbury*, he saw a poor man, with a poorer horse, that was fall'n under his Load; they were both in distress, and needed present help; which Mr. *Herbert* perceiving, put off his Canonical Coat, and help'd the poor man to unload, and after, to load his horse: The poor man blest him for it: and he blest the poor man; and was so like the *good Samaritan*, that he gave him money to refresh both himself and his horse; and told him, *That if he lov'd himself, he should be merciful to his Beast*. – Thus he left the poor man, and at his coming to his musical friends at *Salisbury*, they began to wonder that Mr. *George Herbert* which us'd to be so trim and clean, came into that company so soyl'd and discompos'd; but he told them the occasion:

And when one of the company told him, *He had disparag'd himself by so dirty an employment*; his answer was, *That the thought of what he had done, would prove Musick to him at Midnight; and that the omission of it, would have upbraided and made discord in his Conscience, whensoever he should pass by that place; for, if I be bound to pray for all that be in distress, I am sure that I am bound so far as it is in my power to practise what I pray for. And though I do not wish for the like occasion every day, yet let me tell you, I would not willingly pass one day of my life without comforting a sad soul, or shewing mercy; and I praise God for this occasion*: and now let's tune our Instruments.

IZAAK WALTON The Life of Mr. George Herbert 1675

Pepys was a keen amateur musician and composer, though the one course of musical instruction that he mentions in his diary does not seem to have lasted long

January 15 This morning, Mr. Berchenshaw come again; and after he had examined me and taught me something in my work, he and I went to breakfast in my chamber upon a Collar of brawne. . . .

February 11 . . . at the office in the afternoon. So home to musique, my mind being full of our alteracions in the garden. . . . At night begun to compose songs, and begin with 'Gaze not on swans.'

February 24 Long with Mr. Berchenshaw in the morning at my Musique practice, finishing my song of 'Gaze not on swans,' in two parts, which pleases me well. And I did give him £5 for this month or five weeks that he hath taught me, which is a great deal of money, and troubled me to part with it. . . .

February 27 Come Mr. Berchensha [*sic*] to me; and in our discourse . . . we fell to angry words, so that in a pet he flung out of my chamber and I never stopped him, being entended to have put him off today, whether this had happened or no, because I think I have all the rules that he hath to give. . . .

SAMUEL PEPYS Diary 1662

The *New Grove* says that the 'pet' arose from Pepys's criticism of John Birchenshaw's rules, which he had conceded elsewhere 'the best I believe that ever were yet made'

The Court of *England* is much alter'd. At a solemn Dancing, first you had the grave Measures, then the Corrantoes and the Galliards, and this is kept up with Ceremony, and at length to *Trenchmore*, and the

Cushion Dance, and then all the Company dance, Lord and Groom, Lady and Kitchin-Maid, no distinction. So in our Court in Queen *Elizabeth*'s time, Gravity and State were kept up. In King *James*'s time things were pretty well. But in King *Charles*'s time, there has been nothing but *Trenchmore* and the Cushion Dance, *omnium gatherum*, tolly polly, hoite cum toite.

JOHN SELDEN Table Talk 1689

(The indispensable *Brewer's Dictionary of Phrase and Fable* gives all the terms in the last sentence except 'tolly polly'.)

When Sir James Melvil visited the court of Elizabeth I on an embassy from Mary Queen of Scots in 1564, he found Elizabeth eager for details about her northern cousin: '. . . how my Queen dressed? . . . whether my Queens hair or hers was best, and which of them two was fairest? And which of them was of highest stature?. . . .'

. . . Then she asked what kind of exercises she used? I answered that when I received my dispatch, the Queen was lately come from the High-land hunting. That when her more serious affairs permitted, she was taken up with reading of Histories. That sometimes she recreated her self in playing upon the Lute, and Virginals. She asked if she played well? I said reasonably for a Queen.

That same day after dinner my Lord of *Hunsdean* drew me up to a quiet Gallery, that I might hear some Musick, but he said that he durst not avow it, where I might hear the Queen play upon the Virginals. After I had hearkned awhile, I took by the Tapistry that hung before the door of the Chamber, and seeing her back was toward the door, I entered within the Chamber, and stood a pretty space hearing her play excellently well, but she left off immediately, so soon as she turned her about and saw me. She appeared to be surprized to see me, and came forward, seeming to strike me with her hand, alledging she used not to play before Men, but when she was solitary to shun melancholly. She asked how I came there? I answered, as I was walking with my Lord of *Hunsdean*, as we past by the Chamber door, I heard such melody as ravished me, whereby I was drawn in e're I knew how, excusing my fault of homeliness, as being brought up in the Court of *France*, where such freedom was allowed; declaring my self willing to endure what kind of punishment her Majesty should be pleased to inflict upon me for so great an offence. Then she sate down low upon a Cushion, and I upon my knees by her, but with her own hand she gave me a Cushion, to lay under my knee, which at first I refused, but she compelled me to take it. She then called for my Lady *Strafford* out of the next Chamber, for the Queen was alone. She inquired whether my Queen or she played best? In that I found my self obliged to give her the praise.

SIR JAMES MELVIL 1564 Memoirs

Elizabeth's father was no mean musician, and indeed royal amateurs make a fascinating study of their own. Sandoval, the biographer of the Emperor Charles v, has left this remarkable description of imperial musicianship

. . . he was a great friend to the science of music, and after his abdication, would have the church-offices only accompanied by the organ, and sung by fourteen or fifteen Fryers, who were good musicians, and had been selected from the most expert performers of the order. He was himself so skilful that he knew if any other singer pretended, and if any one made a mistake, he would cry out, such a one is wrong, and immediately mark the man. . . . The Emperor understood music, felt, and tasted its charms; the Fryers often discovered him behind the door, as he sat in his own apartment, near the high altar, beating time, and singing in part with the performers; and if anyone was out, they could overhear him call the offender names, as *Redheaded, Blockhead,* etc. A composer from Seville whose name was Guerrero, presented him with a book of Motets and Masses; and when one of these Compositions had been sung as a specimen, the Emperor called his confessor, and said, see what a thief, what a plagiarist, is this son of a . . . ! Why here, says he, this passage is taken from one Composer, and this from another, naming them as he went on. All this while the Singers stood astonished, as none of them had discovered these thefts, till they were pointed out by the Emperor.

PRUDENCIO DE SANDOVAL Life of Charles v 1614

A careless song, with a little nonsense in it now and then, does not misbecome a monarch.

HORACE WALPOLE Letter 1774

Frederick the Great's musical activities extended from playing the flute (notably the 200 sonatas and 300 concertos of his industrious teacher, Johann Joachim Quantz) to writing libretti (notably *Montezuma* for Graun). He was an excellent spare-time composer, and provided for *The Musical Offering* what must surely be reckoned the best musical theme ever to come out of a crowned head. His admiration for Bach is well known – though it seems doubtful whether it was really best expressed by making the old man try out all the

Silbermann fortepianos at Potsdam 'without even giving him time to change his travelling clothes' (as Wilhelm Friedemann told Forkel, his father's first biographer).

The nineteenth century was a little calmer, partly perhaps because the writing and performing of music had become so much more complicated that royal hands could less easily be turned to it. At least there is no ersatz Wagner written by Ludwig II of Bavaria. That queerest of all royal amateurs expressed his admiration for his pet composer in other ways

In the enormous Opera House in Munich there is some sort of machinery which in case of fire can call an immense water power into play. This could, we are told, place the entire stage under water. On one occasion when the King was the sole audience a curious scene took place. In the piece a great storm is introduced; the theatre thunder rolled, the theatre wind blew, the noise of rain falling began. The King grew more and more excited; he was carried out of himself. He called from his box in a loud voice, 'Good, very good! Excellent! But I wish to have real rain! Turn on the water!'

The manager ventured to remonstrate: he spoke of the ruin to the decorations, the silk and velvet hangings, etc., but the King would not listen. 'Never mind, never mind! I wish to have real rain: turn on the cocks!' So it was done. The water deluged the stage, it streamed over the painted flowers and the painted hedges and the summer-houses; the singers in their fine costumes were wet from head to foot, but they tried to ignore the situation, and, being born and bred actors, succeeded. They sang on bravely. The King was in the seventh heaven; he clapped his hands and cried, 'Bravo! More thunder! More lightning! Make it rain harder! Let all the pipes loose! More! More! I will hang anyone who dares to put up an umbrella.'

MARK TWAIN quoted by Christopher Hogwood

If the King loves music, there is little wrong in the land.

MENG-TZU (c. 372–289 BC)

Brahms cautioned

Never criticize the composition of a Royal Highness; you never know who may have written it.

And there were even worse dangers: Berlioz, after completing the score of his immense *Te Deum*, wrote to a friend

But of England and Prince Albert, to whom the work is dedicated, I have no hopes at all: he is perfectly capable of sending me what he sent Meyerbeer on a similar occasion – HIS OWN COMPLETE WORKS!

Albert's descendants were sometimes less musically inclined. Osbert Sitwell, in a description of the Changing of the Guard outside Buckingham Palace, writes about the part played in the ceremony by the bands of the four regiments of Guards

Each of the four, naturally, had its own specialities, and in those days the band of the Grenadiers used often, rather unexpectedly, but always to my delight, to break into contemporary Spanish marches and selections from current *zarzuelas*: for Prince Alexander of Battenberg, the Queen of Spain's brother, who was in the Grenadiers at the time and possessed that love of music which, since the days of George I, so many members of the Royal Family have shown, used to bring back the scores with him from his visits to Andalusia and Madrid. And these were airs which a musician could like, in no way resembling the popular tunes of Paris and London, cities in this respect so badly served for more than a century, though the tunes whistled and hummed by the people at work, and played at street corners by bands and barrel organs, should form so important an ingredient in the communal happiness and afford its own characteristic rhythm to each city, as they do – or did – in, let us say, Palermo and Seville.[*] Other innovations were not so successful as the Spanish marches. Sometimes the band grew ambitious, and I remember Williams, for many years Bandmaster of the Grenadiers, telling me of how he had made an arrangement for his men of part of the score of *Elektra* by Richard Strauss, and of what happened when first he played it. It had taken them many months to learn, and they had just given it in public for the first time during this long interval in the Changing of the Guard at Buckingham Palace, and had experienced a due sense of elation at their own audacity and at the success that had crowned it, when – a rare event – a scarlet-coated page came out from the Palace with a personal message for Williams from King George v. The note was brief and ran, 'His Majesty does not know what the band has just played, but it is *never* to be played again.'

OSBERT SITWELL *Great Morning* 1948

---

* [We are reminded, in parsing, of Vaughan Williams's comment on a passage in his 4th Symphony: 'It looks wrong, and it sounds wrong; but it's right.']

George v was no music-lover, and a military band arrangement of *Elektra* might well have been too much for him even if he had been. But princely displeasure, in the days when monarchs really had musical views, was a recurring threat to all musicians until the end of the eighteenth century. The altercation between the young Mozart and his patron, the Prince Archbishop of Salzburg, is the classic case, and ended in a famous incident – described here in the decorous language of Otto Jahn's English translator

The Archbishop imagined that Mozart's father would bring his son to a sense of his duty; Count Arco, who had received a letter from the elder Mozart, proposed an interview, in the hope of persuading him in a friendly way. Mozart . . . begged for an audience to take leave, but this was three times refused, because it was feared to irritate the Archbishop, and Mozart's submission was still hoped for. The latter was beside himself when he heard that the Archbishop was to leave next day, and that he had not been informed of it. He drew up a fresh memorial, in which he explained that he had waited four weeks for a final audience; as this had been postponed so long from reasons unknown to him, he had no resource but to beg for it himself at the last moment. When he found himself in the antechamber, in pursuance of this intention, and prayed for an audience, Count Arco put the finishing touch to the brutalities suffered by Mozart. After loading him with abusive epithets, *he pushed him towards the door with his foot!* [Miss Townsend's italics]

                        OTTO JAHN (trans. Pauline Townsend) *Life of Mozart* 1882

Mozart's own comments on the incident are expressed in pithier terms

Well, that will be the last time. What is it to him if I want to get my discharge? And if he was really so well disposed towards me, he ought to have reasoned quietly with me – or have let things take their course, rather than throw such words about as 'clown' and 'knave' and *hoof a fellow out of the room with a kick on his arse.* . . . [our italics]

                                    MOZART Letter to his father 9 June 1781

The trials of polite behaviour at the Pleasure Gardens at Vauxhall

[The widow] perceived now that she had no pretensions in the world to taste, her very senses were vulgar, since she had praised detestable custard, and smacked at wretched wine; she was therefore content to yield the victory, and for the rest of the night to listen and improve. It is true she would now and then forget herself, and confess she was pleased but they soon brought her back again to miserable refinement. She once praised the painting of the box in which we were sitting but was soon convinced that such paltry pieces ought rather to excite horror than satisfaction; she ventured again to commend one of the singers, but Mrs. Tibbs soon let her know, in the style of a connoisseur, that the singer in question had neither ear, voice, nor judgment.

Mr. Tibbs, now willing to prove that his wife's pretensions to music were just, entreated her to favour the company with a song; but to this she gave a positive denial, for you know very well, my dear, says she, that I am not in voice today, and when ones voice is not equal to ones judgment, what signifies singing; besides as there is no accompanyment, it would be but spoiling music. All these excuses however were overruled by the rest of the company who, though one would think they already had music enough, joined in the entreaty. But particularly the widow, now willing to convince the company of her breeding, pressed so warmly, that she seem'd determined to take no refusal. At last then the lady complied, and after humming for some minutes, began with such a voice, and such affectation, as I could perceive gave but little satisfaction to any except her husband. He sate with rapture in his eye, and beat time with his hand on the table.

You must observe, my friend, that it is the custom of this country, when a lady or gentleman happens to sing, for the company to sit as mute and motionless as statues. Every feature, every limb must seem to correspond in fixed attention, and while the song continues, they are to remain in a state of universal petrifaction. In this mortifying situation we had continued for some time, listening to the song, and looking with tranquillity, when the master of the box came to inform us that the water-works were going to begin. At this information I could instantly perceive the widow bounce from her seat; but correcting herself, she sat down again, repressed by motives of good breeding. Mrs. Tibbs, who had seen the water-works an hundred times, resolving not to be interrupted, continued her song without any share of mercy, nor had the smallest pity on our impatience. The widow's face, I own, gave me high entertainment; in it I could plainly read the struggle she felt between good breeding and curiosity; she talked of the water-works the whole evening before, and seemed to have come merely in order to see them, but then she could not bounce out in the very middle of a song, for that would be forfeiting all pretensions to high life, or high-lived company ever after: Mrs. *Tibbs* therefore kept on singing, and we continued to listen, till at last, when

the song was just concluded, the waiter came to inform us that the
water-works were over.

OLIVER GOLDSMITH *Beau Tibbs at Vauxhall* 1762

Colonel Fitzwilliam's manners were very much admired at the Parson-
age, and the ladies all felt that he must add considerably to the
pleasure of their engagements at Rosings. It was some days, however,
before they received any invitation thither, for while there were
visitors in the house, they could not be necessary; and it was not till
Easter-day, almost a week after the gentlemen's arrival, that they were
honoured by such an attention, and then they were merely asked on
leaving church to come there in the evening. . . .

The invitation was accepted, of course, and at a proper hour they
joined the party in Lady Catherine's drawing-room. Her Ladyship
received them civilly, but it was plain that their company was by no
means so acceptable as when she could get nobody else; and she was,
in fact, almost engrossed by her nephews, speaking to them,
especially to Darcy, much more than to any other person in the room.

Colonel Fitzwilliam seemed really glad to see them: anything was a
welcome relief to him at Rosings; and Mrs. Collins's pretty friend had,
moreover, caught his fancy very much. He now seated himself by her,
and talked so agreeably of Kent and Hertfordshire, of travelling and
staying at home, of new books and music, that Elizabeth had never
been half so well entertained in that room before; and they conversed
with so much spirit and flow as to draw the attention of Lady
Catherine herself, as well as Mr. Darcy. *His* eyes had been soon and
repeatedly turned towards them with a look of curiosity; and that her
Ladyship, after a while, shared the feeling, was more openly acknowledged, for she did not scruple to call out, –

'What is that you are saying, Fitzwilliam? What is it you are talking
of? What are you telling Miss Bennet? Let me hear what it is.'

'We are speaking of music, madam,' said he, when no longer able to
avoid a reply.

'Of music! Then pray speak aloud. It is of all subjects my delight. I
must have my share in the conversation, if you are speaking of music.
There are few people in England, I suppose, who have more true
enjoyment of music than myself, or a better natural taste. If I had ever
learnt, I should have been a great proficient. And so would Anne, if
her health had allowed her to apply. I am confident that she would
have performed delightfully. How does Georgiana get on, Darcy?'

Mr. Darcy spoke with affectionate praise of his sister's proficiency.

'I am very glad to hear such a good account of her', said Lady Catherine; 'and pray tell her from me that she cannot expect to excel if she does not practise a great deal.'

'I assure you, madam,' he replied, 'that she does not need such advice. She practises very constantly.'

'So much the better. It cannot be done too much; and when I write next to her, I shall charge her not to neglect it on any account. I often tell young ladies that no excellence in music is to be acquired without constant practice. I have told Miss Bennet several times that she will never play really well unless she practises more; and though Mrs. Collins has no instrument, she is very welcome, as I have often told her, to come to Rosings every day, and play on the pianoforte in Mrs. Jenkinson's room. She would be in nobody's way, you know, in that part of the house.'

Mr. Darcy looked a little ashamed of his aunt's ill-breeding, and made no answer.

When coffee was over, Colonel Fitzwilliam reminded Elizabeth of having promised to play to him; and she sat down directly to the instrument. He drew a chair near her. Lady Catherine listened to half a song, and then talked, as before, to her other nephew; till the latter walked away from her, and, moving with his usual deliberation towards the pianoforte, stationed himself so as to command a full view of the fair performer's countenance. Elizabeth saw what he was doing, and at the first convenient pause turned to him with an arch smile, and said, –

'You mean to frighten me, Mr. Darcy, by coming in all this state to hear me. But I will not be alarmed, though your sister *does* play so well. There is a stubbornness about me that never can bear to be frightened at the will of others. My courage always rises with every attempt to intimidate me.'

JANE AUSTEN *Pride and Prejudice* 1813

An ear for music is a very different thing from a taste for music. I have no ear whatever; I could not sing an air to save my life; but I have the intensest delight in music, and can detect good from bad. Naldi, a good fellow, remarked to me once at a concert, that I did not seem much interested with a piece of Rossini's which had just been performed. I said, it sounded to me like nonsense verses. But I could scarcely contain myself when a thing of Beethoven's followed.

SAMUEL TAYLOR COLERIDGE *Table Talk* 1830

Snob!

I even think that *sentimentally* I am disposed to harmony. But *organically*
I am incapable of a tune. I have been practising *'God save the King'* all my
life; whistling and humming it over to myself in solitary corners; and
am not yet arrived, they tell me, within many quavers of it.

CHARLES LAMB *Essays of Elia* 1823

We were none of us musical, though Miss Jenkyns beat time, out of
time, by way of appearing to be so.

MRS GASKELL *Cranford* 1853

>   . . . How sour sweet music is
>   When time is broke and no proportion kept!
>   So is it in the music of men's lives . . .

SHAKESPEARE *Richard* II

A vile beastly rottenheaded foolbegotten brazenthroated pernicious
piggish screaming, tearing, roaring, perplexing, splitmecrackle
crashmecriggle insane ass of a woman is practising howling below-
stairs with a brute of a singingmaster so horribly, that my head is
nearly off.

EDWARD LEAR Letter to Lady Strachey 24 January 1859

The music teacher came twice each week to bridge the awful gap
between Dorothy and Chopin.

GEORGE ADE 1866–1944

Hamilton Palace
Near Edinburgh
21 Oct. [1848]

. . . Art here means painting, sculpture, and architecture. Music isn't
considered an art, and if you use the word *artist* an Englishman thinks
you are talking about a painter or an architect or a sculptor. For the
English, music is a profession not an art: nobody here would speak or
write of a musician as an artist . . . No doubt it's the musicians' fault,
but just you try to put it right! People here play the most extraordinary
things and think them beautiful; it's hopeless to try and interest them
in anything serious. Lady —, one of the first great ladies of London, is
regarded as very musical. I went to spend a few days at her castle and
one evening, when I had played and she had sung a whole lot of
songs, they brought her a sort of accordion and she settled down, with
an expression of the utmost gravity, to perform the most horrible

tunes on this thing. But what would you? It seems to me that all these creatures are a bit touched. . . . The ones who know my compositions say to me: '*Jouez-moi donc votre second Soupir . . . J'aime beaucoup vos cloches. . . .*' And all their appreciation always ends with '*leik water*', that's to say 'your music flows like water'. I have not yet played to any English woman without her saying '*leik water*'. They all look at their hands and play wrong notes with great feeling. What eccentric folk! God help them.

FRÉDÉRIC CHOPIN
Letter to Albert Grzymala 21 October 1848

For what happened a few moments later you must not blame him. Some measure of force was the only way out of an impossible situation. It was in vain that he commanded the young lady to let go: she did but cling the closer. It was in vain that he tried to disentangle himself of her by standing first on one foot, then on the other, and veering sharply on his heel: she did but sway as though hinged to him. He had no choice but to grasp her by the wrists, cast her aside, and step clear of her into the room.

Her hat, gauzily basking with a pair of long white gloves on one of his arm-chairs, proclaimed that she had come to stay.

Nor did she rise. Propped on one elbow, with heaving bosom and parted lips, she seemed to be trying to realise what had been done to her. Through her undried tears her eyes shone up to him.

He asked: 'To what am I indebted for this visit?'

'Ah, say that again!' she murmured. 'Your voice is music.'

He repeated his question.

'Music!' she said dreamily; and such is the force of habit that 'I don't,' she added, 'know anything about music, really. But I know what I like.'

MAX BEERBOHM *Zuleika Dobson* 1911

'What a beautiful movement!' she murmured, as the music paused.

'Beautiful!' I roused myself to echo, though I hadn't heard a note.

Immediately I found myself again in the dock; and again the trial began, that ever-recurring criminal Action in which I am both Judge and culprit, all the jury, and the advocate on either side.

I now pleaded my other respectable attainments and general good character; and winning a favourable verdict, I dropped back into my dream, letting the violin wail unheard through the other movements, and the Grand Piano tinkle.

LOGAN PEARSALL SMITH 'The Concerto' 1921

Softly, in the dusk, a woman is singing to me;
Taking me back down the vista of years, till I see
A child sitting under the piano, in the boom of the tingling strings
And pressing the small, poised feet of a mother who smiles as she
    sings.

In spite of myself, the insidious mastery of song
Betrays me back, till the heart of me weeps to belong
To the old Sunday evenings at home, with winter outside
And hymns in the cosy parlour, the tinkling piano our guide.

So now it is vain for the singer to burst into clamour
With the great black piano appassionato. The glamour
Of childish days is upon me, my manhood is cast
Down in the flood of remembrance, I weep like a child for the past.

D. H. LAWRENCE 'Piano' 1918

Prodigies

'He does not seem a remarkably clever child in any other respect, but his whole soul is absorbed in music,' wrote an unknown correspondent to Dr Burney in the very first report on one of the most phenomenal of all musical prodigies, the infant Crotch. The *New Grove* corroborates the dates in John Rowe Parker's account of this prodigy's progress

About Christmas, 1776, when Master Crotch was only a year and a half old, he discovered a great inclination for music, by leaving even his food to attend to it, when the organ was playing; and about Midsummer, 1777, he would touch the key note of his particular favorite tunes, in order to persuade his father to play them. Soon after this, as he was unable to name these tunes, he would play the first two or three notes of them, when he thought the key note did sufficiently explain what he wished to have played. But according to his mother's account it seems to have been in consequence of his having heard the superior performance of Mrs. Lulman, a musical lady, who came to try his father's organ, and who not only played on it, but sung to her own accompaniment, that he first attempted to play a tune himself: for, the same evening, after her departure, the child cried and was so peevish that his mother was wholly unable to appease him. At length, passing through the dining room, he screamed and struggled violently to go to the organ, in which, when he was indulged, he eagerly bent down the keys with his little fists, as other children usually do, after finding themselves able to produce a noise, which pleases them more than the artificial performance of real melody or harmony by others. The next day, however, being left, while his mother went out, in the dining room with his brother, a youth about fourteen years old, he would not let him rest till he blew the bellows of the organ, while he sat on his knee and bent down the keys, at first promiscuously, but presently, with one hand, he played enough of *God save the King* to awaken the curiosity of his father, who being in a garret, which was his workshop, hastened down stairs to inform himself who was playing this tune upon the organ. When he found it was the child, he could hardly believe what he heard and saw. At this time, he was exactly two years and three weeks old, as appears by the register, in the parish of St. George, Colgate, Norwich. Although he showed such a decided inclination for music, he could no more be prevailed on to play by persuasion than a bird to sing.

When his mother returned, the father, with a look that at once implied joy, wonder and mystery, desired her to go up stairs with him, as he had something curious to show her. She obeyed, and was as much surprised as was the father, on hearing the child play the first part of *God save the King*. The next day he made himself master of the treble of the second part; and the day after he attempted the base, which he performed nearly correct in every particular, except the note immediately before the close, which being an octave below the preceding sound, was out of the reach of his little hand. In the beginning of November, 1777, he played both the treble and base of *Let Ambition fire thy mind*; an old tune now called, *Hope thou Nurse of Young Desire*.

JOHN ROWE PARKER *A Musical Biography* 1824

Crotch played to a large company at Norwich in February 1778, to the King and Queen in 1779, toured the country with his mother and by the age of 11 was playing the organ for services at King's College, Trinity and Great St Mary's Church, Cambridge.

But alas for Ambition, Hope and Young Desire, the infant Crotch eventually grew up into a really rather ordinary composer. Our next prodigy was something else.

On 11 April 1770, Mozart and his father arrived in Rome, and on the same afternoon went to St Peter's to hear the celebrated *Miserere* of the seventeenth-century composer, Gregorio Allegri, sung in the Sistine Chapel. Leopold Mozart wrote to his wife three days later

You have often heard of the famous *Miserere* in Rome, which is so greatly prized that the performers in the chapel are forbidden on pain of excommunication to take away a single part of it, to copy it or to give it to anyone. *But we have it already*. Wolfgang has written it down and we would have sent it to Salzburg in this letter, if it were not necessary for us to be there to perform it. But the manner of performance contributes more to its effect than the composition itself. So we shall bring it home with us. Moreover, as it is one of the secrets of Rome, we do not wish to let it fall into other hands, *ut non incurramus mediate vel immediate in censuram Ecclesiae*.

The news of Mozart's feat of musical memory seems to have caused some uneasiness in Salzburg, for in a later letter to his wife Leopold Mozart wrote

On reading the article about the *Miserere*, we simply burst out laughing. There is not the slightest cause for anxiety. Everywhere else far more fuss is being made about Wolfgang's feat [than here]. All Rome knows and even the Pope himself that he wrote it down. There is nothing whatever to fear; on the contrary, the achievement has done him great credit, as you will shortly hear. You will see to it that the letter is read out everywhere, so that we may be sure that His Grace [the Archbishop of Salzburg] hears what Wolfgang has done.

This is the original version of one of the best-known anecdotes about Mozart and indeed, about child prodigies. To fill in a few details by no means detracts from a remarkable feat by a boy of fourteen. In the first place, it is not entirely unique, for Mendelssohn did the same thing, at least in part, when he was in Rome in 1831, and besides, Jahn, in his *Life of Mozart*, says that on Good Friday Wolfgang 'took his manuscript with him into the chapel, and holding it in his hat, corrected some passages where his memory had not been quite true.' Nor, in spite of romantic assertions to the contrary, was this the first copy of the *Miserere* to be made: three others are known to have preceded it – one of which, made at the request of the Emperor Leopold 1, much disappointed its recipient because it omitted the elaborate traditional embellishments upon which the greater part of its effect depended. In Mozart's case it does not seem to be certain whether he wrote out only the basic work which, though for double chorus with nine voices, is severe and extremely simple in style, lasting ten minutes, or whether he included the all-important ornamentations: his father's remark about the manner of its performance might be taken as pointing in either direction.

In any case the feat was a remarkable one, and Mozart was of course very young. To the letter in which his father first sent home news of the incident, the composer added a postscript which finishes

I have just now drawn a picture of St Peter with his keys and with him St Paul with his sword and St Luke with my sister and so forth. I have had the honour of kissing St Peter's foot in St Peter's church and as I have the misfortune to be so small, I, that same old dunce,

WOLFGANG MOZART
had to be lifted up.

Postscript to his father's letter 14 April 1770

Mozart is, of course, the archetype of the child prodigy. The stories about him are astonishing, innumerable, and often true. The first written testimony to his extraordinary musical talent is a note in his father's hand in his sister Nannerl's music book, under a *Scherzo* by Georg Christoph Wagenseil

This piece was learnt by Wolfgangerl on 24 January 1761, 3 days before his 5th birthday, between 9 and 9.30 in the evening.

The first written reference outside the family appears in Count Zinzendorf's diary on 9 October 1762, where Mozart is described as 'a little boy who, it is said, is but five and a half years of age . . .'. (Leopold Mozart, unnecessarily some might feel, was already trimming his son's age by a year.) When he played again a few days later, Zinzendorf observes: 'Mlle de Gudenus, who plays the harpsichord well, gave him a kiss and he wiped his face . . .'.

After travels in Germany and a visit to Paris, Leopold Mozart and his two children arrived in London towards the end of April 1764. They didn't lose any time, playing before George III (who apparently gave Mozart some awkward tests at the keyboard) on 27 April, and twice again later. They also appeared in public:

At the Great Room in Spring-Garden near St. James's Park, Tuesday, June 5, will be performed a grand Concert of Vocal and Instrumental Music. For the Benefit of Miss MOZART of Eleven, and Master MOZART of seven Years of Age, Prodigies of Nature; taking the Opportunity of representing to the Public the greatest Prodigy that Europe or that Human Nature has to boast of. Every Body will be astonished to hear a Child of such a tender Age playing the Harpsichord in such a Perfection – It surmounts all Fantastic and Imagination, and it is hard to express which is more astonishing, his Execution upon the Harpsichord, playing at Sight, or his own Composition. His Father brought him to England, not doubting but that he will meet with Success in a Kingdom, where his Countryman, that late famous Vertuoso Handel, received during his Life-time such Particular Protection. Tickets at Half a Guinea each; to be had of Mr. Mozart, at Mr. Couzin's, Hair-Cutter, in Cecil Court, St. Martin's Lane.

Public Advertiser 31 May 1764

The philosopher Daines Barrington, who tested Mozart thoroughly, presented a report on him to the Royal Society in 1769–70

Account of a Very Remarkable Young Musician

Sir,

If I was to send you a well attested account of a boy who measured seven feet in height, when he was not more than eight years of age, it might be considered as not undeserving the notice of the Royal Society.

The instance which I now desire you will communicate to that learned body, of as early an exertion of most extraordinary musical talents, seems perhaps equally to claim their attention.

Joannes Chrysostomus Wolfgangus Theophilus Mozart, was born at Saltzbourg in Bavaria, on the 17th of January, 1756. . . .

At seven years of age his father carried him to Paris. . . . Upon leaving Paris, he came over to England, where he continued more than a year. As during this time I was witness of his most extraordinary abilities as a musician, both at some publick concerts, and likewise by having been alone with him for a considerable time at his father's house; I send you the following account, amazing and incredible almost as it may appear.

I carried to him a manuscript duet, which was composed by an English gentleman to some favourite words in Metastasio's opera of *Demofoonte*.

The whole score was in five parts, viz. accompaniments for a first and second violin, the two vocal parts, and a base. I shall here likewise mention, that the parts for the first and second voice were written in what the Italians stile the *Contralto* cleff . . .

My intention in carrying with me this manuscript composition, was to have an irrefragable proof of his abilities, as a player at sight, it being absolutely impossible that he could have ever seen the music before.

The score was no sooner put upon his desk, than he began to play the symphony in a most masterly manner, as well as in the time and stile which corresponded with the intention of the composer.

I mention this circumstance, because the greatest masters often fail in these particulars on the first trial.

The symphony ended, he took the upper part, leaving the under one to his father.

His voice in the tone of it was thin and infantile, but nothing could exceed the masterly manner in which he sung.

His father, who took the under part in this duet, was once or twice out, though the passages were not more difficult than those in the upper one; on which occasions the son looked back with some anger pointing out to him his mistakes, and setting him right.

He not only however did complete justice to the duet, by singing his own part in the truest taste, and with the greatest precision: he also threw in the accompaniments of the two violins, wherever they were most necessary, and produced the best effects. . . .

When he had finished the duet, he expressed himself highly in its approbation, asking with some eagerness whether I had brought any more such music.

Having been informed, however, that he was often visited with musical ideas, to which, even in the midst of the night, he would give utterance on his harpsichord; I told his father that I should be glad to hear some of his extemporary compositions.

The father shook his head at this, saying, that it depended entirely upon his being as it were musically inspired, but that I might ask him whether he was in humour for such a composition.

Happening to know that little Mozart was much taken notice of by Manzoli, the famous singer, who came over to England in 1764, I said to the boy, that I should be glad to hear an extemporary *Love Song*, such as his friend Manzoli might choose in an opera.

The boy on this (who continued to sit at his harpsichord) looked back with much archness, and immediately began five or six lines of a jargon recitative proper to introduce a love song.

He then played a symphony which might correspond with an air composed to the single word, *Affetto*.

It had a first and second part, which, together with the symphonies, was of the length that opera songs generally last: if this extemporary composition was not amazingly capital, yet it was really above mediocrity, and shewed most extraordinary readiness of invention.

Finding he was in humour, and as it were inspired, I then desired him to compose a *Song of Rage*, such as might be proper for the opera stage.

The boy again looked back with much archness, and began five or six lines of a jargon recitative proper to precede a *Song of Anger*.

This lasted also about the same time with the *Song of Love*; and in the middle of it, he had worked himself up to such a pitch, that he beat his harpsichord like a person possessed, rising sometimes in his chair.

The word he pitched upon for this second extemporary composition was, *Perfido*.

After this he played a difficult lesson, which he had finished a day or two before: his execution was amazing, considering that his little fingers could scarcely reach a fifth on the harpsichord.

His astonishing readiness, however, did not arise merely from great practice; he had a thorough knowledge of the fundamental principles of composition, as, upon producing a treble, he immediately wrote a base under it, which, when tried, had very good effect.

He was also a great master of modulation, and his transitions from one key to another were excessively natural and judicious; he practised in this manner for a considerable time with an handkerchief over the keys of the harpsichord.

The facts which I have been mentioning I was myself an eye witness of; to which I must add, that I have been informed by two or three able musicians, when Bach* the celebrated composer had begun a fugue and left off abruptly, that little Mozart hath immediately taken it up, and worked it after a most masterly manner.

Witness as I was myself of most of these extraordinary facts, I must own that I could not help suspecting his father imposed with regard to the real age of the boy, though he had not only a most childish appearance, but likewise had all the actions of that stage of life.

For example, whilst he was playing to me, a favourite cat came in, upon which he immediately left his harpsichord, nor could we bring him back for a considerable time.

He would also sometimes run about the room with a stick between his legs by way of a horse. . . .

I have therefore for a considerable time made the best inquiries I was able . . . but could never receive any further information than he was born near Saltzbourg, till I was so fortunate as to procure an extract from the register of that place. . . .

It appears from this extract, that Mozart's father did not impose with regard to his age when he was in England, for it was in June, 1765, that I was witness to what I have above related, when the boy was only eight years and five months old.

DAINES BARRINGTON in The Philosophical Transactions of the Royal Society 1771

. . . When the Gramophone Company wished the fifteen-year-old Menuhin to record Elgar's Violin Concerto, feeling that his celebrity would help to send the work all over the world, I was asked to accompany him when he went to play the Concerto to its composer.

The occasion was both interesting and moving. Behind the military appearance and grandeur of manner which have misled many people, Elgar was a deeply sensitive man, extremely lonely and not without

*J. C. Bach, at this time living in London.

some bitterness that a lifetime's work and a series of accepted masterpieces had not been sufficiently accepted by his fellow-countrymen to fill the Queen's Hall for an Elgar 'Prom'. The boy and the old man took to each other at once, and the meeting marked the beginning of a friendship which meant much to Elgar's old age and drew him back to music when he had felt his life work to be over.

We played right through the Concerto except for the *tuttis*; the scoring of the work is so complex and luscious that it cannot be made to sound pianistic, and I was not unduly depressed when Elgar declared that it would be unnecessary to play them. Menuhin and Elgar discussed the music like equals, but with great courtesy and lack of self-consciousness on the boy's part. Listening to the discussion, I could not be other than amazed at his maturity of outlook and his ability to raise points for discussion without ever sounding like anything but a master violinist discussing a work with a composer for whom he had unbounded respect. There is a point at the beginning of the finale where a passage of rushing semiquavers from the soloist goes into octaves which are extremely hard to manage neatly, one of the most uncomfortable passages in a concerto that is a work of extreme difficulty for the violinist. 'Can I make a slight *rallentando* where I go into octaves?' the soloist asked.

'No,' replied the composer. 'No *rallentando*; the music must rush on.'

'If you want it to rush on, why did you put it into octaves?' asked Yehudi.

Most of the time Elgar sat back in a chair with his eyes closed, listening intently, but it was easy to see the impression that Yehudi had made on him. I remember, however, that he referred to the punctiliousness with which he had written directions into his scores. 'Beethoven and Brahms,' he said, 'wrote practically nothing but *allegro* and *andante*, and there seems to be no difficulty. I've done all I can to help players, but my efforts appear only to confuse them.'

Eventually Poppa Menuhin invited me to lunch. Elgar, whose secret vice was a love of racing, claimed an important appointment at Newmarket and departed, so that after lunch I was left to entertain Yehudi as though he were a young prince. 'He must not be left alone,' his father declared, obviously fearing goodness knows what injury to the boy's hands or the even worse scrapes which a high-spirited youngster might find tempting.

'Perhaps you'd like to go through the Concerto again?' I suggested.

'Oh no,' said Yehudi with great decision. 'There's no need for that. I don't want to play it again.' I looked at him in surprise, but his words were assured, not conceited; one could tell that the problems solved that morning were solved for good.

Entertaining young boys is not exactly one of my fortes, so I racked my brains to think of what might please him, and eventually suggested that we walked from Grosvenor House, where the Menuhins were staying, across the Park to the Science Museum; every boy who finds himself there for the first time enjoys his visit, I thought. Yehudi was pleased at the idea, and after his father had insisted that we had our photographs taken together ('This is a day you will remember all your life,' he said), we set off on our walk.

Immediately I discovered a new Yehudi Menuhin, an intelligent, lively boy with a boy's interests. Cars fascinated him and he knew them all, pointing out the differences between this year's model and last. We never reached the Science Museum, for the sight of the Serpentine was too tempting and I spent one of the few athletic afternoons of my life rowing him round the lake while he steered, often into a passing rowing boat from which he would look innocently away when he knew that impact was inevitable.

IVOR NEWTON 1931 At the Piano

Performers

I have wept only three times in my life: the first time when my earliest opera failed, the second time when, with a boating party, a truffled turkey fell into the water, and the third time when I first heard Paganini play.

GIOACCHINO ROSSINI

'Paganini is the turning point of virtuosity,' said Schumann

One must await him in an overcrowded opera house among thousands of visitors and hear the strange rumors running from row to row. And now, after a long pause, see the odd, sickly, wornout man sliding through the orchestra, the face fleshless and bloodless in its entanglement of dark locks and beard, the boldest of noses with an expression of contemptuous scorn, eyes that shine like black jewels out of bluish-white. And now, instantly, the hasty beginning of the *ritornelli*, and then the tenderest and boldest song ever heard on the violin.

A. B. MARX 1829 Allgemeine musikalische Zeitung

The great French lexicographer, François-Joseph Fétis, has left an interesting glimpse of the practical (and curiously sympathetic) man that lay behind the public legend

Most people imagined that he was constantly occupied by his violin. Far from it: he never touched it except to tune it before going to a concert or rehearsal. 'I studied enough when I was working to acquire my talent,' he would say; 'now it's time for me to rest.'

... In spite of the immense number of concerts he had given, Paganini was always worried when the day came to give another. In the morning he would remain idle, staying quietly on his couch. Then before going to the rehearsal in the afternoon, he would open his violin-case to make sure that no strings of the instrument were broken, and to give the violin a preliminary tuning-up; and next he would get ready the orchestra parts of the pieces he was to play. During these operations, he took great quantities of snuff – which, in him, was a certain mark of concern and anxiety. When he arrived at the rehearsal, his first care was to make sure that no outsider was present in the hall;

for if some pushing individuals or some enthusiastic amateurs had
managed to get in, then he would play his solo part only in tones so
soft as to be scarcely audible, or in a light *pizzicato.*

When he came to the beginning of the cadenza, the members of the
orchestra nearly always rose in their seats to watch him as he played:
but on such occasions he would just throw off five or six notes off-
handedly, turn round, smile and say *'Et cetera,* gentlemen!' The full
resources of his talent he kept in reserve for the performance.

After the rehearsal he would have a few minutes' conversation with
the leader of the orchestra, to thank him for his pains and to draw his
attention to certain passages. When he left, he invariably took with
him the orchestral parts, which he would entrust to nobody; as for the
solo part, no one ever saw the music for it, for he always played from
memory, being unwilling to take the risk that someone might make a
copy of his compositions. Back at home, he would have a light meal
and then, throwing himself on his bed, would wait until the carriage
came to take him to the concert. When it arrived, his toilet took but a
moment, and he left straightway for the concert-hall. There, in the
artists' room, he became as gay as he had been grave before. The first
thing he did was to ask if there was a good attendance: if the answer
was that the house was full, he would say 'Excellent! The people here
are a good sort'; but if the house was not full he would say he was
afraid that the sound of the music would go to waste in the empty
boxes.

F. J. FETIS *Notice sur Nicolo Paganini* 1851

Berlioz has left another fascinating 'personal' account of Paganini in the
Memoirs. But the public image was what counted to the vast majority of
Paganini's listeners, and who better than Heine to speak for them all?

Only in crude, black and fugitive strokes can those supernatural
features be limned – features that seem to belong rather to the
sulphurous realm of shadows than to the sunny world of living things.
. . . He wore a dark grey coat which, reaching to his feet, gave the
impression of great height to his figure. His long black hair fell in
twisted curls about his shoulders and formed a dark frame round a
pale, corpse-like face, on which trouble, genius, and hell had graved
their indelible marks.

By his side tripped a short, comfortable figure,* quaintly prosaic,
with a pink puckered face, a little light grey coat with steel buttons,

*Paganini's English manager, George Harrys.

darting irresistibly friendly glances in all directions, at the same time looking up with worried shyness at the gloomy figure that moved meditatively and seriously at his side. It seemed as if we had before us the picture of Retzsch, in which Faust and Wagner promenade outside the gates of Leipzig. . . .

If Paganini appeared to me in broad daylight under the green trees of the Hamburg Jungfernstieg as sufficiently uncanny and romantic, how much more must his creepy and bizarre appearance surprise me when I saw him at his concert in the evening. The Hamburg theatre was the scene of this concert, and the art-loving public had arrived in such numbers and so early, that I could scarcely snatch a seat near the orchestra. Every eye was directed on to the stage. My neighbour, a fur-dealer, removed his dirty plugs of cotton-wool from his ears, the better to suck in the priceless notes he was soon to hear – notes which cost two thalers to approach.

At length a dark form appears on the stage, looking as if it had risen from the underworld. This was Paganini in his black gala-clothes: his black coat and vest of a terrible cut, such as is probably dictated by the hellish etiquette of Proserpine's court; his black trousers flapping disconsolately against his bony legs. His long arms seemed length-ened by the violin he carried in one hand, and the bow in the other – both perpendicular and almost touching the ground, as he trotted out his ungainly acknowledgements before the public. In the angular contortions of his body there was a wooden horror, and at the same time, something stupidly animalistic, that involuntarily called forth our laughter; but his face which, in the garish illumination of the orchestra, seemed still more corpse-like in its pallor, contained an expression so pleading, so idiotically humble, that a horrible sym-pathy crushed the desire to laugh it out of existence.

Did he learn these obeisances from an automaton or from a dog? Is this pleading glance that of a being stricken with a fatal disease, or hides there behind it the scorn of a cunning miser? Is this a living being who wishes to delight his audience at the moment of his dissolution in the art-arena with his last quivering gasp, like a dying gladiator? Or is it a corpse that has risen from the grave – a vampyr with a violin, who would suck, if not the blood from our hearts, at least the money from our pockets?

Such questions crossed our minds while Paganini went through his interminable bending and bowing. But all such thoughts had perforce to vanish instantly, at the moment in which the marvellous master placed his violin under his chin and began to play.

HEINRICH HEINE Review 1829

Alas, how different the virtuosos of today! Or are they?

Zuckerman Dazzles Las Vegans

Wednesday, January 18, Pinchas Zuckerman conducted and performed with the Saint Paul Chamber Orchestra in an all Betthoven [*sic*] concert at Ham Hall. Those Las Vegans lucky enough to attend were treated to an evening of performance of a caliber shamefully rare in a city of half a million people.

The first half of the program, consisting of the Overture to the Creatures of Prometheus and the Symphony No. 4 in B Flat, Op. 60, was somewhat disappointing in that Zuckerman conducted the orchestra with his back to the audience. While one cannot fault him entirely for assuming the traditional posture of the vast majority of great maestros, it must be said that the choice of his stance in combination with his having also elected to wear the traditional 'tails' all but obscured whatever clarity of physique one might have hoped to savor, even from the best seats.

Even so, true genius shines forth. The broad expanse of his shoulders, the abundant wavy dark hair, the well proportioned legs planted oh-so-firmly on the podium were sufficient food for the culture-starved crowd to feast upon throughout even the longest of movements. Perhaps it might even be said that the program order reflected a certain deftness of planning, for it certainly left the audience at intermission clambering to return to their seats in anticipation of the climactic second half which promised the chance to observe Mr Zuckerman from the front for the duration of a whole violin concerto.

What followed was pure magic, as Zuckerman proved that the combination of virtuosity, artistry and a great body can make even the Concerto in D for Violin and Orchestra, Op. 61, seem too short. He inspired his audience where a performer of lesser attributes might have left them bored to death. But who among them could for an instant let her eyes stray from the Maestro as he cradled his violin so gently, yet firmly, with the touch of well proportioned hands made strong and supple by years of torturous practice? Whose eyes could have been other than riveted to the spectacle of the grace and power of the bow arm, the fire in his dark eyes, the tension in his taut thighs as he made ready to launch into some passionate passage with the energy of an athlete. Who could but succumb to the tenderness of his smile as he lost himself in the ecstacy of each undulating sweet melodic phrase that surged and swelled from the instrument at his command? It is only a wonder that the audience managed to suppress both thunderous applause and shrieks of pleasure until the end. We can only hope that it not be an eternity before he again graces our stage with the captivating magic of his talents.

Mr Zuckerman is a native of Israel, Middle East. He has recorded quite a number of musical pieces onto records which are considered quite good by those who listen to them. He is married to a woman of questionable musical ability and character.

LISA COFFEY Review 23 March 1983

(We cannot quite remember where we got this; it was a photocopy of newsprint, but without the name of the paper. When we asked Mr Zuckerman himself whether the article was genuine he said, 'I think so', and changed the subject.)

A seventeenth-century view of violinists

Here is an earwig that creeps into man's ear and torments him, until he is got out again. . . . His fiddle is but a rubber made of a horse's tail to curry sinners with, and he scrubs and firks them till they kick and fling as if the Devil were in them. The noise of cat's guts sets them a caterwauling, as those that are bitten with a mad dog are said to foam at the mouth and bark. . . . He is free of all taverns, as being as useful to relish a glass of wine as anchovies or caviare, serves like stum to help off bad wine, and conduces wonderfully to over-reckoning.

SAMUEL BUTLER 1613–80 *Characters*

It got to a point where I had to get a haircut or a violin.

F. D. ROOSEVELT *Reader's Digest* 1938

Sherlock Holmes (no mean performer on the violin himself if Watson is to be believed) was a great violinist fancier in the late nineteenth century

. . . [Holmes] suddenly sprang out of his chair with the gesture of a man who has made up his mind, and put his pipe down upon the mantelpiece.

'Sarasate plays at the St. James's Hall this afternoon', he remarked. 'What do you think, Watson? Could your patients spare you for a few hours?'

'I have nothing to do to-day. My practice is never very absorbing'.

'Then put on your hat, and come . . . I observe that there is a good deal of German music on the programme, which is rather more to my taste than Italian or French. It is introspective, and I want to introspect. Come along!' . . .

All the afternoon he sat in the stalls wrapped in the most perfect happiness, gently waving his long thin fingers in time to the music, while his gently smiling face and his languid, dreamy eyes were as unlike those of Holmes the sleuth-hound, Holmes the relentless, keen-witted, ready-handed criminal agent, as it was possible to conceive. . . . When I saw him that afternoon so enwrapped in the music at St. James's Hall I felt that an evil time might be coming upon those whom he had set himself to hunt down.

ARTHUR CONAN DOYLE The Red-Headed League 1892

Guy Warrack, conductor and composer, was a dedicated Holmes scholar, and followed up with perspicacity and wit every possible musical reference in the Sherlock Holmes canon. Enthusiasts will relish the following:

We have also observed that Holmes took Watson to hear Sarasate in 1890. . . . the only other known instance of the attendance of either at a concert is in July, 1898, when they spend an evening together at the Albert Hall hearing Carina sing.*

The Retired Colourman, S 1326. I have not so far been able to trace this singer. It is tempting to try to identify her with Annie Louise Cary, a mezzo-contralto. This American singer had, it is true, married Charles Monson Raymond and retired in 1882, but singers are notorious for their returns to the platform. She might, it will be argued, be unlikely to re-appear under a pseudonym, but if for any reason she did so, it would be natural enough to make up a name from the first three letters of her surname and three letters of her Christian name. Holmes had a bias towards violinists who played on Stradivaris: his bias in singers would be towards contraltos, for 'the woman' was such. For information about Annie Louise Cary, see *Grove*, op. cit., Vol. I, pp. 574 and 575.

GUY WARRACK Sherlock Holmes and Music 1947

But the archetype of the romantic virtuoso is, of course, Liszt

We walk through this world in the midst of so many wonders that our senses become indifferent to the most amazing things: light and life, the ocean, the forest, the voice and flight of the pigmy lark, are unheeded commonplaces; and it is only when some comet, some giant, some tiger-tamer, some new Niagara, some winged being appears, that our obdurate faculties are roused into the consciousness that miracles do exist. Of the miracle genus is M. Liszt, the Polyphemus of the pianoforte – the Aurora Borealis of musical effulgence – the Niagara of thundering harmonies!

The Musical World 1841

Liszt's musical contemporaries did not always see him exclusively in this light

[1838] We heard Liszt. He cannot be compared to any other player – he is absolutely unique. He arouses fear and astonishment and yet is a very kind artist. His appearance at the piano is indescribable – he is an original – totally involved with the piano. His passion knows no bounds: he often injures one's sense of beauty by tearing the line apart and using the pedal too much so that his compositions must become even more incomprehensible, if not to the connoisseur, then certainly to the layman. But he has a great soul; one may say of him, 'His art is his life'.

[1840] One could hear and see that he felt most comfortable in the *Hexameron* [his own piece]. He didn't play the first things as freely, and it was disturbing to see him continually looking at the music. He did not play *Carnaval* to my satisfaction and altogether did not make the same impression on me that he had in Vienna. I believe it was my own fault; my expectations were too high.

[1841] I could almost hate him as a composer. As a performer, however, his concert on the 13th absolutely astounded me, especially in his *Don Juan* Fantasy, which he played overpoweringly – his performance of the Champagne Aria will remain unforgettable – the bravado, the pleasure with which he played was unique! One saw Don Juan with the popping champagne corks, in his wantonness, as only Mozart could have imagined him. After the concert we all had supper together. . . . Of Liszt there was not much to be seen, since two women attached themselves to him. I am convinced that the reason Liszt displays such arrogance at times is really the fault of the women, because they pay court to him everywhere in a way that is intolerable to me and that I also find highly improper. I venerate him too, but even veneration must have a limit. On the 16th, Liszt played for the last time and performed Beethoven's E Flat Major Concerto masterfully, but then he played Robert's *Fantaisie* in dreadful taste. . . . [He] came to the soirée [at the Schumanns'], as always, late. He seems to enjoy making people wait for him, which is something I don't like. He strikes me as a spoiled child, good natured, tyrannical, amiable, arrogant, noble, and generous, often hard on others – a strange mixture of characters. Yet we have become very fond of him and he has always treated us in the friendliest way.

In 1848 Liszt blotted his copybook with Clara again. He arrived for a supper party at the Schumanns' two hours late, called Robert's Piano Quintet 'Leipzigerisch', praised Meyerbeer and was so insulting about Mendelssohn that Schumann finally exploded and walked out of the room. Before this, Robert had had nothing but praise for Liszt, especially for his playing of his (Schumann's) own compositions (which in itself upset Clara, who considered the works her own and played them quite differently), and afterwards Liszt continued the soul of generosity towards the Schumanns, going out of his way to perform Robert's works, inviting Clara to play in Weimar and, crowning gesture, dedicating his own B Minor Sonata to Schumann. But it was no good: Clara's comment on the Sonata, after hearing Liszt play it, was:

. . . merely a blind noise – no healthy ideas any more, everything confused, one cannot find one clear harmonic progression – and yet now I must thank him for it. It is really too awful.

[1852] Liszt at his piano . . . no longer music, but like demonic boozing and bluster . . .

CLARA SCHUMANN *Diaries*

The Abbé Liszt
Hit the piano with his fist.
That was the way
He used to play.

E. C. BENTLEY *Biography for Beginners* 1905

Nevertheless, for the world in general Liszt was *the* virtuoso figure, and the model for a generation of romantic audiences and romantic fiction.

Half an hour later Lavretsky was standing before the little garden gate. He found it locked and was obliged to get over the fence. He returned to the town and walked along the slumbering streets. A sense of immense, unhoped-for happiness filled his soul; all his doubts had died away. 'Away, dark phantom of the past,' he thought. 'She loves me, she will be mine.' Suddenly it seemed to him that in the air over his head were floating strains of divine triumphant music. He stood still. The music resounded in still greater magnificence; a mighty flood of melody – and all his bliss seemed speaking and singing in its strains. He looked about him; the music floated down from two upper windows of a small house.

'Lemm?' cried Lavretsky as he ran to the house. 'Lemm! Lemm!' he repeated aloud.

The sounds died away and the figure of the old man in a dressing-gown, with his throat bare and his hair dishevelled, appeared at the window.

'Aha!' he said with dignity, 'is it you?'

'Christopher Fedoritch, what marvellous music! for mercy's sake, let me in.'

Without uttering a word, the old man with a majestic flourish of the arm dropped the key of the street door from the window.

Lavretsky hastened up-stairs, went into the room and was about to rush up to Lemm; but the latter imperiously motioned him to a seat, saying abruptly in Russian, 'Sit down and listen,' sat down himself to the piano, and looking proudly and severely about him, he began to play. It was long since Lavretsky had listened to anything like it. The sweet passionate melody went to his heart from the first note; it was glowing and languishing with inspiration, happiness and beauty; it swelled and melted away; it touched on all that is precious, mysterious, and holy on earth. It breathed of deathless sorrow and mounted dying away to the heavens. Lavretsky drew himself up, and rose cold and pale with ecstasy. This music seemed to clutch his very soul, so lately shaken by the rapture of love, the music was glowing with love too. 'Again!' he whispered as the last chord sounded. The old man threw him an eagle glance, struck his hand on his chest and saying deliberately in his own tongue, 'This is my work, I am a great musician,' he played again his marvellous composition. There was no candle in the room; the light of the rising moon fell aslant on the window; the soft air was vibrating with sound; the poor little room seemed a holy place, and the old man's head stood out noble and inspired in the silvery half light. Lavretsky went up to him and embraced him. At first Lemm did not respond to his embrace, and even pushed him away with his elbow. For a long while without moving in any limb he kept the same severe, almost morose expression, and only growled out twice, 'aha.' At last his face relaxed, changed, and grew calmer, and in response to Lavretsky's warm congratulations he smiled a little at first, then burst into tears, and sobbed weakly like a child.

'It is wonderful,' he said, 'that you have come just at this moment; but I know all, I know all.'

'You know all?' Lavretsky repeated in amazement.

'You have heard me,' replied Lemm, 'did you not understand that I knew all?'

Till daybreak Lavretsky could not sleep – all night he was sitting on his bed. And Lisa too did not sleep; she was praying.

IVAN TURGENEV *A House of Gentlefolk* 1859

Busoni was one of Liszt's greatest successors, though the public image of virtuosi was by this time very different. His set of rules for practising the piano implies a deep seriousness of approach which compares oddly with our impressions of the young Liszt (which may of course be wrong), though it assorts well enough with what we know of Liszt in old age

1   Practise the passage with the most difficult fingering; when you have mastered that, play it with the easiest.

2   If a passage offers some particular technical difficulty, go through all similar passages you can remember in other places; in this way you will bring system into the kind of playing in question.

3   Always join technical practice with the study of the interpretation; the difficulty often does not lie in the notes, but in the dynamic shading prescribed.

4   Never be carried away by temperament, for that dissipates strength, and where it occurs there will always be a blemish, like a dirty spot which can never be washed out of a material.

5   Don't set your mind on overcoming the difficulties in pieces which have been unsuccessful because you have previously practised them badly; it is generally a useless task. But if meanwhile you have quite changed your way of playing, then begin the study of the old piece from the beginning, as if you did not know it.

6   Study everything as if there were nothing more difficult; try to interpret studies for the young from the standpoint of the virtuoso; you will be astonished to find how difficult it is to play a Czerny or Cramer, or even a Clementi.

7   Bach is the foundation of piano playing, Liszt the summit. The two make Beethoven possible.

8   Take it for granted from the beginning that everything is possible on the piano, even when it seems impossible to you, or really is so.

9   Attend to your technical apparatus so that you are prepared and armed for every possible event; then, when you study a new piece, you can turn all your power to the intellectual content; you will not be held up by the technical problems.

10 Never play carelessly, even when there is nobody listening, or the occasion seems unimportant.

11 Never leave a passage which has been unsuccessful without repeating it; if you cannot do it in the presence of others, then do it subsequently.

12 If possible, allow no day to pass without touching your piano.

                                    FERRUCCIO BUSONI Letter 20 July 1898

Brahms's attitude seems to have been very different

The reception given to the composer by his native town was as enthusiastic as we anticipated. His pianoforte playing was not so much that of a finished pianist, as of a composer who despised virtuosity. The skips, which are many and perilous in the solo part, were accomplished regardless of accuracy, and it is not an exaggeration to say that there were handfuls of wrong notes. The touch was somewhat hard, and lacking in force-control; it was at its best in the slow movement, where he produced the true velvety quality, probably because he was not so hampered by his own difficulties. But never since have I heard a rendering of the concerto, so complete in its outlook or so big in its interpretation. The wrong notes did not really matter, they did not disturb his hearers any more than himself. He took it for granted that the public knew that he had written the right notes, and did not worry himself over such little trifles as hitting the wrong ones. His attitude at the piano was precisely that in Professor von Beckerath's sketch. The short legs straight down to the pedals, which they seemed only just to reach, the head thrown back and slightly tilted as if listening to the band rather than to himself, the shoulders hunched up and the arms almost as straight as the legs and well above the keyboard. His figure was curiously ill-proportioned. He had the chest development and height from the waist of a muscular man of five foot ten, but his legs were so short as to reduce him well below middle height. His eyes were, I think, the most beautiful I ever saw; blue, and of a depth so liquid that (as I once heard a friend of his say) 'You could take a header into them.'

C. V. STANFORD *Unwritten Diary* 1880

Many think it a matter of great importance and despise such organists as do not use this or that particular fingering, which in my opinion is not worth the talk: for let a player run up and down with either first, middle, or third finger, aye even with his nose if that could help him, provided everything is done clearly, correctly and gracefully, it does not much matter how or in what manner it is accomplished.

MICHAEL PRAETORIUS *Syntagma Musicum* 1619

Bach, replying to compliments on his organ playing, commented

There is nothing remarkable about it. All you have to do is hit the right notes at the right time, and the instrument plays itself.

J. F. KÖHLER *Historia Scholarum Lipsiensium* 1776

Bach was, of course, one of the greatest performers himself and, characteristically, knew the whole business of the organ inside out (as well as simply hitting the right notes on it)

No one has ever tried out organs so severely and yet at the same time honestly as he. He understood the whole building of organs in the highest degree. When an organ builder had worked conscientiously, and incurred losses by his work, he would persuade the employers to make amends. No one understood registration at the organ as well as he. Organists were terrified when he sat down to play on their organs and drew the stops in his own manner, for they thought that the effect could not be good as he was planning it; but then they heard an effect that astounded them. (These sciences perished with him.)

The first thing he would do in trying an organ was this: he would say, in jest, 'Above all I must know whether the organ has good lungs,' and, to find out, he would draw out every speaking stop, and play in the fullest and richest possible texture. At this the organ builders would often grow quite pale with fright.

The exact tuning of his instruments as well as of the whole orchestra had his greatest attention. No one could tune and quill his instruments to please him. He did everything himself. The placing of an orchestra he understood perfectly. He made good use of any space. He grasped at the first glance the sound properties of any place. A remarkable illustration of that fact is the following:

He came to Berlin to visit me; I showed him the new opera house. He perceived at once its virtues and defects (that is, as regards the sound of music in it). I showed him the great dining hall; we went up to the gallery that goes around the upper part of that hall. He looked at the ceiling, and without further investigation made the statement that the architect had here accomplished a remarkable feat, without intending to do so, and without anyone's knowing about it: namely, that if someone went to one corner of the oblong-shaped hall and whispered a few words very softly upwards against the wall, a person standing in the corner diagonally opposite, with his face to the wall, would hear quite distinctly what was said, while between them, and in the other parts of the room, no one would hear a sound. A feat of architecture hitherto very rare and much admired! This effect was brought about by the arches in the vaulted ceiling, which he saw at once.

C. P. E. BACH Letter 1774

The following notice, by Kenneth Langbell, of a Bach recital given at the Erawan Hotel, Bangkok, by the American pianist Myron Kropp, originally appeared in the *Bangkok Post*

Mr Kropp, the pupil and artistic successor to Straube and Ramin, had chosen the title 'An Evening with Bach' for his performance. Indeed from the very outset, it was an evening the social members of Bangkok would not soon forget, the men in tuxedos and white dinner jackets and the ladies resplendent in floor-length evening gowns with more than one orchid corsage crowning a Lemey or Delmonte original.

. . . A hush fell over the room as Mr Kropp appeared from the right of the stage, attired in black formal evening-wear with a small white poppy in his lapel. With sparse, sandy hair, a sallow complexion and a deceptively frail looking frame, the man who has repopularized Johann Sebastian Bach approached the Baldwin concert grand, bowed to the audience and placed himself upon the stool.

It might be appropriate to insert at this juncture that many pianists, including Mr Kropp, prefer a bench, maintaining that on a screw-type stool they sometimes find themselves turning sideways during a particularly expressive strain. There was a slight delay, in fact, as Mr Kropp left the stage briefly, apparently in search of a bench, but returned when informed that there was none.

The evening opened with the Toccata and Fugue in D Minor, the 'raging storm' as described by Schweitzer, which, even when adapted for piano, gives us an idea of what the young Bach, whose ideas were close to those of Buxtehude, meant by virtuosity; bold melodic figures, surging dynamics, forceful accents and impassioned modulations which not infrequently confounded the church congregations, according to contemporaries, who were alarmed by the intensity of Bach's expressive power.

As I have mentioned on several other occasions, the Baldwin concert grand, while basically a fine instrument, needs constant attention, particularly in a climate such as Bangkok. This is even more true when the instrument is as old as the one provided in the Chamber Music Room of the Erawan Hotel. In this humidity the felts which separate the white keys from the black tend to swell, causing an occasional key to stick, which apparently was the case last evening with the D in the second octave.

During the 'raging storm' Mr Kropp must be complimented for putting up with the awkward D. However, by the time the 'storm' was past [and] he had gotten into the Prelude and Fugue in D Major, in which the second octave plays a major role, Mr Kropp's patience was wearing thin.

Some who attended the performance later questioned whether the awkward key justified some of the language which was heard coming from the stage during softer passages of the fugue. However, one member of the audience, who had sent his children out of the room by the midway point of the fugue, had a valid point when he commented over the music and extemporaneous remarks of Mr Kropp that the workman who greased the stool might have done better to use some of the grease on the second octave D key. Indeed, Mr Kropp's stool had more than enough grease, and during one passage in which the music and lyrics both were particularly violent Mr Kropp was turned completely around. Whereas before his remarks had been aimed largely at the piano and were therefore somewhat muted, to his surprise and that of those in the Chamber Music Room he found himself addressing himself directly to the audience.

But such things do happen, and the person who began to laugh deserves to be severely reprimanded for this undignified behaviour. Unfortunately, laughter is contagious, and by the time it had subsided and the audience had regained its composure Mr Kropp appeared to be somewhat shaken. Nevertheless, he swiveled himself back into position facing the piano and, leaving the D Major Fugue unfinished, commenced on the Fantasia and Fugue in G Minor, whose character is virtually that of a dramatic poem which, in a four-part polyphonic setting, reminds us of the Bach of the Passions.

Why the concert grand piano's G key in the third octave chose that particular time to begin sticking I hesitate to guess. However, it is certainly safe to say that Mr Kropp himself did nothing to help matters when he began using his feet to kick the lower portion of the piano instead of operate the pedals as is generally done.

Possibly it was this jarring, or the un-Bach-like hammering to which the sticking keyboard was being subjected. Something caused the right front leg of the piano to buckle slightly inward, leaving the entire instrument listing at approximately a 35-degree angle from that which is normal. A gasp went up from the audience, for if the piano had actually fallen several of Mr Kropp's toes, if not both his feet, would surely have been broken.

It was with a sigh of relief, therefore, that the audience saw Mr Kropp slowly rise from his stool and leave the stage. A few men in the back of the room began clapping, and when Mr Kropp reappeared a moment later it seemed he was responding to the ovation. Apparently, however, he had left to get the red-handled fire axe which was hung back stage in case of fire, for that was what he had in his hand.

My first reaction at seeing Mr Kropp begin to chop at the left leg of the grand piano was that he was attempting to make it tilt at the same angle as the right leg and thereby correct the list. However, when the weakened legs finally collapsed altogether with a great crash and Mr Kropp continued to chop, it became obvious to all that he had no intention of going on with the concert.

The ushers, who had heard the snapping of piano wires and splintering of sounding board from the dining room, came rushing in and, with the help of the hotel manager, two Indian watchmen and a passing police corporal, finally succeeded in disarming Mr Kropp and dragging him off the stage.

The concensus of those who witnessed Mr Kropp's performance is that it will be a long time before Bangkok concert-goers are again treated to such a spectacular evening.

Bangkok Post n.d.

Of piano virtuosi one of the most eccentric was Vladimir de Pachmann, whose zany performing manner, and fabulous sensitivity of touch in Chopin, can still be detected in the records he made in the early 1930s when he was well over eighty years old. Judging from the memories of those who heard him play, the following eye-witness account is in no way overdone

Arrived at Queen's Hall in time for Pachmann's Recital at 3.15. . . . As usual he kept us waiting for 10 minutes. Then a short, fat, middle-aged man strolled casually on to the platform and everyone clapped violently – so it was Pachmann: a dirty greasy looking fellow with long hair of dirty grey colour, reaching down to his shoulders and an ugly face. He beamed on us and then shrugged his shoulders and went on shrugging them until his eye caught the music stool, which seemed to fill him with amazement. He stalked it carefully, held out one hand to it caressingly, and finding all was well, went two steps backwards, clasping his hands before him and always gazing at the little stool in mute admiration, his eyes sparkling with pleasure, like Mr Pickwick's on the discovery of the archaeological treasure. He approached once more, bent down and ever so gently moved it about ⅞ths of an inch nearer the piano. He then gave it a final pat with his right hand and sat down. . . .

At the close we all crowded around the platform and gave the queer, old-world gentleman an ovation, one man thrusting up his hand which Pachmann generously shook as desired.

As an encore he gave us a Valse – 'Valse, Valse', he exclaimed ecstatically, jumping up and down in his seat in time to the music. It was a truly remarkable sight: on his right the clamorous crowd around the platform; on his left the seat holders of the Orchestra Stalls, while at the piano bobbed this grubby little fat man playing divine Chopin divinely well, at the same time rising and falling in his seat, turning a beaming countenance first to the right and then to the left, and crying, 'Valse, Valse'. He is as entertaining as a tumbler at a variety hall.

As soon as he had finished, we clapped and rattled for more, Pachmann meanwhile standing surrounded by his idolaters in affected despair at ever being able to satisfy us. Presently he walked off and a scuffle was half visible behind the scenes between him and his agent who sent him in once more.

The applause was wonderful. As soon as he began again it ceased on the instant, and as soon as he left off it started again immediately – nothing boisterous or rapturous, but a steady, determined thunder of applause that came regularly and evenly like the roar from some machine.

W. N. P. BARBELLION 5 May 1916 Journal of a Disappointed Man

Incidentally, not only does Pachmann talk on some of those old 78 recordings, but there is also at one point, the weary voice of a technician saying, 'Try it again, sir.' And on another, 'Oh, *do* go on.'

And now for something entirely different

> There was a young fellow from Sparta,
> A really magnificent farter,
> > On the strength of one bean
> > He'd fart 'God save the Queen'
> And Beethoven's Moonlight Sonata.
>
> He was great in the Christmas Cantata,
> He could double-stop fart the Toccata,
> > He'd boom from his ass
> > Bach's B Minor Mass
> And, in counterpoint, *La Traviata*.

ANON.

Monsieur Pujol (known to many as 'Le Pétomane') would have been jealous: even 'La Canonnade' was hardly in this class. Not to mention Barbariccia in Dante's *Inferno* (Canto XXI)

At once he made a trumpet of his arse.

Instrumental performing talent may also take unexpected forms. Kurt Weill, looking for a new subject for a musical after *Lady in the Dark*, happened on F. Anstey's *The Tinted Venus* and persuaded the producer, Cheryl Crawford, that it would make a good show. Ogden Nash was commissioned to write the lyrics, Sam and Bella Spewack the book. The role of Venus seemed tailor-made for Marlene Dietrich, but she would not commit herself: whenever Cheryl Crawford and the composer, Kurt Weill, visited her sumptuous Hollywood home and talked about the show, Dietrich always ended up playing her favourite musical instrument. Years later Cheryl Crawford recalled

I was accustomed to many varieties of eccentric behavior from stars, but I must confess that when Marlene placed that huge saw securely between her elegant legs and began to play, I was more than a little startled. It was an ordinary saw about five feet high and was played with a violin bow. We would talk about the show for a while, then Marlene would take up the musical saw and begin to play; that, we soon found out, was the cue that talk was finished for the evening.

Musical saws usually have no teeth, and a friend of ours who wanted to buy one for her elderly mother (!) found that there was only one manufacturer still extant – in San Francisco. Incidentally, the most talented performer that either of us has heard on the saw is undoubtedly Charles Chaplin's daughter, Victoria

Imagin with your selfe what an unsightly matter it were to see a woman play upon a tabour or drum, or blow in a flute or trumpet, or any like instrument: and this because the boisterousnesse of them doth both cover and take away that sweete mildnesse which setteth so forth everie deede that a woman doth.

BALDASSARE CASTIGLIONE *The Book of the Courtier* 1561

9 May 1967. A Criminal Court Judge in New York City gives a suspended jail sentence to Charlotte Moorman, 28-year-old American cellist for playing a recital in New York on 9 February 1967 in 'topless' attire, with her rounded bosoms fully exposed to potentially innocent eyes.

NICOLAS SLONIMSKY *Music Since 1900*

Composers
on
Composers

We must also take heed of seperating any part of a word from another by a rest, as som dunces have not slackt to do, yea one whose name is *Johannes* Dunstaple (an ancient English author) hath not onlie devided the sentence, but in the verie middle of a word hath made two long rests thus, in a song of foure parts upon these words, *Nesciens virgo mater virum.*' . . .

For these be his owne notes and wordes, which is one of the greatest absurdities which I have seene committed in the dittying of musicke.

THOMAS MORLEY *A Plaine and Easie Introduction to Practicall Musicke* 1597

Never edit the Sonatas for violin and piano of J. S. Bach on a rainy Sunday. I've just finished revising the above, and I feel the rain inside.

When the old Saxon cantor has no ideas, he sets off on anything and is truly merciless. In short, he is unbearable except when he is admirable. That's really something, you'll say.

However, had he had a friend – an editor, perhaps – who would have gently advised him not to write one day a week, for example, we might have been spared several hundred pages, in which we must wander through a thicket of joyless measures which unwind pitilessly, with ever the same little rascal of a 'subject' and 'countersubject'.

Sometimes, frequently even, the prodigious writing which is, after all, but another bit of gymnastics to the old master, does not succeed in filling the terrific void which grows greater from his insistence on turning to account any old idea, no matter what the price.

CLAUDE DEBUSSY Letter to his publisher Jacques Durand 15 April 1917

Carl Philipp Emanuel Bach was a devoted son and took a different view. Here is his defence of his father after receiving a copy of Eschenburg's translation of Dr Burney's book on the Handel Commemoration in 1784. He wrote to Eschenburg on 21 January 1786:

I am very much obliged to you, dear Professor, for your *Handel*. With Mr Burney, I am dissatisfied on several scores. The same thing happens to Handel that happens to others when you want to idolize them: it works usually to their detriment.

Comparisons are difficult and not even necessary. Here, during Handel's time, Keiser surpassed him by far in vocal composition, and Handel would never have become a Hasse, Graun, etc. in this [kind of composition], even had he lived at the same time as these artists. Nor was it necessary that he should; he was great enough, especially in his oratorios.

But to write about organ playing that *he had surpassed my father*: this should not have been said by a man who lives in England where the organ is of slight value, *N.B.*, without pedals, and by one who has, as a consequence, no insight into what constitutes the excellence of organ playing; who perhaps never saw or heard any works for the organ; who, finally, certainly does not know my father's works for the keyboard and more especially for the organ, and in these the obbligato use of the pedal to which now the chief melody, now the alto or the tenor voice is given, [as] always in fugues where *no voice is ever abandoned* and the most difficult passages occur while the feet are occupied with the greatest fire and brilliance, *enfin*, innumerable things about which Burney knows nothing.

Hasse, Faustina, Quantz and others who knew Handel well and heard him play, said in 1728 or 1729, when my father made a public appearance in Dresden: Bach has brought organ playing to its greatest perfection. (*Vide* Quantz's *Method*.)

Seriously, the differences could hardly be greater. Did Handel ever write trios for two manuals and pedals? Did he write fugues for five or six voices for keyboard alone? Certainly not. Consequently, no comparison can be made in this respect, the disparity being too great. People need only look at the clavier and organ compositions of both men!

Excuse my chatter and scribble! The drollest thing of all is the King's gracious precautionary measure, thanks to which everything that Handel wrote in his youth is being preserved. I do not wish to compare myself to Handel, but recently I burned a ream or more of my old compositions and am glad that they no longer exist.

Pray continue to love, all the foregoing notwithstanding,

Your most devoted
Bach

C. P. E. BACH Letter 1774

Gluck, on the other hand, reported by Michael Kelly

One morning, after I had been singing with him, he said, 'Follow me up stairs, Sir, and I will introduce you to one, whom, all my life, I have made my study, and endeavoured to imitate.' I followed him into his bed-room, and, opposite to the head of the bed, saw a full-length picture of Handel, in a rich frame. 'There, Sir,' said he, 'is the portrait of the inspired master of our art; when I open my eyes in the morning, I look upon him with reverential awe, and acknowledge him as such, and the highest praise is due to your country for having distinguished and cherished his gigantic genius.'

MICHAEL KELLY 1786 *Reminiscences*

Handel was regarded with reverence by several of the greatest composers. The Englishman Edward Schulz, who visited Beethoven at Baden in 1823, recorded his interview with the deaf composer

. . . In the whole course of our table-talk there was nothing so interesting as what he said about Handel. I sat close by him and heard him assert very distinctly in German, 'Handel is the greatest composer that ever lived.' I cannot describe to you with what pathos, and I am inclined to say, with what sublimity of language, he spoke of the *Messiah* of this immortal genius. Every one of us was moved when he said, 'I would uncover my head, and kneel down at his tomb!' H. and I tried repeatedly to turn the conversation to Mozart, but without effect. I only heard him say, 'In a monarchy we know who is the first'; which might or might not apply to the subject. . . .

EDWARD SCHULZ *The Harmonicon* January 1824

I take Beethoven twice a week; Haydn four times, Mozart every day. . . . Your Beethoven is a colossus who often gives me a mighty thump in the ribs, but Mozart is always adorable. He was lucky enough to go to Italy when he was very young, at a time, too, when they still knew how to sing.

GIOACCHINO ROSSINI, reported in a letter to Moscheles from his son

This series of aphorisms about Mozart was written by Busoni in 1906; there is one for each year of Mozart's life

He is the most perfect embodiment of musical talent until now; every genuine musician looks up to him, gladdened and disarmed.

His short life and his immense output raise his achievement to the sphere of the phenomenal.

His unclouded beauty disconcerts.

His sense of form borders on the superhuman.

His art is like the sculptor's – every aspect is perfect in itself.

He has the animal's instinct for stretching himself to the utmost limits but never beyond them.

He never risks anything foolhardy.

He finds without seeking and does not seek the undiscoverable – perhaps undiscoverable even to him.

His resources are infinite, but he never uses them all.

He can say very much, but he never says too much.

He is passionate, but the form is *galant*.

He contains within himself all characters, but only to present and portray them.

He gives the solution as well as the riddle.

His proportions are astonishingly right, but they can be measured and verified.

He has light and shade at his command, but his light never blinds and his darkness does not obscure a clear outline.

In the most tragic situations he has a joke ready, in comic ones he can be serious.

In his versatility he is universal.

He can drink from every glass because he never drinks to the dregs.

Standing so high, he can see further than anyone, and therefore sees everything a little diminished.

His palace is immeasurably large, but he never steps outside its walls.

Through its windows he sees Nature; the window frame is his frame too.

Joy is his outstanding quality; he can win over the least well-disposed with a smile.

His smile is not a diplomat's smile or an actor's smile, it is the smile of a pure spirit – and yet of a man of the world.

His spirit is not pure out of ignorance.

He has neither remained simple nor become too refined.

He has temperament without nervousness, idealism without confu-
sion, realism without ugliness.
He is burgher as well as aristocrat, but never peasant or rebel.
He is a friend of order: miracle and devilry last their 16 and 32 bars.
He is religious, as far as religion can be identified with harmony.
In him the Antique and the Rococo are perfectly united, yet without
producing new forms of architecture.
Architecture is the nearest art to his.
He is neither demonic nor transcendental; his kingdom is of this
world.
He is the perfect and rounded figure, the sum total, an end and not a
beginning.
He is as young as a boy, as wise as an old man; never out of date, never
modern; he has gone to his grave yet he is still alive.
His smile, that was so human, is transfigured and shines on us
still. . . .

FERRUCCIO BUSONI 'Mozart-Aphorismen' 1906

What gives Sebastian Bach and Mozart a place apart is that these two
great expressive composers never sacrificed form to expression. As
high as their expression may soar, their musical form remains
supreme and all-sufficient.

CAMILLE SAINT-SAËNS Letter 1907

In the wake of *Amadeus*, the phenomenally successful play and film of the
1980s, this excerpt from Pushkin's little poetic drama, *Mozart and Salieri*,
perhaps makes specially interesting reading. It was written in 1830, only five
years after Salieri's death, at a time when the long-exploded myth that Salieri
had poisoned Mozart was still widely believed: the point of view it expresses
remains a worrying one, however

SALIERI: Justice, they say, does not exist on earth.
But justice won't be found in heaven either:
That's plain as any simple scale to me.
Born with a love of art, when as a child
I heard the lofty organ sound, I listened,
I listened and the sweet tears freely flowed.
Early in life I turned from vain amusements;
All studies that did not accord with music
I loathed, despised, rejected out of hand;
I gave myself to music. Hard as were

The earliest steps, and dull the earliest path,
I rose above reverses. Craftsmanship
I took to be the pedestal of art:
I made myself a craftsman, gave my fingers
Obedient, arid virtuosity,
My ear precision; killing sound, dissecting
Music as if it were a corpse, I checked
My harmony by algebra. At last,
Having achieved a mastery of theory,
I ventured on the rapture of creation.
I started to compose; in secrecy,
Not dreaming yet of glory. Many a time,
When I had sat in silence in my cell
Two days and more, forsaking sleep and food,
Tasting the bliss and pain of inspiration,
I burned my work and watched indifferently
As my ideas, the sounds I had created
Flared up and disappeared in wisps of smoke.
But what of that? For when the mighty Gluck
Revealed to us his new, enchanting secrets,
Did I not put behind me all I knew,
All that I loved, believed so fervently?
Did I not follow promptly in his path,
As trustful as a traveller redirected
By someone he encounters on the way?
Through zealous, unremitting application
I gained a not inconsequential place
In art's infinity. Fame smiled on me;
I found the hearts of men in harmony
With my creations. Happiness was mine;
My toil, success and glory I enjoyed
In peace – as too, success and fame of friends,
My fellows in the majesty of music.
I knew no envy – never! – not when first
I heard the opening of *Iphigenia*,
Not when Piccini tamed Parisian ears.
Who could have called the proud and free Salieri
A wretched envier, a trampled serpent
Alive yet helpless, biting sand and dust?
No-one! . . . But now – and *I* who say it – now
I envy – I profoundly envy. Heaven!

O where is justice when the sacred gift,
Immortal genius, comes not in reward
For toil, devotion, prayer, self-sacrifice –
But shines instead inside a madcap's skull,
An idle hooligan's? O Mozart, Mozart!
. . . .
I cannot bend the course of destiny –
For I am chosen, I must stop him now,
Or he will be the downfall of us all,
Us ministers and acolytes of music,
Not only me, of humble fame . . . What good
If Mozart should live on to reach new heights?
Will music be the better? Not at all;
Music will fall again, he'll leave no heir.
What use is he? He brings us, cherub-like,
Snatches of song from heaven, only to stir
Wingless desire in us poor sons of dust
And fly away . . . Then let him fly away!
The sooner he can spread his wings the better.
Here's poison, my Isora's dying gift,
Kept eighteen years upon me – years when often
My life has seemed a throbbing wound, when often
Some carefree foe and I have sat together,
And never have I yielded to temptation,
Though I'm no coward, though I feel a wrong
Most deeply, though I've little love for life.
When thirst for death tormented me, I waited;
I thought: Why should I die? For life, perhaps,
Will bring me new and unexpected gifts;
I shall be visited, perhaps, with rapture,
With inspiration and creative night;
Perhaps great works will come from some new Haydn
For my delight . . . In hated company
I thought: Perhaps I'll find far worse a foe,
Perhaps far worse a wrong will fall on me
From overbearing heights – and then I know,
Isora's precious gift, you will not fail.
And I was right! I've found my foe at last:
A second Haydn fills my soul with rapture!
The time has come now. Sacred gift of love,
Today the cup of friendship shall receive you!

ALEXANDER PUSHKIN 1830 *Mozart and Salieri*

Beethoven on Schubert, as remembered by Beethoven's friend and factotum, Anton Schindler

Since the illness of which Beethoven finally died, after four months of suffering, made his usual mental activity impossible for him, from its very inception, it was necessary to think of things which might distract him, and which were in harmony with his intellect and his preferences. Thus it happened that I submitted to him a collection of Schubert's songs and melodies, some sixty in all, and among them many still in manuscript. This was done not alone with the intention of providing him with agreeable entertainment; but also to give him an opportunity of becoming acquainted with Schubert's nature and being, so that he might gain a favorable impression of talents which exaggerators, who no doubt took the same stand with regard to others among Schubert's contemporaries, had made objects of suspicion. The great Master, who formerly had not known even five Schubert songs, was astonished at their number, and refused to believe that Schubert up to that time (February, 1827), already had written five hundred melodies. Yet if the number of songs surprised him, his astonishment passed all bounds when he became acquainted with their content. For several days in succession he could not part with them and spent hours, every day, over *Iphigenias Monolog*, the *Grenzen der Allmacht*, the *Junge Nonne*, the *Viola*, the *Müllerlieder* and others more. With joyous enthusiasm he cried again and again: 'In truth, a divine spark lives in Schubert! Had I known of this poem I, too, would have set it to music!' This he said of most of the poems whose subjects, contents and original working-out on Schubert's part he could not sufficiently praise. In the same way he found it almost impossible to understand how Schubert found the leisure 'to attack such long poems, many among them comprising ten others,' as he expressed it. What he wanted to say was, poems, as long as ten others put together; and of these songs in the grand style alone Schubert has supplied no less than a hundred, songs that are by no means only lyric in character, but which contain the most extended ballads and dialogue scenes and which, since they have been treated dramatically, would be in place even in opera and there, too, would not fail of effect. What would the great Master have said, in fact, had he seen the Ossianic songs, *Die Bürgschaft*, *Elysium*, *Der Taucher* and other great songs which have appeared only recently? In short, the respect Beethoven conceived for Schubert's talents was so great, that he now insisted upon also seeing his operas and his piano compositions; but his illness already had made such headway that it no longer was possible for him to gratify this desire. Yet he often spoke of Schubert and prophesied 'that he would yet attract much attention in the world,' while he regretted that he had not made his acquaintance at an earlier date.

ANTON SCHINDLER 1827 *Life of Beethoven*

But Schubert did not always meet with such appreciation. Here is a curious case of mistaken identity

18 April 1817

Sir

. . . I have received your much appreciated letter of ten days ago, in which you enclosed the manuscript of a setting of Goethe's *Erlking*, supposedly by me. With the greatest astonishment, I have to say that this cantata was never composed by me. I am keeping it in my possession in the hope of discovering the fellow who sent you such rubbish, so impertinently trading on my name. Meanwhile, I am most grateful to you for sending me this manuscript, and I remain respectfully.

Your most grateful friend and brother
FRANZ SCHUBERT
Royal Church Composer

Letter to Breitkopf & Härtel

In fact there were three Franz Schuberts: this letter-writing one, 1768–1827, whose compositions have sunk without trace; his son, 1808–78, who at least wrote one pleasant piece of study fodder called 'The Bee', that young violinists play and sometimes think is by *the* Schubert, 1797–1828.

Debussy again, this time in the form of his music critic *alter ego*, Monsieur Croche (literally, Mr Quaver), taking a really rather unexpected line about the Ninth Symphony

A fog of verbiage and criticism surrounds the *Choral Symphony*. It is amazing that it has not been finally buried under the mass of prose which it has provoked. Wagner intended to complete the orchestration. Others fancied that they could explain and illustrate the theme by means of pictures. If we admit to a mystery in this Symphony we might clear it up; but is it worth while? There was not an ounce of literature in Beethoven, not at any rate in the accepted sense of the word. He had a great love for music, representing to him, as it did, the joy and passion piteously absent from his private life. Perhaps we ought in the *Choral Symphony* to look for nothing more than a magnificent gesture of musical pride. A little notebook with over two hundred different renderings of the dominant theme in the *Finale* of this Symphony shows how persistently Beethoven pursued his search and how entirely musical his guiding motive was; Schiller's lines can have only been used for their appeal to the ear. Beethoven determined that his leading idea should be essentially self-developing and, while it is of extraordinary beauty in itself, it becomes sublime because of its perfect response to his purpose. It is the most triumphant example of the moulding of an idea to the preconceived form; at each leap forward there is a new delight, without either effort or appearance of repetition; the magical blossoming, so to speak, of a tree whose leaves burst forth simultaneously. Nothing is superfluous in this stupendous work. . . . The flood of human feeling which overflows the ordinary bounds of the symphony sprang from a soul drunk with liberty, which, by an ironical decree of fate, beat itself against the gilded bars within which the misdirected charity of the great had confined him. Beethoven must have suffered cruelly in his ardent longing that humanity should find utterance through him; hence the call of his thousand-voiced genius to the humblest and poorest of his brethren. Did they hear it? That is the question.

CLAUDE DEBUSSY *Monsieur Croche* 1921

Spohr's view on the Choral Symphony could hardly be more different from Debussy's – though it represents an attitude widely held towards Beethoven's later works for quite a long time after his death

Up to this time [1813], there had been no falling off in Beethoven's creative powers. But as of this moment, owing to his constantly increasing deafness, he could no longer hear any music, and that must of necessity have had a prejudicial effect upon his creative imagination. His constant endeavor to be original and to open new paths could no longer, as formerly, be saved from error by the guidance of the ear. Was it, then, to be wondered at that his works became more eccentric, disconnected, and incomprehensible? It is true that there are people who imagine they can understand them, and in their pleasure at that claim, rank them far above his earlier masterpieces. But I am not of their number and freely confess that I have never been able to relish the last works of Beethoven. Yes, I must even reckon that much admired *Ninth Symphony* among these, the three first movements of which seem to me, despite some solitary flashes of genius, worse than all the eight previous symphonies. The fourth movement is, in my opinion, so monstrous and tasteless and, in its grasp of Schiller's *Ode*, so trivial that I cannot understand how a genius like Beethoven could have written it. I find in it another proof of what I had already noted in Vienna, that Beethoven was wanting in aesthetic feeling and in a sense of the beautiful.

LOUIS SPOHR *Autobiography* 1860

There are some people, like Churchill or Beecham or Dorothy Parker, to whom stories become attached whether they are true or not. Handel is one of these, and so is Rossini.

We *hope* it is true that, when Rossini was shown the score of Berlioz's *Symphonie Fantastique* for the first time, he said, 'Mon Dieu, it's lucky it's not music.' And was he really the author, or (for he was actually a kind man) did he just like it to be thought that he was the author, of the greatest put-down in musical history when, being shown a Funeral March written for Meyerbeer by Meyerbeer's nephew, he examined it carefully and then said: 'Very nice, but tell me frankly, don't you think it would have been better if it had been *you* who had died, and your *uncle* who had written the Funeral March?'. This was apparently a favourite story of Verdi's.

Though it doesn't really belong here, perhaps this is as good a place as any to quote a letter written by Rossini in the last year of his life to Costantino Dall' Argine, a young Italian composer, who had had the 'audacity' to make a new setting of *The Barber of Seville*, remembering how he had written his own *Barber* in the teeth of Paisiello's even earlier setting of the same subject. It is a model of charm and kindness from an older to a younger man

8 August 1868

. . . Even if your name is not unknown to me, since for some time I have been aware of the brilliant success that you obtained with your opera *I Due Orsi* [The Two Bears], I am deeply touched to find that an audacious young man (as you call yourself) holds me in some esteem – intending as you do to dedicate to me the opera to which you are now putting the final touches. This word 'audacity' is the only one that I find superfluous in your most charming letter. I certainly didn't regard myself as audacious when, after Papa Paisiello . . . I set Beaumarchais' delightful subject to music. So why should you be if, after half a century and more, you bring a new style to the musical setting of the *Barber*?

Not long ago Paisiello's version was revived at a theatre in Paris: sparkling as it is with spontaneous melody and theatrical invention, it obtained a brilliant and well-deserved success. Many polemics and many discussions have passed, and still pass, between the admirers of the old music and of the new, but you should remember (at least, I advise you to) the ancient proverb which says, *Fra due litiganti il terzo gode*. Be assured that I should like nothing better in this case than to see the third of us turn out to be the one who rejoices.

And so may your new *Barber* join the *Due Orsi* in forming a Great Bear in the musical heavens, and secure imperishable glory for its author and for our common country. Such are the cordial wishes offered to you by the old man of Pesaro whose name is

ROSSINI

(It is sad, after this, to read in the *New Grove* that Dall' Argine's opera 'aroused sharp but short-lived controversy, followed by rapid and complete oblivion for this mediocre score'.)

Brahms could be a devastating critic of his contemporaries. Max Bruch was a favourite target, though it is fair to add that Bruch tended to get a bad press all round: Tchaikovsky described him as 'a most sickeningly arrogant figure' when he met him at Cambridge in 1893 (where the two of them were described as looking like 'an ambassador and a store keeper from the Middle West')

'The first performance of my Second Violin Concerto in D Minor took place in a semi-private manner in Baden-Baden last summer. All the prominent musical personalities who generally assemble there at that time of the year were present, and among them Brahms. The Concerto, against the rule usually adopted, commences with a slow movement. The work had a great success, and at the end of the performance I was warmly congratulated by all present with the exception of Brahms, who only exclaimed, "My dear Bruch, how can one commence a Violin Concerto with an Adagio?" Not content with this, he followed me round during the afternoon and kept on tugging at my coat-tails and repeating the words, "How can one commence a Violin Concerto with an Adagio?" An unsupportable fellow.'

Here is another story about the two. Brahms chanced to visit Bruch in Cologne, and Bruch put into his hands a MS score of considerable dimensions with a request for his opinion and a solemn admonition to secrecy. It was the score of an oratorio entitled *Arminius*, founded on an episode in early German history, which eventually enjoyed a short-lived popularity. Bruch waited anxiously for the verdict, but all Brahms said after a seemingly close scrutiny was: 'I say, what splendid music-paper this is! Where did you get it?' A few days later Brahms and Bruch met again at a large dinner-party as the guests of a wealthy patron of music. When the sound of a barrel-organ in the street reached the ears of the company, Brahms called across the dinner-table in stentorian tones: 'Listen, Bruch. The fellow has got hold of *Arminius.'*

EDWARD SPEYER *My Life and Friends* 1937

Concertos often seem to arouse violent criticism, particularly Tchaikovsky's

Tchaikovsky's Violin Concerto gives us for the first time the hideous notion that there can be music that stinks to the ear.

EDUARD HANSLICK Review 1881

In December, 1874, I had written a pianoforte concerto. As I am not a pianist, I needed to consult some virtuoso as to what might be technically ineffective, ungrateful, impractical and so on. I needed a serious, but at the same time a friendly, critic for the pianistic aspects of my composition only. Now Rubinstein is not only the first pianist in Moscow, but also an excellent all round musician; knowing that he would, in any case, be deeply offended if he heard I had gone to anyone else with my concerto, I decided to ask him to listen to it and give me a soloist's opinion – though I must confess that some inner voice warned me against my choice of him as judge. It was Christmas Eve of 1874; as we were both invited to a Christmas tree that evening at the Albrechts, Nikolay Grigoryevich suggested that we go to one of the classrooms at the Conservatoire beforehand. And so we did. I arrived with my manuscript, and soon afterwards Nikolay Gr. with Hubert. . . .

I played the first movement. Not a word, not a single comment! If you only knew how foolish, how unbearable it feels for a man to offer his friend a dish of his own preparation, and the friend just eats and says nothing! Say something, tear it to pieces in a constructive way – but for God's sake, just one kind word, even if it isn't praise! While Rubinstein prepared his thunder, Hubert waited for the situation to clarify, so that he would know which way to jump. I didn't, after all, want a verdict on artistic quality, but a pianist's advice on technique. And Rubinstein's eloquent silence had immense significance. It was as if he was saying: 'My friend, how can I speak of details when the thing as a whole disgusts me?' I armed myself with patience, and played on to the end. Again silence. I got up and said, 'Well?' Then from the lips of Nikolay Grigoryevich began a stream of words – quiet at first, but gathering volume until it burst into the fury of a *Jupiter tonans*. It appeared that my concerto was worthless, that it was unplayable, that the passage work was so commonplace, unskillfully written and awkward that it would be impossible to put it right, that the composition itself was bad and trivial, that I had stolen this bit from here and that bit from there, that there were only two or three pages worth keeping, and that the rest would have to be scrapped or else completely rewritten. 'Look at this, for instance – what on earth does it mean?' (and he plays the passage, caricaturing it). 'And then this – is this really possible?', and so on, and so on, and so on. What I cannot convey, the most significant thing, is the *tone* in which all this was spoken. Any outsider, dropping into the room by chance, would have assumed I was an imbecile, some utterly untalented scribbler with no knowledge of composition who was pestering an eminent musician with his rubbish. . . .

I was not only stunned, I was deeply offended by the whole performance. I am no longer a boy, trying his hand at composition – I don't need lessons, particularly lessons administered in such a sharp and unsympathetic manner. I do need, and always shall need, friendly criticism, but that's not in the least what this was. It was a decisive, outright condemnation, expressed so as to touch me in a sensitive spot. I left the room without a word and went upstairs. I could not speak for anger and emotion. Presently Rubinstein joined me and, seeing how upset I was, took me off to a distant room. There he told me once again that my concerto was impossible, pointed out many places that would need to be radically changed, but said that, if I would revise the work according to his wishes by such-and-such a date, he would do me the honour of performing it at one of his concerts. '*I won't change a single note*', I replied, '*and I'll publish it exactly as it is now!*' And so I did!

TCHAIKOVSKY Letter 2 February 1878

Compare Tchaikovsky in his diary on 9 October 1886

Played over the music of that scoundrel Brahms. What a giftless bastard! It irritates me that this self-conscious mediocrity should be recognized as *a genius*. In comparison with him, Raff was a giant, not to mention Rubinstein, a much bigger and more vital personality. And Brahms is so chaotic, so dry and meaningless!

I like best to think of Brahms at the piano, playing his own compositions or Bach's mighty organ fugues, sometimes accompanying himself with a sort of muffled roar, as of Titans stirred to sympathy in the bowels of the earth. The veins in his forehead stood out, the wonderful bright blue eyes became veiled, and he seemed the incarnation of the restrained power in which his own work is forged. For his playing was never noisy, and when lifting a submerged theme out of a tangle of music he used jokingly to ask us to admire the gentle sonority of his 'tenor thumb'.

ETHEL SMYTH *Impressions that Remained* 1919

Another composer on Brahms

Sitting at the piano, he began to reveal wonderful landscapes. We were drawn into more and more magical circles. The impression was heightened by his masterly playing, which transformed the piano into an orchestra of mourning or rejoicing voices. There were sonatas, or rather, veiled symphonies – songs, whose poetry could be understood without the words being known, although a deep singing melody pervades all his music – separate piano pieces, partly demonic in nature under their very attractive form – then sonatas for violin and piano – string quartets – and each work so different from the others that each seemed to flow from a different source. And then it seemed as if, roaring on like a torrent, he gathered them all together into one cascade, that bore a quiet rainbow over furious waves, falling between banks where butterflies played and nightingale voices sang.

ROBERT SCHUMANN 1853 *New Paths*

This was written by Schumann in 1853, in the famous notice which first hailed the young Brahms as 'the chosen spirit' of German music; it was Schumann's last article as a music critic.

Criticism

The band of composers who are also professional (or at least practising) music critics is a small but select one. Schumann, at fifteen, was regarded by his friends almost more as a poet than as a musician, and he remained a writer all his life. His first published article, under the title 'An Opus 2', appeared in the Leipzig *Allgemeine musikalische Zeitung* in 1831: its subject is the *Là ci darem* Variations by the 21-year-old Chopin and it opens almost like a novel

Eusebius walked quietly in at the door the other day. You know his pale face, and the ironical smile with which he tries to arouse attention. I was sitting at the piano with Florestan. Florestan, as you know, is one of those rare musicians who as it were divine things to come, the new, the unexpected, long in advance. But that day he was to have a surprise. With the words, 'Hats off, gentlemen, a genius!' Eusebius laid a piece of music on the piano. He would not let us see the title. I turned the pages over carelessly; there is something fascinating in this partaking of music without sound. Besides, it seems to me that each composer's music has a look of its own, simply to the eye: Beethoven looks different on the page from Mozart, rather as Jean Paul's prose looks different from Goethe's. But in this case I felt as if nothing but strange eyes – eyes of flowers, eyes of basilisks, eyes of peacocks, eyes of girls – were miraculously looking at me. In some places there was more light – I thought I saw Mozart's *Là ci darem la mano* winding through a hundred chords. Leporello seemed quite to wink at me, and Don Juan flew past me in his white cloak. 'Now play it,' Florestan said. Eusebius agreed. We listened, sitting close together in a window-niche. Eusebius played as if inspired, and countless figures, alive with the utmost intensity of life, passed by. . . .

ROBERT SCHUMANN *An Opus 2* 1831

Some turned to criticism more willingly than others. Berlioz was another of the great prose writers among composers, yet 'this self-perpetuating task poisons my life' he wrote, and elsewhere:

It can take eight or nine attempts before I am rid of an article for the *Journal des débats*. I have to set aside two days for it, even when the subject excites or amuses me. And then, the blots and the scratchings-out! The first draft is like a battlefield.

It is surprising, in one who poured so much wit, critical perception and musical understanding into his *feuilletons*, to find him making a disparaging distinction between his own métier and what he obviously regarded as 'real' criticism

The critic – let us suppose him intelligent and honest – writes only when he has something to say: when he wishes to illuminate some question, challenge some theory, bestow well-merited praise or blame. He always has reasons, to him genuine, for airing his opinions and dispensing his accolades or his thunderbolts. The wretched feuilletonist, obliged to write on anything and everything within the domain of his feuilleton (gloomy domain, bog-ridden, infested with toads and grass-hoppers), wishes for one thing only – to be done with the labour that weighs upon him. More often than not he has no opinion about the objects on which he is compelled to give an opinion; they stir him to neither anger nor admiration; they do not exist. Yet he has to behave as if he believed in their existence and felt strongly about them and had powerful motives for bringing his whole mind to bear upon them. Most of my colleagues can extricate themselves without difficulty and often with a dexterity which it is a pleasure to watch. But for me, it is a long and painful struggle to keep up the pretence. Once, when I had to write a feuilleton about the Opéra-Comique, I spent three days immured in my room, unable to begin. I do not remember what opus I was supposed to be discussing (within a week of the opening night its name had faded from my mind for ever), but the torture I went through during those three days before I could write the first three lines of my article – that I have not forgotten. The lobes of my brain seemed about to disintegrate; I felt as if burning embers were scorching my veins. Sometimes I stayed sitting with my elbows on the table, holding my head in my hands. Sometimes I strode up and down like a sentry on duty in twenty-five degrees of frost. I stood at the window and looked out at the neighbouring gardens and the heights of Montmartre and the setting sun – and at once my thoughts flew off and I was carried a thousand miles from that hideous opéra-comique. Then I turned back and my eye fell once more on the accursed sheet of paper, blank except for the accursed title at the top and waiting obstinately for the other words to cover it – and a feeling of despair surged over me. . . .

That was fifteen years ago, and the rack still turns. Ruin and destruction! To be always at it! Let me only be given scores to compose, orchestras to conduct, rehearsals to direct; be made to stay on my feet eight or ten hours at a stretch, baton in hand, training choirs, without an instrument to accompany them, giving the leads myself while I beat time, until I cough blood and my arm is rigid with cramp; be made to carry desks, double basses, harps, to shift platforms, nail planks, like a porter or a carpenter; and then be forced, as a relaxation, to sit up all night correcting the mistakes of engravers and copyists: I have done it, I do it, I will do it again; it is part of my life as a musician, and I bear it without complaint, without even a thought, as a sportsman endures cold, heat, hunger, thirst, sunshine and downpour, mud, dust and all the countless exertions of the chase. But eternally to scratch feuilletons for a living! to write nothing about nothing! to give tepid approval to insufferable insipidities! to speak one evening of a great master and the next of an idiot in the same language, with the same gravity of utterance! to spend your time, intelligence, spirit and patient endeavour on this drudgery, without even the compensation of knowing that you are at least serving a useful artistic purpose by helping to abolish a few abuses, eradicate prejudices, enlighten opinion, refine public taste and put men and things in their true place and perspective – oh, it is the most horrible humiliation! Better to be – to be finance minister in a republic!

HECTOR BERLIOZ *Memoirs* 1865

In spite of the brilliance and originality of his mind, Berlioz still had his limitations as a critic. Wagner, for instance, was too much for him: the *Tristan* Prelude had 'no other theme than a sort of chromatic sigh'. This recalls the Viennese music critic Eduard Hanslick's wonderful comment: 'With scrupulous avoidance of all closing cadences, this boneless tonal mollusk, self-renewing, swims ever on into the immeasurable. . . .'

Here is Hanslick, not on Wagner, but on a composer whom he regarded as a close follower of the master of Bayreuth, after a concert conducted by Hans Richter in Vienna on 18 December 1892

The Philharmonic Orchestra devoted its entire concert to a new symphony by Bruckner. It is the eighth in the series and similar to its predecessors in form and mood. I found this newest one, as I have found the other Bruckner symphonies, interesting in detail but strange as a whole and even repugnant. The nature of the work consists – to put it briefly – in applying Wagner's dramatic style to the symphony.

Not only does Bruckner fall continually into Wagnerian devices, effects, and reminiscences; he seems even to have accepted certain Wagnerian pieces as models for symphonic construction, as, for example, the Prelude to *Tristan and Isolde*. Bruckner begins with a short chromatic motive, repeats it over and over again, higher and higher in the scale and on into infinity, augments it, diminishes it, offers it in contrary motion, and so on, until the listener is simply crushed under the sheer weight and monotony of this interminable lamentation. Alongside these upward surging lamentations we have the subsiding lamentation (after the model of the *Tannhäuser* Overture). Wagnerian orchestral effects are met on every hand, such as the tremolos of the violins *divisi* in the highest position, harp arpeggios over muffled chords in the trombones, and, added to all that, the newest achievements of the Siegfried tubas.

Also characteristic of Bruckner's newest symphony is the immediate juxtaposition of dry schoolroom counterpoint with unbounded exaltation. Thus, tossed about between intoxication and desolation, we arrive at no definite impression and enjoy no artistic pleasure. Everything flows, without clarity and without order, willy-nilly, into dismal long-windedness. In each of the four movements, and most frequently in the first and third, there are interesting passages and flashes of genius – if only all the rest were not there! It is not out of the question that the future belongs to this muddled hangover style – which is no reason to regard the future with envy. For the time being, however, one would prefer that symphonic and chamber music remain undefiled by a style only relatively justified as an illustrative device for certain dramatic situations.

Even before the performance we had heard such provocative reports of the extraordinary profundity of the new symphony that I took care to prepare myself through study of the score and attendance at the dress rehearsal. I must confess, however, that the mysteries of this all-embracing composition were disclosed to me only through the helpful offices of an explanatory program handed to me prior to the concert. The author of this dissertation is anonymous, but we easily discerned the fine hand of Schalk. From him we learned that the irksome humming theme of the first movement represents the figure of the Aeschylean Prometheus. An especially tiresome part of this movement is charmingly described as 'most awful loneliness and quiet'. Right next to Prometheus stands *Der deutsche Michl*. Had a critic uttered this blasphemy, he would probably have been stoned by the Bruckner disciples. But it was the composer himself who gave the Scherzo the name of *Der deutsche Michl*, as is plain to be seen in black and white in the program. With this authentic pronouncement before him, however, the commentator (Schalk) doesn't hesitate to find in the *Michl*-Scherzo 'the deeds and sufferings of Prometheus reduced in parody to the smallest scale'.

What follows is even more exalted. In the Adagio we behold nothing less than 'the all-loving Father of Mankind in all His infinite mercy!' Since this Adagio lasts exactly twenty-eight minutes, or about as long as an entire Beethoven symphony, we cannot complain of being denied ample time for the contemplation of the rare vision. At long last, the Finale – which, with its baroque themes, its confused structure and inhuman din, strikes us only as a model of tastelessness – represents, according to the program, 'Heroism in the Service of the Divine!' The blaring trumpet figures are 'heralds of the Gospel truth and the conception of God'. The childish, hymnal character of this program characterizes our Bruckner community, which consists of Wagnerites and some added starters for whom Wagner is already too simple and intelligible. One sees how Wagnerism educates, not only musically but also in literature.

And the reception of the new symphony? A storm ovation, waving of handkerchiefs from the standees, innumerable recalls, laurel wreaths, etc.! For Bruckner, the concert was certainly a huge success. Whether Hans Richter performed a similar favor for his subscribers by devoting an entire concert to the Bruckner symphony is doubtful. The program seems to have been chosen only for the sake of a noisy minority. The test is easy: just give the symphony in a special concert outside the subscription series. This would be helpful to all concerned, save probably the Philharmonic Orchestra.

EDUARD HANSLICK Review 1892

Richard Specht records Brahms's comments about two of his contemporaries, which are fascinating (if Specht's memory is really to be trusted)

Bruckner? That is a swindle which will be forgotten a year or two after my death. Take it as you will, Bruckner owes his fame solely to me, and but for me nobody would have cared a brass farthing for him. Of course I had nothing to do with it; in fact it happened very much against my will. Nietzsche once declared that I had become famous through a mere chance, because the anti-Wagner party required me as an anti-pope. That is nonsense, for I am not the man to be placed at the head of any party whatsoever. . . . But in Bruckner's case it was so. That is to say, after Wagner's death his party naturally had need for another pope, and they managed to find no better one than Bruckner. Do you really believe that anyone in this immature crowd has the least notion what these symphonic boa-constrictors are about? And do you not think that I am the musician who knows and understands Wagner's work best to-day, certainly better than any of his so-called followers, who would like nothing better than to poison me? I once told Wagner himself that I was the best Wagnerian of our time. Do you take me to be too dull to have been as enchanted as anyone by the joyousness and sublimity of the *Mastersingers*? Or dishonest enough to conceal my view that I consider a few bars of this work as of more value than all the operas that have been written since? I an anti-pope? It is too silly! And Bruckner's works immortal, and 'symphonies'? It is ludicrous!

BRAHMS in RICHARD SPECHT *Johannes Brahms* 1928

Here is a curious little footnote to the Bruckner/Wagner relationship. (Curious, too, to discover that the boy Kreisler was a pupil of Bruckner)

'Bruckner had a chubby, fat pug dog named Mops,' Kreisler recalled. 'He would leave us with Mops munching our sandwiches while he himself hastened off to luncheon. We decided we'd play a joke on our teacher which would flatter him. So while the *Meister* was away, we'd play a motif by Wagner, and as we did so, would slap Mops and chase him. Next we'd start Bruckner's *Te Deum*, and while this music was in progress, would give Mops something to eat. He soon showed a convincing preference for the *Te Deum*! When we thought we had trained him sufficiently so that he would automatically run away when Wagner was played and joyfully approach us at the sound of a Bruckner strain, we deemed the moment appropriate for our prank.

'"Meister Bruckner," we said one day as he returned from lunch, "we know that you are devoted to Wagner, but to our way of thinking he cannot compare with you. Why, even a dog would know that you are a greater composer than Wagner."

'Our guileless teacher blushed. He thought we were serious. He reproved us, paid tribute to Wagner as the unquestionably greatest contemporary, but was nevertheless filled with enough curiosity to ask what we meant by claiming even a dog could tell the difference.

'This was the moment we had waited for. We played a Wagner motif. A howling, scared Mops stole out of the room. We started in on Bruckner's *Te Deum*. A happy canine returned, wagging his tail and pawing expectantly at our sleeves. Bruckner was touched.'

LOUIS LOCHNER *Fritz Kreisler* 1950

Specht also remembers an incident which highlights one of the great dangers of professional musical criticism – musical politics – and makes one wary of Hanslick, brilliant and immensely readable though he is. (He was, of course, the established champion of Brahms in the Brahms–Wagner battles of the later nineteenth century.)

Richard Heuberger once showed me a postcard addressed to him by Hanslick, for whom he often deputized as critic in the *Neue Freie Presse*, and I can vouch for its contents. It may still be among the papers left by Heuberger, who for good reasons would not risk the publication for which I begged him. It said: 'I have just come from the Rosé Quartet's concert, where Brahms's new Quintet was played. I could scarcely endure to remain to the end, so much did this music bore me. . . . The trouble is that Brahms no longer has any ideas and that he is becoming more and more leathern. After this piece, the Suite by Brüll that followed was a veritable feast with its Bachish euphony.' (I only quote from memory, but would answer for the actual words.) That the master's 'leathern' work was afterwards honoured by high praise in the paper – and justly so, since it is a wonderfully fresh composition of sovereign workmanship, – while the 'Bachish euphony' was dismissed with a few parenthetic words, speaks sufficiently for the method of making musical history that obtained in Vienna during more than a quarter of a century.

RICHARD SPECHT Johannes Brahms 1928

No music critic was further from *musical* politics than Bernard Shaw – though it must be admitted that he had a persistent and obstinate blind spot where Brahms was concerned

. . . a sentimental voluptuary with a wonderful ear . . . gifted enough to play with harmonies that would baffle most grown-up men . . . and rather tiresomely addicted to dressing himself up as Handel or Beethoven and making a prolonged and intolerable noise.

To a friend he privately described him as 'just like Tennyson, an extraordinary musician, with the brains of a third-rate village policeman'. The German Requiem, which 'is patiently borne only by the corpse', was an especial *bête noire*. He seems only to have heard it once

The Bach Choir gave a concert on the 16th. I was not present. There are some sacrifices which should not be demanded twice from any man; and one of them is listening to Brahms' Requiem. On some future

evening, perhaps, when the weather is balmy, and I can be accommodated with a comfortable armchair, an interesting book, and all the
evening papers, I may venture; but last week I should have required a
requiem for myself if I had attempted such a feat of endurance. I am
sorry to have to play the 'disgruntled' critic over a composition so
learnedly contrapuntal, not to say so fugacious; but I really cannot
stand Brahms as a serious composer. It is nothing short of a European
misfortune that such prodigious musical powers should have nothing
better in the way of ideas to express than incoherent commonplace.

And the memory was still fresh in his mind when the Leeds Festival came
round again in 1892

The forthcoming performances in October will be welcomed by all
except those who incautiously attended the benumbing fourth day of
the 1889 Festival, on which occasion the whole West Riding was
plunged into listless gloom by an unprovoked performance of Brahms'
Requiem.

It was in May of the same year that he first came across the Clarinet Quintet

I shall not attempt to describe this latest exploit of the Leviathan
Maunderer. It surpassed my utmost expectations: I never heard such a
work in my life. Brahms' enormous gift of music is paralleled by
nothing on earth but Mr Gladstone's gift of words: it is a verbosity
which outfaces its own commonplaceness by dint of sheer magnitude.
The first movement of the quintet is the best; and had the string
players been on sufficiently easy terms with it, they might have
softened it and given effect to its occasional sentimental excursions
into dreamland. Unluckily they were all preoccupied with the difficulty of keeping together; and they were led by a violinist whose bold,
free, slashing style, though useful in a general way, does more harm
than good when the strings need to be touched with great tenderness
and sensitiveness.
  Mr Clinton played the clarionet part with scrupulous care, but
without giving any clue to his private view of the work, which, though
it shews off the compass and contrasts the registers of the instrument
in the usual way, contains none of the haunting phrases which Weber,
for instance, was able to find for the expression of its idiosyncrasy. The
presto of the third movement is a ridiculously dismal version of a lately
popular hornpipe. I first heard it at the pantomime which was
produced at Her Majesty's Theatre a few years ago; and I have always

supposed it to be a composition of Mr Solomon's. Anyhow, the street-pianos went through an epidemic of it; and it certainly deserved a merrier fate than burying alive in a Brahms quintet.

BERNARD SHAW 1890–92 *Music in London*

Shaw began 'ghosting' for the music critic of *The Hornet* in 1876, when he was twenty, later writing in *The Star* (as 'Corno di Bassetto') and from 1890 to 1894 in *The World* (as himself). He told T. P. O'Connor, the editor of *The Star*, that he could make a deaf stockbroker read his two columns on music, and he probably could. There never was such a readable music critic. It is, of course, always tempting to quote him when he is being witty or caustic or indignant. Here, instead, is his marvellously perceptive reaction after a first look through the score of Verdi's last (and possibly greatest) opera

Falstaff is lighted and warmed only by the afterglow of the fierce noonday sun of *Ernani*; but the gain in beauty conceals the loss in heat – if, indeed, it be a loss to replace intensity of passion and spontaneity of song by fullness of insight and perfect mastery of workmanship. Verdi has exchanged the excess of his qualities for the wisdom to supply his deficiencies; his weaknesses have disappeared with his superfluous force; and he is now, in his dignified competence, the greatest of living dramatic composers. It is not often that a man's strength is so immense that he can remain an athlete after bartering half of it to old age for experience; but the thing happens occasionally, and need not so greatly surprise us in Verdi's case, especially those of us who, long ago, when von Bülow and others were contemptuously repudiating him, were able to discern in him a man possessing more power than he knew how to use, or indeed was permitted to use by the old operatic forms imposed on him by circumstances.

BERNARD SHAW 1893 *ibid.*

Shaw's flights of indignation can be very exhilarating; they often gain by being read aloud, with a slight brogue and (as in this case) a rising inflection of the voice as the climax approaches

Il Trovatore, Un Ballo, Ernani, etc., are no longer read at the piano at home as the works of the *Carmen* genre are, and as Wagner's are. The popular notion of them is therefore founded on performances in which the superb distinction and heroic force of the male characters, and the tragic beauty of the women, have been burlesqued by performers with every sort of disqualification for such parts, from age and obesity to the most excruciating phases of physical insignificance and modern cockney vulgarity. I used often to wonder why it was that whilst every asphalt contractor could get a man to tar the streets, and every tourist could find a gondolier rather above the average of the House of Lords in point of nobility of aspect, no operatic manager, after Mario vanished, seemed able to find a Manrico with whom any exclusively disposed Thames mudlark would care to be seen grubbing for pennies. When I get on this subject I really cannot contain myself. The thought of that dynasty of execrable imposters in tights and tunics, interpolating their loathsome B flats into the beautiful melodies they could not sing, and swelling with conceit when they were able to finish *Di quella pira* with a high C capable of making a stranded man-of-war recoil off a reef into mid-ocean, I demand the suspension of all rules as to decorum of language until I have heaped upon them some little instalment of the infinite abuse they deserve.

                                        BERNARD SHAW 1892 *ibid*.

The ultimate apology for the passionate critic

People have pointed out evidences of personal feeling in my notices as if they were accusing me of a misdemeanour, not knowing that a criticism written without personal feeling is not worth reading. It is the capacity for making good or bad art a personal matter that makes a man a critic. The artist who accounts for my disparagement by alleging personal animosity on my part is quite right: when people do less than their best, and do that less at once badly and self-complacently, I hate them, loathe them, detest them, long to tear them limb from limb and strew them in gobbets about the stage or platform. . . .

   In the same way, really fine artists inspire me with the warmest personal regard, which I gratify in writing my notices without the smallest reference to such monstrous conceits as justice, impartiality, and the rest of the ideals. When my critical mood is at its height, personal feeling is not the word: it is passion: the passion for artistic perfection – for the noblest beauty of sound, sight, and action – that rages in me. Let all young artists look to it, and pay no heed to the idiots who declare that criticism should be free from personal feeling. The true critic, I repeat, is the man who becomes your personal enemy on the sole provocation of a bad performance, and will only be appeased by good performances.

                                        BERNARD SHAW 1890 *ibid*.

It is a point of view that would have been echoed by one at least of the composer-critics' band

'I love music too much,' [Debussy] proclaimed once, 'to speak of it otherwise than passionately.' So we must not be surprised at the bold, disrespectful judgments which he passed equally on the gods of music – universally (and conventionally) adored – and on the consecrated reputations of his own time. We heard him just now making some concession to the 'worthy man' Sebastian Bach, for whom he was, I really think, full of a certain respect. But Gluck was for him only a 'pedant', not less than Wagner; he called the Tetralogie *bottin* and found Wagner's masterpieces 'manufactured'. Of songs of Schubert he cries, 'They are inoffensive; they have the odor of bureau drawers of provincial old maids – ends of faded ribbon – flowers forever faded and withered – out-of-date photographs! Only they repeat the same effect for interminable stanzas and, at the end of the third, one wonders if one could not set to music our national Paul Delmet.' In Schumann's *Faust*, 'one stumbles on Mendelssohn', Beethoven is 'a deaf old man', Berlioz a 'monster', César Franck 'a Belgian'. . . . Of the new Italian school and the performance of *I Pagliacci* at the Opera in 1903, Debussy wrote: 'There are jokes on which it is bad taste to insist'; elsewhere one finds in Puccini and Leoncavallo 'an almost complete imitation of the manias of our most notorious master' – that is, Massenet, for whom Debussy has nowhere else a cruel word.

J. G. PROD'HOMME *The Musical Quarterly* 1918

But neither Shaw nor Debussy laid claim to the actual bodily discomfort of Wagner's most famous critic

My objections to Wagner's music are physiological – why disguise them as usual behind aesthetic formulas? Aesthetics is nothing else than applied physiology. I base myself upon fact – indeed it is my 'small, real fact' when I say that I breathe with difficulty as soon as Wagner's music begins to act upon me. I say that my *foot* gets annoyed and rebels against the music; my foot wants rhythm, dancing, marching. The rhythm of Wagner's 'Kaisermarsch' keeps even the young emperor from marching in time with it. My foot asks of music, above all, the pleasure of *good* pacing, stepping, dancing, capering.

And then is not my stomach in revolt as well? my heart and the circulation of my blood? It seems as if my bowels were saddened too, and my throat made hoarse by imperceptible degrees: in order to listen to Wagner I need medicated lozenges. And so I ask myself the question: What, in the last analysis, does *my body as a whole* require of music? For there is no such thing as the soul. Well, I think my body needs lift, lightening, it needs all the animal functions accelerated by light, bold, heedless, and proud rhythms; so that our leaden life, our cast-iron existence shall lose its gravity under the influence of golden melodies, delicate, fluent as oil. My melancholy wants to find surcease in the crannies and abysses of *perfection*.

FRIEDRICH NIETZSCHE *Nietzsche contra Wagner* 1888

Among the more devastating English music critics of the 1920s and 1930s was Constant Lambert. Here he is on the Cello Concerto by the eminent scholar, composer and pianist Donald Tovey, played by Casals at a BBC concert in 1937

I am told by those who had the moral, physical and intellectual stamina to sit it out to the end that Professor Donald Tovey's *Cello Concerto* lasts for over an hour. This I cannot vouch for as, like several other musicians, I was compelled to leave at the end of the first movement, which seemed to last as long as my first term at school . . .

CONSTANT LAMBERT *The Sunday Referee* 21 November 1937

Some critics, of course, go *too* far

6 December 1950. President Truman, infuriated by the disparaging review by Paul Hume in the *Washington Post* of a song recital by Truman's daughter Margaret, dispatches a letter to him written in longhand on White House stationery, as follows: 'Mr Hume: I have just read your lousy review of Margaret's concert. I've come to the conclusion that you are an eight-ulcer man on four-ulcer pay. . . . Some day I hope to meet you. When that happens, you'll need a new nose, a lot of beefsteak for black eyes, and perhaps a supporter below.'

NICOLAS SLONIMSKY *Music Since 1900*

Criticism does what it is its duty to do. It judges, and must judge, according to existing rules and forms. The artist, however, must cope with the future, see new worlds in chaos; and when, far, far ahead on his new path, he perceives a little light, he must not be frightened by the darkness that still shrouds it. He must march forward; and if he often stumbles and falls, he must rise again and press on forward.

GIUSEPPE VERDI Letter quoted by Max Graf

In the 1940s Benjamin Britten and Michael Tippett started a friendship that began very warmly and survived cooler moments. On Britten's fiftieth birthday Tippett dedicated his *Concerto for Orchestra* to him; on Tippett's sixtieth Britten returned the compliment with *Curlew River*, and this letter of greeting – which ended with the famous *cri de coeur*: 'PS I wish your piano parts weren't so difficult!'

Evaluations, comparisons – the whole apparatus; does it mean anything to you? It doesn't to me, much. Slaps or bouquets, they come too late to help, long after the work is over. What matters to us now is that people want to use our music. For that, as I see it, is our job – to be useful, and to the living. Criticism likes to separate, to dislodge, to imply rivalries, to provoke jealousies. But I don't think I am jealous – (yes, envious, possibly of the man who can do something much better than I can), and the colleagues whom I admire, I regard as friends on the side of the angels rather than as rivals. Do you remember the story of Haydn banging the table and rushing from the room when someone poked fun at *Don Giovanni* (I think it was)? He knew very well the problems of finding the right notes and balancing forms. Schumann, too, who later found such difficulty in getting the courage to write at all, was the tenderest of critics. What does it matter if some of the people he admired mean little to us? His first duty was to his contemporaries, not to us.

BENJAMIN BRITTEN 1965 in Michael Tippett, A Symposium

Comparisons and groupings of composers or performers have always been a part of the critic's technique. The Haydn, Mozart, Beethoven trinity was an early example

Haydn created [by] drawing from the clear, pure source of his charming original personality. He remains therefore always unique. . . . Mozart's more vigorous and richer fancy encompassed more, and in several pieces expressed the highest and deepest feeling of his inner self; moreover, he was more the virtuoso himself, and expected more from players; he attributed more significance to elaborate development, and thus built his palace upon Haydn's charming garden house of fancy. Beethoven early made himself at home in this palace, and so it was left to him to express his own personality in his own forms, the bold, defiant building of the tower to which no one could add without breaking his neck.

J. F. REICHARDT quoted by Max Graf

Haydn comprehends the humanity in human life romantically; it is easier for the majority to understand him. Mozart strives for the superhuman and the miraculous that dwell in the depths of the mind. Beethoven's music sets in motion the levers of fear, stirs shuddering, terror, and anguish, and rouses the infinite longing that forms the essence of romanticism.

E. T. A. HOFFMANN quoted by Max Graf

The quartets were perfectly clear and easy to understand. One was by Mozart and the other by Beethoven, so that I could compare the two masters. Their individuality seemed to become plain to me: Mozart – grace, liberty, certainty, freedom, and precision of style – an exquisite and aristocratic beauty – serenity of soul – the health and talent of the master, both on a level with his genius; Beethoven – more pathetic, more passionate, more torn with feeling, more intricate, more profound, less perfect, more the slave of his genius, more carried away by his fancy or his passion, more moving and more sublime than Mozart. Mozart refreshes you, like the *Dialogues* of Plato; he respects you, reveals to you your strength, gives you freedom and balance. Beethoven seizes upon you: he is more tragic and oratorical, while Mozart is more disinterested and poetical. Mozart is more Greek, and Beethoven more Christian. One is serene, the other serious. The first is stronger than destiny, because he takes life less profoundly; the second is less strong, because he dares to measure himself against deeper sorrows. His talent is not always equal to his genius, and pathos is his dominant feature, as perfection is that of Mozart. In Mozart the balance of the whole is perfect; in Beethoven feeling governs everything, and emotion troubles his art in proportion as it deepens it.

HENRI-FRÉDÉRIC AMIEL *Journal intime* 1883

. . . I like Mozart best when I have the sensation I am watching him think. The thought processes of other composers seem to me different: Beethoven grabs you by the back of the head and forces you to think with him; Schubert, on the other hand, charms you into thinking his thoughts. But Mozart's pellucid thinking has a kind of sensitized objectivity all its own: one takes delight in watching him carefully choose orchestral timbres or in following the melodic line as it takes flight from the end of his pen.

Mozart in his music was probably the most reasonable of the world's great composers. It is the happy balance between flight and control, between sensibility and self-discipline, simplicity and sophistication of style that is his particular province. By comparison Bach seems weighted down with the world's cares, Palestrina other-worldly in his interests. Composers before him had brought music a long way from its primitive beginnings, proving that in its highest forms the art of music was to be considered on a par with other strict disciplines as one of man's grandest achievements.

Mozart, however, tapped once again the source from which all music flows, expressing himself with a spontaneity and refinement and breath-taking rightness that has never since been duplicated.

AARON COPLAND *Copland on Music* 1960

I think I see in Haydn, the Tintoret of music. Like the Venetian painter, he unites to the energy of Michel Angelo, fire, originality, and fertility of invention. All this is invested with a loveliness of colouring, which renders pleasing even the minutest details. I am, nevertheless, of opinion, that the Tintoret of Eisenstadt, was more profound in his art than the Venetian one; more particularly, he knew how to work slowly.

The mania of comparisons seizes me. I trust you with my collection, on condition that you will not laugh at it too much. I fancy, then that

Pergolese, and Cimarosa are the Raphaels of music
Paesiello is Guido
Durante – Lionardo da Vinci
Hasse – Rubens
Handel – Michel Angelo
Galluppi – Bassano
Jomelli – Lewis Caracci
Gluck – Caravaggio
Piccini – Titian
Sacchini – Correggio
Vinci – Fra Bartolommeo
Mozart – Dominichino

The least imperfect resemblance, is that of Paesiello and Guido. As for Mozart, Dominichino should have a still stronger cast of melancholy, to resemble him entirely.

JOHN ROWE PARKER *A Musical Biography* 1824

It has often occurred to me to compare our composers to the works of
the days of creation. Chaos – Beethoven. Let there be light! –
Cherubini. Let the mountains appear! (great but very uncouth masses)
– Joseph Haydn. Every singing bird after his kind – the Italian school.
Bears – Albrechtsberger. Every thing that creepeth upon the earth –
Gyrowetz. Man – Mozart!

FRANZ GRILLPARZER *Diary* 1809

Paul Henry Lang on the *Eroica*

. . . Beethoven himself never again approached this feat of fiery
imagination; he wrote other, perhaps greater, works, but he never
again took such a fling at the universe. . . .

PAUL HENRY LANG *Music in Western Civilization* 1942

Lenin on Opus 57

I know nothing more beautiful than the 'Appassionata,' I could hear it
every day. It is marvellous, unearthly music. Every time I hear these
notes, I think with pride and perhaps childlike *naïveté*, that it is
wonderful what man can accomplish. But I cannot listen to music
often, it affects my nerves. I want to say amiable stupidities and stroke
the heads of the people who can create such beauty in a filthy hell. But
today is not the time to stroke people's heads; today hands descend to
split skulls open, split them open ruthlessly, although opposition to all
violence is our ultimate ideal – it is a hellishly hard task. . . .

LENIN quoted by Maxim Gorky in *Days with Lenin* 1933

Opus 131

The Quartet in C Sharp Minor is the greatest of Beethoven's quartets,
as he himself thought. It is also the most mystical of the quartets, and
the one where the mystical vision is most perfectly sustained. It counts
seven movements, but, regarded as an organic unity, it is the most
complete of Beethoven's works. For the purposes of description,
however, it is convenient to divide it into three parts. The opening
fugue is the most superhuman piece of music that Beethoven has ever
written. It is the completely unfaltering rendering into music of what
we can only call the mystic vision. It has that serenity which, as
Wagner said, speaking of these quartets, passes beyond beauty.
Nowhere else in music are we made so aware, as here, of a state of
consciousness surpassing our own, where our problems do not exist,

and to which even our highest aspirations, those that we can formulate, provide no key. Those faint and troubling intimations we sometimes have of a vision different from and yet including our own, of a way of apprehending life, passionless, perfect and complete, that resolves all our discords, are here presented with the reality they had glimpsed. This impression of a superhuman knowledge, of a super-human life being slowly frozen into shape, as it were, before our eyes, can be ambiguous. That passionless, remote calm can seem, as it did to Wagner, like a melancholy too profound for any tears. To Berlioz it was terrifying. To Beethoven himself it was the justification of, and the key to, life. In the light of this vision he surveys the world. That this vision was permanent with Beethoven is inconceivable. No man ever lived who could maintain such a state of illumination. This, we may be sure, is the last and greatest of Beethoven's spiritual discoveries, only to be grasped in the moments of his profoundest abstraction from the world. But it was sufficiently permanent to enable him to write the C Sharp Minor Quartet in the light of it, a feat of concentration, of abstraction, of utter truthfulness, that is without equal.

J. W. N. SULLIVAN *Beethoven: his Spiritual Development* 1927

Literary
Views

If a literary man puts together two words about music, one of them will be wrong.

AARON COPLAND

A long-drawn organ-stop. . .

GEORGE ELIOT

> I chatter over stony ways
> In little sharps and trebles
>
> ALFRED, LORD TENNYSON 'The Brook'

> Sliding by semitones, till I sink to the minor. . .
>
> ROBERT BROWNING *Abt Vogler*

Browning's version of Abt Vogler's views is well known

> But here is the finger of God, a flash of the will that can,
>   Existent behind all laws, that made them and, lo, they are!
> And I know not if, save in this, such gift be allowed to man,
>   That out of three sounds he frame, not a fourth sound, but a star.
> Consider it well: each tone of our scale in itself is nought;
>   It is everywhere in the world – loud, soft, and all is said:
> Give it to me to use! I mix it with two in my thought:
>   And, there! Ye have heard and seen: consider and bow the head!
>
> ROBERT BROWNING *Abt Vogler (After he has been extemporizing upon the musical instrument*
> *of his invention)* 1864

'In chord studies,' says the *New Grove*, 'Vogler proposed that the triad must be the basis for all chords' – which is, after all, much what Browning has him propose, if on a rather different poetic level. The 'musical instrument of his invention' was presumably the 'orchestrion', a small, portable organ which he

used on his concert tours, though Browning, who was only two when Vogler
died, cannot actually have heard him play on anything. He was greatly
admired as an extemporizer by most of his contemporaries, though one at
least demurred

The organ in the Lutheran church which has just been tried today is
very good, both in the full and in single stops. Vogler played it. He is,
to put it bluntly, a trickster pure and simple. As soon as he tries to play
maestoso, he becomes as dry as dust; and it is a great relief that playing
upon the organ bores him and that therefore it doesn't last long. But
what is the result? An unintelligible muddle . . .

MOZART Letter to his father 18 December 1777

Dr Johnson was not a music-lover

After we had exhausted the Erse poems, of which Dr Johnson said
nothing, Mis M'Lean gave us several tunes on a spinnet, which,
though made so long ago as in 1667, was still very well toned. She
sung along with it. Dr Johnson seemed pleased with the music,
though he owns he neither likes it, nor has hardly any perception of it.
At Mr M'Pherson's, in Slate, he told us, that, 'he knew a drum from a
trumpet, and a bagpipe from a guitar, which was about the extent of
his knowledge of music.' To-night he said, that, 'if he had learned
music, he should have been afraid he would have done nothing else
but play. It was a method of employing the mind, without the labour
of thinking at all, and with some applause from a man's self.'

We had the music of the bagpipe every day, at Armidale, Dunvegan
and Col. Dr Johnson appeared fond of it, and used often to stand for
some time with his ear close to the great drone.

JAMES BOSWELL *Journal of a Tour to the Hebrides* 1785

Nor was Charles Lamb

> Some cry up Haydn, some Mozart,
> Just as the whim bites; for my part,
> I do not care a farthing candle
> For either of them, or for Handel. –
> Cannot a man live free and easy,
> Without admiring Pergolesi?
> Or thro' the world with comfort go,
> That never heard of Doctor Blow?
> So help me heaven, I hardly have;

And yet I eat, and drink, and shave,
Like other people, if you watch it,
And know no more of stave or crotchet,
Than did the primitive Peruvians;
Or those old ante-queer-diluvians
That lived in the unwash'd world with Jubal,
Before that dirty blacksmith Tubal
By stroke on anvil, or by summ'at,
Found out, to his great surprise, the gamut.
I care no more for Cimarosa,
Than he did for Salvator Rosa,
Being no painter; and bad luck
Be mine, if I can bear that Gluck!
Old Tycho Brahe, and modern Herschel,
Had something in them; but who's Purcel?
The devil, with his foot so cloven,
For aught I care, may take Beethoven;
And, if the bargain does not suit,
I'll throw him Weber in to boot.
There's not the splitting of a splinter
To chuse 'twixt him last named, and Winter.
Of Doctor Pepusch old queen Dido
Knew just as much, God knows, as I do.
I would not go four miles to visit
Sebastian Bach (or Batch, which is it?);
No more I would for Bononcini.
As for Novello, or Rossini,
I shall not say a word to grieve 'em,
Because they're living; so I leave 'em.

CHARLES LAMB Poem addressed to William Ayrton 1836

Lamb's distaste for music was positively physical

Scientifically I could never be made to understand (yet have I taken some pains) what a note in music is; or how one note should differ from another. Much less in voices can I distinguish a soprano from a tenor. Only sometimes the thorough bass I contrive to guess at, from its being supereminently harsh and disagreeable. I tremble, however, for my misapplication of the simplest terms of *that* which I disclaim. While I profess my ignorance, I scarce know what to *say* I am ignorant of. I hate, perhaps, by misnomers. *Sostenuto* and *adagio* stand in the like relation of obscurity to me; and *Sol, Fa, Mi, Re,* is as conjuring as *Baralipton*.

It is hard to stand alone – in an age like this, – (constituted to the quick and critical perception of all harmonious combinations, I verily believe, beyond all preceding ages, since Jubal stumbled upon the gamut), to remain, as it were, singly unimpressible to the magic influences of an art, which is said to have such an especial stroke at soothing, elevating, and refining the passions. – Yet rather than break the candid current of my confessions, I must avow to you, that I have received a great deal more pain than pleasure from this so cried-up faculty.

I am constitutionally susceptible of noises. A carpenter's hammer, in a warm summer noon, will fret me into more than midsummer madness. But those unconnected, unset sounds are nothing to the measured malice of music. The ear is passive to those single strokes; willingly enduring stripes, while it hath no task to con. To music it cannot be passive. It will strive – mine at least will – 'spite of its inaptitude, to thrid the maze; like an unskilled eye painfully poring upon hieroglyphics. I have sat through an Italian Opera, till, for sheer pain, and inexplicable anguish, I have rushed out into the noisiest places of the crowded streets, to solace myself with sounds, which I was not obliged to follow, and get rid of the distracting torment of endless, fruitless, barren attention! I take refuge in the unpretending assemblage of honest, common-life sounds; – and the purgatory of the Enraged Musician becomes my paradise.

I have sat at an Oratorio (that profanation of the purposes of the cheerful playhouse) watching the faces of the auditory in the pit (what a contrast to Hogarth's Laughing Audience!) immovable, or affecting some faint emotion, – till (as some have said, that our occupations in the next world will be but a shadow of what delighted us in this) I have imagined myself in some cold Theatre in Hades, where some of the *forms* of the earthly one should be kept up, with none of the *enjoyment*; or like that –

> ———party in a parlour,
> All silent, and all DAMNED:

Above all, those insufferable concertos, and pieces of music, as they are called, do plague and embitter my apprehension. – Words are something; but to be exposed to an endless battery of mere sounds; to be long a-dying, to lie stretched upon a rack of roses; to keep up languor by unintermitted effort; to pile honey upon sugar, and sugar upon honey, to an interminable tedious sweetness; to fill up sound with feeling, and strain ideas to keep pace with it; to gaze on empty frames, and be forced to make the pictures for yourself; to read a book, *all stops*, and be obliged to supply the verbal matter; to invent extempore tragedies to answer to the vague gestures of an inexplicable rambling mime – these are faint shadows of what I have undergone from a series of the ablest-executed pieces of this empty *instrumental music*.

CHARLES LAMB *Essay of Elia* 1823

Ruskin had quite a (tin) ear for music; in a letter to his friend John Brown in 1881 he wrote: 'Beethoven always sounds to me like the upsetting of a bag of nails, with here and there an also dropped hammer.' Here is his reaction to *Die Meistersinger*

Of all the bête, clumsy, blundering, boggling, baboon-blooded stuff I ever saw on a human stage, that thing last night beat – as far as the story and acting went: and of all the affected, sapless, soulless, beginningless, endless, topless, bottomless, topsiturviest, tongs and boniest doggerel of sounds I ever endured the deadliness of, that eternity of nothing was the deadliest – as far as the sound went. I never was so relieved, so far as I can remember in my life, by the stopping of any sound – not excepting railway whistles – as I was by the cessation of the cobbler's bellowing; even the serenader's carica-ture twangle was a rest after it. As for the great Lied, I never made out where it began, or where it ended – except by the fellow's coming off the horse block.

JOHN RUSKIN Letter to Mrs Burne-Jones 30 June 1882

No musicians excel, like Wagner, in *painting* space and depth, both material and spiritual. This is a remark which severe intellectuals, and some of the best, could not help making on more than one occasion. His is the art of translating, by subtle gradations, all that is excessive, immense, ambitious in spiritual and natural mankind. On listening to this ardent and despotic music one feels at times as though one discovered again, painted in the depths of a gathering darkness torn asunder by dreams, the dizzy imaginations induced by opium.

CHARLES BAUDELAIRE *Richard Wagner et Tannhäuser à Paris* 1861

One of the great writers who really did understand music was Thomas Mann. Perhaps the single classic example is the lecture on Beethoven's Piano Sonata, Opus 111, in *Doctor Faustus*. It is delivered by one of Adrian Leverkühn's teachers, the German-American cathedral organist at Kaiseraschern, and apart from anything else is a noble example of triumph over a k-k-king sized speech defect

. . . Wendell Kretschmar honoured the principle, which we repeatedly heard from his lips, first formed by the English tongue, that to arouse interest was not a question of the interest of others, but of our own; it could only be done, but then infallibly was, if one was fundamentally interested in a thing oneself, so that when one talked about it one could hardly help drawing others in, infecting them with it, and so creating an interest up to then not present or dreamed of. And that was worth a great deal more than catering to one already existent.

It was a pity that our public gave him almost no opportunity to prove his theory. With us few, sitting at his feet in the yawning emptiness of the old hall with the numbered chairs, he proved it conclusively, for he held us charmed by things of which we should never have thought they could so capture our attention; even his frightful impediment did in the end only affect us as a stimulating and compelling expression of the zeal he felt. Often did we all nod at him consolingly when the calamity came to pass, and one or the other of the gentlemen would utter a soothing 'There, there!' or 'It's all right,' or 'Never mind!' Then the spasm would relax in a merry, apologetic smile and things would run on again in almost uncanny fluency, for a while.

What did he talk about? Well, the man was capable of spending a whole hour on the question: Why did Beethoven not write a third movement to the Piano Sonata Opus 111? It is without doubt a matter worth discussing. But think of it in the light of the posters outside the hall of activities for the Common Weal, or inserted in the Kaiseraschern *Railway Journal*, and ask yourself the amount of public interest it could arouse. People positively did not want to know why Op. 111 has only two movements. We who were present at the explanation had indeed an uncommonly enriching evening, and this although the sonata under discussion was to that date entirely unknown to us. Still it was precisely through these lectures that we got to know it, and as a matter of fact very much in detail; for Kretschmar played it to us on the inferior cottage piano that was all he could command, a grand piano not being granted him. He played it capitally despite the rumbling noise the instrument made: analysing its intellectual content with great impressiveness as he went, describing the circumstances under which it – and two others – were written and expatiating with caustic wit upon the master's own explanation of the reason why he had not done a third movement corresponding to the first. Beethoven, it seems, had calmly answered this question, put by his famulus, by saying that he had not had time and therefore had somewhat extended the second movement. No time! And he had said it 'calmly', to boot. The contempt for the questioner which lay in such an answer had obviously not been noticed, but it was justified contempt. And now the speaker described Beethoven's condition in the year 1820, when his hearing, attacked by a resistless ailment, was in progressive decay, and it had already become clear that he could no longer conduct his own works. Kretschmar told us about the rumours that the famous author was quite written out, his productive powers exhausted, himself incapable of larger enterprises, and busying himself like the old Haydn with writing down Scottish songs. Such reports had continually gained ground, because for several years no work of importance bearing his name had come on the market. But in the late autumn, returning to Vienna from Mödling, where he had spent the summer, the master had sat down and written these three compositions for the piano without, so to speak, once looking up from the notes, all in one burst, and gave notice of them to his patron, the Count of Brunswick, to reassure him as to his mental condition. And then Kretschmar talked about the Sonata in C minor, which indeed it was not easy to see as a well-rounded and intellectually digested work, and which had given his contemporary critics, and his friends as well, a hard aesthetic nut to crack. These friends and admirers, Kretschmar said, simply could not follow the man they revered beyond the height to which at the time of his maturity he had brought the symphony, the piano sonata, and the classical string quartet. In the works of the last period they stood with heavy hearts before a process of dissolution or alienation, of a mounting into an air no longer familiar or safe to meddle with: even before a *plus ultra*, wherein they had been able to see nothing else than a degeneration of tendencies previously present, an excess of introspection and speculation, an extravagance of minutiae and scientific musicality – applied sometimes to such simple material as the arietta theme of the monstrous movement of variations which forms the second part of this sonata. The theme of this movement goes through a hundred vicissitudes, a hundred worlds of rhythmic contrasts, at length outgrows itself, and is finally lost in giddy heights that one might call other-worldly or abstract. And in just that very way Beethoven's art had outgrown itself, risen out of the habitable regions of tradition, even before the startled gaze of human eyes, into spheres of the entirely and utterly and nothing-but personal – an ego painfully isolated in the absolute, isolated too from sense by the loss of his hearing; lonely prince of a realm of spirits, from whom now only a chilling breath issued to terrify his most willing contemporaries, standing as they did aghast at these communications of which only at moments, only by exception, they could understand anything at all.

So far, so good, said Kretschmar. And yet again, good or right only conditionally and incompletely. For one would usually connect with the conception of the merely personal, ideas of limitless subjectivity and of radical harmonic will to expression, in contrast to polyphonic objectivity (Kretschmar was concerned to have us impress upon our minds this distinction between harmonic subjectivity and polyphonic objectivity) and this equation, this contrast, here as altogether in the masterly late works, would simply not apply. As a matter of fact, Beethoven had been far more 'subjective', not to say far more 'personal', in his middle period than in his last, had been far more bent on taking all the flourishes, formulas, and conventions, of which music is certainly full, and consuming them in the personal expression, melting them into the subjective dynamic. The relation of the later Beethoven to the conventional, say in the last five piano sonatas, is, despite all the uniqueness and even uncanniness of the formal language, quite different, much more complaisant and easy-going. Untouched, untransformed by the subjective, convention often appeared in the late works, in a baldness, one might say exhaustiveness, an abandonment of self, with an effect more majestic and awful than any reckless plunge into the personal. In these forms, said the speaker, the subjective and the conventional assumed a new relationship, conditioned by death.

At this word Kretschmar stuttered violently; sticking fast at the first sound and executing a sort of machine-gun fire with his tongue on the roof of his mouth, with jaw and chin both quivering, before they settled on the vowel which told us what he meant. But when we had guessed it, it seemed hardly proper to take it out of his mouth and shout it to him, as we sometimes did, in jovial helpfulness. He had to say it himself and he did. Where greatness and death come together, he declared, there arises an objectivity tending to the conventional, which in its majesty leaves the most domineering subjectivity far behind, because therein the merely personal – which had after all been the surmounting of a tradition already brought to its peak – once more outgrew itself, in that it entered into the mythical, the collectively great and supernatural.

He did not ask if we understood that, nor did we ask ourselves. When he gave it as his view that the main point was to hear it, we fully agreed. It was in the light of what he had said, he went on, that the work he was speaking of in particular, Sonata Op. 111, was to be regarded. And then he sat down at the cottage piano and played us the whole composition out of his head, the first and the incredible second movement, shouting his comments into the midst of his playing and in order to make us conscious of the treatment demonstrating here and there in his enthusiasm by singing as well; altogether it made a spectacle partly entrancing, partly funny; and repeatedly greeted with merriment by his little audience. For as he had a very powerful attack and exaggerated the *forte*, he had to shriek extra loud to make what he said half-way intelligible and to sing with all the strength of his lungs to emphasize vocally what he played. With his lips he imitated what the hands played. 'Tum-tum, tum-tum tum-tr-r!' he went, as he played the grim and startling first notes of the first movement; he sang in a high falsetto the passages of melodic loveliness by which the ravaged and tempestuous skies of the composition are at intervals brightened as though by faint glimpses of light. At last he laid his hands in his lap, was quiet a moment, and then said: 'Here it comes!' and began the variations movement, the *'adagio molto semplice e cantabile'*.

The arietta theme, destined to vicissitudes for which in its idyllic innocence it would seem not to be born, is presented at once, and announced in sixteen bars, reducible to a motif which appears at the end of its first half, like a brief soul-cry – only three notes, a quaver, a semiquaver, and a dotted crotchet to be scanned as, say: 'heav-en's blue, lov-ers' pain, fare-thee well, on a-time, mead-ow-land' – and that is all. What now happens to this mild utterance, rhythmically, harmonically, contrapuntually, to this pensive, subdued formulation; with what its master blesses and to what condemns it; into what black nights and dazzling flashes, crystal spheres wherein coldness and heat, repose and ecstasy are one and the same, he flings it down and lifts it up; all that one may well call vast, strange, extravagantly magnificent, without thereby giving it a name, because it is quite truly nameless: and with labouring hands Kretschmar played us all those enormous transformations, singing at the same time with the greatest violence, 'Dim-dada!' and mingling his singing with shouts. 'These chains of trills! he yelled. 'These flourishes and cadenzas! Do you hear the conventions that are left in? Here – the language – is no longer – purified of the flourishes – but the flourishes – of the appearance – of their subjective – domination – the appearance – of art is thrown off – at last – art always throws off the appearance of art. Dim-dada! Do listen, how here – the melody is dragged down by the centrifugal weight of chords! It becomes static, monotonous – twice D, three times D, one after the other – the chords do it – dim-dada! Now notice what happens here –'

It was extraordinarily difficult to listen to his shouts and to the highly complicated music both at once. We all tried. We strained, leaning forward, hands between knees, looking by turn at his hands and his mouth. The characteristic of the movement of course is the wide gap between bass and treble, between the right and the left hand, and a moment comes, an utterly extreme situation, when the poor little motif seems to hover alone and forsaken above a giddy yawning abyss – a procedure of awe-inspiring unearthliness, to which then succeeds a distressful making-of-itself-small, a start of fear as it were, that such a thing could happen. Much else happens before the end. But when it ends and while it ends, something comes, after so much rage, persistence, obstinacy, extravagance: something entirely unexpected and touching in its mildness and goodness. With the motif passed through many vicissitudes, which takes leave and so doing becomes itself entirely leave-taking, a parting wave and call, with this D G G occurs a slight change, it experiences a small melodic expansion. After an introductory C, it puts a C sharp before the D, so that it no longer scans 'heav-en's blue', 'mead-owland', but 'O-thou heaven's blue', 'Green-est meadowland', 'Fare-thee well for aye'; and this added C sharp is the most moving, consolatory, pathetically reconciling thing in the world. It is like having one's hair or cheek stroked, lovingly, understandingly, like a deep and silent farewell look. It blesses the object, the frightfully harried formulation, with overpowering humanity, lies in parting so gently on the hearer's heart in eternal farewell that the eyes run over. 'Now for-get the pain,' it says. 'Great was – God in us.' ''Twas all – but a dream.' 'Friendly – be to me.' Then it breaks off. Quick, hard triplets hasten to a conclusion with which any other piece might have ended.

Kretschmar did not return from the piano to his desk. He sat on his revolving stool with his face turned towards us, in the same position as ours, bent over, hands between his knees, and in a few words brought to an end his lecture on why Beethoven had not written a third movement to Op. 111. We had only needed, he said, to hear the piece to answer the question ourselves. A third movement? A new

approach? A return after this parting – impossible! It had happened
that the sonata had come, in the second, enormous movement, to an
end, an end without any return. And when he said 'the sonata', he
meant not only this one in C minor, but the sonata in general, as a
species, as traditional art-form; it itself was here at an end, brought to
its end, it had fulfilled its destiny, reached its goal, beyond which
there was no going, it cancelled and resolved itself, it took leave – the
gesture of farewell of the D G G motif, consoled by the C sharp, was a
leave-taking in this sense too, great as the whole piece itself, the
farewell of the sonata form.

With this Kretschmar went away, accompanied by thin but prolonged applause, and we went too, not a little reflective, weighted
down by all these novelties. Most of us, as usual, as we put on our
coats and hats and walked out, hummed bemusedly to ourselves the
impression of the evening, the theme-generating motif of the second
movement, in its original and its leave-taking form, and for a long time
we heard it like an echo from the remoter streets into which the
audience dispersed, the quiet night streets of the little town: 'Fare –
thee well,' 'fare thee well for aye,' 'Great was God in us.'

THOMAS MANN *Doctor Faustus* 1947

But literary attitudes, even to Beethoven, vary to an astonishing degree

'They played Beethoven's Kreutzer Sonata,' he continued. 'Do you
know the first presto? You do?' he cried. 'Ugh! Ugh! It is a terrible
thing, that sonata. And especially that part. And in general music is a
dreadful thing! What is it? I don't understand it. What is music? What
does it do? And why does it do what it does? They say music exalts the
soul. Nonsense, it is not true! It has an effect – an awful effect – I am
speaking of myself – but not of an exalting kind. It has neither an
exalting nor a debasing effect, but it produces agitation. How can I put
it? Music makes me forget myself, my real position; it transports me to
some other position, not my own. Under the influence of music it
seems to me that I feel what I do not really feel, that I understand what
I do not understand, that I can do what I cannot do. I explain it by the
fact that music acts like yawning, like laughter: I am not sleepy, but I
yawn when I see someone yawning; there is nothing for me to laugh
at, but I laugh when I hear people laughing.

'Music carries me immediately and directly into the mental condition in which the man was who composed it. My soul merges with
his, and together with him I pass from one condition into another; but

why this happens, I don't know. You see, he who wrote, let us say, the Kreutzer Sonata – Beethoven – knew of course why he was in that condition; that condition caused him to do certain actions, and therefore that condition had a meaning for him, but for me – none at all. That is why music only agitates and doesn't lead to a conclusion. Well, when a military march is played, the soldiers step to the music, and the music has achieved its object. A dance is played, I dance, and the music has achieved its object. Mass has been sung, I receive Communion, and that music too has reached a conclusion. Otherwise it is only agitating, and what ought to be done in that agitation is lacking. That is why music sometimes acts so dreadfully, so terribly. In China, music is a State affair. And that is as it should be. How can one allow anyone who pleases to hypnotize another, or many others, and do what he likes with them? And especially that this hypnotist should be the first immoral man who turns up?

'It is a terrible instrument in the hands of any chance user! Take that Kreutzer Sonata, for instance, how can that first presto be played in a drawing room among ladies in low-necked dresses? To hear that played, to clap a little, and then to eat ices and talk of the latest scandal? Such things should only be played on certain important significant occasions, and then only when certain actions answering to such music are wanted; play it then and do what the music has moved you to. Otherwise an awakening of energy and feeling unsuited both to the time and the place, to which no outlet is given, cannot but act harmfully.

LEO TOLSTOY The Kreutzer Sonata 1889

The Song Against Songs

The song of the sorrow of Melisande is a weary
    song and a dreary song,
The glory of Mariana's grange had got into great
    decay,
The song of the Raven Never More has never been
    called a cheery song,
And the brightest things in Baudelaire are anything
    else but gay.

But who will write us a riding song
Or a hunting song or a drinking song,
Fit for them that arose and rode
When day and the wine were red?
But bring me a quart of claret out,
And I will write you a clinking song,
A song of war and a song of wine
And a song to wake the dead.

The song of the fury of Fragolette is a florid song
    and a torrid song,
The song of the sorrow of Tara is sung to a harp
    unstrung,
The song of the cheerful Shropshire Lad I consider
    a perfectly horrid song,
And the song of the happy Futurist is a song that
    can't be sung.

But who will write us a riding song
Or a fighting song or a drinking song,
Fit for the fathers of you and me,
That know how to think and thrive?
But the song of Beauty and Art and Love
Is simply an utterly stinking song,
To double you up and drag you down
And damn your soul alive.

G. K. CHESTERTON *The Flying Inn* 1914

Singers

The silver Swan, who living had no Note,
When death approached unlocked her silent throat,
Leaning her breast against the reedy shore,
Thus sung her first and last, and sung no more.
Farewell all joys, O death come close mine eyes,
More Geese then Swans now live, more fools than wise.

ANON. from Orlando Gibbons' *First Set of Madrigals* 1612

Swans sing before they die. 'Twere no bad thing
Should certain persons die before they sing.

SAMUEL TAYLOR COLERIDGE

Orpheus with his lute made trees
  And the mountain-tops that freeze
Bend themselves; that's more than you
  With your disgusting voice can do.

J. B. MORTON 'On a lady singing' 1932

Nor cold, nor stern, my soul! yet I detest
  These scented rooms where, to a gaudy throng,
Heaves the proud harlot her distended breast
  In intricacies of laborious song.

SAMUEL TAYLOR COLERIDGE

So bright is thy beauty, so charming thy song,
As had drawn both the beasts and their Orpheus along;
But such is thy avarice, and such is thy pride,
That the beasts must have starved, and the poet have died.

ALEXANDER POPE 'On Mrs Tofts, a celebrated opera singer'

Reasons briefly set downe by th'auctor, to perswade every one to learne to sing.

First it is a Knowledge easely taught, and quickly learned where there is a good Master, and an apt Scoller.

2 The exercise of singing is delightfull to Nature & good to preserve the health of Man.

3 It doth strengthen all the parts of the brest, & doth open the pipes.

4 It is a singular good remedie for a stuttering & stammering in the speech.

5 It is the best meanes to procure a perfect pronunciation & to make a good Orator.

6 It is the onely way to know where Nature hath bestowed the benefit of a good voyce: which guift is so rare, as there is not one among a thousand, that hath it: and in many, that excellent guift is lost, because they want Art to expresse Nature.

7 There is not any Musicke of Instruments whatsoever, comparable to that which is made of the voyces of Men, where the voyces are good, and the same well sorted and ordered.

8 The better the voyce is, the meeter it is to honour and serve God there-with: and the voyce of man is chiefly to be imployed to that ende.

> *omnis spiritus laudet Dominum.*

Since singing is so good a thing,
I wish all men would learne to sing.

WILLIAM BYRD *Psalmes, Sonets, & Songs* 1588

I have never met a single German Kapellmeister or musical-director who could really *sing* a melody, be his voice good or bad. No, music to them is an abstraction, a mixture of syntax, arithmetic and gymnastics. . . .

The human voice is the practical foundation of music, and however far the latter may progress upon the path of its choice, the boldest expressions of the composer or the most daring bravura of the instrumental virtuoso must always return to the essence of song for its ultimate vindication. Thus I maintain that elementary instruction in singing must be made obligatory for every musician, and in the successful organisation of a singing-school upon these lines should be found the basis for the intended all-embracing school of music. Only then should it extend frontiers which it has been seen to reach with the need to instruct the singer in the elements of harmony and rudimentary analysis of musical composition.

RICHARD WAGNER *About Conducting* 1869

The Physitians will tell you, that the exercise of Musicke is a great lengthner of the life, by stirring and reviving of the Spirits, holding a secret sympathy with them; Besides, the exercise of singing openeth the breast and pipes; it is an enemy to melancholly and dejection of the mind, which St. *Chrysostome* truely calleth, *The Devils Bath*. Yea, a curer of some diseases: in *Apuglia*, in *Italy*, and thereabouts, it is most certaine, that those who are stung with the *Tarantula*, are cured onely by Musicke. Beside, the aforesaid benefit of singing, it is a most ready helpe for a bad pronunciation, and distinct speaking, which I have heard confirmed by many great Divines: yea, in my selfe have knowne many Children to have bin holpen of their stammering in speech, onely by it.

HENRY PEACHAM *The Compleat Gentleman* 1634

There is a good Wodehouse story about a diffident young man who overcomes a chronic stammer by singing at a totally unknown young lady in a train. And there is another nice stuttering incident recorded by Michael Kelly, the Irish tenor who doubled the roles of Don Basilio and Don Curzio in the first performance of *Le Nozze di Figaro*. Tradition in the making?

In the sestetto, in the second act, (which was Mozart's favourite piece of the whole opera,) I had a very conspicuous part, as the Stuttering Judge. All through the piece I was to stutter; but in the sestetto, Mozart requested I would not, for if I did, I should spoil his music. I told him, that although it might appear very presumptuous in a lad like me to differ with him on this point, I did, and was sure, the way in which I intended to introduce the stuttering, would not interfere with the other parts, but produce an effect; besides, it was certainly not in nature, that I should stutter all through the part, and when I came to the sestetto speak plain; and after that piece of music was over, return to stuttering; and, I added, (apologizing at the same time, for my apparent want of deference and respect in placing my opinion in opposition to that of the great Mozart,) that unless I was allowed to perform the part as I wished, I would not perform it at all.

Mozart at last consented that I should have my own way, but doubted the success of the experiment. Crowded houses proved that nothing ever on the stage produced a more powerful effect; the audience were convulsed with laughter, in which Mozart himself joined. The Emperor repeatedly cried out Bravo! and the piece was loudly applauded and encored. When the opera was over, Mozart came on the stage to me, and shaking me by both hands, said, 'Bravo! young man, I feel obliged to you; and acknowledge you to have been in the right and myself in the wrong.' There was certainly a risk run, but I felt within myself I could give the effect I wished, and the event proved that I was not mistaken.

MICHAEL KELLY 1786 *Reminiscences*

Between the late seventeenth and early nineteenth centuries the tenor voice, of which Michael Kelly's was an example, became something of a rarity in opera – and almost unknown in the serious variety, where it was forced ruthlessly out of all the best male roles by those Hollywood glamour boys of the eighteenth century, the castrati

At Ranelagh I heard the famous Tenducci, a thing from Italy: it looks for all the world like a man, though they say it is not. The voice, to be sure, is neither man's nor woman's; but it is more melodious than either, and it warbled so divinely, that, while I listened, I really thought myself in paradise.

TOBIAS SMOLLETT *Humphrey Clinker* 1771

By far the most famous of all the castrati was Carlo Broschi, known as Farinelli. Though no actor ('during the time of his singing he was as motionless as a statue' says Dr Burney), his vocal agility and, in particular, the amazing length of his breath were such as to

excite incredulity even in those who heard him, who, though unable to detect the artifice, imagined him to have had the latent help of some instrument by which the tone was continued, while he renewed his powers by respiration.

Burney paid a personal visit to Farinelli, then living in retirement at Bologna, on 25 August 1770

His large room, in which is a billiard-table, is furnished with pictures of great personages, chiefly sovereign princes, who have been his patrons, among whom are two emperors, one empress, three kings of Spain, two princes of Asturias, a king of Sardinia, a prince of Savoy, a king of Naples, a princess of Asturias, two queens of Spain, and Pope Benedict the XIVth. . . . He shewed me a number of pictures of himself, painted during that time, from one of which, by Amiconi, there is a print. He has an English sweep-chimney boy playing with a cat, and an apple-woman with a barrow by the same hand . . . he has likewise a curious English clock, with little figures playing in concert on the guitar, the violin, and violoncello, whose arms and fingers are always moved by the same pendulum.

He speaks much of the respect and gratitude he owes to the English. When I dined with him it was on an elegant service of plate, made in England at the time he was there.

They spoke of Farinelli's remarkable career, and Burney no doubt took the opportunity of checking at first hand one of its most famous episodes, from the singer's early years in Rome

During the run of an opera, there was a struggle every night between him and a famous player on the trumpet, in a song accompanied by that instrument: this, at first, seemed amicable and merely sportive, till the audience began to interest themselves in the contest, and to take different sides: after severally swelling out a note, in which each manifested the power of his lungs, and tried to rival the other in brilliancy and force, they both had a swell and a shake together, by thirds, which was continued so long, while the audience eagerly awaited the event, that both seemed to be exhausted; and in fact, the trumpeter, wholly spent gave it up, thinking, however, his antagonist as much tired as himself, and that it would be a drawn battle; when Farinelli with a smile on his countenance, shewing he had been only sporting with him all this time, broke out all at once in the same breath, with fresh vigour, and not only swelled and shook the note, but ran the most rapid and difficult divisions, and was at last silenced only by the acclamations of the audience.

. . . In the year 1734, he came into England, where every one knows who heard, or has heard of him, what an effect his surprising talents had upon the audience: it was extasy! rapture! enchantment!

In the famous air *Son qual Nave*, which was composed by his brother, the first note he sung was taken with such delicacy, swelled by minute degrees to such an amazing volume, and afterwards diminished in the same manner to a mere point, that it was applauded for full five minutes. After this he set off with such brilliancy and rapidity of execution, that it was difficult for the violins of those days to keep pace with him. In short, he was to all other singers as superior as the famous horse Childers was to all other running-horses; but it was not only in speed that he excelled, for he had now every excellence of every great singer united. In his voice, strength, sweetness and compass; in his style, the tender, the graceful and the rapid. Indeed he possessed such powers as never met before, or since, in any one human being; powers that were irresistible, and which must have subdued every hearer; the learned and the ignorant, the friend and the foe.

With these talents he went into Spain in the year 1737, with a full design to return into England . . . but the first day he performed before the king and queen of Spain, it was determined that he should be taken into the service of the court, to which he was ever after wholly appropriated, not once being suffered to sing again in public. A pension was then settled on him of upwards of £2000 sterling a year.

He told me, that for the first ten years of his residence at the court of Spain, during the life of Philip the Vth, he sung every night to that monarch the same four airs, of which two were composed by Hasse, *Pallido il sole*, and *Per questo dolce amplesso*. I forget the others, but one was a minuet which he used to vary at his pleasure . . .

CHARLES BURNEY The Present State of Music in France and Italy 1773

Eighteenth-century sopranos, unlike the tenors, did not find themselves totally eclipsed by the castrati. Indeed they counted some redoubtable champions among their number

Mrs. BILLINGTON's fame continued to spread while her never ceasing ardour and assiduity were day by [day] enlarging her stocks of knowledge acquirement and facility. She was a constant performer at the concerts of the metropolis, and she sung at the memorable Westminster Abbey performances. She remained at Covent Garden till 1793, when she adopted a resolution to retire from public life, which she vainly imagined she had firmness enough to adhere to. At the instigation of her husband and her brother she was induced to make a continental tour, with a view solely to amusement, and to this intent she declined all letters of introduction, intending to travel incognito. For some time they succeeded and passed along without notice; but at Naples, the English Ambassador, Sir W. Hamilton, penetrated their secret and persuaded Mrs. B. and Mr. W. to perform in private before the King and Queen, at Caserto, a country residence. The gratification they received induced their Majesties to request Mrs. BILLINGTON to perform at the Great Theatre of St. Carlo, then thought to be the finest opera establishment in the world. She accordingly in May, 1794, made her debut in *Inez di Castro*, which was composed expressly for her, by the Maestro Francesco Bianchi, who wrote an opera worthy the supereminent ability of his primadonna. Her success was complete, for indeed her celebrity had made her name known in Italy, and previous to her quitting England the Venetian Ambassador had been in treaty with her to accept an engagement, which however she broke.

Mrs. BILLINGTON's performance at Naples was interrupted by a sudden and affecting event. On the second night as Mr. BILLINGTON was seeking his hat, to accompany his wife to the theatre, he fell down in a fit of appoplexy and died in the arms of Bianchi, at the residence of the Bishop of Winchester. Nor was this the only circumstance that impeded her progress. About this time an eruption of Mount Vesuvius took place, and the superstitious bigotry of the Neapolitans attributed the visitation to the permission granted to a Heretic to perform at St. Carlo. Serious apprehensions were entertained by Mrs. B's. friends for the consequences of such an impression. Her talents, however triumphed, she renewed her performance, and no prima donna was ever more rapturously received in the country where the opera is best cultivated and best understood.

JOHN S. SAINSBURY A Dictionary of Musicians 1825

Not all English sopranos were equally well received, however

. . . my servant informed me that a lady and gentleman had called upon me, who said they came from England, and requested to see me at their hotel. I called the next morning, and saw the gentleman, who said his name was Botterelli, that he was the Italian poet of the King's Theatre in the Haymarket, and that his wife was an English woman, and a principal singer at Vauxhall, Ranelagh, the Pantheon, &c. Her object in visiting Vienna was to give a concert, to be heard by the Emperor, and if she gave that satisfaction, (which she had no doubt she would,) to accept of an engagement at the Royal Theatre; and he added, that she had letters for the first nobility in Vienna.

The lady came into the room; she was a very fine woman, and seemed sinking under the conscious load of her own attractions. – She really had powerful letters of recommendation. Prince Charles Lichtenstein granted her his protection, and there was such interest made for her, that the Emperor himself signified his Royal intention of honouring her concert with his presence. Every thing was done for her; – the orchestra and singers were engaged; – the concert began to a crowded house, but, I must premise we had no rehearsal.

At the end of the first act, the beauteous Syren, led into the orchestra by her caro sposo, placed herself just under the Emperor's box, the orchestra being on the stage. She requested me to accompany her song on the piano-forte. – I of course consented. Her air and manner spoke 'dignity and love.' The audience sat in mute and breathless expectation. The doubt was, whether she would melt into their ears in a fine cantabile, or burst upon them with a brilliant bravura. I struck the chords of the symphony – silence reigned – when, to the dismay and astonishment of the brilliant audience, she bawled out, without feeling or remorse, voice or time, or indeed one note in tune, the hunting song of 'Tally ho!' in all its pure originality. She continued shrieking out Tally ho! tally ho! in a manner and tone so loud and dissonant, that they were enough to blow off the roof of the house. The audience jumped up terrified; some shrieked with alarm, some hissed, others hooted, and many joined in the unknown yell, in order to propitiate her. The Emperor called me to him, and asked me in Italian (what tally ho! meant?) – I replied I did not know, and literally, at that time, I did *not*.

His Majesty, the Emperor, finding, that even *I*, a native of Great Britain, either could not, or would not, explain the purport of the mysterious words, retired with great indignation from the theatre, and the major part of the audience, convinced by His Majesty's sudden retreat that they contained some horrible meaning, followed the Royal example. The ladies hid their faces with their fans, and mothers were heard in the lobbies cautioning their daughters on the way out, never to repeat the dreadful expression of 'tally ho,' nor venture to ask any of their friends for a translation of it.

The next day, when I saw the husband of 'tally ho,' he abused the taste of the people of Vienna, and said that the song which they did not know how to appreciate, had been sung by the celebrated Mrs. Wrighton at Vauxhall, and was a great favourite all over England. Thus, however, ended the exhibition of English taste; and Signora Tally ho! with her Italian poet, went *hunting* elsewhere, and never returned to Vienna, at least during my residence.

MICHAEL KELLY *c.* 1784 *Reminiscences*

Here is Dickens (or rather, Boz) at Vauxhall, just about fifty years after Mme Botterelli's reputed successes there

At this moment the bell rung; the people scampered away, pell-mell, to the spot from whence the sound proceeded; and we, from the mere force of habit, found ourself running among the first, as if for very life.

It was for the concert in the orchestra. A small party of dismal men in cocked hats were 'executing' the overture to *Tancredi*, and a numerous assemblage of ladies and gentlemen, with their families, had rushed from their half-emptied stout mugs in the supper boxes, and crowded to the spot. Intense was the low murmur of admiration when a particularly small gentleman, in a dress coat, led on a particularly tall lady in a blue sarcenet pelisse and bonnet of the same, ornamented with large white feathers, and forthwith commenced a plaintive duet.

We knew the small gentleman well; we had seen a lithographed semblance of him, on many a piece of music, with his mouth wide open as if in the act of singing; a wine-glass in his hand; and a table with two decanters and four pine-apples on it in the background. The tall lady, too, we had gazed on, lost in raptures of admiration, many and many a time – how different people *do* look by daylight, and without punch, to be sure! It was a beautiful duet: first the small gentleman asked a question, and then the tall lady answered it; then the small gentleman and the tall lady sang together most melodiously; then the small gentleman went though a little piece of vehemence by himself, and got very tenor indeed, in the excitement of his feelings, to which the tall lady responded in a similar manner; then the small gentleman had a shake or two, after which the tall lady had the same, and then they both merged imperceptibly into the original air: and the band wound themselves up to a pitch of fury, and the small gentleman handed the tall lady out, and the applause was rapturous.

CHARLES DICKENS *Sketches by Boz* 1836

And then there were the great divas of the nineteenth and indeed the twentieth centuries

Melba's reign at Covent Garden lasted for many years, and her power over the management was so real that she was consulted about such details as the colour and design of new curtains. Sir Thomas Beecham (another autocrat) described the situation which arose when he ordered that 'her' dressing-room in Covent Garden was to be repainted without her knowledge. For a long time her contract contained a clause declaring that no artist appearing at Covent Garden was to receive more than she did, so that she was paid in guineas to Caruso's pounds. This was the age when every well-dressed man wore a tie-pin, and it was with tie-pins that Melba rewarded her male colleagues and subordinates. A tenor or a baritone high in her favour would receive a tie-pin with her initial 'M' in diamonds; the less exalted found that the initial was in gold, while for attentive stage-door keepers it was in blue enamel.

Melba had all the experienced artist's sensitivity to an audience's reactions. Once at an afternoon concert in Caernarvon, the audience was stolid rather than responsive. With half the programme behind her, she determined to break down the barriers. She addressed her apparently staid Welsh listeners. 'All my life,' she said, 'I've been hearing about the wonderful voices of the Welsh, and their magnificent choral singing. I wonder, may I ask you to sing for me? Perhaps you would sing *Aberystwyth*.'

The audience rose like one man and the splendid tune rolled overpoweringly forth with a fervour that almost raised the roof. The rest of the concert was an overwhelming triumph for Melba.

In Australia as well as in England she imposed authority over the country and its social life as well as over the musical theatre. 'The Melba Opera Company' toured the Australian cities with artists of the first rank, drawn to the antipodes by Melba's prestige.

After she had sung with Dino Borgioli at Monte Carlo, she ensured his engagement in Australia by means of a telegram which read: 'We must have Borgioli. Fine voice, good legs.' Borgioli told me of Dame Nellie's speech on the last night of the season in Melbourne that year. She stood, surrounded by bouquets, thanked the audience for its support and gave her special thanks to her 'dear public' for attending performances on the nights when she was not singing. But it was not only Melba's voice which made her Australian operatic ventures successful, although the Australian tradition of music began with her; her sheer efficiency as an organiser made a real success of whatever she handled with concentration . . .

Only once did Melba shake the Australian people's devotion to their star. When Clara Butt and Kennerley Rumford were about to tour Australia for the first time, draining the country of money with fourteen concerts in Sydney, another fourteen in Melbourne and as many in every other city as its population warranted, the Rumfords asked Melba's advice. What sort of programmes, they wondered, would Australians like? 'Sing 'em muck,' said Melba, bluntly. 'It's all they understand.'

Forty years later, when Clara Butt wrote her *Memoirs*, she recalled the advice she had been given by the greatest musical personality Australia had produced, and caused an uproar. Cables of denial sped across the oceans from Australia, for loyalty had somehow to be recovered. 'How could I have said that?' asked Melba plaintively of the Australian press. 'I have always had the greatest admiration for the taste and discrimination of my Australian audiences.' A mutual friend asked Melba if it were true that she had really given Clara Butt this dangerous advice. 'Of course not,' retorted Melba; 'in Clara's case, it wasn't necessary.'

IVOR NEWTON At the Piano 1966

Callas had an absolute contempt for merely beautiful singing. Although she was preoccupied all her career with bel canto, that is, beautiful singing, she was one of the few Italian artists in my memory who quite deliberately produced significant signs of a particular dramatic intensity or meaning on a syllable or even on a single consonant – sometimes over a long phrase to convey dramatic meaning. She herself often said, 'After all, some of the texts we have to sing are not distinctive poetry. I know that to convey the dramatic effect to the audience and to myself I must produce sounds that are not beautiful. I don't mind if they are ugly as long as they are true.'

I am afraid that Callas may harm a generation of singers. Young singers try to imitate not her virtues but some of those things that she did deliberately and could only do because of her intelligence and because she knew the dramatic purpose.

Most admirable of all her qualities, however, were her taste, elegance and deeply musical use of ornamentation in all its forms and complications, the weighting and length of every appoggiatura, the smooth incorporation of the turn in melodic lines, the accuracy and pacing of her trills, the seemingly inevitable timing of her portamentos, varying their curve with enchanting grace and meaning. There were innumerable exquisite felicities – minuscule portamentos from one note to its nearest neighbor, or over widespread intervals – and changes of color that were pure magic. In these aspects of bel canto she was supreme mistress of that art.

But . . . can you, dear reader, swear that you have never winced at or flinched from some of her high notes, those that were more like pitched screams than musical sounds? Or those she waved at you like Isolde's scarf, so unsteady they could be mistaken for labored trills? They were brave triumphs of will, but remote from the beauty that the term bel canto implies. A couple of years ago, I asked her what she was doing with her time – 'I play and study our records of *Lucia* and *Tosca* and then try to get back to those vocal positions I used then.' She would not or could not accept the fact that after fifty no woman can expect to have the upward range and facility she had at thirty. She was particularly interesting about the pirated recordings made in Mexico in 1951 and 1952. 'Don't listen to them – they're awful! I was singing like a wildcat. Something must have happened to me between these and our *Lucia*, *Puritani* and *Tosca*.' That something was the contract with La Scala, which she had been hoping and striving for in the four years since her debut in Verona, and the luxury and discipline of working under ideal conditions with de Sabata. She knew she had arrived.

Great directors, particularly Visconti and Zeffirelli, like great conductors, invariably got the best out of her. The challenge of a great conductor and/or stage director curiously paralleled her reactions to a less enthusiastic reception than she expected and felt she deserved after a first act. She would pace her dressing room with a hard glint in her eyes and mutter, 'I'll teach those stinkers out there,' or sometimes, 'Don't worry! When I'm furious I'm always at my best.' Then she would sing the rest of the performance with incandescent inner fire and aggressive flamboyance. During several *Sonnambulas* I sat in Ghiringhelli's box watching her move down to the footlights to hurl 'Ah, non giunge' into the very teeth of the gallery. The Scala gallery was a vital factor in Meneghini's operations, especially the seats near the proscenium, which he infiltrated with young fans to throw bouquets to his wife when she took curtain calls. One evening the opponents got there first: fewer floral tributes were mixed in the rain of bunches of small vegetables from the gallery. Callas, trading on her well-known myopia, sniffed each bunch as she picked it up; vegetables she threw into the orchestra pit, while flowers were graciously handed to her colleagues. Not even Strehler could have staged that improvised scene better.

WALTER LEGGE in *On and Off the Record* 1982

Verdi himself, of course, had provided the precedent for less than beautiful singing a century earlier

I know that you are rehearsing *Macbeth*, and as this is an opera that interests me more than all my others, I hope that you will allow me to say a few words about it. The part of Lady Macbeth has been given to Madame Tadolini, and I am surprised that she should have agreed to do it. You know how highly I esteem Mme Tadolini, and she knows it herself; but in the interests of everybody concerned I think I must make one or two comments. La Tadolini has too many gifts for this part! Perhaps you will think this absurd!! . . . But la Tadolini is good and beautiful in appearance, and I want Lady Macbeth evil and ugly. La Tadolini sings perfectly, but I want *Lady* not to sing. La Tadolini has a stupendous voice, clear, limpid and powerful, but I want for Lady a voice that is harsh, suppressed, sullen. About la Tadolini's voice there is something angelic; for Lady I want something devilish. . . .

Please note that there are two crucial pieces in the opera: the duet between Lady and her husband, and the sleep-walking scene. If these fail to come off, the whole opera collapses – and these pieces must absolutely not be sung.

GIUSEPPE VERDI Letter 23 November 1848

Nevertheless, the divas of the nineteenth century preferred to ignore this kind of realism in favour of a cosier operatic tradition that kept their audiences happy. Shaw, as usual, complained. Here he is on *Traviata* with Emma Albani, the great Victorian soprano of Canadian origin, and the French baritone Victor Maurel, who had already been Verdi's first Iago and was, two years later, to be the first Falstaff

After a fortnight of Gluck, Gounod, Bizet, and Wagner, Covent Garden relapsed exhausted into the arms of La Traviata; and the audience promptly dwindled. Albani played Violetta on the occasion; and it is proper, if somewhat personal, to say that on her part too there has been a certain dwindling which does much to reconcile the imagination to her impersonations of operatic heroines. Not, of course, that she can by any conceivable stretch of fancy be accepted as a typical case of pulmonary consumption. But one has only to recall the eminent prima donnas who began their careers needing only a touch of blue under the eyes to make them look plausibly phthisical, and progressed with appalling rapidity to a condition in which no art of the maker-up could prevent them from looking insistently dropsical, to feel abundantly grateful to Albani for having so trained herself that nobody can say anything worse of her than that she is pleasingly plump. Indeed, in one way her figure is just the thing for La Traviata, as it does away with the painful impression which the last act produces whenever there is the faintest realism about it. Even in the agonies of death Albani robs the sick bed and the medicine bottles of half their terrors by her reassuring air of doing as well as can be expected.

. . . I read the promise of Maurel's appearance as Germont with some hope of witnessing a beginning of reform. Maurel is courageous in matters of costume: his Holbein dress as Valentine, his mouse-coloured Mephistopheles, his stupendous helmet in Lohengrin, which reminded us all of the head-dress of the Indian in West's picture of the death of Wolfe, had proved him ready for any sacrifice of tradition to accuracy. I fully expected to see Germont enter fearlessly in frock-coat, tall hat, and primrose gloves with three braids down the back. Judge of my disappointment when he marched forward in a magnificent Vandyke costume, without even an umbrella to save appearances. I knew then that he wanted, not to play Germont, but simply to sing *Di provenza*. However, to do him justice, he did not treat the part with utter frivolity. He came in rudely with his hat on; and when he found that Violetta had a noble soul, he took the hat off, like a gentleman, and put it on a chair. I instantly foresaw that Albani, when next overcome by emotion, would sit on it. So breathless became my anticipation that I could hardly attend to the intervening duet. At last she did sit on it; and never ·would that hat have graced Maurel's temples again if it had been historically accurate. This, then, I presume, is the explanation of the anachronism on Maurel's part. Albani must have refused to give up the business of sitting on Germont's hat, thereby forcing him to adopt one that would bend but not break under an exceptional pressure of circumstances . . .

BERNARD SHAW 1891 *Music in London*

Nineteenth-century audience loyalties became passionate, and farewell performances tended to become a farce

Great was the applause . . . and then the comedy began. Mr Ganz, whilst the house was shouting and clapping uproariously, deliberately took up his *bâton* and started Moszkowski's Serenata in D. The audience took its cue at once, and would not have Moszkowski. After a prolonged struggle, Mr Ganz gave up in despair; and out tripped the *diva*, bowing her acknowledgments in the character of a petted and delighted child. When she vanished there was more cheering than ever. Mr Ganz threatened the serenata again; but in vain. He appealed to the sentinels of the greenroom; and these shook their heads, amidst roars of protest from the audience, and at last, with elaborate gesture, conveyed in dumb show that they dare not, could not, would not, must not, venture to approach Patti again. Mr Ganz, with well-acted desolation, went on with the serenata, not one note of which was heard. Again he appealed to the sentinels; and this time they waved their hands expansively in the direction of South America, to indicate that the prima donna was already on her way thither. On this the audience showed such sudden and unexpected signs of giving in that the diva tripped out again, bowing, wafting kisses, and successfully courting fresh thunders of applause. Will not some sincere friend of Madame Patti's tell her frankly that she is growing too big a girl for this sort of thing, which imposes on nobody – not even on the infatuated gentlemen who write columns about her fans and jewels. No: the queens of song should leave the coquetry of the footlights to the soubrettes.

BERNARD SHAW Review 23 January 1889

Loyalties often transcended the opera house

. . . Housemaids are notoriously early risers, and can usually count upon three clear hours when a house belongs to them alone. But not at Alconleigh. Uncle Matthew was always, winter and summer alike, out of his bed by five a.m., and it was then his habit to wander about, looking like Great Agrippa in his dressing-gown, and drinking endless cups of tea out of a thermos flask, until about seven, when he would have his bath. Breakfast for my uncle, my aunt, family and guests alike, was sharp at eight, and unpunctuality was not tolerated. Uncle Matthew was no respecter of other people's early morning sleep, and after five o'clock one could not count on any, for he raged round the house, clanking cups of tea, shouting at his dogs, roaring at the housemaids, cracking the stock whips which he had brought back from Canada on the lawn with a noise greater than gun-fire, and all to the accompaniment of Galli Curci on his gramophone, an abnormally loud one with an enormous horn, through which would be shrieked 'Una voce poco fa' – 'The Mad Song' from *Lucia* – 'Lo, hear the gen-tel lar-ha-hark' – and so on, played at top speed, thus rendering them even higher and more screeching than they ought to be.

Nothing reminds me of my childhood days at Alconleigh so much as those songs. Uncle Matthew played them incessantly for years, until the spell was broken when he went all the way to Liverpool to hear Galli Curci in person. The disillusionment caused by her appearance was so great that the records remained ever after silent, and were replaced by the deepest bass voices that money could buy.

'Fearful the death of the diver must be,
Walking alone in the de-he-he-he-he-epths of the sea'
or
'Drake is going West, lads'.

These were, on the whole, welcomed by the family, as rather less piercing at early dawn. . . .

NANCY MITFORD *The Pursuit of Love* 1945

. . . Recently the twelve [red-bearded] dwarfs bought a female sing-ing-mouse called Royal Gertrude on the hire-purchase system – ninepence a year for fifty-one years. The mouse broke its foot against a sugar-tongs, and, instead of singing, bawled. Only the first ninepence has been paid, and the dwarfs are claiming the money back. The firm of Hustington and Chaney, importers of singing mice, refuse to take the mouse back or refund the money, and the Boycott Japan League is organising a mass-meeting of novelists and professional agitators to petition for the deportation of the mouse to the island of Capri, where a mouse-lover, Miss Webbe-Ffoote, has offered to house, feed, clothe, and educate it. . .

J. B. MORTON A Diet of Thistles 1938

Talking of performing mice, Larry Adler tells the story of ten mice brought by an agent for audition to the impresario Sol Hurok. They played the third of Bach's Brandenburg Concertos – nine string players and one harpsichord continuo. Mr Hurok turned them down: 'Yeah, they play well enough but they look too Jewish.'

Here is a nice instance of self-confidence in a singer – at the Teatro Nuovo in Florence about 1780

Signor Morigi [was] the primo buffo, who had been so popular in London in the part of the German Soldier, in Piccini's La Buona Figliola. He was still a great actor, though infirm. He never sung his old song, 'Paterio Giudizzio,' without applause; for if the audience failed, he never failed to applaud himself. He would make his exit, clapping his hands loudly, and saying, 'Well! if they want taste, I do not!' . . .

MICHAEL KELLY 1826 Reminiscences

And another?

Baccaloni was unquestionably the hit of this and the succeeding seasons. Fat, jovial, and I think intelligent – I had no way to know: there was no language in which we could communicate – he brought to Glyndebourne the blessing of absolutely perfect comic timing, and a plummy voice of incomparable richness. He could be a trouble to directors, conductors, and general managers. For four seasons a regular feature of my life at Glyndebourne was the arrival of a furious Baccaloni in my office, sputtering streams of rapid Italian despite his knowledge that I did not understand a word of the language, furious about something that had just happened. I would listen until he seemed to have completed what he had to say, then reach into the desk and give him a five-pound note. That always seemed to be the right reply, and he would go away content.

SIR RUDOLF BING 5,000 Nights at the Opera 1972

Sir Rudolf Bing, of Glyndebourne, Edinburgh and New York Metropolitan fame, wrote one of the more entertaining impresarios' autobiographies; to get the full flavour it should be read with a light Viennese accent and a gently bantering tone. Here is another episode (this time in New York)

The size of Miss Nilsson's triumph placed me in a quandary . . . when I found myself without a Tristan to partner her third Isolde. Ramon Vinay had been scheduled, but he was having vocal difficulties: he had barely made it through the previous performance, and simply did not feel well enough to undertake this killing role after only four days' rest. All right: we had a cover: Karl Liebl, who had in fact sung Tristan ten days before on the occasion of Miss Nilsson's debut. But this was New York in December: Liebl had a cold. The Metropolitan being the company it is, we even had a *third* Tristan lined up, the young tenor Albert Da Costa. By now it was four o'clock of the day of the performance, and I was beginning to get quite worried. I called Da Costa, and my worst fears were realized – he, too, was sick.

Even if I could have imagined myself stepping in front of the curtain to announce a change of opera to that sold-out and over-stimulated house, and I couldn't imagine it, we no longer had time to put anything else onstage. I consulted with Miss Nilsson and then spoke with my three tenors again. None of them felt up to an entire *Tristan*; could each of them take an act? They agreed. When the house lights went down, before the music began, I came on to the stage, and was greeted by a great moan from all corners of the house – the general manager appears only to make the most important announcements, and everyone thought he knew that this announcement had to be: Miss Nilsson has cancelled.

So I began by saying, 'Ladies and gentlemen, Miss Nilsson is very well', which brought a sigh of relief from almost four thousand people. Then I went on: 'However, we are less fortunate with our Tristan. The Metropolitan has three distinguished Tristans available, but all three are sick. In order not to disappoint you, these gallant gentlemen, against their doctors' orders, have agreed to do one act each.' There was laughter in the house. I added, 'Fortunately, the work has only three acts', and there was a roar of laughter. Never has *Tristan und Isolde* started so hilariously. But Miss Nilsson sang gloriously and to this day I am grateful to my three tenors for saving a terrible situation.

SIR RUDOLF BING *ibid*.

Accompanists have found themselves involved in strange incidents, too

An English singer, named Gordon, once found fault with [Handel's] method of accompanying. High words ensued; and Gordon finished by saying, that if Handel persisted in accompanying him in that manner, he would jump upon his harpsichord and smash it to pieces. 'Oh!' replied Handel, 'let me know when you will do that, and I will advertise it; for I am sure more people will come to see you jump, than to hear you sing.'

w. s. ROCKSTRO The Life of George Frederick Handel 1883

One morning I was told . . . that Kammersänger Burian wished to have a piano rehearsal for his Herod (*Salome* was on the programme for the following evening), but wasn't well enough to come to the theatre. Would I therefore go to him? I went. He lived in the Hotel Royal, not far from the Opera House. Entering his room, I was choked by the awful stench, and shocked by the disorder and filth in which this man lived. The bed was unmade, the floor was littered with old newspapers, crumpled and dirty clothes, and remnants of several days' food and drink. The windows and shutters were closed. Burian himself was in a red velvet robe over a nightshirt. He was barefoot and unshaven, but apparently in good spirits.

'Ah, my young friend, here you are! Good! Let's start rehearsing!'
I looked around for a piano. In vain. There was none in the room.
'Very well, Mr Burian. Where shall we go?'
'Go – why?'
'Hm – eh –'
'Oh, the piano! We won't need any!'
'???'
'Let me tell you how we will do it. You sit here and beat the time. I will remain sitting where I am, look at you and think over my part. When I make a mistake I will stop you and we will do that bit over again in the same way.'

Never had I heard of such a manner of rehearsing. But I did as he wanted.

That dingy room must have presented an eerie spectacle: a young man, sitting with a big score on his lap, silently beating out varied tempi, while, two paces away from him, his glassy eyes fixed on the young man's moving hands, an elderly figure, looking like a king of tramps, sat slumped, immobile.

This strange pantomime went on for as long as it took to 'rehearse' the entire part.

At the end Burian said: 'I did not make any mistake.'
What could I do but offer my congratulations?

ANTAL DORATI *Notes of Seven Decades* 1979

It is in *lieder* that most accompanists really show their quality. Ivor Newton,
who accompanied most of the great artists in his day, left an autobiography
that is a model of its kind: modest, entertaining and shrewd, and occasionally
passing on wisdom learned from those he had worked with – as here, from the
German-born singer and teacher Raimund von zur Mühlen who had himself
been a pupil of Clara Schumann

'The relationship of a singer to his accompanist,' von zur Mühlen told
me, 'must be a marriage of two minds; it must be a sympathetic,
deeply felt, mutually understood partnership. Both must be humble.
They must love, honour and obey the composer. Their performance,
with the composer's music and the poet's words, must be a holy
trinity.' His teaching was that every song must first be approached
through its poem, which always called for study. Singer and pianist
first, he declared, must think out the scene, the mood and the
atmosphere of the poem. 'You should build a programme,' he said, 'as
though you were arranging a picture gallery, in which each song is a
picture – of a mood, an age, an emotion, a season. As you perform a
song, you should think always of the picture you wish to create, and as
you finish it, you must forget it at once and concentrate on the next
picture which you have to paint from your imagination. The accompanist should, as it were, set the scene and arrange the lighting with his
introduction, and, with his postlude must suggest the dropping of the
curtain – sometimes he has to contrive a slow curtain; sometimes it
falls very abruptly. . . .

I remember once that he took me to task for my accompaniment to
Schubert's *Wohin* during a lesson. 'Your accompaniment does not
sparkle enough; it is muddy, it doesn't suggest the crystal clearness of
the brook which inspires and encourages the miller's apprentice to
wander and wander – the craving of all youth. Later on, he may suffer
from unrequited love as only a young man can suffer, but in this song
in particular he's completely free from care or worry.'

To illustrate this, he began to sing and to saunter youthfully round
the room as he did so; he moved with the utmost grace, as lithe as any
country lad. Then, the illustration over, he said, 'I sing like a young old
man; you are playing like an old young one.' 'When you play the
Schöne Müllerin,' he said, 'you must always think of a clear brook. In
the *Winterreise* you must think, perhaps, of a deep river.' . . .

[Von zur Mühlen's] language at times could be extraordinarily crude
– his description of some of the most beloved singers of the day would
have surprised many of their admirers – but at the same time he was
capable of poetic refinements of speech. A passage in Brahms's
Requiem was to him, when properly sung, 'so delicate that you should
hear the beat of angel's wings'. 'Never weep at a performance,' he
would tell emotional pupils. 'You should shed tears only at rehearsals.
Tears shed in study can always be heard at the concert.'

IVOR NEWTON *At the Piano* 1966

There are some singers who need no accompanist at all

The Solitary Reaper

Behold her, single in the field,
  Yon solitary Highland Lass!
Reaping and singing by herself;
  Stop here, or gently pass!
Alone she cuts and binds the grain,
And sings a melancholy strain;
O listen! for the Vale profound
Is overflowing with the sound.

No Nightingale did ever chaunt
  More welcome notes to weary bands
Of travellers in some shady haunt,
  Among Arabian sands:
A voice so thrilling ne'er was heard
In spring-time from the Cuckoo-bird,
Breaking the silence of the seas
Among the farthest Hebrides.

Will no one tell me what she sings? –
  Perhaps the plaintive numbers flow
For old, unhappy, far-off things,
  And battles long ago:
Or is it some more humble lay,
Familiar matter of to-day?
Some natural sorrow, loss, or pain,
That has been, and may be again?

Whate'er the theme, the Maiden sang
  As if her song could have no ending;
I saw her singing at her work,
  And o'er the sickle bending; –
I listen'd, motionless and still;
And, as I mounted up the hill,
The music in my heart I bore,
Long after it was heard no more.

WILLIAM WORDSWORTH *A Tour in Scotland* 1803

Opera

A good opera will never be written. Music does not know how to narrate.

NICOLAS BOILEAU

No good opera plot can be sensible, for people do not sing when they are feeling sensible.

W. H. AUDEN

Good operas have always been rare, in all periods, now they are almost non-existent. Why? you will ask. Because we make too much music; because we search too hard; because by peering into the obscurity we lose touch with the sun. . . .

GIUSEPPE VERDI

The theatre is not the place for the musician. When the curtain is up the music interrupts the actor, and when it is down the music interrupts the audience.

SIR ARTHUR SULLIVAN

How wonderful opera would be if there were no singers.

GIOACCHINO ROSSINI

To his friend Maister R. L. In praise of Musique and Poetrie

If Musique and sweet Poetrie agree,
As they must needes (the Sister and the Brother)
Then must the Loue be great, twixt thee and mee,
  Because thou lou'st the one, and I the other.
  Dowland to thee is deare; whose heauenly tuch
Vpon the Lute, doeth rauish humaine sense:
Spenser to mee; whose deepe Conceit is such,
  As passing all Conceit, needs no defence.
  Thou lou'st to heare the sweete melodious sound,
That *Phœbus* Lute (the Queene of Musique) makes:
And I in deepe Delight am chiefly drownd,
  When as himselfe to singing he betakes.
  One God is God of Both (as Poets faigne)
  One Knight loues Both, and Both in thee remaine.

RICHARD BARNFIELD Poems: In divers humors 1598

Musick and Poetry have ever been acknowledg'd Sisters, which walking hand in hand, support each other; As Poetry is the harmony of Words, so Musick is that of Notes: and as Poetry is a Rise above Prose and Oratory, so is Musick the exaltation of Poetry. Both of them may excel apart, but sure they are most excellent when they are joyn'd, because nothing is then wanting to either of their Perfections: for thus they appear like Wit and Beauty in the same Person. Poetry and Painting have arrived to their perfection in our own Country: Musick is yet but in its Nonage, a forward Child, which gives hope of what it may be hereafter in *England*, when the Masters of it shall find more Encouragement. 'Tis now learning *Italian*, which is its best Master, and studying a little of the *French* Air, to give it somewhat more of Gayety and Fashion. Thus being farther from the Sun, we are of later Growth than our Neighbour Countries, and must be content to shake off our Barbarity by degrees. The present Age seems already dispos'd to be refin'd, and to distinguish betwixt wild Fancy, and a just, numerous Composition. So far the Genius of Your Grace has already prevail'd on Us: Many of the Nobility and Gentry have follow'd Your Illustrious Example in the Patronage of Musick. Nay even our Poets begin to grow asham'd of their harsh and broken Numbers, and promise to file our uncouth Language into smoother Words.

HENRY PURCELL Dedication of Dioclesian 1690

At least it's nice to think this is by Purcell – though many believe that Dryden ghosted it. But the following piece is genuine Dryden and displays an attitude rare among librettists:

There is nothing better, than what I intended, than the Musick; which has since arrived at a greater perfection in England, than ever formerly; especially passing through the artful hands of Mr. Purcell, who has composed it with so great a genius, that he has nothing to fear but an ignorant, ill-judging audience. But the numbers of poetry and vocal musick are sometimes so contrary, that in many places I have been obliged to cramp my Verses, and make them rugged to the Reader, that they may be harmonious to the Hearer; of which I have no reason to repent me, because these sorts of Entertainments are principally designed for the ear and the eye; and therefore, in reason, my art on this occasion ought to be subservient to his.

JOHN DRYDEN Dedication of King Arthur 1691

Such good sense is less rare, perhaps, in the twentieth century

If the librettist is a practicing poet, the most difficult problem, the place where he is most likely to go astray, is the composition of the verse. Poetry is in its essence an act of reflection, of refusing to be content with the interjections of immediate emotion in order to understand the nature of what is felt. Since music is in essence immediate, it follows that the words of a song cannot be poetry. Here one should draw a distinction between lyric and song proper. A lyric is a poem intended to be chanted. In a chant the music is subordinate to the words which limit the range and tempo of the notes. In song, the notes must be free to be whatever they choose and the words must be able to do what they are told.

The verses of *Ah non credea* in *La Sonnambula*, though of little interest to read, do exactly what they should: suggest to Bellini one of the most beautiful melodies ever written and then leave him completely free to write it. The verses which the librettist writes are not addressed to the public but are really a private letter to the composer. They have their moment of glory, the moment in which they suggest to him a certain melody; once that is over, they are as expendable as infantry to a Chinese general: they must efface themselves and cease to care what happens to them.

W. H. AUDEN The Dyer's Hand 1963

Auden, 'this big, blond intellectual bloodhound' as Stravinsky called him, produced with Chester Kallman one of the best of all twentieth-century librettos in *The Rake's Progress*, as well as the text for Britten's first opera, *Paul Bunyan*, a couple of librettos for Hans Werner Henze and an important new translation of *Die Zauberflöte*.

Mozart might well have appreciated Auden's qualities as a librettist, though he was far too instinctive an artist to be able, as a rule, to put his ideas into words with comparable clarity. Nevertheless, the comments inspired by the verses which Gottlob Stephanie provided for *Die Entführung aus dem Serail* have remained one of the central statements about the relationship between words and music in opera

. . . Now as to the libretto of the opera. You are quite right so far as Stephanie's work is concerned. Still, the poetry is perfectly in keeping with the character of stupid, surly, malicious Osmin. I am well aware that the verse is not of the best, but it fitted in and agreed so well with the musical ideas which were already buzzing in my head, that it could not fail to please me; and I would like to wager that when it is performed, no deficiencies will be found. . . . Besides, I should say that in opera the poetry must be altogether the obedient daughter of the music. Why do Italian comic operas please everywhere – in spite of their miserable libretti – even in Paris, where I myself witnessed their success? Just because there the music reigns supreme and when one listens to it all else is forgotten. Why, an opera is sure of success when the plot is well worked out, the words written solely for the music and not shoved in here and there to suit some miserable rhyme (which, God knows, never enhances the value of any theatrical performance, be what it may, but rather detracts from it) – I mean, words or even entire verses which ruin the composer's whole idea. Verses are indeed the most indispensable element for music – but rhymes – solely for the sake of rhyming – the most detrimental. Those high and mighty people who set to work in this pedantic fashion will always come to grief, both they and their music. The best thing of all is when a good composer, who understands the stage and is talented enough to make sound suggestions, meets an able poet, that true phoenix; in that case no fears need be entertained as to the applause even of the ignorant. Poets almost remind me of trumpeters with their professional tricks! If we composers were always to stick so faithfully to our rules (which were very good at a time when no one knew better), we should be concocting music as unpalatable as their libretti.

MOZART Letter to his father 13 October 1781

The relationship between composer and librettist was never an easy one, even in the seventeenth century. Here is Pepys's impression of Henry Cooke, one of the composers who contributed to the very first English opera, William Davenant's *The Siege of Rhodes*

Discoursed most about plays and the Opera, where, among other vanities, Captain Cooke, had the arrogance to say that he was fain to direct Sir W. Davenant in the breaking of his verses into such and such lengths, according as would be fit for musick, and how he used to swear at Davenant, and command him that way, when W. Davenant would be angry, and find fault with this or that note – a vain coxcomb I perceive he is, though he sings and composes so well.

SAMUEL PEPYS *Diary* 1667

A letter from the librettist of Handel's *Saul* (and of *Messiah*):

Queen's Square
London
19 September 1738

To the Earl of Guernsey

. . . Mr. Handel's head is more full of maggots than ever. I found yesterday in his room a very queer instrument which he calls carillon (Anglice, a bell) and says some call it a Tubalcain, I suppose because it is both in the make and tone like a set of Hammers striking upon anvils. 'Tis played upon with keys like a Harpsichord and with this Cyclopean instrument he designs to make poor Saul stark mad. His second maggot is an organ of £500 price which (because he is overstocked with money) he had bespoke of one Moss of Barnet. This organ, he says, is so constructed that as he sits at it he has a better command of his performers than he used to have, and he is highly delighted to think with what exactness his Oratorio will be performed by the help of this organ; so that for the future instead of beating time at his oratorios, he is to sit at the organ all the time with his back to the Audience. His third maggot is a Hallelujah which he has trump'd up at the end of his oratorio since I went into the Country, because he thought the conclusion of the oratorio was not Grand enough . . . I could tell you more of his maggots: but it grows late and I must defer the rest till I write next, by which time, I doubt not, more new ones will breed in his Brain. . . .

CHARLES JENNENS

Handel must have presented a very special sort of problem to his librettists

I heard [Thomas Morell] say that one fine summer morning he was aroused out of bed at five o'clock by Handel, who came in his carriage a short distance from London. The doctor went to the window and spoke to Handel, who would not leave his carriage. Handel was at the

time composing an oratorio. When the doctor asked him what he
wanted, he said, 'What de devil means de vord billow?' which was in
the oratorio the doctor had written for him. The doctor, after laughing
at so ludicrous a reason for disturbing him, told him that billow meant
wave, a wave of the sea. 'Oh, de vave,' said Handel, and bade his
coachman return, without addressing another word to the doctor.

JOHN TAYLOR Records of my Life 1832

Samuel Butler, who confessed to having 'worshipped Handel' since the age of
twelve, could really find very little good to say of any other composer, even
Bach. Butler produced a number of musical compositions of his own, of which
the most important are two earnestly Handelian 'dramatic cantatas'. Here is
the synopsis prefixed to the score of the first

Narcissus, a simple shepherd, and Amaryllis, a prudent shepherdess,
with companions who form the chorus, have abandoned pastoral
pursuits and embarked on a course of speculation upon the Stock
Exchange. This results in the loss of the hundred pounds upon which
Narcissus and Amaryllis had intended to marry. Their engagement is
broken off, and the condolences of the chorus end Part I. In the
interval between the parts, the aunt and godmother of Narcissus has
died at an advanced age, and is discovered to have been worth one
hundred thousand pounds, all of which she has bequeathed to her
nephew and godson. This removes the obstacle to the union with
Amaryllis; but the question arises in what securities the money is to be
invested. At first he is inclined to resume his speculations and to buy
Egyptian Bonds, American railways, mines, etc.; but, yielding to the
advice of Amaryllis, he resolves to place the whole of it in the Three
per cent. Consolidated Bank Annuities, to marry at once and to live
comfortably upon the income. With the congratulations and approbation of the chorus, the work is brought to a conclusion.

SAMUEL BUTLER 1886 Narcissus

In *Narcissus* and *Ulysses* [wrote Butler] I made an attempt, the failure of
which has yet to be shown, to return to the principles of Handel and
take them up where he left off

Note-Books 1912

We particularly like the idea of a fugal chorus on the words

> How blest the prudent man, the maiden pure,
> Whose income is both ample and secure;
> Arising from Consolidated Three
> Per cent. Annuities paid quarterly.

SAMUEL BUTLER 1886 Narcissus

It was Butler who suggested that, since all faith is a matter of speculation, the words of the soprano air in *Messiah* should be amended to 'I *bet* that my Redeemer liveth'.

The setting of everyday language to music is something the English have always found hard to accept

There is nothing that has more startled our *English* Audience, than the *Italian Recitativo* at its first Entrance upon the Stage. People were wonderfully surprised to hear Generals singing the Word of Command, and Ladies delivering Messages in Musick. Our Countrymen could not forbear laughing when they heard a Lover chanting out a Billetdoux, and even the Superscription of a Letter set to a Tune. . . .

JOSEPH ADDISON *The Spectator* 1711

I am ravished by opera, on condition that I have only a vague idea of what it is about. In this I wholly agree with Arnold Bennett, who maintained that opera was tolerable only when sung in a language he didn't understand.

JAMES AGATE *Ego 8* 24 June 1945

Opera in English is, in the main, about as sensible as baseball in Italian.

H. L. MENCKEN 1880–1956

In the period between Purcell and the twentieth century English opera more or less gave up in the face of Italian and, later, German competition. About French opera, at least in the eighteenth century, the English were less sure

You figure us in a set of pleasures, which, believe me, we do not find; cards and eating are so universal, that they absorb all variation of pleasures. The operas, indeed, are much frequented three times a week; but to me they would be a greater penance then eating maigre: their music resembles a gooseberry tart as much as it does harmony.

HORACE WALPOLE Letter 21 April 1739

Native opera suffered from a dearth of both librettists and composers, which lasted well into the nineteenth century. Later there were exceptions, even if sometimes they were the wrong way round. Shaw's review of 'Mr Robert Buchanan's opera, The Piper of Hamelin' begins with two pages that read like a paean of sober approval, until it dawns on the reader that Mr Buchanan was in fact only the *librettist* of the opera . . .

But – for I am loth to have to add that all this is only leading up to a great BUT – why did not Mr Buchanan, Wagner-like, compose the music to his own play? Mr F. W. Allwood, the composer who relieved him of that task, is a gentleman with a very great knowledge of Italian opera and English drawing room ballad music, from Mercadante down to Mr Cowen; and he has used his knowledge unsparingly. Unfortunately, his memory is not note perfect. He repeatedly tried to make the Piper play *It was a dream*; but not even at the end, when he brought the whole orchestra to aid him in two heroic final attempts, did he succeed in getting it right. Only for this unlucky infirmity Mr Allwood would have produced a passable *pot pourri*.

As it was, from the opening reminiscence of the exordium to Mendelssohn's *Ruy Blas*, and the bold resurrection of 'Regnava nel silenzio', which immediately follows, down to the curiously unsuccessful shot at 'God Save the Queen', which closes the opera, I heard hardly a theme which did not differ from the authentic version by several notes, and differ for the worse, too. No doubt the truth is that Mr Allwood honestly mistook his memory for his invention; but I do not see how I could have mistaken his invention for my memory; and therefore I am reluctantly compelled to except his score from my otherwise favourable verdict on *The Piper of Hamelin*.

BERNARD SHAW 1893 *Music in London*

With characteristic delicacy, and punctuation, another literary figure refuses a request from George Henschel, the eminent singer, conductor and composer (and Brahms's swimming companion, see pp 49–51)

Your flattering dream is beautiful – but, I fear, alas, delusive. When I say 'fear' it, I mean I only too completely feel it. It is a charming idea, but the root of the libretto is not in me. We will talk of it – yes: because I will talk with you, with joy, of *anything* – will even play to myself that I have convictions I haven't, for that privilege. But I am unlyrical, unmusical, unrhythmical, unmanageable. And I hate 'old New England stories'! – which are lean and pale and poor and ugly. But let us by all means talk – and the more the better. I am touched by your thinking so much good of me – and I embrace you, my dear Henschel, for such rich practical friendship and confidence. I congratulate you afresh on your glorious wife, I await you with impatience, and I stretch out to you across the wintry wastes the very grateful hand of yours always,

HENRY JAMES

Letter 22 January 1895

To get back to the more serious librettists, here is a picture of one of the most famous of them all, Mozart's librettist, Lorenzo Da Ponte; there seems to be some doubt as to whether Michael Kelly has remembered the right opera for the incident, but it has the ring of truth none the less

The last of these operas was composed by Signor Righini, and written by the poet of the theatre, the Abbé da Ponte, by birth a Venetian. It was said, that originally he was a Jew, turned Christian, – dubbed himself an Abbé, and became a great dramatic writer. In his opera, there was a character of an amorous eccentric poet, which was allotted to *me*; at the time I was esteemed a good mimic, and particularly happy in imitating the walk, countenance, and attitudes of those whom I wished to resemble. My friend, the poet, had a remarkably aukward gait, a habit of throwing himself (as he thought) into a graceful attitude, by putting his stick behind his back, and leaning on it; he had also, a very peculiar, rather dandyish, way of dressing; for in sooth, the Abbé stood mighty well with himself, and had the character of a consummate coxcomb; he had also, a strong lisp and broad Venetian dialect.

The first night of the performance, he was seated in the boxes, more conspicuously than was absolutely necessary, considering he was the author of the piece to be performed. As usual, on the first night of a new opera, the Emperor was present, and a numerous auditory. When I made my *entrée* as the amorous poet, dressed exactly like the Abbé in the boxes, imitating his walk, leaning on my stick, and aping his gestures, and his lisp, there was a universal roar of laughter and applause; and after a buzz round the house, the eyes of the whole audience were turned to the place where he was seated. The Emperor enjoyed the joke, laughed heartily, and applauded frequently during the performance; the Abbé was not at all affronted, but took my imitation of him in good part, and ever after we were on the best of terms.

MICHAEL KELLY *c.* 1785 *Reminiscences*

Da Ponte, in his own Memoirs, describes Kelly as 'not a man of much education or learning' and makes no mention of the incident. (He himself died at the age of eighty-nine in New York, where he had opened up as a grocer after his bookshop and printing works in London had come to grief.)

He has left a graphic description of the problems confronting a librettist in the latter part of the eighteenth century. Recently arrived in Vienna, he had just received his first commission

As this, my first production, was to be set to music by Salieri, who was, to tell the truth, a most accomplished and able man, I suggested various plots and subjects and then left the choice to him. Unfortunately he liked the one that was perhaps least likely to prove attractive and interesting on the stage. This was the 'Ricco d'un Giorno'.

I set to work courageously, but I very soon found out how much more difficult it is to carry out a piece of work than it is to conceive it. My difficulties were endless. The subject did not furnish enough characters and variety of incident to make an interesting plot that would last about two hours, my dialogues seemed dull, the *arie* affected, the sentiment commonplace, the action halting, and the effect lifeless. In fine, I seemed to be no longer able to write prose or verse and to have undertaken to wield the club of Hercules with but the hand of a child.

I finished at last nearly all the first act, for better or worse. There only remained the finale. The finale, besides having to be closely bound up with the rest of the opera, is a kind of little comedy or play by itself, demanding a fresh plot and some special interest. It is here chiefly that the genius of the Kapellmeister, the worth of the singers and the greatest dramatic effect must show themselves. There is no recitative, everything is sung, and every kind of singing has to be introduced: *adagio, allegro, andante, amabile, armonioso, strepitoso, arci-strepitoso, strepitosissimo,* with which nearly always the finale closes. This in technical musical language is called the *chiusa,* or *stretta,* I know not whether because in it the play draws to a close, or because it generally puts the brain of the poor poet who has to write the words into such straits not once but a hundred times. According to theatrical dogma, in the finale all the singers must appear on the stage, even if there were three hundred of them, one at a time, or two, or three, or six, or ten, or sixty at a time, to sing solos or duets or trios or sestets or sessantets. And if the plot of the play does not allow of it, then the poet must find a way to make it do so, in despite of good sense and reason and all the Aristotles on earth. And if then it proves to go badly, so much the worse for him.

After this, it will not be hard to imagine my perplexity in writing my first finale. A dozen times I was on the point of throwing what I had written on the fire and going to offer my resignation. At last by dint of biting my nails, rolling my eyes, scratching my head and invoking the aid of Lucina and all the divinities and midwives of Pindus, I finished both the first finale and the whole opera. I put it away in my cupboard and left it there for a fortnight before reading it over in a calmer mood. It seemed to me worse and more lifeless than ever. I was bound, however, to give it to Salieri, for he had already written the music for some scenes and asked me every day for the remainder. I went to him very crestfallen and handed him the libretto without speaking. He read it in my presence and then said, 'It is well written, but we must see how it goes on the stage. It has some very good songs and scenes which I like very much, but I shall want a few small alterations made, more for the musical effect than for anything else'.

I parted from him feeling as pleased as Punch, and as it is easy to believe what one wishes to believe, I began to hope my play was not so bad as I had at first judged. But what did these 'small alterations' amount to? They meant shortening or lengthening most of the scenes, introducing new duets, trios, quartets, etc., changing metres in the middle of a song, inserting choruses (to be sung by Germans!), cutting out nearly all the recitative and therefore all the plot and interest which the play possessed, such as it had, so that when it was put on the stage I do not believe there were a hundred of my original lines left.

LORENZO DA PONTE 1784 Memoirs

But the composer was only the first hurdle. Da Ponte later describes the second: confrontation with the singers (though on this occasion, because he had made himself so unpopular in the Viennese theatre, he had concealed his name as librettist)

Directly the parts were distributed, it was pandemonium let loose. One had too many recitatives, another not enough; for one the music was too high, for another it was too low; this one had no part in the concerted pieces, the other had to sing in too many; one was sacrificed to the prima donna, another to the first or second or third or fourth *buffo*. There was a general flare-up. The words, however, they said, were very good – this was meant as a hit at both Martín and me for they did not know I was the author – the characters were interesting, and the subject entirely new; the play was, in short, a masterpiece, but the music was very poor and trivial. 'Take note, Signor Da Ponte', a certain singer said seriously to me one day, 'how a *libretto buffo* should be written'. You may guess how I laughed.

LORENZO DA PONTE ibid.

Meanwhile, the original author of Da Ponte's most famous libretto was already expressing his views

Nowadays what is not worth saying is sung.

PIERRE-AUGUSTIN CARON DE BEAUMARCHAIS Le Mariage de Figaro 1784

Saint-Evrémond had put it succinctly in a famous dictum half a century earlier

If you wish to know what an OPERA is, I shall tell you that it is a *fantastical work of Poetry and of Music, in which the Poet and the Musician, equally embarrassed the one with the other, take great pains to turn out an evil Work.*

CHARLES DE SAINT-DENIS SAINT-EVRÉMOND Letter to the Duke of Buckingham 1678

The opposite point of view has, of course, always existed. Here is Monteverdi, within twenty years of the first opera of all, complaining about the libretto for a piece entitled *Le Nozze di Tetide* (which he subsequently abandoned)

I see that the personages [of this drama] are to be Winds, *Amoretti, Zeffiretti* and Sirens, so that a lot of sopranos will be needed, and what is more that the Winds – that is, the North winds and the Zephyrs – actually have to sing. But how, dear Sir, can I imitate the speech of winds, when winds do not speak! And how am I going to be able to use them to move the emotions? Arianna moved us because she was a woman, Orfeo because he was a man – not a wind. Music, without any words, can suggest the sound of the wind, or the bleating of sheep or the neighing of horses, or whatever else you choose, but it cannot imitate the speech of winds because there is no such thing. . . .

As to the story taken as a whole, it may be my own ignorance, but I do not find that it moves me in any way; indeed, I can only understand it with difficulty – and I don't feel that it carries me, with any natural progression, to an end that moves me. Arianna led me naturally to a lament, Orfeo naturally to a prayer, but where this leads me I do not know. So what is it that Your Lordship, in this case, would like the music to do?

CLAUDIO MONTEVERDI Letter 1616

The first great revolt against the excesses of the eighteenth century, however, came with Gluck and his librettist Ranieri de' Calzabigi – a somewhat unlikely figure for an operatic reformer, who ran a lottery in Paris shady enough to bring him under the eyes of the police. His later writings about his collaboration with Gluck tend to be heavily tipped in his own favour, but here is part of a less well known letter, which came to light in 1938 and has received little attention since; it was written after *Orfeo*, shortly before the première of *Alceste*, and two years before the famous preface to the score of that opera

When it is the pleasure of H.I.M. and Your Highness to order that *Alceste* be put on the stage, it is of paramount importance to choose for the opera really suitable executants. Alceste and Admetus cannot be represented by just any singers, partly by reason of the texture of this new species of drama in which all depends on the eye of the spectator and consequently on the action, but also because the music is exactly fitted to what is happening on the stage and depends much more on expression than anything the Italians are nowadays pleased to call 'song'.

Only the dramas of the Abbé Metastasio, whose length – by reason of the large number of verses and of musical arabesques – is such that they cannot from the outset hope to hold the attention of the spectator, enjoy the privilege of being saddles for all horses. There it matters not whether a character in the drama is sung by a Farinelli, Caffarelli, Guadagni or Toschi, or by a Tesi, Gabrielli or Bianchi, since the audience does not expect, nor demand from the singers more than a couple of arias and a duet, having from the start abandoned all hope of taking an interest in the action; no one, after all, can listen attentively for five hours to six performers, four of whom are usually so inept that they hardly know how to enunciate, for the mere pleasure of getting excited over an insipid Clelia, a cold Ersilia, an imaginary Aristea, a saucy Emira, an indecent Onoria and a shameless Mandane, all of whom are at bottom no more than little Roman or Neapolitan courtesans who sentimentalize about love in polite language on the stage. As for those unnatural, philosophizing heroes like Metastasio's Horace, Themistocles, Cato and Romulus – they are simply not to be met with in this world, and about them I prefer to hold my tongue altogether.

Since these dramas could not, in performance, please the mind, they had need to entertain the senses: the eye by the sight of live horses in cardboard forests, by real battles fought on painted battle-fields, by conflagrations of coloured paper; the ear by using the voices as if they were violins and producing whole concerts with the mouth alone – thus giving rise to that musical gargling which in Naples they call *trocciolette* (because it closely resembles the noise of the wheels passing over the ropes of a pulley) – and a mass of other musical whimsies comparable to those stone tit-bits with which Gothic architecture decorated (or rather, disfigured) its monuments and which, once so admired, are now objects of laughter and contempt to anyone who bothers to stop and look at them. To make room for these strange embellishments the poet lent himself to the filling of his libretti with wonders, storms, tempests, lions, war horses and nightingales which fit about as well into the mouths of passionate, desperate or furious heroes as beauty-spots, powder, make-up and diamonds on the face, head and neck of an ape.

Matters are entirely different in the new plan of musical drama which has been, if not invented, at least first put into practice by me in *Orfeo*, then in *Alceste*, and continued by Signor Coltellini. All is nature here, all is passion; there are no sententious reflections, no philosophy or politics, no paragons of virtue and none of those descriptions or amplifications which are only an avoidance of difficulties and are to be found in all libretti. The duration is limited to what does not tire or make the attention wander. The plots are simple, not romanticized; a few verses are enough to inform the spectators of the progress of the action which is never complicated or duplicated in servile, uncalled-for obedience to the silly rule concerning the 'secondo uomo' and the 'seconda donna', but reduced to the dimensions of Greek tragedy, and therefore has the unique advantage of exciting terror and compassion in the same way as spoken tragedy. According to this plan, as your Highness will perceive, the music has no other function than to express what arises from the words, which are therefore neither smothered by notes nor used to lengthen the spectacle unduly, because it is ridiculous to prolong the sentence 'I love you' (for instance) with a hundred notes when nature has restricted it to three (I am of the opinion that a note can never have the value of more than one syllable).

If this new plan, with the addition of pantomime in the choruses and ballets in imitation of the Greek, should find the approval of the public and of the exalted taste of H.I.M. (who was after all present fourteen times at *Orfeo* and signified his extreme pleasure by making gifts to the conductor and composer), it is essential to adhere to it properly and not to confound it with that of Signor Metastasio, because ornaments for brunettes do not suit blondes. In one of the Abbé's dramas, let the Gabriellis, the Bastardellas and suchlike *zufolatrici* warble and scream their heads off in an aria about a murmuring brook so that you can't hear a word, it is no matter; but in *Orfeo*, in *Telemaco* and in *Alceste* we need actresses who will sing what the maestro has written and not take it upon themselves to add to the score by repeating thirty or forty times over a 'Farewell' or 'I leave you' in their personal musical hieroglyphics of which, not to be discourteous, one might perhaps say: 'Pulcrum est, sed non erat hic locus'.

RANIERI DE' CALZABIGI Letter to Count Kaunitz 1767

The too great ascendancy of the solo voice had been a bone of contention since early days, as well as the undue subjugation of the orchestra. Doesn't this sound like Wagner *avant la lettre*?

One thing I dislike is the laying too much stress upon some one voice, wch is purchased at a dear rate. Were it not as well If somewhat of that was abated & added to the rest to bring ye orchestre to a neerer equality? Many persons come to hear that single voice, who care not for all the rest, especially If it be a fair Lady; And observing ye discours of the Quallity crittiques, I found it runs most upon ye point, who sings best? and not whither ye musick be good, and wherein? and it is a sorry case to sitt by one who during a recitativo, sighs & groans at what he is to endure, before this favourite ariette, or that ballett, comes up. And it is a fault in ye composition to overcalculate for ye prime voice, as If no other part were worth Regarding, whereupon the whole enterteinment consists of solos, and very little or no consorts of voices: where is there a chorus of 4 full voices Interwoven with ye proper consort ornaments to be heard? I am sure nature affords not means for musick to be so good any other way. If they say It is not suitable to a Drama to have many sing together. The contrary of that is most apparently true; for (excepting ye comedys) wch of ye Ancient Dramatiques had not a chorus that sang what was proper to the subject? And now at last, from what I can perceiv, the Operas made In England of ye latter date, are more substantially musicall, then those wch are used notati out of Itally, wch latter have of late diverted from the Lofty style downe to the Ballad, fitt for the streets that receivs them, whereby it appears that the Itallian vein is much degenerated.

ROGER NORTH *The Musicall Gramarian c.* 1728

Wagner's own attitude to his interpreters is touchingly expressed in a notice which appeared in the wings, wardrobe and dressing rooms of the Bayreuth Festival Theatre, on the first day of the First Bayreuth Festival, 13 August 1876

Last request to my faithful artists!

Distinctness!

The big notes will take care of themselves; the little notes, and their words, are the things to watch. Never address anything to the public, but always to each other. In monologues look either up or down, but never straight in front of you.
And a last wish: be good to me, you dear children!

RICHARD WAGNER

For the orchestra, he had a shorter admonition

No preluding! Piano, pianissimo, and all will be well!
Quoted by CAROLINE V. KERR in *The Bayreuth Letters of Richard Wagner*

A visitor to backstage Bayreuth in the late 1960s observed a notice which said (in English)

> There is, in the whole house, no microphone;
> therefore, the singers must fulfil the utmost.

There were some who (like Rossini in another context) thought that Wagner would be even better without the singers

The entire overture, long as it was, was played to a dark house with the curtain down. It was exquisite; it was delicious. But straightway thereafter, of course, came the singing, and it does seem to me that nothing can make a Wagner opera absolutely perfect and satisfactory to the untutored but to leave out the vocal parts. I wish I could see a Wagner opera done in pantomime once. Then one would have the lovely orchestration unvexed to listen to and bathe his spirit in, and the bewildering beautiful scenery to intoxicate his eyes with, and the dumb acting couldn't mar these pleasures, because there isn't often anything in the Wagner opera that one would call by such a violent name as acting; as a rule all you would see would be a couple of silent people, one of them standing still, the other catching flies. Of course I do not really mean that he would be catching flies; I only mean that the usual operatic gestures which consist in reaching first one hand out into the air and then the other might suggest the sport I speak of if the operator attended strictly to business and uttered no sound.

This present opera was 'Parsifal'. Madame Wagner does not permit its representation anywhere but in Bayreuth. The first act of the three occupied two hours, and I enjoyed that in spite of the singing.

I trust that I know as well as anybody that singing is one of the most entrancing and bewitching and moving and eloquent of all the vehicles invented by man for the conveying of feeling; but it seems to me that the chief virtue in song is melody, air, tune, rhythm, or what you please to call it, and that when this feature is absent what remains is a picture with the color left out. I was not able to detect in the vocal parts of 'Parsifal' anything that might with confidence be called rhythm or tune or melody; one person performed at a time – and a long time, too – often in a noble, and always in a high-toned, voice; but he only pulled out long notes, then some short ones, then another long one, then a sharp, quick, peremptory bark or two – and so on and so on; and when he was done you saw that the information which he had conveyed had not compensated for the disturbance. Not always, but pretty often. If two of them would but put in a duet occasionally and blend the voices; but no, they don't do that. The great master, who knew so well how to make a hundred instruments rejoice in unison and pour out their souls in mingled and melodious tides of delicious sounds, deals only in barren solos when he puts in the vocal parts. It may be that he was deep, and only added the singing to his operas for the sake of the contrast it would make with the music. Singing! It does seem the wrong name to apply to it. Strictly described, it is a practising of difficult and unpleasant intervals, mainly. An ignorant person gets tired of listening to gymnastic intervals in the long run, no matter how pleasant they may be.

MARK TWAIN 'At the Shrine of St Wagner' 1891

Some found that the singers didn't really get enough of a look in

. . . through four evenings we hear singing upon the stage without independent, distinct melodies, without a single duet, trio, ensemble, chorus or finale. The exceptions vanish as fleeting moments in the whole. This alone demonstrates that the knife is applied not to an outward form but to the living roots of dramatic music. Opera lovers who do not know *Tristan* and the *Ring* are prone to suspect that the opponents of these late works are opponents of Wagner altogether. They think only in terms of *Holländer* or *Tannhäuser*, which are as different from this newest music as two things can be within the same art. One can regard *Tannhäuser* as one of the most beautiful of operas and think the opposite of the *Ring*; and, indeed, one must. For what made the fortune of Wagner's earlier operas, and continues to make it, is the firm bond of the descriptive, specifically dramatic element with the charm of the comprehensible melody, the alternation of dialogue with ensembles, choruses and finales. In the *Ring* Wagner has removed all trace of anything reminiscent of these virtues. Even *Meistersinger*, in which separate vocal melody occurs less frequently but, for all that, in certain magnificent examples, seems by comparison a musically charming and popularly comprehensible work.

The *Ring* is, in fact, something entirely new, something essentially different from all that has gone before, a thing alone and apart. As such, as an imaginative experiment, inexhaustibly instructive for the musician, it has enduring significance. That it will ever become popular in the way that Mozart's or Weber's operas are popular appears improbable. Three main considerations distinguish this music in principle from all previous operas, including Wagner's – first, the absence of independent, separate vocal lines, replaced here by a kind of exalted recitative with the 'endless melody' in the orchestra as a basis; second, the dissolution of all form, not just the usual forms (arias and duets, etc.) but of symmetry, of musical logic developed in accordance with laws; third, the exclusion of multiple-voiced pieces, of duets, trios, choruses, and finales, not counting a few passing entrances.

EDUARD HANSLICK *Review* 1876

Others clearly thought that it was less what the singers sang than what they did that mattered. Here is the announcement of the first performance of *Tristan und Isolde* in the local Munich press

On Friday next Adultery with Drums and Trumpets, complete with the entire Music of the Future, is to appear at the Court and National Theatre. Some, it is true, take the liberty of saying that it is neither courtly nor national to extol a breach of the sixth commandment with glitter and with glory, while others pretend to know that insanity is to display itself on the Ramersdorfer Lüften,* its natural environment.

MÜNCHNER VOLKSBOTE 1865

*The site of the Munich lunatic asylum, although this reference is not exactly clear. And isn't it the *seventh* commandment?

Meanwhile, in Paris, there were others who held quite different views

'I don't feel tempted to imitate what I admire in Wagner. My idea of dramatic form is different: in it, music begins at the point where speech has no power to express. Music is made for the inexpressible; I would have her seem to emerge from the shadows and then retire back into them from time to time; I would have her always discreet.

'What kind of poet could provide you with a libretto?'

'One who, only hinting at things, enables me to graft my dream onto his; one who creates characters whose history and abode belong to no time and no place; one who does not despotically impose upon me formal scenes, who allows me, now and then, to outdo him in artistry and perfect his own work. Not that he need be afraid. I won't fall into the bad old ways of the *théâtre lyrique*, where music insolently takes precedence and the text is pushed into second place and stifled by a musical garb that is too heavy for it. In the musical theatre there is too much singing. One should only sing when there is something *worth* singing about; the accents of emotion should be held in reserve. And there must be different levels in the energy of expression: it is sometimes necessary to paint in monochrome, to be content with a *grisaille*. . . . Nothing must interfere with the progress of the drama: all musical development that is not called for by the words is a fault. And this without counting the fact that any musical development, however little it is prolonged, is incapable of matching the mobility of the words. . . .

'I dream of a libretto which does not condemn me to perpetrating long, heavy acts, which offers me constantly changing scenes, varied both in place and in atmosphere, where the characters do not argue but submit to life and to fate. . . .'

CLAUDE DEBUSSY 1889 quoted by Maurice Emmanuel 1933

Incredibly, it was not until three years after this conversation that Debussy, walking down the Boulevard des Italiens, stopped at a bookstall and for the first time picked up a copy of Maeterlinck's *Pelléas et Mélisande*.

In 1907, also in Paris, Richard Strauss attended a performance of *Pelléas*, sitting in a box between Ravel and Romain Rolland from whose diary these paragraphs are taken

Strauss hardly talks to anyone but me, whispering his impressions . . . he listens with the greatest attention, his face cupped in one hand and with my opera glasses in the other. Not for an instant does he stop looking at the artists and the orchestra. But he does not understand anything. After the first Act (the first three scenes), he says to me: 'Is it always like that?' – 'Yes' – 'Nothing more? . . . nothing . . . no music . . . it does not follow on . . . it doesn't hold together . . . no musical phrases. No development.' Marnold tries to join in our conversation and says in his usual heavy manner: 'There are musical phrases, but they are not stressed or underlined so that the general public can appreciate them'. Strauss, a little put out, but quite calmly, answers: 'But I am a musician and I hear nothing . . .' We carry on our whispered conversation and I try to make Strauss understand the modesty of this art, all nuance and half-colours, this impressionism, delicate and poetic, using little touches of colour juxtaposed, discreet and vibrant. He says: 'Myself, I am a musician before everything else. Whenever there is music in a work of art I want it to be master; I do not like it to be subordinated to anything else. This would be too modest. I do not say that poetry is inferior to music. But real poetic dramas, Schiller, Goethe, Shakespeare, are self-sufficient, they do not need music. When there is music it must carry all before it; it must not be inferior to the poetry. I make use of the Wagnerian method. Take *Tristan*. There is not enough music for me here. . . . There are very fine harmonies, very good orchestral effects in very good taste. But it is nothing; nothing at all. I find that it is just Maeterlinck's drama by itself without music'. He starts to listen again. . . . 'But that is completely *Parsifal*,' he says at one point. However the scene with the hair, the prelude to the scene in the grotto and the scene that follows give him a certain pleasure. Of the whole score these are clearly what he likes best. But he returns always to his slightly disdainful praise: 'It's very "fin"'. . . . (In the café later) the conversation turns to ancient music, a subject in which Strauss is profoundly uninterested. He says somewhat disdainfully that he knows nothing of Frescobaldi nor of Monteverdi, indeed nothing before Bach and that the subject does not interest him; certain little things by Rameau perhaps. We try to make him understand that there are works of quite modern genius like Monteverdi's *Orfeo*. He listens politely but he is bored.

ROMAIN ROLLAND *Diary* 22 May 1907

One of the most famous of all operatic collaborations was that between Richard Strauss and his librettist, Hugo von Hofmannsthal – the one, good-humoured, extrovert, essentially instinctive, the other sophisticated, intelligent, highly sensitive and devastatingly articulate: 'we seem to be watching a Siamese cat working out a *modus vivendi* with a Labrador' wrote Edward Sackville-West in his introduction to the English edition of their correspondence. Here is Hofmannsthal in the early stages of one of their greatest successes, *Ariadne auf Naxos*

Aussee, Obertressen
July 1911

My dear Doctor Strauss

I must confess I was somewhat piqued by your scant and cool reception of the finished manuscript of *Ariadne*, compared with the warm welcome you gave to every single act of *Rosenkavalier* – which stands out in my memory as one of the most significant pleasures connected with that work. I believe that in *Ariadne* I have produced something at least equally good, equally original and novel, and although we certainly agree in wishing to shun anything like the false show of mutual adulation in which mediocre artists indulge, I cannot help asking myself whether any praise in all the world could make up to me for the absence of yours.

You may of course have written your letter or read the manuscript when you were somewhat out of sorts, as happens so easily to creative artists; nor do I overlook the fact that a fairly subtle piece of work like this inevitably suffers seriously by being presented in manuscript rather than clear typescript (unfortunately my typist was ill). And so I am not without hope that closer acquaintance with my libretto will bring home to you its positive qualities. Set pieces like, say, the intermezzo, Zerbinetta's aria and the ensemble will not, I venture to say, be surpassed in their own line by anyone writing in Europe today. The way in which this work – though it adheres to the conventional form (which, properly understood, is full of appeal even to the librettist) – indicates and establishes its central idea quite naturally by making Ariadne and Zerbinetta represent diametrical contrasts in female character, or the manner in which I have led up to the arrival of Bacchus, first by the trio of the three women cutting each other short, next by the little Circe song, and finally by Zerbinetta's announcement which, though important in itself, gives the orchestra predominance in that hymn-like march theme – all this, I must say, seemed to me to deserve some expression of appreciation on the part of the one person for whom my work was visualized, conceived and executed. I doubt, moreover, if one could easily find in any other libretto for a one-act opera three songs of comparable delicacy, and at the same time equally characteristic in tone, as Harlekin's song, the rondo for Zerbinetta and the Circe song of Bacchus.

Not unnaturally I would rather have heard all this from you than be obliged to write it myself.

No doubt it will be possible to find a way of heightening the intensity of the end along the lines you indicate, but before we proceed to settle the degree and the manner of any such climax-building, let me try and explain in a few sentences the underlying idea or meaning of this little poetic work. What it is about is one of the straightforward and stupendous problems of life: fidelity; whether to hold fast to that which is lost, to cling to it even unto death – or to live, to live on, to get over it, to transform oneself, to sacrifice the integrity of the soul and yet in this transmutation to preserve one's essence, to remain a human being and not to sink to the level of the beast, which is without recollection. It is the fundamental theme of *Elektra*, the voice of Electra opposed to the voice of Chrysothemis, the heroic voice against the human. In the present case we have the group of heroes, demi-gods, gods – Ariadne, Bacchus, (Theseus) – facing the human, the merely human group consisting of the frivolous Zerbinetta and her companions, all of them base figures in life's masquerade. Zerbinetta is in her element drifting out of the arms of one man into the arms of another; Ariadne could be the wife or mistress of *one* man only, just as she can be only *one* man's widow, can be forsaken only by *one* man. One thing, however, is still left even for her: the miracle, the God. To him she gives herself, for she believes him to be Death: he is both Death and Life at once; he it is who reveals to her the immeasurable depths in her own nature, who makes of her an enchantress, the sorceress who herself transforms the poor little Ariadne; he it is who conjures up for her in this world another world beyond, who preserves her for us and at the same time transforms her.

But what to divine souls is a real miracle, is to the earth-bound nature of Zerbinetta just an everyday love-affair. She sees in Ariadne's experience the only thing she *can* see: the exchange of an old lover for a new one. And so these two spiritual worlds are in the end ironically brought together in the only way in which they can be brought together: in non-comprehension.

In this experience of Ariadne's, which is really the monologue of her lonely soul, Bacchus represents no mere *deus ex machina*; for him, too, the experience is vital. Innocent, young and unaware of his own divinity he travels where the wind takes him, from island to island. His first affair was typical, with a woman of easy virtue, you may say or you may call her Circe. To his youth and innocence with its infinite potentialities the shock has been tremendous: were he Harlekin, this would be merely the beginning of one long round of love affairs. But he is Bacchus; confronted with the enormity of erotic experience all is laid bare to him in a flash – the assimilation with the animal, the transformation, his own divinity. So he escapes from Circe's embraces still unchanged, but not without a wound, a longing, not without knowledge. The impact on him now of this meeting with a being whom he can love, who is mistaken about him but is enabled by this very mistake to give herself to him wholly and to reveal herself to him in all her loveliness, who entrusts herself to him completely, exactly as one entrusts oneself to Death, this impact I need not expound further to an artist such as you.

It would be a very great joy to me if, by an early reply to this personal, friendly letter, you were to restore to me that sense of fine and intimate contact between us which I so much enjoyed during our earlier collaboration and which has by now become indispensable to me.

Very sincerely yours,
HOFMANNSTHAL

Opera is, of course, the classic source for the funnier musical stories: we have all heard about Siegfrieds whose anvils won't break (or break too soon), Toscas who bounce back into view of the audience after casting themselves off the top of Castel Sant'Angelo, snow which falls relentlessly into Mimi's bedroom or Boris's council chamber, and Lohengrins whose swans sail off before they have a chance to get on board. Most people probably know Leo Slezak's famous reaction in the last instance: 'What time's the next swan?' – but here is another *Lohengrin* incident that may not be so well known

A very special adventure was my meeting with Karl Burian, the remarkable Czech tenor, who died in the same year that my operatic work started. He drank himself to death, dying horribly of delirium tremens. His stage presence was magical. Imagine a short, ugly, middle-aged man, with sparse red-grey hair (sometimes covered by a wig), a ravaged face distorted by drink (which no make-up could hide), stooped shoulders and at best a lurching, somewhat insecure gait. And imagine this gnome-like figure side-by-side – or worse, embracing – one of the huge, over-bosomy Brünnhildes or Isoldes of those times. Grotesque – a Hoffnung cartoon come alive – and yet his audiences were completely enraptured, hearing and seeing the young Siegfried or Tristan. Such is the power of a great stage talent. And such was Burian's power. At rehearsals he was sleepy and absent-minded, if sober; or heart-breakingly funny when slightly drunk.

Every performance in which he appeared was like a huge game of roulette. Until he actually appeared on the scene, and sometimes not then, no one knew what state he would be in. One evening, singing Lohengrin, and even more unsteady than usual, he almost capsized the swan-boat. Then, stepping out of it with surprising assurance, he sang *Nun sei bedankt, mein lieber Schwan* with such ethereal beauty that our terror turned to delight. The anxious watchers backstage began congratulating each other, shaking hands, embracing. Thank God, all was well!

But – what was this? His song finished, Burian got up from his kneeling position, took a long, ominous look round the stage, and started a deliberate, pompous walk towards Elsa and King Heinrich. Arriving in front of them he took Elsa's hand, carried it to his lips, kissed it gallantly, clicked his heels like a lieutenant of Dragoons, and – rendering Richard Wagner's elaborate three-act effort completely superfluous – introduced himself loud and clear: 'Lohengrin!'

ANTAL DORATI *Notes of Seven Decades* 1979

At Wexford, on the south-east tip of Eire, there is a festival round about Hallowe'en each year. In a pretty little Georgian theatre tucked in between two rows of fishermen's houses the rafters resound to obscure operas by Giordano, Humperdinck, Massenet or, *annus mirabilis*, Spontini – and, thank God, Bernard Levin was there

Well, in 1979 it was *La Vestale*. The set for Act I of the opera consisted of a platform laid over the stage, raised about a foot at the back and sloping evenly to the footlights. This was meant to represent the interior of the Temple where burned the sacred flame, and had therefore to look like marble; the designer had achieved a convincing alternative by covering the raised stage in Formica. But the Formica was slippery; to avoid the risk of a performer taking a tumble, designer and stage manager had between them discovered that an ample sprinkling of lemon juice would make the surface sufficiently sticky to provide a secure foothold. The story now forks; down one road, there lies the belief that the member of the stage staff whose duty it was to sprinkle the lifesaving liquid, and who had done so without fail at rehearsal and at the earlier performances (this was the last one of the Festival), had simply forgotten. Down the other branch in the road is a much more attractive rumour: that the theatre charlady, inspecting the premises in the afternoon, had seen to her horror and indignation that the stage was covered in the remains of some spilt liquid, and, inspired by professional pride, had thereupon set to and given it a good scrub and polish all over.

The roads now join again, for apart from the superior charm of the second version, it makes no difference what the explanation was. What matters is what happened.

What happened began to happen very early. The hero of the opera strides on to the stage immediately after the curtain has gone up. The hero strode; and instantly fell flat on his back. There was a murmur of sympathy and concern from the audience for his embarrassment and for the possibility that he might have been hurt; it was the last such sound that was to be heard that night, and it was very soon to be replaced by sounds of a very different nature.

The hero got to his feet, with considerable difficulty, and, having slid some way down the stage in falling, proceeded to stride up-stage to where he should have been in the first place; he had, of course, gone on singing throughout, for the music had not stopped. Striding up-stage, however, was plainly more difficult than he had reckoned on, for every time he took a step and tried to follow it with another, the foot with which he had taken the first proceeded to slide down-stage again, swiftly followed by its companion; he may not have known it, but he was giving a perfect demonstration of what is called *marcher sur place*, a graceful manoeuvre normally used in mime, and seen at its best in the work of Marcel Marceau.

Finding progress uphill difficult, indeed impossible, the hero wisely decided to abandon the attempt and stay where he was, singing bravely on, no doubt calculating that, since the stage was brightly lit, the next character to enter would notice him and adjust his own movements accordingly. So it proved, in a sense at least, for the next character to enter was the hero's trusted friend and confidant, who, seeing his hero further down-stage than he was supposed to be, loyally decided to join him there. Truth to tell, he had little choice, for from the moment he had stepped on to the stage he had begun to slide downhill, arms semaphoring, like Scrooge's clerk on the way home to his Christmas dinner. His downhill progress was arrested by his fetching up against his friend with a thud; this, as it happened, was not altogether inappropriate, as the opera called for them to embrace in friendly greeting at that point. It did not, however, call for them, locked in each other's arms and propelled by the impetus of the friend's descent, to career helplessly further down-stage with the evident intention of going straight into the orchestra pit with vocal accompaniment – for the hero's aria had, on the arrival of his companion, been transformed into a duet.

On the brink of ultimate disaster they managed to arrest their joint progress to destruction and, working their way along the edge of the stage like mountaineers seeking a route round an unbridgeable crevasse, most gallantly began, with infinite pain and by a form of progress most aptly described in the title of Lenin's famous pamphlet, *Four Steps Forward, Three Steps Back*, to climb up the terrible hill. It speedily became clear that this hazardous ascent was not being made simply from a desire to retain dramatic credibility; it had a much more practical object. The only structure breaking the otherwise all too smooth surface of the stage was a marble pillar, a yard or so high, on which there burned the sacred flame of the rite. This pillar was embedded firmly in the stage, and it had obviously occurred to both mountaineers at once that if they could only reach it it would provide a secure base for their subsequent operations, since if they held on to it for dear life they would at any rate be safe from any further danger of sliding downhill and/or breaking their necks.

It was soon borne in upon them that they had undertaken a labour of truly Sisyphean proportions, and would have been most heartily

pardoned by the audience if they had abandoned the librettist's words
at this point, and fitted to the music instead the old moral verse:

> The heights by great men reached and kept,
> Were not attained by sudden flight;
> But they, while their companions slept,
> Were toiling upwards in the night.

By this time the audience – all 440 of us – were in a state of such
abandon with laughter that several of us felt that if this were to
continue a moment longer we would be in danger of doing ourselves a
serious internal mischief; little did we know that the fun was just
beginning, for shortly after Mallory and Irvine reached their longed-
for goal, the chorus entered, and instantly flung themselves *en masse*
into a very freely choreographed version of *Les Patineurs*, albeit to the
wrong music. The heroine herself, the priestess Giulia, with a survival
instinct strong enough to suggest that she would be the one to get
close to, should any reader of these lines happen to be shipwrecked
along with the Wexford opera company, skated into the wings and
kicked her shoes off and then, finding on her return that this had
hardly improved matters, skated back to the wings and removed her
tights as well.

Now, however, the singing never having stopped for a moment, the
chorus had come to the same conclusion as had the hero and his
friend, namely that holding on to the holy pillar was the only way to
remain upright and more or less immobile. The trouble with this
conclusion was that there was only one such pillar on the stage, and it
was a small one; as the cast crowded round it, it seemed that there
would be some very unseemly brawling among those seeking a hand-
hold, a foothold, even a bare finger-hold, on this tiny island of security
in the terrible sea of impermanence. By an instinctive understanding
of the principles of co-operation, however, they decided the matter
without bloodshed; those nearest the pillar clutched it, those next
nearest clutched the clutchers, those farther away still clutched those,
and so on until, in a kind of daisy-chain that snaked across the stage,
everybody was accommodated.

The condition of the audience was now one of fully extended
hysteria, which was having the most extraordinary effect – itself
intensifying the audience's condition – on the orchestra. At Wexford,
the orchestra pit runs under the stage; only a single row of players –
those at the edge of the pit nearest the audience, together, of course,
with the conductor – could see what was happening on the stage. The
rest realized that *something* out of the ordinary was going on up there,

and would have been singularly dull of wit if they had not, for many members of the audience were now slumped on the floor weeping helplessly in the agony of their mirth, and although the orchestra at Wexford cannot see the stage, it can certainly see the auditorium.

Theologians tell us that the delights of the next world are eternal. Perhaps; but what is certain is that all earthly ones, alas, are temporary, and duly, after giving us a glimpse of the more enduring joy of Heaven that must have strengthened the devout in their faith and caused instant conversion among many of the unbelievers, the entertainment came to an end when the first act of the opera did so, amid such cheering as I had never before heard in an opera house, and can never hope to hear again. In the interval before Act II, a member of the production staff walked back and forth across the stage, sprinkling it with the precious nectar, and we knew that our happiness was at an end. But he who, after such happiness, would have demanded more, would be greedy indeed, and most of us were content to know that, for one crowded half-hour, we on honeydew had fed, and drunk the milk of Paradise.

BERNARD LEVIN *Conducted Tour* 1981

I love Italian opera – it's so reckless. Damn Wagner, and his bellowings at Fate and death. Damn Debussy, and his averted face. I like the Italians who run all on impulse, and don't care about their immortal souls, and don't worry about the ultimate.

D. H. LAWRENCE Letter 1911

The Italian opera . . . an exotick and irrational entertainment . . .

SAMUEL JOHNSON *Lives of the Poets* 1779–81

PS – They have been crucifying Othello into an Opera (*Otello* by Rossini) – Music good but lugubrious – but as for the words! – all the real scenes with Iago cut out – & the greatest nonsense instead – the handkerchief turned into a billet doux, and the first Singer would not *black* his face – for some exquisite reasons assigned in the preface. – Scenery – dresses – & Music very good –

BYRON Letter from Venice 1818

Let me explain the inner workings of the theatrical system in Italy. A *contractor* – usually the wealthiest burgher of some petty township, for this particular office carries with it considerable social prestige and not a few other advantages, although it frequently turns out to be financially ruinous! – undertakes to run the theatre in the town whose leading citizen he has the honour to be; so to start with, he forms a company, which consists invariably of: a *prima donna*, a *tenore*, a *basso cantante*, a *basso buffo*, a second (female), and a third (male) *buffo* singer. Next, the *impresario* engages a *maestro* (composer) to write an original opera for him, having always due regard, in the setting of the *arias*, to the particular characteristics of the voices of the singers who are to perform them. The *impresario* then purchases a text (the *libretto*: always in verse), which may cost him anything from sixty to eighty francs, the author being usually some wretched *abbé* parasitically attached to one of the wealthier households in the neighbourhood; for in Lombardy, where the meanest of petty provincial towns invariably counts some half dozen landed estates bringing in a hundred thousand *livres* a year and upwards, the undignified profession of *parasite*, so brilliantly satirized by Terence, still flourishes in all its glory. Next, the *impresario*, himself the owner of one of these estates, proceeds to hand over all the business management of the theatre to his agent, who is usually a lawyer, and in fact the same arch-scoundrel who manages his personal business in private life; while *he* (the impresario) is more properly occupied in falling in love with the *prima donna*; at which point, the great question which arises to tickle the curiosity of the entire neighbourhood, is whether or not he will offer her his arm in public.

Thus 'organized', the company eventually gives its first performance, but not without previously having survived a whole month of utterly burlesque intrigues, thus furnishing an inexhaustible supply of gossip to entertain the entire countryside. This *prima recita* is the greatest public happening in all the long, dull existence of the town concerned – so momentous indeed, that I can think of nothing in Paris which could offer anything like an adequate comparison. For three weeks on end, eight or ten thousand persons will argue the merits and defects of the opera with all the powers of sustained concentration with which heaven has seen fit to endow them, and above all, with the maximum force of which their lungs are capable. This *première*, unless blasted at the very outset by some scandal of positively catastrophic dimensions, would normally be followed by some thirty or forty others, at the conclusion of which, the company disbands. A run of this type is usually called a 'season' (*una stagione*); and the best season is that which coincides with the Carnival. Any singers who have not been engaged (*scritturati*), usually hang about in Bologna or in Milan, where they have theatrical agents who make it their business to secure them contracts, and to rob them unashamedly in the process.

Furnished with this little sketch of the life and manners prevailing in the Italian theatre, the reader will now have no difficulty in picturing the singular existence which Rossini led between the years 1810 and 1816, and which has no equivalent in France. One after the other, he visited every town in Italy, spending some two or three months in each. As soon as he set foot in the place, he would be welcomed, banqueted and generally adulated by every *dilettante* in the neighbourhood, so that the first two or three weeks would be gaily frittered away in the consumption of gala dinners, spiced with sighs and shrugs over the unspeakable imbecility of the librettist. Rossini, over and above the extraordinary and penetrating intelligence with which he was gifted by nature, was indebted to his earliest mistress (the countess P— in Pesaro) for a thorough training in literary appreciation, which he had perfected through reading the works of Ariosto, the comedies of Machiavelli, the *Fiabe* of Gozzi, and the satires of Buratti; and in consequence, he was exquisitely sensitive to the nicer absurdities of the average *libretto*. . . .

After two or three weeks spent in these and similar dissipations, Rossini begins to refuse invitations to banquets and *soirées musicales*, under the pretext that he must seriously give his attention to studying the vocal potentialities of his company. With this end in view, he commandeers a piano, and makes them sing; and on such occasions the observer may witness the depressing spectacle of a great composer compelled to distort and mutilate the finest flights of musical inspiration which have ever been known, for the simple reason that the *tenore* cannot reach the note which some noble vista of creative imagination has suggested, or else because the *prima donna* invariably sings off pitch in the course of transition from one key to the next! Frequently the only competent singer in the whole company turns out to be the *basso*.

Finally, three weeks before the *première* is billed, Rossini, who is by now quite sufficiently familiar with the voices of his company, starts to compose in earnest. He rises late, and settles down to work through a perpetual barrage of conversation maintained by his new-found acquaintances, who, despite every protest he can venture to make, obstinately refuse to leave him in peace for a single instant during the whole of the live-long day. He dines with them at the local *osteria*, and as often as not, sups with them as well; he returns home late at night, his friends convoying him back to the very door of his lodgings, all singing at the tops of their voices some song which he has improvised during the course of the evening; on occasions, they have even been known to indulge in an impromptu *miserere*, to the inexpressible scandal of all pure and pious church-goers in the neighbourhood. But eventually he does manage to retreat to the peace of his own room, and this is the hour – often towards three in the morning – when his most brilliant musical inspirations tend to come upon him. He scribbles them down, hastily and without a piano, on any odd scraps of paper which may chance to be handy, and tosses them aside until the morning, when, amid the roar and hubbub of convivial conversation, he may find time to 'instrument' them (to use his own favourite expression). He must be pictured as a spirit of quicksilver agility, as a character of the most fiery temperament, perpetually subject to new impressions, perpetually on the alert for new ideas; the sort of man for whom nothing ever seems too difficult.

. . . To the best of my knowledge, there is only one thing which reduces this ever-brilliant, ever-fertile, ever-active genius to a state of utter paralysis, and that is the importunate presence of some pedantic *purist*, in whose conversation flattery alternates with an airing of theories, and who is only happy if he can overwhelm his victim with compliments decked out in academic verbiage. . . .

One such pedant, a full-blown *monsignore* by trade, who, in order to badger him with civilities, had tracked him down right into the very bedchamber of the inn where he was staying, and had effectively prevented him from getting out of bed, received the following admonition: '*Ella mi vanta per mia gloria* . . . you are pleased to mention my celebrity; yet do you know, my lord Bishop, wherein lies my *fundamental* claim to immortality? I will tell you: it is because I am the handsomest man alive! Canova has promised me that, one day, he will use me as a model for a statue of Achilles!' – saying which, Rossini leapt eagerly out of bed, and stood before the dazed stare of that noble prelate in the very costume in which Achilles is usually depicted, and whose public exhibition, in Italy, is considered monumentally disrespectful. 'Observe, my Lord, this *leg*,' he went on. 'When a man possesses a limb so exquisitely turned, is he not *certain* of immortality? . . .' The remainder of the harangue, I omit; for once launched on a thoroughly bad joke, Rossini gets drunk with the sound of his own voice, intoxicated with the wild gusts of laughter which are inspired by his own grotesque fancies; he seems to be inexhaustibly fertile in the invention of nonsensical inanities, which usually veer rapidly towards the obscene; and once he is set on *that* course, nothing in the

world can stop him. The pedantic prelate soon discovered that there
was no alternative but to retreat.

Composing, according to Rossini, is mere child's play; the real
drudgery of the job comes with *rehearsal*. Then begins the agony, for
on such distressing occasions the poor *maestro* has to endure the
torments of the damned, as, one by one, he hears his most inspired
ideas, his most brilliant, his suavest *cantilenas*, distorted and disfigured in every key the human voice can embrace. 'It is quite enough,'
Rossini maintains, 'to make one want to boo oneself out of the
profession for good and all.' Invariably, after each rehearsal, he falls
into a fit of black depression, utterly disgusted with music which, only
the previous day, had seemed delightful.

Nevertheless, these rehearsal-sessions, painful as they must be for
any sensitive young composer, are to my mind symbolic, for they
reflect the triumph of Italian musical sensibility. On such occasions,
gathered together around some evil, broken-backed piano in a decre-
pit shanty, known as the *ridotto*, belonging to the local theatre of some
unspeakable little provincial town – say Reggio or Velletri – I have
watched eight or ten fourth-rate, down-at-heel opera-singers proceed-
ing to rehearsal, invariably to the accompaniment of a full concerto for
saucepans and roasting-jack from some neighbouring kitchen, and,
under such appalling circumstances, both *experience* and *express* the
subtlest and the most intimately moving emotional nuances of which
the art of music is capable; and it is precisely on occasions such as these
that we cold Northerners must stand amazed to see a plain set of
ignorant dolts, all totally incapable of picking out a simple waltz on the
piano, or of telling the difference between one key and the next,
singing and accompanying *by instinct alone*, and with such magnificent
brio, music which is new, original and completely unfamiliar to them,
and which, in fact, the *maestro* himself composes, alters and re-
arranges before their very eyes while they are actually in course of
rehearsal. They make countless mistakes, of course; but in music,
mistakes which are due to over-enthusiasm are soon forgotten and
forgiven – as quickly as the lover forgives his mistress faults which
arise from loving too well. . . .

The critical evening arrives at last. The *maestro* takes his seat at the
piano; the auditorium is stuffed to bursting-point. The crowds have
come pouring in from every town and village within twenty miles'
radius; enthusiasts bivouac in their open carriages in the middle of the
streets; the inns have been overflowing ever since the previous day,
and the customary Italian courtesy of these establishments is showing

a tendency to wear a bit thin. Everyone has downed tools long ago. As the hour of the performance draws near, the town seems like a deserted, hollow shell; the passions, the wavering hopes and fears, the entire life of a whole thriving population is focused upon the *theatre*.

As the overture begins, you could hear a pin drop; as it bangs its way triumphantly to an end, the din bursts with unbelievable violence. It is extolled to high heaven; or alternately, it is whistled, nay rather *howled* into eternity with merciless shrieks and ulutations. There is no parallel in Paris, where cautious vanity anxiously eyes a neighbouring vanity beside it; these are men possessed of seven devils, determined at all costs, by dint of shrieking, stamping and battering with their canes against the backs of the seats in front, to enforce the triumph of *their* opinion, and above all, to prove that, come what may, *none but their opinion is correct*; for, in all the world, there is no intolerance like that of a man of artistic sensibility. . . .

Each *aria* of the new opera, in its turn, is listened to in perfect silence; after which, the cataclysm is let loose once more; and the bellowing of a storm-tormented sea is nothing but the feeblest comparison. The audience makes its opinion of the singers on the one hand, and of the composer on the other, distinctly audible. There are cries of *Bravo Davide! Bravo Pisaroni!*, or on other occasions, the whole theatre will echo with daemonic shrieks of *Bravo maestro!* Rossini rises from his seat at the piano, his handsome face assuming an unwonted expression of gravity. He bows thrice, submitting to storms of applause, and deafened by a most unlikely variety of acclamations, for whole sentences of adulation may be flung at his unresisting head; after which, the company proceeds to the next item.

Rossini always appears in person at the piano for the first three nights of each new opera; but, at the conclusion of this statutory period, having received his salary of seventy *sequins* (about eight hundred francs) and attended a grand farewell dinner given in his honour by all his new friends (that is to say, by the entire population of the town) he at length drives away in a *vettura*, his bags up beside him stuffed far more tightly with music than with personal belongings, only to begin the same procedure all over again at the next port of call, perhaps forty miles distant. . . .

STENDHAL *Life of Rossini* 1824

Last night a theatre that Torlonia has undertaken and organized, was opened with a new opera of Pacini's. The crowd was great, and every box filled with handsome, well-dressed people; young Torlonia appeared in a stage-box with his mother, the old Duchess, and they were immensely applauded. The audience call out *Bravo, Torlonia, grazie, grazie!* Opposite to him was Jerome, with his suite, and covered with orders; in the next box Countess Samoilow, etc. Over the orchestra is a picture of Time pointing to the dial of the clock, which revolves slowly, and is enough to make any one melancholy. Pacini then appeared at the piano, and was kindly welcomed. He had prepared no overture, so the opera began with a chorus, accompanied by strokes on an anvil tuned in the proper key. The Corsair came forward, sang his *aria*, and was applauded, on which the Corsair above, and the Maestro below, bowed (this pirate is a contralto, and sung by Mademoiselle Mariani); a variety of airs followed, and the piece became very tiresome. This seemed to be also the opinion of the public, for when Pacini's grand *finale* began, the whole pit stood up, talking to each other as loud as they could, laughing and turning their backs on the stage. Madame Samoilow fainted in her box, and was carried out. Pacini glided away from the piano, and at the end of the act, the curtain fell in the midst of a great tumult. Then came the grand ballet of *Barbe Bleue*, followed by the last act of the opera. As the audience were now in a mood for it, they hissed the whole ballet from the very beginning, and accompanied the second act also with hooting and laughter. At the close Torlonia was called for, but he would not appear.

This is the matter-of-fact narrative of a first performance, at the opening of a theatre in Rome. I had anticipated much amusement, so I came away considerably out of humour; still, if the music had made *furore*, I should have been very indignant, for it is so wretched that it really is beneath all criticism. But that they should turn their backs on their favourite Pacini, whom they wished to crown in the Capitol, parody his melodies, and sing them in a ludicrous style, this does, I confess, provoke me not a little, and is likewise a proof of how low such a musician stands in the public opinion. Another time they will carry him home on their shoulders; but this is no compensation. They would not act thus in France with Boieldieu; independent of all love of art, a sense of propriety would prevent their doing so. . . .

FELIX MENDELSSOHN Letter 1831

Operatic performances made favourite backdrops for scenes of social or
amorous intention in many of the romantic novels of the nineteenth century.
Perhaps the most famous is Tolstoy's description of the meeting between
Natasha Rostov and Anatole Kurágin at the opera in Moscow. Here, for a
change, is Turgenev's description of a young runaway couple at the opera in
Venice, the husband already far gone with the fatal disease that was to kill him
on the following day

One of Verdi's operas was being performed; it was *Traviata*, in truth
rather a commonplace piece, but one which had already successfully
made the round of all the European cities, and which is well known
even to us Russians. The Venice season was over, and none of the
singers achieved more than a dull mediocrity; they just shouted their
parts as loud as they could. Violetta was taken by a singer without any
particular reputation, and judging by the way the public received her
she was not much liked, though she was not without talent. She was a
young girl with dark eyes and no great beauty; her voice was not quite
steady and had already lost its purity of tone. She was dressed with an
almost painful *naïveté* in a motley assortment of garments; a red hair-
net on her head, a dress of faded sky-blue satin fitting too tightly
round her bosom, thick suède gloves reaching up to her pointed
elbows; and indeed, how should a girl like this, the daughter of some
peasant from Bergamo, know how the Parisian courtesans dress? She
did not even know how to carry herself on the stage; but there was
much sincerity and artless simplicity in her playing, and she sang with
that peculiarly passionate expression and rhythm which belongs to
the Italians alone. Elena and Insarov were sitting alone in the dark box,
next to stage. The gay frame of mind which had taken possession
of them in the Accademia di Belle Arti was still with them. When a
man in a pea-green tail-coat and a tousled white wig appeared on the
scene – he was the father of the unfortunate youth who falls into the
clutches of a temptress – opened his mouth slantwise, and, in obvious
confusion, gave vent to a dismal bass *tremolo*, both Insarov and Elena
almost burst into laughter; but the Violetta made a real impression on
them.

'They hardly applaud the poor girl at all,' Elena said, 'yet I prefer her
a thousand times to some self-assured, minor celebrity who would just
be posing and giving herself airs and striving after effect. It's as if she is
really experiencing what she is acting; you can see she doesn't notice
the audience.'

Insarov leaned over the box and gazed intently at Violetta.

'Yes,' he said, 'it's the real thing with her; there's a reek of death in
the air.'

At that Elena was silent.

The curtain rose on the third act. Elena shuddered at the sight of the bed, the drawn curtains, the medicine bottles, the shaded lamp – it all brought to mind visions of the recent past. 'And what of the present, the future?' The grim question flashed through her mind . . . As if in answer to the assumed cough of the actress on the stage came the hollow sound of Insarov's unfeigned cough at her side. Elena looked at him surreptitiously, and at once her face assumed a calm, serene expression; Insarov read her thoughts, he smiled and began to accompany the singing under his breath.

But he was soon silent again. The young singer's performance was gaining in strength and freedom all the time. She seemed to rid herself of everything unnecessary, everything irrelevant, and – what is the rarest, highest pleasure for any artist – to *find herself*. Suddenly she seemed to have stepped across that line, that indefinable line, beyond which beauty lies. The audience was surprised, startled; this plain-looking girl with the husky voice began to grip it, to gain possession of it. Indeed, her voice had lost its impurity of tone, it had grown warmer and more powerful. When Alfredo appeared, Violetta's cry of joy almost brought forth that storm of applause which goes by the name of *fanatismo*, and beside which all our northern acclamations are as nothing. A moment later, and the audience was plunged in silence again. The duet began, the best thing in the opera: in it the composer has expressed all the regrets of a youth senselessly squandered, the last struggle of hopeless, helpless love. Seized, carried away on a gust of feeling in which all shared, with tears of joy, the artist's joy, and of real suffering in her eyes, she gave herself up to the surge of her emotions; her face was transfigured, and as, confronted by the sudden spectre of approaching death, the words of her impassioned prayer to heaven broke from her: '*Lascia mi vivere . . . morir si giovane*' (Let me live – to die so young) the whole theatre echoed with frantic clapping and rapturous applause.

Elena had turned quite cold. She sought Insarov's hand, held it tight and felt his answering pressure – but neither looked at the other. This time there was a different meaning underlying the caress, a different motive from that which, earlier in the evening, had inspired him to take her hand in the gondola.

IVAN TURGENEV *On the Eve* 1859

Moving to France, here is Emma Bovary, inexpertly accompanied to the opera at Rouen by her boorish, though adoring husband

Charles went straight off to buy tickets. He got the stalls mixed up with the gallery, the pit with the boxes; he asked for explanations but failed to understand them, was sent from the box-office to the manager, returned to the inn, set out for the theatre once more, and measured the length of the town, between the theatre and the boulevard, several times.

Madame bought herself a hat, gloves, and a bouquet. Monsieur was in dread of missing the start, and, without stopping even to gulp down a plate of broth, they arrived at the theatre to find the doors still shut.

The crowds were lining up along the wall, penned symmetrically inside the railings. Gigantic posters at the corners of the neighbouring streets announced in gaudy lettering: 'Bride of Lammermoor – Lagardy – Opera', and so on. It was a fine day, everyone felt hot, curls ran with perspiration, handkerchiefs were being fetched out to mop red foreheads. Now and then a warm breeze from the river set the fringe of the drill awnings fluttering over the tavern doors. A little farther down, however, came a refreshing draught of ice-cold air, bringing a smell of tallow, oil and leather with it. This was the emanation from the Rue des Charrettes, a street of great dark warehouses and trundling barrels.

So as not to stand there looking foolish, Emma suggested a stroll by the harbour before going in. Bovary kept the tickets cautiously clutched in his hand inside his trousers pocket, which he held tight against his belly.

Her heart beat as she entered the foyer. She smiled involuntarily, out of vanity, as she saw people jostling down the passage on the right while she went up to the boxes. She took a child's delight in pushing open the large upholstered doors with one finger, she breathed deep into her lungs the dusty smell of the corridors, and when she was ensconced in her box she drew herself up in her seat as to the manner born.

The theatre was beginning to fill up. Opera-glasses emerged from their cases; seat-holders, catching sight of their friends, waved greetings. They had come to find relaxation in the arts from the cares of business. Nevertheless they were still talking shop – cotton, proof spirit, indigo, they couldn't forget it. There were old men with peaceful, expressionless faces, bleached hair and bleached complexions, heads like silver medals tarnished by a leaden vapour. There were young bloods strutting about in the stalls, showing off their rose-pink or apple-green cravats in the opening of their waistcoats, and being admired from up above by Madame Bovary as they leaned on their gold-knobbed walking-canes, with the palms of their yellow gloves stretched taut.

Then the orchestra candles were lit and the chandelier was let down from the ceiling, its glittering facets shedding a sudden gaiety upon the house. The musicians filed in; and after a confused din of rumbling double-basses, scraping fiddles, braying cornets, chirruping flutes and flageolets, there came three taps from the stage: a roll of drums: sustained chords from the brasses, and the curtain rose upon a country scene.

It was a crossways in a wood, with a fountain on the left shaded by an oak-tree. Peasants and chieftains with plaids over their shoulders were singing a hunting-chorus. A captain came on and, raising both arms to Heaven, invoked the Spirit of Evil. A second character appeared. Then both departed, and the huntsmen struck up again.

Emma found herself back in the books of her youth, in the land of Sir Walter Scott. She seemed to hear the skirl of the bagpipes echoing through the mist across the heather. Remembering the novel, she could understand the libretto without difficulty, and as she followed the plot, sentence by sentence, elusive thoughts came back to her, to be dispersed immediately by the thunder of the music. She let herself be lulled by the melodies: she felt a vibration pass through her whole being, as if the bows of the violins were being drawn across her own nerves. She hadn't eyes enough to take in all the costumes and the scenery, the characters, the painted trees that shook when anyone took a step, the velvet caps, the cloaks and swords, the whole creation moving to the music as in the atmosphere of another world. A young woman came forward and threw a purse to a squire in green. She was left alone, and a flute started playing, like the murmur of a fountain or the warbling of birds. Gravely Lucy entered upon her cavatina in G major. She plained of love, she longed for wings. So too Emma would have liked to escape from life and fly away in an embrace. . . . Suddenly Edgar Lagardy made his entrance.

He had a splendid pallor of the sort that lends a marmoreal majesty to the ardent races of the South. His vigorous frame was tightly clad in a brown-coloured jerkin. A small carved dagger swung at his left thigh. He rolled his eyes languorously and showed his white teeth. It was said that a Polish princess had fallen in love with him hearing him sing one night on the beach at Biarritz, where he had been a boat-mender. She had thrown everything to the winds for him. He had left her for other women; and his fame as a lover served but to enhance his reputation as an artist. This canny player was always careful to slip into the advertisements some lyric phrase about the fascination of his person and the sensitivity of his soul. A fine voice, imperturbable self-possession, more personality than intelligence and more power than poetry, went to complete the armoury of this admirable mountebank-type, with its ingredients of the hairdresser and the toreador.

He cast an immediate spell. He clasped Lucy in his arms, he left her, returned to her, seemed in despair. He burst out in anger, then agonized with an infinite elegiac tenderness, and the notes rolled forth from his bare throat laden with sobs and kisses. Emma leaned forward to watch him, her fingernails clutching at the plush on the box, and took her heart's fill of those melodious lamentations that poured out to the accompaniment of the double-basses like cries of the drowning amid the tumult of the tempest. She recognized the ecstasy and the anguish of which she had all but died. The heroine's voice seemed simply the echo of her own consciousness, and all this fascinating make-believe a part of her own life. Yet none on earth had ever loved with a love like that. *He* had not wept like Edgar, that last evening in the moonlight when they had said, 'Till tomorrow! Till tomorrow!' . . . The theatre was ringing with applause. The whole of the finale was begun over again. The lovers spoke of the flowers on their tomb, of vows, exile, fate, hope. When they sang their last *adieu* Emma uttered a sharp cry which was drowned in the reverberations of the final chords.

'Why is that lord being cruel to her?' asked Bovary.

'No, no, no, he's her lover,' she answered.

'Well, he's swearing vengeance on her family, whereas the other one, the one that came on just now, said "I love Lucy and believe that she loves me", and then he went off arm-in-arm with her father. That *is* her father, isn't it, the ugly little chap with the cock's feather in his hat?'

Emma explained. But when they got to the duet in which Gilbert unfolds his nefarious schemes to his master Ashton, Charles, seeing the supposed wedding-ring that was to deceive Lucy, imagined it to be a love-token from Edgar. Not that he claimed to understand the story: the music did so interfere with the words.

'What does it matter?' said Emma. 'Be quiet!'

'You know I always like to get things straight,' he answered, leaning over her shoulder.

'Quiet, quiet!' she said impatiently.

Lucy came forward, half-supported by her women, with a wreath of orange-blossom in her hair, her face paler than her white satin dress. Emma thought of her own wedding-day; she saw herself back in the cornfields again, walking along the little path on the way to church. Oh, why, why hadn't she resisted, entreated, like that girl there?

Instead she had plunged blindly, blithely, over the precipice. . . . If only in the freshness of her beauty, before the soilure of marriage and the disillusionment of adultery, she could have grounded her life upon some great, strong heart – then everything would have gone together, virtue and love, the pleasures and the duties, never would she have descended from that height of felicity. But, of course, such happiness must be a fiction, invented to be the despair of all desire. She knew now the littleness of those passions that art exaggerates. Accordingly, Emma strove to deflect her thoughts, to see no more in this reproduction of her sorrows than an embodied fantasy, an ornament for the eye. And she was actually smiling to herself, a smile of contemptuous pity, when from the velvet hangings at the back of the stage a man in a black cloak appeared.

He made a gesture and his broad-brimmed Spanish hat fell to the floor. Immediately orchestra and singers attacked the sextet. Edgar, flashing fury, dominated them all with his clear tenor. Ashton hurled his murderous challenge in deeper notes, Lucy moaned her shrill plaint; Arthur modulated aside in the middle register, the Minister's baritone pealed forth like an organ, while the women's chorus echoed his words deliciously. All the characters were now gesticulating in a line across the stage; and anger and vengeance, jealousy, pity, terror and astonishment all breathed forth together from their parted lips. The outraged lover brandished his naked sword. His lace ruffle jerked up and down with the heaving of his chest as he crossed from left to right with great strides, in buckskin boots that folded back over the ankles, clanking his spurs on the boards. There must, thought Emma, be an endless fund of love within him, that he should lavish it upon the audience in such plenteous draughts. She lost all wish to cavil as the romance of the role took hold of her. Drawn to the man by his creation of the character, she tried to picture to herself the life he led, that extraordinary, hectic, splendid life, that might have been hers if only chance had so ordained it. For they might have met, and loved. With him she would have visited all the kingdoms of Europe, travelling from capital to capital, sharing the fatigue and the glory, gathering up the flowers they flung at his feet, embroidering his costumes with her own hand; in the evening sitting at the back of a box, behind the gilt trellis-work, listening with parted lips to the profusion of that man who would be singing for none but her. He would look up at her as he sang his part on the stage. . . . A wild idea seized her: he was looking at her now, yes, she was certain he was! She longed to run to his arms, to shelter in his strength as in the very incarnation of love, and to say to him, to cry out to him, 'Take me! Carry me away! Away! Yours, yours be all my ardour, all my dreams!'

The curtain fell.

The smell of gas mingled with the smell of breath, the waving of fans made the air still stuffier. Emma wanted to go out, but the corridors were jammed with people; she sank back into her seat with palpitations that took her breath away. Afraid that she was going to faint, Charles went off to the refreshment-room to fetch her a glass of barley-water.

He had the greatest difficulty in getting back to the box. Carrying the glass in both hands, he got his elbows jogged at every step and spilt three-quarters of it over the shoulders of a Rouen lady in a short-sleeved dress, who screamed like a peacock, as though she were being murdered, when she felt the cold liquid running down her back. Her husband, a mill-owner, got furious with the clumsy fellow, and while she took her handkerchief and dabbed at the stains on her beautiful cherry taffeta, he muttered surlily the words compensation, expense, repayment. . . .

At last Charles reached his wife.

'Heavens,' he gasped, 'I thought I'd never get here! It's packed! Packed! . . . And you'll never guess,' he added, 'whom I ran into up there! Monsieur Léon!'

'Léon?'

'Himself! He's coming along to pay you his respects.'

The words were hardly out of his mouth when the ex-clerk of Yonville entered their box.

He held out his hand with an aristocratic nonchalance, and Madame Bovary mechanically extended hers, yielding no doubt to the attraction of a stronger will. She had not touched that hand since that spring evening when the rain pattered on the green leaves and they stood at the window saying goodbye. . . . In an instant, however, she recalled herself to the requirements of the situation, shook herself out of her trance with an effort and began to stammer a few hurried phrases.

'Oh! Good evening! Well! fancy you here!'

'Ssh!' came a voice from the pit, for the third act was beginning.

'So you're at Rouen now.'

'Yes.'

'How long have you been here?'

'Ssh!' 'Quiet there!' 'Go outside!' People were looking round at them. They stopped talking.

But from that moment she listened no more. The wedding chorus, the scene between Ashton and his manservant, the great duet in D Major, for her it all happened at a distance, as though the instruments had been muted and the stage set farther back. She was thinking of those card-games at the chemist's, their walk to the nurse's house, the times when he had read to her in the arbour, or when they had sat together by the fireside: all that sorry little love, so quiet and so patient, so tactful and so tender – which she had none the less forgotten. Why had they met again? What chain of circumstance had brought him back into her life? He sat behind her, leaning against the partition, and every now and then a little shiver ran down her spine as she felt the warm breath of his nostrils on her hair.

'Does this stuff amuse you?' he said, leaning over so close that the point of his moustache brushed her cheek.

'Oh, heavens, no, not much,' she answered indifferently.

He suggested that they should go off and have ices somewhere.

'Oh, not yet! Stay a bit!' said Bovary. 'She's got her hair down – looks like being tragic, this does.'

But the mad scene was little to Emma's taste, and Lucy seemed to her to be overacting.

'She shouts,' said Emma, turning to Charles, who was drinking it in.

'Yes – maybe – a bit,' he answered, torn between the genuineness of his pleasure and the respect he felt for his wife's opinion.

'The heat – !' said Léon with a sigh.

'You're right, it's unbearable.'

'Is it too much for you?' Bovary asked.

'Suffocating! Let's go.'

Monsieur Léon arranged her long lace shawl daintily over her shoulders, and they all three went down to the quayside and sat outside a café in the open air.

GUSTAVE FLAUBERT *Madame Bovary* 1857

Italy (and, as it happens, the same opera) through English eyes

Philip had been to this theatre many years before. . . . Since then it had been thoroughly done up, in the tints of the beetroot and the tomato, and was in many other ways a credit to the little town. The orchestra had been enlarged, some of the boxes had terracotta draperies, and over each box was now suspended an enormous tablet, neatly framed, bearing upon it the number of that box. There was also a drop-scene, representing a pink and purple landscape, wherein sported many a lady lightly clad, and two more ladies lay along the top of the proscenium to steady a large and pallid clock. So rich and so appalling was the effect that Philip could scarcely suppress a cry.

There is something majestic in the bad taste of Italy; it is not the bad taste of a country which knows no better; it has not the nervous vulgarity of England, or the blinded vulgarity of Germany. It observes beauty, and chooses to pass it by. But it attains to beauty's confidence. This tiny theatre of Monteriano spraddled and swaggered with the best of them, and these ladies with their clock would have nodded to the young men on the ceiling of the Sistine.

Philip had tried for a box, but all the best were taken; it was rather a grand performance, and he had to be content with stalls. Harriet was fretful and insular. Miss Abbott was pleasant, and insisted on praising everything; her only regret was that she had no pretty clothes with her.

'We do all right,' said Philip, amused at her unwonted vanity.

'Yes, I know; but pretty things pack as easily as ugly ones. We had no need to come to Italy like guys.' . . .

Harriet, meanwhile, had been coughing ominously at the drop-scene, which presently rose on the grounds of Ravenswood, and the chorus of Scotch retainers burst into cry. The audience accompanied with tappings and drummings, swaying in the melody like corn in the wind. Harriet, though she did not care for music, knew how to listen to it. She uttered an acid 'Shish!'

'Shut it,' whispered her brother.

'We must make a stand from the beginning. They're talking.'

'It is tiresome,' murmured Miss Abbott; 'but perhaps isn't for us to interfere.'

Harriet shook her head and shished again. The people were quiet, not because it is wrong to talk during a chorus, but because it is natural to be civil to a visitor. For a little time she kept the whole house in order, and could smile at her brother complacently.

Her success annoyed him. He had grasped the principle of opera in Italy – it aims not at illusion but at entertainment – and he did not want this great evening party to turn into a prayer-meeting. But soon the boxes began to fill, and Harriet's power was over. Families greeted each other across the auditorium. People in the pit hailed their brothers and sons in the chorus, and told them how well they were singing. When Lucia appeared by the fountain there was loud applause, and cries of 'Welcome to Monteriano!' . . .

Lucia began to sing, and there was a moment's silence. She was stout and ugly; but her voice was still beautiful, and as she sang the theatre murmured like a hive of happy bees. All through the coloratura she was accompanied by sighs, and its top note was drowned in a shout of universal joy.

So the opera proceeded. The singers drew inspiration from the audience, and the two great sextets were rendered not unworthily. . . .

Harriet, like M. Bovary on a more famous occasion, was trying to follow the plot. Occasionally she nudged her companions, and asked them what had become of Walter Scott. She looked round grimly. The audience sounded drunk, and even Caroline, who never took a drop, was swaying oddly. Violent waves of excitement, all arising from very little, went sweeping round the theatre. The climax was reached in the mad scene. Lucia, clad in white, as befitted her malady, suddenly gathered up her streaming hair and bowed her acknowledgements to the audience. Then from the back of the stage – she feigned not to see it – there advanced a kind of bamboo clothes-horse, stuck all over with bouquets. It was very ugly, and most of the flowers in it were false. Lucia knew this, and so did the audience; and they all knew that the clothes-horse was a piece of stage property, brought in to make the performance go year after year. None the less did it unloose the great deeps. With a scream of amazement and joy she embraced the animal, pulled out one or two practicable blossoms, pressed them to her lips, and flung them to her admirers. They flung them back, with loud melodious cries, and a little boy in one of the stage-boxes snatched up his sister's carnations and offered them. 'Che carino!' exclaimed the singer. She darted at the little boy and kissed him. Now the noise became tremendous. 'Silence! Silence!' shouted many old gentlemen behind. 'Let the divine creature continue!' But the young men in the adjacent box were imploring Lucia to extend her civility to them. She refused, with a humorous expressive gesture. One of them hurled a bouquet at her. She spurned it with her foot. Then, encouraged by the roars of the audience, she picked it up and tossed it to them. Harriet was always unfortunate. The bouquet struck her full in the chest, and a little *billet-doux* fell out of it into her lap.

'Call this classical?' she cried, rising from her seat. 'It's not even respectable! Philip! Take me out at once.'

E. M. FORSTER Where Angels Fear to Tread 1905

This description was in fact based on a performance of *Lucia* in Florence on 12 May 1903, to which Forster went with the Cambridge musicologist, E. J. Dent. Forster later wrote

. . . Lucia was sung by a little known soprano. Her name was Tetrazzini. She had come along in a travelling company from Faenza.

We all thought her splendid, but had no conception of her great future and international fame. It is amusing that I should have popped her into my little book without the least idea of her approaching celebrity. As the years passed and she was singing over the world, I sometimes thought I would write to her, for I believe that she was an amiable lady as well as a great artist. I decided not to write and I think you will agree I was wise. No artist, however great, no lady, however amiable, likes to be called ugly and stout.

E. M. FORSTER from a typescript at King's College, Cambridge

And finally Wagner, through Wagnerian eyes. Siegmund and Sieglinde Aarenheld – rich, narcissistic twins – attend a performance of *Die Walküre*, and life runs perilously near to art in Thomas Mann's tale *The Blood of the Walsungs*

The lackey pushed their plush-upholstered chairs beneath them; at that moment the lights went down and below their box the orchestra broke into the wild pulsating notes of the prelude.

Night, and tempest. . . . And they, who had been wafted hither on the wings of ease, with no petty annoyances on the way, were in exactly the right mood and could give all their attention at once. Storm, a raging tempest, without in the wood. The angry god's command resounded, once, twice repeated in its wrath, obediently the thunder crashed. The curtain flew up as though blown by the storm. There was the rude hall, dark save for a glow on the pagan hearth. In the centre towered up the trunk of the ash tree. Siegmund appeared in the doorway and leaned against the wooden post beaten and harried by the storm. Draggingly he moved forwards on his sturdy legs wrapped round with hide and thongs. He was rosy-skinned, with a straw-coloured beard; beneath his blond brows and the blond forelock of his wig his blue eyes were directed upon the conductor, with an imploring gaze. At last the orchestra gave way to his voice, which rang clear and metallic, though he tried to make it sound like a gasp. He sang a few bars, to the effect that no matter to whom the hearth belonged he must rest upon it; and at the last word he let himself drop heavily on the bearskin rug and lay there with his head cushioned on his plump arms. His breast heaved in slumber. A minute passed, filled with the singing, speaking flow of the music, rolling its waves at the feet of the events on the stage . . . Sieglinde entered from the left. She had an alabaster bosom which rose and fell marvellously beneath her muslin robe and deerskin mantle. She displayed surprise at sight of the strange man; pressed her chin upon her breast until it was double, put her lips in position and expressed it, this surprise, in tones which swelled soft and warm from her white throat and were given shape by her tongue and her mobile lips. She tended the stranger; bending over him so that he could see the white flower of her bosom rising from the rough skins, she gave him with both hands the drinking-horn. He drank. The music spoke movingly to him of cool refreshment and cherishing care. They looked at each other with the beginning of enchantment, a first dim recognition, standing rapt while the orchestra interpreted in a melody of profound enchantment.

She gave him mead, first touching the horn with her lips, then watching while he took a long draught. Again their glances met and mingled, while below, the melody voiced their yearning. Then he rose, in deep dejection, turning away painfully, his arms hanging at his sides, to the door, that he might remove from her sight his affliction, his loneliness, his persecuted, hated existence and bear it back into the wild. She called upon him but he did not hear; heedless of self she lifted up her arms and confessed her intolerable anguish. He stopped. Her eyes fell. Below them the music spoke darkly of the bond of suffering that united them. He stayed. He folded his arms and remained by the hearth, awaiting his destiny.

Announced by his pugnacious motif, Hunding entered, paunchy and knock-kneed, like a cow. His beard was black with brown tufts. He stood there frowning, leaning heavily on his spear, and staring ox-eyed at the stranger guest. But as the primitive custom would have it he bade him welcome, in an enormous, rusty voice.

Sieglinde laid the evening meal, Hunding's slow, suspicious gaze moving to and fro between her and the stranger. Dull lout though he was, he saw their likeness: the selfsame breed, that odd, untrammelled rebellious stock, which he hated, to which he felt inferior. They sat down, and Hunding, in two words, introduced himself and accounted for his simple, regular, and unorthodox existence. Thus he forced Siegmund to speak of himself – and that was incomparably more difficult. Yet Siegmund spoke, he sang clearly and with wonderful beauty of his life and misfortunes. He told how he had been born with a twin sister – and as people do who dare not speak out, he called himself by a false name. He gave a moving account of the hatred and envy which had been the bane of his life and his strange father's life, how their hall had been burnt, his sister carried off, how they had led in the forest a horrid, persecuted, outlawed life; and how finally he had mysteriously lost his father as well. . . . And then Siegmund sang the most painful thing of all: he told of his yearning for human beings, his longing and ceaseless loneliness. He sang of men and women, of friendship and love he had sometimes won, only to be thrust back again into the dark. A curse had lain upon him for ever, he was marked by the brand of his strange origins. His speech had not been as others' speech nor theirs as his. What he found good was vexation to them, he was galled by the ancient laws to which they paid honour. Always and everywhere he had lived amid anger and strife, he had borne the yoke of scorn and hatred and contempt – all because he was strange, of a breed and kind hopelessly different from them.

Hunding's reception of all this was entirely characteristic. His reply showed no sympathy and no understanding, but only a sour disgust and suspicion of all Siegmund's story. And finally understanding that the stranger standing here on his own hearth was the very man for whom the hunt had been called up today, he behaved with the four-square pedantry one would have expected of him. With a grim sort of courtesy he declared that for tonight the guest-right protected the fugitive; tomorrow he would have the honour of slaying him in battle. Gruffly he commanded Sieglinde to spice his night-drink for him and to await him in bed within; then after a few more threats he followed her, taking all his weapons with him and leaving Siegmund alone and despairing by the hearth.

Up in the box Siegmund bent over the velvet ledge and leaned his dark boyish head on his narrow red hand. His brows made two black furrows, and one foot, resting on the heel of his patent-leather shoe, was in constant nervous motion. But it stopped as he heard a whisper close to him.

'Gigi!'

His mouth, as he turned, had an insolent line.

Sieglinde was holding out to him a mother-of-pearl box with maraschino cherries.

'The brandy chocolates are underneath,' she whispered. But he accepted only a cherry, and as he took it out of the waxed paper she said in his ear:

'She will come back to him again at once.'

'I am not entirely unaware of the fact,' he said, so loud that several heads were jerked angrily in his direction. . . . Down in the darkness big Siegmund was singing alone. From the depths of his heart he cried out for the sword – for a shining haft to swing on that day when there burst forth at last the bright flame of his anger and rage, which so long had smouldered deep in his heart. He saw the hilt glitter in the tree, saw the embers fade on the hearth, sank back in gloomy slumber – and started up in joyful amaze when Sieglinde glided back to him in the darkness.

Hunding slept like a stone, a deafened, drunken sleep. Together they rejoiced at the outwitting of the clod; they laughed, and their eyes had the same way of narrowing as they laughed. Then Sieglinde stole a look at the conductor, received her cue, and putting her lips in position sang a long recitative: related the heartbreaking tale of how they had forced her, forsaken, strange and wild as she was, to give herself to the crude and savage Hunding and to count herself lucky in an honourable marriage which might bury her dark origins in oblivion. She sang too, sweetly and soothingly, of the strange old man in the hat and how he had driven the sword-blade into the trunk of the ash tree, to await the coming of him who was destined to draw it out. Passionately she prayed in song that it might be he whom she meant, whom she knew and grievously longed for, the consoler of her sorrows, the friend who should be more than friend, the avenger of her shame, whom once she had lost, whom in her abasement she wept for, her brother in suffering, her saviour, her rescuer. . . .

But at this point Siegmund flung about her his two rosy arms. He pressed her cheek against the pelt that covered his breast and, holding her so, sang above her head – sang out his exultation to the four winds, in a silver trumpeting of sound. His breast glowed hot with the oath that bound him to his mate. All the yearning of his hunted life found assuagement in her; all that love which others had repulsed, when in conscious shame of his dark origins he forced it upon them – in her it found its home. She suffered shame as did he, dishonoured was she like to himself – and now, now their brother-and-sister love should be their revenge!

The storm whistled, a gust of wind burst open the door, a flood of white electric light poured into the hall. Divested of darkness they stood and sang their song of spring and spring's sister, love!

Crouching on the bearskin they looked at each other in the white light, as they sang their duet of love. Their bare arms touched each other's as they held each other by the temples and gazed into each other's eyes, and as they sang their mouths were very near. They compared their eyes, their foreheads, their voices – they were the same. The growing, urging recognition wrung from his breast his father's name; she called him by his: Siegmund! Siegmund! He freed the sword, he swung it above his head, and submerged in bliss she told him in song who she was: his twin sister, Sieglinde. In ravishment he stretched out his arms to her, his bride, she sank upon his breast – the curtain fell as the music swelled into a roaring, rushing, foaming whirlpool of passion – swirled and swirled and with one mighty throb stood still.

Rapturous applause. The lights went on. A thousand people got up, stretched unobtrusively as they clapped, then made ready to leave the hall, with heads still turned towards the stage, where the singers appeared before the curtain, like masks hung out in a row at a fair. Hunding too came out and smiled politely, despite all that had just been happening.

Siegmund pushed back his chair and stood up. He was hot; little red patches showed on his cheek-bones, above the lean, sallow, shaven cheeks.

'For my part,' said he, 'what I want now is a breath of fresh air. Siegmund was pretty feeble, wasn't he?'

'Yes,' answered Sieglinde, 'and the orchestra saw fit to drag abominably in the Spring Song.'

'Frightfully sentimental,' said Siegmund, shrugging his narrow shoulders in his dress coat. 'Are you coming out?' She lingered a moment, with her elbows on the ledge, still gazing at the stage. He looked at her as she rose and took up her silver scarf. Her soft, full lips were quivering.

[They leave, but the parallel with art does not stop. There is a bearskin rug in the Aarenheld mansion too.]

THOMAS MANN *The Blood of the Walsungs* 1905

One of the things many people find difficult to take about opera during the whole of this period is the existence of the *claque* – that is, a group of audience members hired by the performers to applaud them in the theatre. The necessity (or inevitability) of this system was accepted by composers as well as artists for a couple of centuries at least, though its influence has waned since the 1930s. Some composers even used it to advantage: here is Meyerbeer, the sharpest business man of them all, remembered by one of his greatest interpreters

In the course of a long talk with Madame Viardot she told me many interesting stories of Meyerbeer, and of the extraordinary precautions he took to insure a success for his operas. He always sat at the final rehearsal next Père David, the 'Chef de Claque', and arranged with him the places where the applause was to come in. He even altered passages which David did not think quite effective enough to give him his cue. He used to wander about the back of the stage to hear if the scene-shifters had any criticisms to make amongst themselves, and to note if they whistled or hummed any of his tunes.

C. V. STANFORD *Unwritten Diary* 1914

Even Verdi, an artist of a very different stamp but equal theatrical intuition, deliberately withheld the music of *La donna é mobile* from the tenor at rehearsals of *Rigoletto* until the last possible moment, so as not to risk revealing his trump card before its time.

The activities and duties of the claque have been entertainingly described by Joseph Wechsberg, an Austrian-American who was himself a member of the famous Vienna claque of the 1920s

A great many people whom I have talked to during intermissions at the Metropolitan Opera House seem opposed to the idea of a permanent claque, some going so far as to call it a cheap, disgraceful racket. There was, of course, a permanent claque at the Metropolitan when Gatti-Casazza was director, and there were permanent claques at La Scala, Milan, the Paris Opéra, the Prague National Theatre, and the Warsaw Opera, where at one time a fellow by the name of Artur Rodzinski acted as claque chef. And there was nothing disgraceful about the claque at the Vienna Staatsoper, which I had the honour of belonging to in the middle 'twenties.

The claque was far more exclusive than the aristocratic Jockey Club. Anybody with a good family tree and who had not been caught stealing silver spoons could get into the Jockey Club. To become a member of the claque you had to know by heart the scores of popular operas – all arias, recitatives, solo numbers. In addition, some courage and diplomacy were essential.

The claque chef's name was Schostal. He had become a claqueur under Gustav Mahler and at one time or another he had worked for Scotti, Hesch, Tita Ruffo, Chaliapin, Farrar, and Caruso. The claque consisted of thirty or forty regulars, youthful lovers of good opera, most of whom, like myself, were somewhat insolvent students at the Vienna Conservatory or the *Akademie für Musik und Darstellende Kunst*. If we had two schilling, we would rather spend them for an opera ticket than for a dinner. However, we had to eat now and then, so we all tried to get into the claque. The 'work' was fun, and we were given free admission to the standing-room. Schostal was a citizen of the world and liked foreigners, so at one time there were two Frenchmen, a Czech, a Chinese, an Ethiopian prince, and Childs, an American pianist from Cleveland, among his employees. . . .

A claqueur's operatic perspective is really upside down. *Tristan und Isolde, Walküre, Götterdämmerung, Pelléas et Mélisande,* and *Elektra* are extremely 'light' operas. The claque works only at the end of each act; there is no other applause. On the other hand, Rossini, Massenet,

Verdi, Puccini, and Bizet operas are very 'difficult'. Take, for instance, the second act of *Carmen*, a claqueur's nightmare. You start working right after Carmen's gypsy song, *Les tringles des sistres tintaient*, and you applaud after her dance with the castanets. Then Escamillo enters (applause), sings his famous *Couplets* (applause), and leaves (more applause). By that time the public is likely to applaud spontaneously after each number – the quintet (Carmen, Mercédès, Frasquita, and the smugglers), Don José's off-stage *a capella* song, Carmen's dance for Don José, and the tenor's famous *La fleur que tu m'avais jetée*. The trouble is that enthusiastic listeners are apt to break into 'wild' applause in the wrong places, such as in the middle of an aria, after an effective high C. In Vienna, where opera was a way of life and even the small boys discussed opera as they discuss baseball in America, 'wild' applause was considered heresy and one of the claque's functions was to influence public acclaim into orderly channels. . . .

Schostal had a perfect sense of timing and he had a showman's instinct for the mood of the public. He could feel whether an aria was going over or not. A claqueur's most unpardonable crime is to start applause which is not taken up by the public and perhaps is even drowned out by enraged hisses. Schostal seldom made a mistake. He himself never applauded during a performance – generals do not shoot rifles – but at the end of an exceptionally good one he would step down to the breastwork and benevolently clap his hands for the stars. They never failed to look up and give him a smile. During the ordinary, more or less routine performance, Schostal would get up from his seat shortly before he had to give a cue, and the claqueurs, throughout the balcony, could see his bald skull shining under the pillar lamp. There would be from ten to thirty of us, depending on how many clients we had in the cast. At the critical moment he would give the cue, a short nod to three lieutenants standing behind him, and they would start applauding in a cautious, subdued manner; the rest of us would fall in, and within three seconds a wave of applause would sweep the house. . . .

Members of the claque never got anything except the ticket. We had nothing to do with business details, which were attended to by Schostal. Of course, everybody knew that he was given money by the singers and that he bought the tickets and kept part of the money for himself, but this seemed fair enough. There was no set fee. The artists gave him as much as they thought applause in a particular role was worth. They all knew that Schostal was incorruptible and never took money from singers who were not good enough for special applause. . . . If Schostal really liked a great singer, he did not mind working without any compensation. When Kirsten Flagstad sang for the first time in Vienna, Schostal went to see her and offered her his services, as he always did in the case of famous singers who had not appeared in Vienna before. Madame Flagstad refused, unaware of the local practice. After the first act of *Tristan*, Schostal said, 'She's great. Get going, boys.'

The claque was frequently denounced by the critics, who were reluctant to share with us their right to influence the public, but it was nevertheless tolerated by the directors of the Opera. Some of them, like Felix von Weingartner and Franz Schalk, preferred regulated applause to the enthusiastic outbursts of amateurs. Bruno Walter always had some kind word for us. (Schostal never took money from any conductor.) Richard Strauss considered the claque a necessary evil, like the ladies of the chorus, the ticket-jobbers outside the Opera, and the cockroaches under the plush seats of the Kaiserloge. When Clemens Krauss became the director of the Opera, he publicly threatened to 'rub out the claque'. Schostal took up the challenge. The following evening Krauss conducted *Don Giovanni*. Schostal bought thirty expensive orchestra seats, which he distributed among those of us who owned tuxedos. When Krauss entered, we started a terrific ovation. During the intermission Schostal asked Krauss how he liked our work.

'Don't be ridiculous,' Krauss said. 'The applause was made by my followers in the orchestra pit. Since when do your boys sit in orchestra seats?'

During the second act, we applauded too early after Don Giovanni's *Deh vieni alla finestra* and after Don Ottavio's beautiful *Il mio tesoro intanto* and started several 'wild' salvos. After the cemetery scene several of our boys shouted 'Bravo, Walter!' and when told by kindly neighbours that Krauss, not Bruno Walter, was conducting, they looked dumbfounded and unhappy. The midday papers played up the story and for weeks thereafter Krauss was greeted by malicious friends with 'Bravo, Walter!' After that, Krauss did not object to the claque any more.

JOSEPH WECHSBERG Looking for a Bluebird 1946

Audiences

To *The Times*
London   3 July 1905

Sir, – The Opera management at Covent Garden regulates the dress of its male patrons. When is it going to do the same to the women?

On Saturday night I went to the Opera. I wore the costume imposed on me by the regulations of the house. I fully recognize the advantage of those regulations. Evening dress is cheap, simple, durable, prevents rivalry and extravagance on the part of male leaders of fashion, annihilates class distinctions, and gives men who are poor and doubtful of their social position (that is, the great majority of men) a sense of security and satisfaction that no clothes of their own choosing could confer, besides saving a whole sex the trouble of considering what they should wear on state occasions. The objections to it are as dust in the balance in the eyes of the ordinary Briton. These objections are that it is colourless and characterless; that it involves a whitening process which makes the shirt troublesome, slightly uncomfortable, and seriously unclean; that it acts as a passport for undesirable persons; that it fails to guarantee sobriety, cleanliness, and order on the part of the wearer; and that it reduces to a formula a very vital human habit which should be the subject of constant experiment and active private enterprise. All such objections are thoroughly un-English. They appeal only to an eccentric few, and may be left out of account with the fantastic objections of men like Ruskin, Tennyson, Carlyle, and Morris to tall hats.

But I submit that what is sauce for the gander is sauce for the goose. Every argument that applies to the regulation of the man's dress applies equally to the regulation of the woman's. Now let me describe what actually happened to me at the Opera. Not only was I in evening dress by compulsion, but I voluntarily added many graces of conduct as to which the management made no stipulation whatever. I was in my seat in time for the first chord of the overture. I did not chatter during the music nor raise my voice when the Opera was too loud for normal conversation. I did not get up and go out when the statue music began. My language was fairly moderate considering the number and nature of the improvements on Mozart volunteered by Signor Caruso, and the respectful ignorance of the dramatic points of the score exhibited by the conductor and the stage manager – if there is such a functionary at Covent Garden. In short, my behaviour was exemplary.

At 9 o'clock (the Opera began at 8) a lady came in and sat down very conspicuously in my line of sight. She remained there until the beginning of the last act. I do not complain of her coming late and going early; on the contrary, I wish she had come later and gone earlier. For this lady, who had very black hair, had stuck over her right ear the pitiable corpse of a large white bird, which looked exactly as if someone had killed it by stamping on its breast, and then nailed it to the lady's temple, which was presumably of sufficient solidity to bear the operation. I am not, I hope, a morbidly squeamish person, but the spectacle sickened me. I presume that if I had presented myself at the doors with a dead snake round my neck, a collection of blackbeetles pinned to my shirtfront, and a grouse in my hair, I should have been refused admission. Why, then, is a woman to be allowed to commit such a public outrage? Had the lady been refused admission, as she should have been, she would have soundly rated the tradesman who imposed the disgusting headdress on her under the false pretence that 'the best people' wear such things, and withdrawn her custom from him; and thus the root of the evil would be struck at; for your fashionable woman generally allows herself to be dressed according to the taste of a person whom she would not let sit down in her presence. I once, in Drury Lane Theatre, sat behind a *matinée* hat decorated with the two wings of a seagull, artificially reddened at the joints so as to produce an illusion of being freshly plucked from a live bird. But even that lady stopped short of the whole seagull. Both ladies were evidently regarded by their neighbours as ridiculous and vulgar; but that is hardly enough when the offence is one which produces a sensation of physical sickness in persons of normal humane sensibility.

I suggest to the Covent Garden authorities that, if they feel bound to protect their subscribers against the danger of my shocking them with a blue tie, they are at least equally bound to protect me against the danger of a woman shocking me with a dead bird.

Yours truly,
G. BERNARD SHAW

It is not for me to say precisely in what the superiority of the Anglo-Saxons consists, but, amongst other things, they have Covent Garden. . . . An English audience listens with almost rapt attention. If any boredom is felt there is no sign of it. On the other hand the theatre is plunged into darkness throughout the acts, so that it is possible to sleep in perfect safety. . . .

CLAUDE DEBUSSY *Monsieur Croche* 1921

Of all audiences, the German and the Japanese are the most disciplined and polite. The Japanese especially are reverently inaudible beyond belief – one simply doesn't know they are there. Two Americans appropriate more space and effect more distraction than a thousand Japanese, whose rapt attention and quasi-invisibility are such as might unnerve the unaccustomed artist. It used not to be the manner of their country to applaud, but applause like other Western habits, good and bad, has taken root in postwar Japan and ovations now are respectably enthusiastic. The Germans' love of music prompts a reaction I have found in no other country: at the end of a piece, applause never comes immediately, but a fractional pause is made, balancing the pause before the music starts, framing it in silence; then the hall applauds as one man, for there is no dissenter in a German audience. In Israel, in contrast, there are only dissenters. As one looks along the front row of the Frederick Mann Auditorium in Tel Aviv, one sees as many varieties of expression as there are people. Someone is madly applauding; his neighbour, arms folded, remains unconvinced. A whole recital usually contrives to weld these unrepentent individuals into a unity, but one feels one must win from each his personal surrender.

Unfairly in my view, the English audience has the reputation of saving its coughs and sneezes for slow movements. This has not been my experience. I have found, even in the smallest British towns, a very touching genuine response, a vein of true sentiment which resists pretension. It may be that I am biased toward the English: so many tributes have reached me, backstage and through the mail, that I play to the English audience persuaded they are already my friends. I have, too, a special tenderness for the Moscow public, associated in my memory with students who seem to be familiar with corners and crevices of the auditorium unknown to other people, whose heads, like the Baron's illegitimate children in the last act of *Rosenkavalier*, pop out of the most unexpected places. The Russian audience can also surprise: once in Odessa – in a hall, therefore, full of as many Jews as Russians, all of them cognoscenti – the well-wishers gathered in the

artists' room after the recital offered few compliments on my playing,
few comments on my interpretations, but, to a man, demanded to
know how I fingered this or that passage.

YEHUDI MENUHIN Unfinished Journey 1976

Audience inattention can of course take various forms. There is a famous story
of Liszt, refusing to play at the Russian court because the Tsar and his friends
were talking. When he stopped playing an *aide-de-camp* came up and told him
to continue, to which Liszt replied with perfect courtesy: 'Quand le Tsar parle,
tout le monde se tait'. But it seems that Liszt may not have been the first to use
this delicate form of criticism. Mainwaring, in his *Memoirs of the Life of Handel*,
records of Corelli

He was requested one evening to play, to a large and polite company,
a fine solo which he had lately composed. Just as he was in the midst of
his performance, some of the number began to discourse together a
little unseasonably; Corelli gently lays down his instrument. Being
asked whether any thing was the matter with him? Nothing, he
replied, he was only afraid that he interrupted conversation.

This recalls the reaction of the audience imagined by Browning in 'A Toccata of
Galuppi's'

So, an octave struck the answer. Oh, they praised you, I dare say!
'Brave Galuppi! that was music! good alike at grave and gay!
'I can always leave off talking when I hear a master play!'

In 1875, at the Festspielhaus in Bayreuth, the acoustics of the still unfinished
auditorium were tried out for the first time. In order to provide for the physical
presence of an audience, soldiers were brought in to listen; they squatted on
the floor, and Wagner described them as the ideal audience on three counts

1 They were all in their places before the music began.
2 They did not talk or fidget while it was being played.
3 When it was over they made no pretence of having understood
   anything of what they had seen or heard, and so refrained from
   airing their opinions about it.

RICHARD WAGNER in ROBERT HARTFORD Bayreuth: The Early Years 1980

Wagner, surprisingly, seems to have been concerned about audience reaction

In one respect opera at Baireuth in the lifetime of [Wagner] had a virtue
which has gradually tended to disappear since his death. The com-

poser did not permit his conductor to exaggerate slowness of pace. This was especially noticeable, when Levi directed 'Parsifal' in 1883 (the year of the composer's death). Dannreuther, who stayed at 'Wahnfried' for the rehearsals in 1882, told me that Wagner frequently called out from the stalls, 'Schneller! Schneller! Die Leute werden sich langweilen.' (Quicker, quicker, the people will be bored). With the advent of Mottl, every movement became slower and slower. His playing of the Prelude was, by my watch, five minutes slower than Levi's. . . . The disease of exaggerated Adagios spread to an alarming extent, and Mottl's fad became a cult.

C. V. STANFORD Unwritten Diary 1914

In art (music, painting, above all, sculpture) as in letters, what makes success is talent, and not ideas. The public (and I speak of intelligent people, the rest don't count: that's my democracy for you) – the public understands the idea *later*. To achieve this *later*, the artist's talent must manifest itself in an agreeable form and so ease the road for the public, not repel it from the outset.

Thus Auber, who had so much talent and few ideas, was almost always understood, while Berlioz, who had genius but no talent at all, was almost never understood.

GEORGES BIZET Letter 1871

Reggio Emilia
7 May 1872

Much honoured Signor Verdi,

The 2nd of this month I went to Parma, drawn there by the sensation made by your opera *Aida*. So great was my curiosity, that one half-hour before the commencement of the piece I was already in my place, No. 120. I admired the *mise en scène*, I heard with pleasure the excellent singers, and I did all in my power to let nothing escape me. At the end of the opera, I asked myself if I was satisfied, and the answer was 'No'. I started back to Reggio and listened in the railway carriage to the opinions given upon *Aida*. Nearly all agreed in considering it a work of the first order.

I was then seized with the idea of hearing it again, and on the 4th I returned to Parma; I made unheard-of efforts to get a reserved seat; as the crowd was enormous, I was obliged to throw away five lire to witness the performance in any comfort.

I arrived at this decision about it: it is an opera in which there is absolutely nothing which causes any enthusiasm or excitement, and without the pomp of the spectacle, the public would not stand it to the end. When it has filled the house two or three times, it will be banished to the dust of the archives.

You can now, dear Signor Verdi, picture to yourself my regret at having spent on two occasions thirty-two lire; add to this the aggravating circumstance that I depend on my family, and that this money troubles my rest like a frightful spectre. I therefore frankly address myself to you, in order that you may send me the amount. The account is as follows:

	Lire
Railroad – going	2.60
" – returning	3.30
Theatre	8
Detestable supper at the station	2
	15.90
Twice	31.80

Hoping that you will deliver me from this embarrassment, I salute you from my heart.

BERTANI

My address: Bertani Prospero, Via San Domenico, No. 5.

Disgusted – Reggio Emilia?

Verdi at once wrote to his publisher, Giulio Ricordi, in Milan, enclosing this letter

[May 1872]

You may well imagine that to protect the son of a family from the spectres which pursue him, I will willingly pay the little bill which he sends me. I therefore beg you to forward by one of your correspondents to this M. Prospero Bertani, Via San Domenico No. 5, the sum of 27 lire 80 centimes. It is not the amount he demands; but that in addition I should be expected to pay for his supper, certainly not! He might very well take his meals at home.

It is understood that he will give you an acknowledgement, and further a short letter in reply, undertaking to hear my new operas no more, exposing himself no more to the menace of spectres, and sparing me further travelling expenses. . . .

GIUSEPPE VERDI in ARTHUR POUGIN Verdi 1887

To know whether you are enjoying a piece of music or not you must see whether you find yourself looking at the advertisements of Pears' soap at the end of the programme.

SAMUEL BUTLER *Note-Books* 1912

Mr Prince sighed, and said: 'I was thinking of going up to the Promenades to-night.' George took fire at once. 'The Glazounov Ballet music?' 'Glazounov?' repeated Mr Prince, uncertainly. 'No. I rather wanted to hear the new Elgar.' . . .

When they got to the Hall the band was sending forth a tremendous volume of brilliant, exhilarating sound. A vast melody seemed to ride on waves of brass. . . . Then came a final crash. . . . 'What was that piece?' she asked. 'I don't know,' he said. . . . The music resumed. He listened, ready to put himself into the mood of admiration if it was the Glazounov item. Was it Glazounov? He could not be certain. It sounded fine. Surely it sounded Russian. Then he had a glimpse of a programme held by a man standing near, and he peered at it. . . . 'It's only the Elgar,' he said, with careless condescension, perceiving at once, by the mere virtue of a label, that the music was not fine, and not Russian.

ARNOLD BENNETT *The Roll Call* 1918

. . . And if it be lawful to tell the truth, you your selfe and all wee here have many times, and doe at this present credite the opinion of others, more than our owne.

And that it is true, not long agoe there were certain verses shewed here, that bore the name of Senazarus, and were thought of every body very excellent, and praysed out of reason, afterwarde when they were certainely knowne to be an other mans doing, they lost by and by their reputation, and seemed worse than meane.

And where there was song in the Dutchesse presence here a certaine Antheme, it never delyted nor was reckned good, until it was knowne to be the doing of Josquin de Pris.

BALDASSARE CASTIGLIONE *The Book of the Courtier* 1561

A rose by any other name?

And it works the other way

For certain people the mere sight of my name on a placard or in a paper
is a red rag to a bull. They attribute to me a whole world of absurdities
hatched in their own little brains; they hear things in my works which
don't exist, and fail to hear the things that do. If they were asked their
opinion of the chord of D Major (being warned beforehand that I had
written it) they would exclaim with indignation: 'A detestable chord!'

HECTOR BERLIOZ *Memoirs* 1870

In the end, perhaps incomprehension is the clue

I found myself gazing in blank amazement at the row of decorous
middle-class people in front of me who appeared to be listening with
pleasure and edification. There were broad matronly backs, reverent
bald heads, here and there a gaunt clerical neck, and in every line of
head and shoulder one could decipher rectitude, propriety, and
virtue. Pillars of their churches, stern members of Charity Organisation Societies, teetotallers, models of thrift, self-discipline and self-
help – one asked oneself in amazement what they were doing in that
particular gallery. For, decadent and artificial as Debussy is, there is no
mistaking his meaning, and for those whose imagination is defective
there is, after all, the programme. The programme is bald, uncom-
promising, literal. The faun with whom Debussy invites us to spend
an afternoon was by no means a virtuous biped. . . .

H. N. BRAILSFORD *Adventures in Prose* 1911

To the Gentleman in Row E

Dear Sir, we in Row E are well aware
Your soul is steeped in music to the core.
You love, we notice, each succeeding air
More deeply than the one which came before.

You lead the orchestra in perfect time,
With ever-nodding head you set the pace,
We in Row E consider it a crime
You are not in Sir Thomas Beecham's place.

Your lily hands most delicately haver,
Each phrase is ended with a graceful twist,
You know, it seems, each breve and semi-quaver,
And play them gently on your other wrist.

Sometimes you hum the least familiar portions,
And beat upon the floor a faint tattoo,
Though we can stand a lot of your contortions,
We shouldn't tap too much if we were you!

Dear Sir, we need no musical instructor,
We also sang in oratorio,
And if you were a really good conductor,
Our lightning would have struck you hours ago!

VIRGINIA GRAHAM *Consider the Years* 1946

In spite of the taxi, in spite of the gobbled dinner, they were late. The concert had begun.

'Never mind,' said Gumbril. 'We shall get in in time for the minuetto. It's then that the fun really begins.'

'Sour grapes,' said Emily, putting her ear to the door. 'It sounds to me simply too lovely.'

They stood outside, like beggars waiting abjectly at the doors of a banqueting-hall – stood and listened to the snatches of music that came out tantalizingly from within. A rattle of clapping announced at last that the first movement was over; the doors were thrown open. Hungrily they rushed in. The Sclopis Quartet and a subsidiary viola were bowing from the platform. There was a chirrup of tuning, then preliminary silence. Sclopis nodded and moved his bow. The minuetto of Mozart's G Minor Quintet broke out, phrase after phrase, short and decisive, with every now and then a violent sforzando chord, startling in its harsh and sudden emphasis.

Minuetto – all civilization, Mr Mercaptan would have said, was implied in the delicious word, the delicate, pretty thing. Ladies and precious gentlemen, fresh from the wit and gallantry of Crebillon-haunted sofas, stepping gracefully to a pattern of airy notes. To this passion of one who cries out, to this obscure and angry argument with fate how would they, Gumbril wondered, how would they have tripped it?

How pure the passion, how unaffected, clear and without clot or pretension the unhappiness of that slow movement which followed! Blessed are the pure in heart, for they shall see God. Pure and unsullied; pure and unmixed, unadulterated. 'Not passionate, thank

God; only sensual and sentimental.' In the name of earwig. Amen. Pure, pure. Worshippers have tried to rape the statues of the gods; the statuaries who made the images were generally to blame. And how deliciously, too, an artist can suffer! and, in the face of the whole Albert Hall, with what an effective gesture and grimace! But blessed are the pure in heart, for they shall see God. The instruments come together and part again. Long silver threads hang aerially over a murmur of waters; in the midst of muffled sobbing a cry. The fountains blow their architecture of slender pillars, and from basin to basin the waters fall; from basin to basin, and every fall makes somehow possible a higher leaping of the jet, and at the last fall the mounting column springs up into the sunlight, and from water the music has modulated up into a rainbow. Blessed are the pure in heart, for they shall see God; they shall make God visible, too, to other eyes.

Blood beats in the ears. Beat, beat, beat. A slow drum in the darkness, beating in the ears of one who lies wakeful with fever, with the sickness of too much misery. It beats unceasingly, in the ears, in the mind itself. Body and mind are indivisible, and in the spirit blood painfully throbs. Sad thoughts droop through the mind. A small, pure light comes swaying down through the darkness, comes to rest, resigning itself to the obscurity of its misfortune. There is resignation, but blood still beats in the ears. Blood still painfully beats, though the mind has acquiesced. And then, suddenly, the mind exerts itself, throws off the fever of too much suffering and laughing, commands the body to dance. The introduction to the last movement comes to its suspended, throbbing close. There is an instant of expectation, and then, with a series of mounting trochees and a downward hurrying, step after tiny step, in triple time, the dance begins. Irrelevant, irreverent, out of key with all that has gone before. But man's greatest strength lies in his capacity for irrelevance. In the midst of pestilences, wars and famines, he builds cathedrals; and a slave, he can think the irrelevant and unsuitable thoughts of a free man. The spirit is slave to fever and beating blood, at the mercy of an obscure and tyrannous misfortune. But irrelevantly, it elects to dance in triple measure – a mounting skip, a patter of descending feet.

The G Minor Quintet is at an end; the applause rattles out loudly. Enthusiasts stand up and cry bravo. And the five men on the platform rise and bow their acknowledgements. Great Sclopis himself receives his share of the plaudits with a weary condescension; weary are his poached eyes, weary his disillusioned smile. . . .

'Strange,' said Gumbril, 'to think that those ridiculous creatures could have produced what we've just been hearing.'

The poached eye of Sclopis lighted on Emily, flushed and ardently applauding. He gave her, all to herself, a weary smile. He would have a letter, he guessed, to-morrow morning signed 'Your little Admirer in the Third Row'. She looked a choice little piece. He smiled again to encourage her. Emily, alas! had not even noticed. She was applauding the music.

ALDOUS HUXLEY *Antic Hay* 1923

It will be generally admitted that Beethoven's Fifth Symphony is the most sublime noise that has ever penetrated into the ear of man. All sorts and conditions are satisfied by it. Whether you are like Mrs Munt, and tap surreptitiously when the tunes come – of course, not so as to disturb the others; or like Helen, who can see heroes and shipwrecks in the music's flood; or like Margaret, who can only see the music; or like Tibby, who is profoundly versed in counterpoint, and holds the full score open on his knee; or like their cousin, Fräulein Mosebach, who remembers all the time that Beethoven is 'echt Deutsch'; or like Fräulein Mosebach's young man, who can remember nothing but Fräulein Mosebach: in any case, the passion of your life becomes more vivid, and you are bound to admit that such a noise is cheap at two shillings. It is cheap, even if you hear it in the Queen's Hall, dreariest music-room in London, though not as dreary as the Free Trade Hall, Manchester; and even if you sit on the extreme left of that hall, so that the brass bumps at you before the rest of the orchestra arrives, it is still cheap.

'Who is Margaret talking to?' said Mrs Munt, at the conclusion of the first movement. She was again in London on a visit to Wickham Place.

Helen looked down the long line of their party, and said that she did not know.

'Would it be some young man or other whom she takes an interest in?'

'I expect so,' Helen replied. Music enwrapped her, and she could not enter into the distinction that divides young men whom one takes an interest in from young men whom one knows.

'You girls are so wonderful in always having – oh dear! We mustn't talk.'

For the Andante had begun – very beautiful, but bearing a family likeness to all the other beautiful Andantes that Beethoven has written, and, to Helen's mind, rather disconnecting the heroes and shipwrecks of the first movement from the heroes and goblins of the third. She heard the tune through once, and then her attention wandered, and she gazed at the audience, or the organ, or the architecture. Much did she censure the attenuated Cupids who encircle the ceiling of the Queen's Hall, inclining each to each with vapid gesture, and clad in sallow pantaloons, on which the October sunlight struck. 'How awful to marry a man like those Cupids!' thought Helen. Here Beethoven started decorating his tune, so she heard him through once more, and then she smiled at her cousin Frieda. But Frieda, listening to Classical Music, could not respond. Herr Liesecke, too, looked as if wild horses could not make him inattentive; there were lines across his forehead, his lips were parted, his pince-nez at right angles to his nose, and he had laid a thick, white hand on either knee. And next to her was Aunt Juley, so British, and wanting to tap. How interesting that row of people was! What diverse influences had gone to their making! Here Beethoven, after humming and hawing with great sweetness, said 'Heigho' and the Andante came to an end. Applause, and a round of wunderschöning and prachtvolleying from the German contingent. Margaret started talking to her new young man; Helen said to her aunt: 'Now comes the wonderful movement: first of all the goblins, and then a trio of elephants dancing'; and Tibby implored the company generally to look out for the transitional passage on the drum.

'On the what, dear?'

'On the *drum*, Aunt Juley.'

'No; look out for the part where you think you have done with the goblins and they come back,' breathed Helen, as the music started with a goblin walking quietly over the universe, from end to end. Others followed him. They were not aggressive creatures; it was that that made them so terrible to Helen. They merely observed in passing that there was no such thing as splendour or heroism in the world. After the interlude of elephants dancing, they returned and made the observation for the second time. Helen could not contradict them, for, once at all events, she had felt the same, and had seen the reliable walls of youth collapse. Panic and emptiness! Panic and emptiness! The goblins were right.

Her brother raised his finger: it was the transitional passage on the drum.

For, as if things were going too far, Beethoven took hold of the goblins and made them do what he wanted. He appeared in person. He gave them a little push, and they began to walk in a major key instead of in a minor, and then – he blew with his mouth and they were scattered! Gusts of splendour, gods and demigods contending with vast swords, colour and fragrance broadcast on the field of battle, magnificent victory, magnificent death! Oh, it all burst before the girl, and she even stretched out her gloved hands as if it was tangible. Any fate was titanic; any contest desirable; conqueror and conquered would alike be applauded by the angels of the utmost stars.

And the goblins – they had not really been there at all? They were only the phantoms of cowardice and unbelief? One healthy human impulse would dispel them? Men like the Wilcoxes, or President Roosevelt, would say yes. Beethoven knew better. The goblins really had been there. They might return – and they did. It was as if the splendour of life might boil over and waste to steam and froth. In its dissolution one heard the terrible, ominous note, and a goblin, with increased malignity, walked quietly over the universe from end to end. Panic and emptiness! Panic and emptiness! Even the flaming ramparts of the world might fall.

Beethoven chose to make all right in the end. He built the ramparts up. He blew with his mouth for the second time, and again the goblins were scattered. He brought back the gusts of splendour, the heroism, the youth, the magnificence of life and of death, and, amid vast roarings of a superhuman joy, he led his Fifth Symphony to its conclusion. But the goblins were there. They could return. He had said so bravely, and that is why one can trust Beethoven when he says other things.

Helen pushed her way out during the applause. She desired to be alone. The music had summed up to her all that had happened or could happen in her career. She read it as a tangible statement, which could never be superseded. The notes meant this and that to her, and they could have no other meaning, and life could have no other meaning. She pushed right out of the building, and walked slowly down the outside staircase, breathing the autumnal air, and then she strolled home.

'Margaret,' called Mrs Munt, 'is Helen all right?'

'Oh yes.'

'She is always going away in the middle of a programme,' said Tibby.

E. M. FORSTER *Howard's End* 1910

Into this world of romanticizing audiences Stravinsky comes like a refreshing draught of cool water

I have always had a horror of listening to music with my eyes shut, with nothing for them to do. The sight of the gestures and movements of the various parts of the body producing the music is fundamentally necessary if it is to be grasped in all its fullness. All music created or composed demands some exteriorization for the perception of the listener. In other words, it must have an intermediary, an executant. That being an essential condition, without which music cannot wholly reach us, why wish to ignore it, or try to do so – why shut the eyes to this fact which is inherent in the very nature of musical art? Obviously one frequently prefers to turn away one's eyes, or even close them, when the superfluity of the player's gesticulations prevents the concentration of one's faculties of hearing. But if the player's movements are evoked solely by the exigencies of the music, and do not tend to make an impression on the listener by extramusical devices, why not follow with the eye such movements as those of the drummer, the violinist, or the trombonist, which facilitate one's auditory perceptions? As a matter of fact, those who maintain that they only enjoy music to the full with their eyes shut do not hear better than when they have them open, but the absence of visual distractions enables them to abandon themselves to the reveries induced by the lullaby of its sounds, and that is really what they prefer to the music itself.

IGOR STRAVINSKY An Autobiography 1936

This sharp clarity of ear and intellect had not always earned Stravinsky the immediate allegiance of his audiences

> Who wrote this fiendish 'Rite of Spring,'
> What right had he to write the thing,
> Against our helpless ears to fling
> Its crash, clash, cling, clang, bing, bang, bing?
>
> And then to call it 'Rite of Spring.'
> The season when on joyous wing
> The birds melodious carols sing
> And harmony's in everything!
>
> He who could write the 'Rite of Spring'
> If I be right, by right should swing!

from the Boston Herald 1924

It's extraordinary, though, how quickly these things change

The audience pricks an intellectual Ear . . .
Stravinsky . . . Quite the Concert of the Year!

Forgetting now that none-so-distant date
When they (or folk facsimilar in state
Of mind) first heard with hisses – hoots – guffaws –
This abstract Symphony (they booed because
Stravinsky jumped their Wagner palisade
With modes that seemed cacophonous and queer),
Forgetting now the hullabaloo they made,
The Audience pricks an intellectual ear.

Bassoons begin . . . Sonority envelops
Our auditory innocence; and brings
To Me, I must admit, some drift of things
Omnific, seminal, and adolescent.
Polyphony through dissonance develops
A serpent-conscious Eden, crude but pleasant;
While vibro-atmospheric copulations
With mezzo-forte mysteries of noise
Prelude Stravinsky's statement of the joys
That unify the monkeydom of nations.

This matter is most indelicate indeed!
Yet one perceives no symptom of stampede.
The Stalls remain unruffled: craniums gleam:
Swept by a storm of pizzicato chords,
Elaborate ladies re-assure their lords
With lifting brows that signify 'Supreme!'
While orchestrated gallantry of goats
Impugns the astigmatic programme-notes.

In the Grand Circle one observes no sign
Of riot: peace prevails along the line.
And in the Gallery, cargoed to capacity,
No tremor bodes eruptions and alarms.
They are listening to this not-quite-new audacity
As though it were by someone dead, – like Brahms.

But savagery pervades Me; I am frantic
With corybantic rupturing of laws.
Come, dance, and seize this clamorous chance to function
Creatively, – abandoning compunction
In anti-social rhapsodic applause!

Lynch the conductor! Jugulate the drums!
Butcher the brass! Ensanguinate the strings!
Throttle the flutes! . . . Stravinsky's April comes
With pitiless pomp and pain of sacred springs . . .
Incendiarize the Hall with resinous fires
Of sacrificial fiddles scorched and snapping! . . .

Meanwhile the music blazes and expires;
And the delighted Audience is clapping.

SIEGFRIED SASSOON *Concert-Interpretation* 1926

The first performance of *Le Sacre du Printemps* by Diaghilev's Ballets Russes, in
Paris in 1913, produced one of the most violent of all musical upheavals.
Nijinsky was the choreographer, Pierre Monteux the conductor

According to Carl van Vechten, 'a certain part of the audience was
thrilled by what it considered to be a blasphemous attempt to destroy
music as an art, and, swept away with wrath, began, very soon after
the rise of the curtain, to make cat-calls and to offer audible suggestions as to how the performance should proceed. The orchestra played
unheard, except occasionally when a slight lull occurred. The young
man seated behind me in the box stood up during the course of the
ballet to enable himself to see more clearly. The intense excitement
under which he was labouring betrayed itself presently when he
began to beat rhythmically on the top of my head with his fists. My
emotion was so great that I did not feel the blows for some time.'
Romola Pulsky (later Nijinsky's wife), who was in the auditorium
during the first part of the ballet, describes how 'people whistled,
insulted the performers and the composer, shouted, laughed. Monteux threw desperate glances towards Diaghilev, who sat in Astruc's
box and made signs to him to keep on playing. Astruc in this
indescribable noise ordered the lights to be turned on, and the fights
and controversy did not remain in the domain of sound, but actually
culminated in bodily conflict. One beautifully dressed lady in an
orchestra box stood up and slapped the face of a young man who was
hissing in the next box. Her escort arose, and cards were exchanged
between the men. A duel followed next day.' Jean Cocteau saw the old
Comtesse de Pourtalès stand up in her box with her face aflame and
her tiara awry and heard her cry out, as she brandished her fan, 'This
is the first time in sixty years that anyone has dared to make fun of
me!' . . . Cocteau has given a memorable account of how, about two
o'clock in the morning, Stravinsky, Diaghilev, Nijinsky and himself
got into a cab and were driven to the Bois de Boulogne. 'No one spoke;

the night was fresh and kindly. From the scent of acacias, we knew we had reached the first trees. When we came to the lakes, Diaghilev, who was thickly clad in a coat of opossum, began to murmur in Russian; I felt that Stravinsky and Nijinsky were listening and, as the coachman lit his lantern, I saw tears on Diaghilev's face. He went on murmuring, slowly, indefatigably.

'"What is it?" I asked.

'"Pushkin."

'There was a long silence; and then Diaghilev stammered another short phrase, and the emotion of my two companions seemed so deep that I couldn't help interrupting him to know why.

'"It's difficult to translate," said Stravinsky, "really difficult: too Russian . . . too Russian. . . . It means more or less, 'Will you come for a trip to the islands?' Yes, that's it. It's typically Russian because, you know, at St Petersburg we are accustomed to go to the islands, just as this evening we have come to the Bois de Boulogne; and it is while we were on our way to the islands that we conceived the idea of *The Rite of Spring*."

'For the first time we alluded to the evening's scandal. It was dawn when we returned. No one can imagine how quiet and nostalgic these three men were; and, whatever Diaghilev may have done afterwards, I shall never forget him sitting in that cab reciting Pushkin in the Bois de Boulogne with his cheeks wet with tears.'

E. W. WHITE *Stravinsky, A Critical Survey* 1947

Later, Stravinsky's own memory of the occasion was curiously different

I was sitting in the fourth or fifth row on the right and the image of Monteux's back is more vivid in my mind today than the picture of the stage. He stood there apparently impervious and as nerveless as a crocodile. It is still almost incredible to me that he actually brought the orchestra through to the end. I left my seat when the heavy noises began – light noise had started from the very beginning – and went backstage behind Nijinsky in the right wing. Nijinsky stood on a chair, just out of view of the audience, shouting numbers to the dancers. I wondered what on earth these numbers had to do with the music for there are no 'thirteens' and 'seventeens' in the metrical scheme of the score.

From what I heard of the musical performance it was not bad. Sixteen full rehearsals had given the orchestra at least some security. After the 'performance' we were excited, angry, disgusted, and . . . happy. I went with Diaghilev and Nijinsky to a restaurant. So far from

weeping and reciting Pushkin in the Bois de Boulogne as the legend is,
Diaghilev's only comment was: 'Exactly what I wanted.' He certainly
looked contented. No one could have been quicker to understand the
publicity value and he immediately understood the good thing that
had happened in that respect. Quite probably he had already thought
about the possibility of such a scandal when I first played him the
score, months before, in the east corner ground room of the Grand
Hotel in Venice.

IGOR STRAVINSKY AND ROBERT CRAFT *Conversations* 1959

And now, a description of another classic musical fracas, masterminded by
Jeeves with an astute regard for programme building

I can't say I exactly saw eye to eye with young Tuppy in his admiration
for the Bellinger female. Delivered on the mat at one-twenty-five, she
proved to be an upstanding light-heavyweight of some thirty sum-
mers, with a commanding eye and a square chin which I, personally,
would have steered clear of. She seemed to me a good deal like what
Cleopatra would have been after going in too freely for the starches
and cereals. I don't know why it is, but women who have anything to
do with Opera, even if they're only studying for it, always appear to
run to surplus poundage.

Tuppy, however, was obviously all for her. His whole demeanour,
both before and during lunch, was that of one striving to be worthy of
a noble soul. When Jeeves offered him a cocktail, he practically
recoiled as from a serpent. It was terrible to see the change which love
had effected in the man. The spectacle put me off my food.

At half-past two, the Bellinger left to go to a singing lesson. Tuppy
trotted after her to the door, bleating and frisking a goodish bit, and
then came back and looked at me in a goofy sort of way.

'Well, Bertie?'

'Well, what?'

'I mean, isn't she?'

'Oh, rather,' I said, humouring the poor fish.

'Wonderful eyes?'

'Oh, rather.'

'Wonderful figure?'

'Oh, quite.'

'Wonderful voice?'

Here I was able to intone the response with a little more heartiness.

The Bellinger, at Tuppy's request, had sung us a few songs before digging in at the trough, and nobody could have denied that her pipes were in great shape. Plaster was still falling from the ceiling.

'Terrific,' I said.

Tuppy sighed, and, having helped himself to about four inches of whisky and one of soda, took a deep, refreshing draught.

. . . 'Do you remember Beefy Bingham who was at Oxford with us?'

'I ran into him only the other day. He's a parson now.'

'Yes. Down in the East End. Well, he runs a Lads' Club for the local toughs – you know the sort of thing – cocoa and backgammon in the reading-room and occasional clean, bright entertainments in the Oddfellows' Hall: and I've been helping him. I don't suppose I've passed an evening away from the backgammon board for weeks. Cora is extremely pleased. I've got her to promise to sing on Tuesday at Beefy's next clean, bright entertainment.'

'You have?'

'I absolutely have. And now mark my devilish ingenuity, Bertie. I'm going to sing, too.'

'Why do you suppose that's going to get you anywhere?'

'Because the way I intend to sing the song I intend to sing will prove to her that there are great deeps in my nature, whose existence she has not suspected. She will see that rough, unlettered audience wiping the tears out of its bally eyes and she will say to herself, 'What ho! The old egg really has a soul!' For it is not one of your mouldy comic songs, Bertie. No low buffoonery of that sort for me. It is all about angels being lonely and what not –'

I uttered a sharp cry.

'You don't mean you're going to sing "Sonny Boy"?'

'I jolly well do.'

Tuppy is in fact already engaged to Angela, the daughter of Bertie's Aunt Dahlia, and Aunt Dahlia is not one to take this sort of in-and-out running lying down. Like all Bertie's friends, she comes to Jeeves for advice, and gets it

'Well, sir, if I may say so, the thing that struck me most forcibly about Miss Bellinger when she was under my observation was that hers was a somewhat hard and intolerant nature. I could envisage Miss Bellinger applauding success. I could not so easily see her pitying and sympathizing with failure. . . . I think, therefore, that, should Miss Bellinger be a witness of Mr Glossop appearing to disadvantage in public, she would cease to entertain affection for him. In the event, for instance, of his failing to please the audience on Tuesday with his singing –'

I saw daylight.

'By Jove, Jeeves! You mean if he gets the bird, all will be off?'

'I shall be greatly surprised if such is not the case, sir.'

I shook my head.

'We cannot leave this thing to chance, Jeeves. Young Tuppy, singing "Sonny Boy", is the likeliest prospect for the bird that I can think of – but, no – you must see for yourself that we can't simply trust to luck.'

'We need not trust to luck, sir. I would suggest that you approach your friend, Mr Bingham, and volunteer your services as a performer at his forthcoming entertainment. It could readily be arranged that you sang immediately before Mr Glossop. I fancy, sir, that, if Mr Glossop were to sing "Sonny Boy", directly after you, too, had sung "Sonny Boy", the audience would respond satisfactorily. By the time Mr Glossop began to sing, they would have lost their taste for that particular song and would express their feelings warmly.'

'Jeeves,' said Aunt Dahlia, 'you're a marvel!'

'Thank you, madam.'

'Jeeves,' I said, 'you're an ass!'

. . . And so that afternoon I sent a pre-paid wire to Beefy Bingham, offering my services in the cause, and by nightfall the thing was fixed up. I was billed to perform next but one after the intermission. Following me, came Tuppy. And, immediately after him, Miss Cora Bellinger, the well-known operatic soprano.

. . . I must admit that there was a moment, just after I had entered the Oddfellows' Hall at Bermondsey East and run an eye over the assembled pleasure-seekers, when it needed all the bull-dog pluck of the Woosters to keep me from calling it a day and taking a cab back to civilization. The clean, bright entertainment was in full swing when I arrived, and somebody who looked as if he might be the local undertaker was reciting 'Gunga Din'. And the audience, though not actually chi-yiking in the full technical sense of the term, had a grim look which I didn't like at all. . . .

'A nice, full house, sir,' said a voice at my elbow. It was Jeeves, watching the proceedings with an indulgent eye.

'You here, Jeeves?' I said, coldly.

'Yes, sir. I have been present since the commencement.'

'Oh?' I said. 'Any casualties yet?'

'Sir?'

'You know what I mean, Jeeves,' I said sternly, 'and don't pretend you don't. Anybody got the bird yet?'

'Oh, no, sir.'

'I shall be the first, you think?'

'No, sir. I see no reason to expect such a misfortune. I anticipate that you will be well received.'

A sudden thought struck me.

'And you think everything will go according to plan?'

'Yes, sir.'

'Well, I don't,' I said. 'And I'll tell you why I don't. I've spotted a flaw in your beastly scheme.'

'A flaw, sir?'

'Yes. Do you suppose for a moment that, if Mr Glossop hears me singing that dashed song, he'll come calmly on a minute after me and sing it too? Use your intelligence, Jeeves. He will perceive the chasm in his path and pause in time. He will back out and refuse to go on at all.'

'Mr Glossop will not hear you sing, sir. At my advice, he has stepped across the road to the Jug and Bottle, an establishment immediately opposite the hall, and he intends to remain there until it is time for him to appear on the platform.'

'Oh?' I said.

'If I might suggest it, sir, there is another house named the Goat and Grapes only a short distance down the street. I think it might be a judicious move –'

'If I were to put a bit of custom in their way?'

'It would ease the nervous strain of waiting, sir.' . . .

The treatment worked like magic. . . . And shortly afterwards I was on the platform with about a million bulging eyes goggling up at me. There was a rummy sort of buzzing in my ears, and then through the buzzing I heard the sound of a piano starting to tinkle: and, commending my soul to God, I took a good, long breath and charged in.

Well, it was a close thing. The whole incident is a bit blurred, but I seem to recollect a kind of murmur as I hit the refrain. I thought at the time it was an attempt on the part of the many-headed to join in the chorus, and at the moment it rather encouraged me. I passed the thing over the larynx with all the vim at my disposal, hit the high note, and off gracefully into the wings. I didn't come on again to take a bow. I just receded and oiled round to where Jeeves awaited me among the standees at the back.

'Well, Jeeves,' I said, anchoring myself at his side and brushing the honest sweat from the brow, 'they didn't rush the platform.'

'No, sir.'

'But you can spread it about that that's the last time I perform outside my bath. My swan-song, Jeeves. Anybody who wants to hear me in future must present himself at the bathroom door and shove his ear against the keyhole. I may be wrong, but it seemed to me that towards the end they were hotting up a trifle. The bird was hovering in the air. I could hear the beating of its wings.'

'I did detect a certain restlessness, sir, in the audience. I fancy they had lost their taste for that particular melody.'

'Eh?'

'I should have informed you earlier, sir, that the song had already been sung twice before you arrived.'

'What!'

'Yes, sir. Once by a lady and once by a gentleman. It is a very popular song, sir.'

I gaped at the man. That, with this knowledge, he could calmly have allowed the young master to step straight into the jaws of death, so to speak, paralysed me. It seemed to show that the old feudal spirit had passed away altogether. I was about to give him my views on the matter in no uncertain fashion, when I was stopped by the spectacle of young Tuppy lurching on to the platform.

Young Tuppy had the unmistakable air of a man who has recently been round to the Jug and Bottle. A few cheery cries of welcome, presumably from some of his backgammon-playing pals who felt that blood was thicker than water, had the effect of causing the genial smile on his face to widen till it nearly met at the back. He was plainly feeling about as good as a man can feel and still remain on his feet. He waved a kindly hand to his supporters, and bowed in a regal sort of manner, rather like an Eastern monarch acknowledging the plaudits of the mob.

Then the female at the piano struck up the opening bars of 'Sonny Boy', and Tuppy swelled like a balloon, clasped his hands together, rolled his eyes up at the ceiling in a manner denoting Soul, and began.

I think the populace was too stunned for the moment to take immediate steps. It may seem incredible, but I give you my word that young Tuppy got right through the verse without so much as a murmur. Then they all seemed to pull themselves together.

A costermonger, roused, is a terrible thing. I had never seen the proletariat really stirred before, and I'm bound to say it rather awed me. I mean, it gave you some idea of what it must have been like during the French Revolution. From every corner of the hall there proceeded simultaneously the sort of noise which you hear, they tell me, at one of those East End boxing places when the referee disqualifies the popular favourite and makes the quick dash for life. And then they passed beyond mere words and began to introduce the vegetable motive.

I don't know why, but somehow I had got it into my head that the first thing thrown at Tuppy would be a potato. One gets these fancies. It was, however, as a matter of fact, a banana, and I saw in an instant that the choice had been made by wiser heads than mine. These blokes who have grown up from childhood in the knowledge of how to treat a dramatic entertainment that doesn't please them are aware by a sort of instinct just what to do for the best, and the moment I saw that banana splash on Tuppy's shirtfront I realized how infinitely more effective and artistic it was than any potato could have been.

Not that the potato school of thought had not also its supporters. As the proceedings warmed up, I noticed several intelligent-looking fellows who threw nothing else.

The effect on young Tuppy was rather remarkable. His eyes bulged and his hair seemed to stand up, and yet his mouth went on opening and shutting, and you could see that in a dazed, automatic way he was still singing 'Sonny Boy'. Then, coming out of his trance, he began to pull for the shore with some rapidity. The last seen of him, he was beating a tomato to the exit by a short head. . . .

But alas for human ambition: all unknown to Jeeves and Bertie, Cora Bellinger's car has broken down on the way to the Oddfellows' Hall, and she has entirely missed the spectacle of Tuppy's discomfiture. Bertie returns home disconsolate

It must have been about half past ten, and I was in the old sitting-room sombrely sucking down a more or less final restorative, when the front door bell rang, and there on the mat was young Tuppy. He looked like a man who has passed through some great experience and stood face to face with his soul. He had the beginnings of a black eye.

'Oh, hullo, Bertie,' said young Tuppy.

He came in, and hovered about the mantelpiece as if he were looking for things to fiddle with and break.

'I've just been singing at Beefy Bingham's entertainment,' he said after a pause.

'Oh?' I said. 'How did you go?'

'Like a breeze,' said young Tuppy. 'Held them spellbound.'

'Knocked 'em, eh?'

'Cold,' said young Tuppy. 'Not a dry eye.'

And this, mark you, a man who had had a good upbringing and had, no doubt, spent years at his mother's knee being taught to tell the truth.

'I suppose Miss Bellinger is pleased?'

'Oh, yes. Delighted.'

'So now everything's all right?'

'Oh, quite.'

Tuppy paused.

'On the other hand, Bertie –'

'Yes?'

'Well, I've been thinking things over. Somehow I don't believe Miss Bellinger is the mate for me after all.'

'You don't?'

'No, I don't.'

'Why don't you?'

'Oh, I don't know. These things sort of flash on you. . . .'

'Jeeves,' I called.

'Sir?' said Jeeves, manifesting himself.

'Jeeves, a remarkably rummy thing has happened. Mr Glossop has just been here. He tells me that it is all off between him and Miss Bellinger.'

'Yes, sir.'

'You don't seem surprised.'

'No, sir. I confess I had anticipated some such eventuality.'

'Eh? What gave you that idea?'

'It came to me, sir, when I observed Miss Bellinger strike Mr Glossop in the eye.'

'Strike him!'

'Yes, sir.'

'In the eye?'

'The right eye, sir.'

I clutched the brow.

'What on earth made her do that?'

'I fancy she was a little upset, sir, at the reception accorded to her singing.'

'Great Scott! Don't tell me she got the bird, too?'

'Yes, sir.'

'But why? She's got a red-hot voice.'

'Yes, sir. But I think the audience resented her choice of a song.'

'Jeeves!' Reason was beginning to do a bit of tottering on its throne. 'You aren't going to stand there and tell me that Miss Bellinger sang

"Sonny Boy", too!'

'Yes, sir. And – rashly, in my opinion – brought a large doll on to the platform to sing it to. The audience affected to mistake it for a ventriloquist's dummy, and there was some little disturbance.'

'But, Jeeves, what a coincidence!'

'Not altogether, sir. I ventured to take the liberty of accosting Miss Bellinger on her arrival at the hall and recalling myself to her recollection. I then said that Mr Glossop had asked me to request her that as a particular favour to him – the song being a favourite of his – she would sing "Sonny Boy". And when she found that you and Mr Glossop had also sung the song immediately before her, I rather fancy that she supposed that she had been the victim of a practical pleasantry by Mr Glossop. Will there be anything further, sir?'

'No, thanks.'

'Good night, sir.'

'Good night, Jeeves,' I said reverently.

P. G. WODEHOUSE *Jeeves and the Song of Songs* 1930

Church Music

   . . . Some to church repair,
Not for the doctrine, but the music there.

ALEXANDER POPE *Essay on Criticism* 1711

It has always been a sore point with the Church authorities. Here is the Abbot of Rievaulx on the subject in the twelfth century

Let me speak now of those who, under the show of religion, doe obpalliate the business of pleasure. . . . Whence hath the Church so many Organs and Musicall Instruments? To what purpose, I pray you, is that terrible blowing of Belloes, expressing rather the crakes of Thunder, than the sweetnesse of a voyce? To what purpose serves that contraction and inflection of the voyce? This man sings a base, this a small meane, another a treble, a fourth divides and cuts asunder, as it were, certaine middle notes. One while the voyce is strained, anon it is remitted, now it is dashed, and then againe it is inlarged with a lowder sound. Sometimes, which is a shame to speake, it is enforced into a horse's neighings; sometimes, the masculine vigour being laid aside, it is sharpened into the shrilnesse of a woman's voyce; now and then it is writhed, and retorted with a certaine artificiall circumvolution. Sometimes thou may'st see a man with an open mouth, not to sing, but, as it were, to breathe out his last gaspe, by shutting in his breath, and by a certaine ridiculous interception of his voyce, as it were to threaten silence, and now again to imitate the agonies of a dying man, or the extasies of such as suffer. . . . In the meantime, the common people standing by, trembling and astonished, admire the sound of the Organs, the noyse of the Cymballs and Musicall Instruments, the harmony of the Pipes and Cornets.

AILRED, ABBOT OF RIEVAULX *Speculum Charitatis*

A letter to the Spectator, signed R. S. (presumably Richard Steele) and dated 25 October 1711.

'Mr. Spectator'

I am a Country Clergyman, and hope you will lend me your Assistance in ridiculing some little Indecencies which cannot so properly be exposed from the Pulpit.

A Widow Lady, who straggled this Summer from London into my Parish for the Benefit of the Air, as she says, appears every Sunday at Church with many fashionable extravagancies, to the great Astonishment of my Congregation.

But what gives us the most Offence is her Theatrical manner of singing the Psalms. She introduces above fifty Italian Airs into the Hundredth Psalm, and whilst we begin 'All People' in the old Solemn Tune of our Forefathers, she in quite a different Key runs Divisions on the Vowels, and adorns them with the Graces of Nicolini; if she meets with Eke or Aye, which are frequent in the Metre of Hopkins and Sternhold, we are certain to hear her quavering them half a Minute after us to some sprightly Airs of the Opera.

I am very far from being an Enemy to Church Musick, but I fear this Abuse of it may make my Parish ridiculous, who already look on the Singing Psalms as an Entertainment, and not part of their Devotion: besides, I am apprehensive that the Infection may spread, for Squire Squeekum, who by his Voice seems (if I may use the Expression) to be cut out for an Italian Singer, was last Sunday practising the same Airs.

I know the Lady's Principles, and that she will plead the Toleration, which (as she fancies) allows her Non-Conformity in this Particular; but I beg you to Acquaint her, that Singing the Psalms in a different Tune from the rest of the Congregation, is a sort of Schism not tolerated by that Act.

I am, Sir, Your Very Humble Servant,
R.S.

Occasionally the irregularities in church music arise from other sources.

Absent-mindedness in a Parish Choir

'It happened on Sunday after Christmas – the last Sunday ever they played in Longpuddle church gallery, as it turned out, though they didn't know it then. As you may know, sir, the players formed a very good band – almost as good as the Mellstock parish players that were led by the Dewys; and that's saying a great deal. There was Nicholas Puddingcome, the leader, with the first fiddle; there was Timothy Thomas, the bass-viol man; John Biles, the tenor fiddler; Dan'l Hornhead, with the serpent; Robert Dowdle, with the clarionet; and Mr. Nicks, with the oboe – all sound and powerful musicians, and strong-winded men – they that blowed. For that reason they were very much in demand Christmas week for little reels and dancing parties; for they could turn a jig or a hornpipe out of hand as well as ever they could turn out a psalm, and perhaps better, not to speak irreverent. In short, one half-hour they could be playing a Christmas carol in the squire's hall to the ladies and gentlemen, and drinking tay and coffee with 'em as modest as saints; and the next, at The Tinker's Arms, blazing away like wild horses with the "Dashing White Sergeant" to nine couple of dancers and more, and swallowing rum-and-cider hot as flame.

'Well, this Christmas they'd been out to one rattling randy after another every night, and had got next to no sleep at all. Then came the Sunday after Christmas, their fatal day. 'Twas so mortal cold that year that they could hardly sit in the gallery; for though the congregation down in the body of the church had a stove to keep off the frost, the players in the gallery had nothing at all. So Nicholas said at morning service, when 'twas freezing an inch an hour, "Please the Lord I won't stand this numbing weather no longer: this afternoon we'll have something in our insides to make us warm, if it cost a king's ransom."

'So he brought a gallon of hot brandy and beer, ready mixed, to church with him in the afternoon, and by keeping the jar well wrapped up in Timothy Thomas's bass-viol bag it kept drinkably warm till they wanted it, which was just a thimbleful in the Absolution, and another after the Creed, and the remainder at the beginning o' the sermon. When they'd had the last pull they felt quite comfortable and warm, and as the sermon went on – most unfortunately for 'em it was a long one that afternoon – they fell asleep, every man jack of 'em; and there they slept on as sound as rocks.

''Twas a very dark afternoon, and by the end of the sermon all you could see of the inside of the church were the pa'son's two candles alongside of him in the pulpit, and his spaking face behind 'em. The sermon being ended at last, the pa'son gie'd out the Evening Hymn. But no quire set about sounding up the tune, and the people began to turn their heads to learn the reason why, and then Levi Limpet, a boy who sat in the gallery, nudged Timothy and Nicholas, and said, "Begin! begin!"

'"Hey? what?" says Nicholas, starting up; and the church being so dark and his head so muddled he thought he was at the party they had played at all the night before, and away he went, bow and fiddle, at "The Devil among the Tailors," the favourite jig of our neighbourhood at that time. The rest of the band, being in the same state of mind and nothing doubting, followed their leader with all their strength, according to custom. They poured out that there tune till the lower bass notes of "The Devil among the Tailors" made the cobwebs in the roof shiver like ghosts; then Nicholas, seeing nobody moved, shouted out as he scraped (in his usual commanding way at dances when the folk didn't know the figures), "Top couples cross hands! And when I make the fiddle squeak at the end, every man kiss his pardner under the mistletoe!"

'The boy Levi was so frightened that he bolted down the gallery stairs and out homeward like lightning. The pa'son's hair fairly stood on end when he heard the evil tune raging through the church, and thinking the quire had gone crazy he held up his hand and said: "Stop, stop, stop! Stop, stop! What's this?" But they didn't hear'n for the noise of their own playing, and the more he called the louder they played.

'Then the folks came out of their pews, wondering down to the ground, and saying: "What do they mean by such wickedness! We shall be consumed like Sodom and Gomorrah!"

'And the squire, too, came out of his pew lined wi' green baize, where lots of lords and ladies visiting at the house were worshipping along with him, and went and stood in front of the gallery, and shook his fist in the musicians' faces, saying, "What! In this reverent edifice! What!"

'And at last they heard'n through their playing, and stopped.

'"Never such an insulting, disgraceful thing – never!" says the squire, who couldn't rule his passion.

'"Never!" says the pa'son, who had come down and stood beside him.

'"Not if the Angels of Heaven," says the squire (he was a wickedish man, the squire was, though now for once he happened to be on the Lord's side) – "not if the Angels of Heaven come down," he says, "shall one of you villainous players ever sound a note in this church again; for the insult to me, and my family, and my visitors, and the parson, and God Almighty, that you've a-perpetrated this afternoon!"

'Then the unfortunate church band came to their senses, and remembered where they were; and 'twas a sight to see Nicholas Puddingcome and Timothy Thomas and John Biles creep down the gallery stairs with their fiddles under their arms, and poor Dan'l Hornhead with his serpent, and Robert Dowdle with his clarionet, all looking as little as ninepins; and out they went. The pa'son might have forgi'ed 'em when he learned the truth o't, but the squire would not. That very week he sent for a barrel-organ that would play two-and-twenty new psalm-tunes, so exact and particular that, however sinful inclined you was, you could play nothing but psalm-tunes whatso-mever. He had a really respectable man to turn the winch, as I said, and the old players played no more.'

THOMAS HARDY *A Few Crusted Characters* 1894

There is another perennial source of trouble in village churches. The following letter, addressed to Mrs John Betjeman, wife of the late Poet Laureate, speaks for itself as well as for many other unhappy incumbents in the same situation

Baulking Vicarage

My dear Penelope,

I have been thinking over the question of the playing of the harmonium on Sunday evenings here and have reached the conclusion that I must now take it over myself.

I am very grateful to you for doing it for so long and hate to have to ask you to give it up, but, to put it plainly, your playing has got worse and worse and the disaccord between the harmonium and the congregation is becoming destructive of devotion. People are not very sensitive here, but even some of them have begun to complain, and they are not usually given to doing that. I do not like writing this, but I think you will understand that it is my business to see that divine worship is as perfect as it can be made. Perhaps the crankiness of the instrument has something to do with the trouble. I think it does require a careful and experienced player to deal with it.

Thank you ever so much for stepping so generously into the breach when Sibyl was ill; it was the greatest possible help to me and your results were noticeably better then than now.

Yours ever,
F. P. Harton
quoted in MAURICE BOWRA *Memories 1898–1939*

Milton was a poet who knew what church music was, or anyhow ought to be, about

. . .

And as I wake, sweet musick breath
Above, about, or underneath,
Sent by som spirit to mortals good,
Or th'unseen Genius of the Wood.
    But let my due feet never fail,
To walk the studious Cloysters pale,
And love the high embowèd Roof,
With antick Pillars massy proof,
And storied Windows richly dight,
Casting a dimm religious light.
There let the pealing Organ blow,

To the full voic'd Quire below,
In Service high, and Anthems cleer,
As may with sweetnes, through mine ear,
Dissolve me into extasies,
And bring all Heav'n before mine eyes.
And may at last my weary age
Find out the peacefull hermitage,
The Hairy Gown and Mossy Cell,
Where I may sit and rightly spell
Of every Star that Heaven doth shew,
And every Herb that sips the dew;
Till old experience do attain
To somthing like Prophetic strain.
These pleasures *Melancholy* give,
And I with thee will choose to live.

JOHN MILTON Il Penseroso c. 1631

It seems irresistible to pass from Milton to Handel at this point, even if the next piece doesn't really have anything to do with church music

Handel, late in life, like the great poets Homer and Milton, was afflicted with blindness; which, however it might dispirit and embarrass him at other times, had no effect on his nerves or intellect in public, as he continued to play concertos and voluntaries between the parts of his oratorios to the last, with the same vigor of thought and touch for which he was ever so justly renowed. To see him, however, led to the organ after this calamity at upward of seventy years of age, and then conducted toward the audience to make his accustomed obeisance, was a sight so truly afflicting and deplorable to persons of sensibility as greatly diminished their pleasure in hearing him perform.

During the oratorio season, I have been told that he practiced almost incessantly; and, indeed, that must have been the case, or his memory uncommonly retentive; for after his blindness he played several of his *old* organ concertos, which must have been previously impressed on his memory by practice. At last, however, he rather chose to trust to his inventive powers than those of reminiscence; for, giving the band only the skeleton or ritornelles of each movement, he played all the solo parts *extempore, ad libitum,* while the other instruments left him, they waiting for the signal of a trill before they played such fragments of symphony as they found in their books.

CHARLES BURNEY . . . in Commemoration of Handel 1785

The organist and choirmaster bear the brunt of the problems that beset music in church. A practising (and suffering) member of the profession has compiled a list of some of them, from which we quote a selection

ABSENCE The only quality of an organist which is generally recognized.

AMEN This may be plagal, perfect, Gibbons, Smith, sevenfold or said. The important thing is for everyone to know what is intended, since one thing is certain – they don't mix.

ANISEED BALLS These confections are not recommended for ecclesiastical use for three reasons: (i) they outlast the longest sermon, (ii) their scent is unmistakable and cannot even be masked by incense, (iii) they are too easily ejected from the cassock pocket and, on reaching ground level, tend to roll into public view. The writer has known one come to a halt at the feet of a hypnotized bishop.

ARPISCHORD The accepted pronunciation of 'harpsichord' among vergers, sextons and caretakers. Some slight criticism is implied.

BOYS Unsatisfactory alternatives to girls (*q.v.*).

CHAMADE Ranks of organ pipes, usually of the trumpet kind, may be mounted *en chamade*. They stick out straight and frighten passers-by. Village choirs often have a tenor who sounds as though he is *en chamade*, though unlikely to be mounted.

CIPHER This is when a note on the organ refuses to stop. Organists of many years' experience vouch that the only thing to do is switch off, write a note to the tuner and go home. This is the quickest way to (a) a rebuild, (b) lunch.

DESCANT One of the two major church nuisances, the other being pigeons. At least no descant has yet spoilt a hat.

FEET Many organists make use of both of these. Generally speaking, the left one is in charge of vibrations, whilst the right cruises gently in sympathy. A good organist does little damage with his right foot.

GIRLS Unsatisfactory alternatives to boys (*q.v.*).

HYMNS These are of two kinds, long and short. They are bound together in volumes which are either too big or too little. Both kinds are sensitive to the pull of gravity at solemn moments.

JELLY BABIES have many advantages over aniseed balls (*q.v.*) particularly in the matters of (i) speed, (ii) scent and (iii) silence. Resist, however, the temptation to contemplate before consumption. Construction is identical and whatever the colour they all taste the same.

LAY CLERKS There are many theories about the origin of this term for cathedral choirmen. The title may bear some relation to the traditional posture of the appellant. It may refer to the one factor common to all his actions in the choir stalls – a sense of reclining, which no doubt induces a feeling of relaxation. The use of the archaic form 'lay' instead of 'lie' has caused confusion. There is no evidence that it could refer to ovulation. Records reveal no instance of any lay clerk, not even an alto, actually laying anything.

MEN These are what choirboys are intended to grow into. Their traditional privileges include arriving later than the boys on rehearsal nights, counting rests audibly, visibly or wrongly (or any combination of all three) and improvising. They also take snuff, mints or umbrage, according to taste. There are three main varieties – altos (whose origin is shrouded in mystery), tenors (glamorous, fickle and rare) and basses (solid, dependable, tenacious of note, opinion and often, unfortunately, life). In mixed choirs, the men do not arrive late, and they leave with the women.

OFFERTORY The process of collecting a wholly inadequate amount of money from a congregation. The resultant tintinnabulation (rarely, alas, a rustle) is covered up in many churches by a hymn, in others by an organ voluntary. In the latter case, the organist needs to watch the progress of the bags or plates, so that appropriate climaxes may be engineered whenever the collectors approach the most promising pews. It is, however, considered bad taste to stop playing and peer into the mirror. At organ recitals, the offertory is taken as the congregation leaves the church. A better idea would be to take it during an interval – and count it publicly. The organist could then play the second half or not, at his discretion.

RECITAL This is usually a performance given by the organist, with heavy emphasis on the word 'given'. Practising for a recital is one of the least understood activities in the church. The start of such a session may be the signal for three other things to happen – the

Vicar wanders in for a chat, the Verger switches on the Hoover, and a student from the Royal College of Music pops up to enquire if practice is allowed.

SWITCHES No one should embark (or embach) upon playing a strange organ without understanding the siting and function of these. There will usually be one for the music desk light, one for the pedal light (but no bulb) and one for the blower. They may be placed anywhere in the church. The blower switch may even be in the adjoining vicarage, thus giving the incumbent the power to protest against inordinate decibels. Sometimes a mains switch in the porch may be thrown by a departing verger. Many an organist has had a foretaste of the end of the world in this way.

TENORS Most choirs have either (a) none or (b) too many. When wholly absent they leave an aching void. When too numerous they fill the void without removing the ache. Tenors rarely sing words and often produce regional sensations rather than actual notes. During the mating season, they draw attention to themselves by a practice known as *rubato*.

USUAL OFFICES Mattins and Evensong. Few churches possess any other usual, or even unusual offices. Choristers would be well advised to make sure before leaving home, especially in winter.

VERGERS These were originally meant to lead processions (and subdue rioters) with their wands or verges. Nowadays they also make strong sweet tea, sweep dust and pencils under the organ pedals – and acquire keys to everything. No verger, however officious, should ever be crossed. His range of retaliations includes inadequate fuses, wrong hymn numbers and, in extreme cases, tidying up the choir stalls.

WOMEN are acceptable in church choirs provided that their ages and vital statistics can be kept to a reasonable minimum. Unfortunate vocal characteristics may ensue if this rule is ignored. Old women of both sexes should be retired.

ZERO When the thermometer beside the organ reaches this mark, the organist should increase the wattage of the pedal light, trim the wick of his paraffin stove, polish up his cold-weather toccatas and lay in a store of glycerine to prevent hoar frost on the altos.

GORDON REYNOLDS *Organo Pleno* 1970

An epitaph on an organist at York Minster, who died about 1573

> Musician and logician both
> John Wynal lieth here
> Who made the organs erst to speak
> As if, or as it were.

And another from Norwich Cathedral, 1621

> Here William Inglott, Organist, doth rest,
> Whose art in Music this Cathedral blest;
> He passed on Organ, Song, and Virginall.
> He left this life at age of sixty-seven,
> And now 'mongst Angels all sings first in Heaven.
> His fame flies far, his Name shall never die,
> See, Art and Age here crown his memorie.

Here, on the other hand, is a note in the Minute Book of the Chapter of Lincoln Cathedral about Thomas Kingston, organist there from 1599–1616

He is verye often drunke and by means thereof he hathe by unorderlye playing on the organs putt the quire out of time and disordered them.

They don't seem to have had much luck with organists at Lincoln. The following plea from the Precentor to the Dean concerned one called Mudd, who was organist from 1662 to 1663

I wish you would be pleased to send us downe an able and more civill organist. We dare trust him no more with our organ, but request you (if you can) to help us to another; and with what speed be.

all quoted by NORMAN DEMUTH in *An Anthology of Musical Criticism* 1947

The Organist in Heaven

[SAMUEL SEBASTIAN WESLEY]

> When Wesley died, the Angelic orders,
>   To see him at the state,
> Press'd so incontinent that the warders
>   Forgot to shut the gate.
> So I, that hitherto had follow'd
>   As one with grief o'ercast,

Where for the doors a space was hollow'd,
　　Crept in, and heard what pass'd.
And God said: – 'Seeing thou hast given
　　Thy life to my great sounds,
Choose thou through all the cirque of Heaven
　　What most of bliss redounds.'
Then Wesley said: – 'I hear the thunder
　　Low growling from Thy seat –
Grant me that I may bind it under
　　The trampling of my feet.'
And Wesley said: – 'See, lightning quivers
　　Upon the presence walls –
Lord, give me of it four great rivers,
　　To be my manuals.'
And then I saw the thunder chidden
　　As slave to his desire;
And then I saw the space bestridden
　　With four great bands of fire;
And stage by stage, stop stop subtending,
　　Each lever strong and true,
One shape inextricable blending,
　　The awful organ grew.
Then certain angels clad the Master
　　In very marvellous wise,
Till clouds of rose and alabaster
　　Conceal'd him from mine eyes.
And likest to a dove soft brooding,
　　The innocent figure ran;
So breathed the breath of his preluding,
　　And then the fugue began –
Began; but, to his office turning,
　　The porter swung his key;
Wherefore, although my heart was yearning,
　　I had to go; but he
Play'd on; and, as I downward clomb,
　　I heard the mighty bars
Of thunder-gusts, that shook heaven's dome,
　　And moved the balanced stars.

T. E. BROWN 1876

This almost suggests De Quincey in his purplest mood

Then was completed the passion of the mighty fugue. The golden tubes of the organ, which as yet had but muttered at intervals – gleaming amongst clouds and surges of incense – threw up, as from fountains unfathomable, columns of heart-shattering music. Choir and anti-choir were filling fast with unknown voices. Thou also, Dying Trumpeter! – with thy love that was victorious, and thy anguish that was finishing – didst enter the tumult; trumpet and echo – farewell love, and farewell anguish – rang through the dreadful *sanctus*. Oh, darkness of the grave! that from the crimson altar and from the fiery font wert visited and searched by the effulgence in an angel's eye – were these indeed thy children? Pomps of life, that from the burials of centuries, rose again to the voice of perfect joy, did ye indeed mingle with the festivals of Death? Lo! as I looked back for seventy leagues through the mighty cathedral, I saw the quick and the dead that sang together to God, together that sang to the generations of man. All the hosts of jubilation, like armies that ride in pursuit, moved with one step. Us, that, with laurelled heads, were passing from the cathedral, they overtook, and, as with a garment, they wrapped us round with thunders greater than our own. . . .

THOMAS DE QUINCEY *The English Mail-Coach* 1849

It is a celebrated piece of fine writing, but are we alone in being nagged by irrepressible memories of, well, Walt Disney, and *Fantasia*?

For most English people, congregational singing is the core of church music

Abundance of people of the best rank and quality being shut up in the city, namely, lords, knights, and gentlemen of the countries round about, besides the souldiers and citizens, who, all or most of them, came constantly every Sunday to hear public prayers and sermon, the number was so exceedingly great, that the church was (as I may say) even cramming and squeezing full. Now here you must take notice that they had then a custom in that church (which I hear not of in any other Cathedral which was) that always before the sermon, the whole congregation sang a psalm, together with the quire and the organ; and you must also know, that there was then a most excellent-large-plump-lusty-full-speaking organ which cost (as I am credibly informed) a thousand pounds. This organ I say, (when the psalm was set before the sermon), being let out into all its fullness of stops, together with the quire, began the psalm. But when that vast-conchording-unity of the whole congregational-chorus, came (as I may say) thundering in, even so it made the very ground shake under us; (oh the unutterable ravishing soul's delight!) in the which I was so transported, and wrapt up into high contemplation, that there was no room left in my whole man, namely, body and spirit, for any thing below divine and heavenly raptures.

THOMAS MACE 'On the Psalm singing at York Cathedral during the Siege' from *Music's Monument* 1676

The attitude is implanted early

The moment had now come for the Hymn. This being the first Sunday of the Summer term, they sang that special hymn, written by the headmaster, with music by Dr Jolly, on purpose to be sung on the first Sundays of terms. The organ quietly sketched out the tune. Simple it was, uplifting and manly.

> One, two, three, four; one, two THREE – 4.
> One, two-and three-and four-and; One, two THREE – 4.
> ONE – 2, THREE – 4; ONE – 2 – 3 – 4,
> and-ONE – 2, THREE – 4; ONE – 2 – 3 – 4.
> One, two-and three, four; One, two THREE – 4.

Five hundred flawed adolescent voices took it up. For good example's sake, Gumbril opened and closed his mouth; noiselessly, however. It was only at the third verse that he gave rein to his uncertain baritone. He particularly liked the third verse; it marked, in his opinion, the Headmaster's highest poetical achievement.

> (*f*) For slack hands and (*dim.*) idle minds
> (*mf*) Mischief still the Tempter finds.
> (*ff*) Keep him captive in his lair.

At this point Dr Jolly enriched his tune with a thick accompaniment in the lower registers, artfully designed to symbolize the depth, the gloom and general repulsiveness of the Tempter's home.

> (*ff*) Keep him captive in his lair.
> (*f*) Work will bind him. (*dim.*) Work is (*pp*) prayer.

Work, thought Gumbril, work. Lord, how passionately he disliked work! Let Austin have his swink to him reserved! Ah, if only one had work of one's own, proper work, decent work – not forced upon one by the griping of one's belly! Amen! Dr Jolly blew the two sumptuous jets of reverence into the air; Gumbril accompanied them with all his heart. Amen, indeed.

ALDOUS HUXLEY *Antic Hay* 1923

Hymns can sometimes be a source of unexpected pleasure, even the most famous: how many fathers, standing docile and correctly dressed at their daughter's side, have really considered the supplication of their assembled guests

> Be present, awful Father,
> To give away this bride . . .
>> 'The voice that breathed o'er Eden' *English Hymnal*

Others may be less well known

> By whom shall Jacob now arise?
> For Jacob's friends are few;
> And what may fill us with surprise,
> They seem divided too.

Or this, from Boston

> Ye monsters of the bubbling deep,
> Your Maker's praises shout,
> Up from the sands, ye codlings, leap
> And wag your tails about.
>> both quoted by D. B. Wyndham Lewis and
>> Charles Lee in *The Stuffed Owl* 1930

Or this

> Our life contains a thousand springs,
> And dies if one be gone.
> Strange! that a harp of thousand strings
> Should keep in tune so long.
>> ISAAC WATTS *Hymns* 1707

And here is a *trouvaille,* used in a church near Cambridge in the 1880s, and preserved in a letter of George Lyttelton

> Milk of the breast that cannot cloy
> He, like a nurse, will bring;
> And when we see His promise nigh,
> Oh how we'll suck and sing!
>> quoted in *The Lyttelton–Hart-Davis Letters* 1956–57

But there are some marvellous poems buried in the volumes of English hymnology too

> The spacious firmament on high,
> With all the blue ethereal sky,
> And spangled heavens, a shining frame,
> Their great Original proclaim.
> Th' unwearied Sun from day to day
> Does his Creator's power display,
> And publishes to every land
> The works of an Almighty hand.
>
> Soon as the evening shades prevail
> The Moon takes up the wondrous tale,
> And nightly to the listening Earth
> Repeats the story of her birth;
> Whilst all the stars that round her burn,
> And all the planets in their turn,
> Confirm the tidings as they roll,
> And spread the truth from pole to pole.
>
> What though in solemn silence all
> Move round the dark terrestrial ball;
> What though nor real voice nor sound
> Amidst their radiant orbs be found?
> In Reason's ear they all rejoice
> And utter forth a glorious voice;
> For ever singing as they shine,
> 'The Hand that made us is Divine'.
>
> JOSEPH ADDISON *Ode* 1712

At the end of *Noye's Fludde* Britten married these words to the tune known as Tallis's *Canon* (happily disregarding the fact that they were written about 150 years after it), and nobody who has been to a performance will forget the overwhelming effect of audience and performers singing in eight-part canon with bugles calling and handbells clashing.

On the north wall of the nave in Norwich Cathedral is a memorial to one Osbert Parsley, an old choirman who died in 1585

> Here lies the Man whose Name in Spight of Death
> Renowned lives by Blast of Golden Fame;
> Whose Harmony survives his vital Breath,
> Whose Skill no Pride did spot, whose Life no Blame;
> Whose low Estate was blest with quiet Mind

As our sweet Cords with Discords mixed be:
Whose life in *Seventy* and *Four* Years entwind
As falleth mellowed Apples from the Tree.
Whose Deeds were Rules, whose Words were Verity;
Who here a Singing-Man did spend his Days.
Full *Fifty* Years in our Church Melody
His Memory shines bright whom thus we praise.

This is an old favourite, but there is some doubt about Parsley's abilities as a composer. William Jackson of Exeter is quoted as saying (of Parsley's canon on the plainsong *Salvator Mundi*): 'A canon upon a plain song is the most difficult part of composition . . . This of Parsley's has many faults which nothing can excuse but its being a canon upon a plain song.'

In fact, this piece seems to have got a fairly grudging reception wherever it was mentioned. Morley quotes it as a musical example in *A Plaine and Easie Introduction to Practicall Musicke*, and then adds: '. . . as concerning the descanting, although I cannot commend it for the best in the musicke, yet is it praiseworthie; and though in some places it be harsh to the eare, yet is it more tollerable in this waie, than in two partes in one. . . .'

And here is a tale told, perhaps, about some latter-day, village Osbert Parsley

He often would ask us
That, when he died,
After playing so many
To their last rest,
If out of us any
Should here abide,
And it would not task us,
We would with our lutes
Play over him
By his grave-brim
The psalm he liked best –
The one whose sense suits
'Mount Ephraim' –
And perhaps we should seem
To him, in Death's dream,
Like the seraphim.

As soon as I knew
That his spirit was gone
I thought this his due,
And spoke thereupon.

'I think,' said the vicar,
'A read service quicker
Than viols out-of-doors
In these frosts and hoars.
That old-fashioned way
Requires a fine day,
And it seems to me
It had better not be.'

Hence, that afternoon,
Though never knew he
That his wish could not be,
To get through it faster
They buried the master
Without any tune.

But 'twas said that, when
At the dead of next night
The vicar looked out,
There struck on his ken
Thronged roundabout,
Where the frost was graying
The headstoned grass,
A band all in white
Like the saints in church-glass,
Singing and playing
The ancient stave
By the choirmaster's grave.

Such the tenor man told
When he had grown old.

THOMAS HARDY 'The Choirmaster's Burial'

from *Moments of Vision* 1917

Mortality

Here lyes Henry Purcell Esqre, who left this Lyfe and is gone to that Blessed Place where only his Harmony can be exceeded.

In Westminster Abbey

Another touching epitaph is Schubert's, written by Grillparzer

The art of music here entombed a rich possession, but even far fairer hopes. Franz Schubert lies here.

In Währing cemetery, only two memorial stones away from Beethoven's

Enterred here doth ly a worthy Wyght
Who for long Tyme in Musick bore the bell:
His Name to shew was Thomas Tallys hyght,
In honest vertuous Lyff he did excel.
He serv'd long Time in Chappell with grete prayse,
Fower Sovereynes Reynes (a Thing not often seen)
I mean Kyng Henry and Prynce Edward's Dayes,
Queene Mary, and Elizabeth our Quene.
He maryed was, though Children he had none,
And lyv'd in Love full thre and thirty Yeres,
Wyth loyal Spowse, whos Name yclyipt was Jone,
Who here entomb'd him Company now bears.
As he dyd lyve, so also did he dy,
In myld and quyet Sort (O! happy Man)
To God ful oft for Mercy did he cry,
Wherefore he lyves, let Death do what he can.

From a tombstone c. 1585 in Greenwich Old Church, destroyed about 1720

To Mr. H. Lawes, *on his Aires*

Harry, whose tuneful and well measur'd Song
   First taught our English Musick how to span
   Words with just note and accent, not to scan
   With *Midas'* Ears, committing short and long;
Thy worth and skill exempts thee from the throng,
   With praise enough for Envy to look wan;
   To after age thou shalt be writ the man,
   That with smooth aire couldst humor best our tongue.
Thou honour'st Verse, and Verse must send her wing
   To honour thee, the Priest of *Phœbus* Quire
   That tun'st their happiest lines in Hymn, or Story.
Dante shall give Fame leave to set thee higher
   Than his *Casella,* whom he woo'd to sing
   Met in the milder shades of Purgatory.

JOHN MILTON 1648

Henry Lawes's reputation did not remain at this exalted level for very long, however. Here is Dr Burney in the *History of Music,* published only ten years after Lawes's death

I have examined with care and candour all the works I can find of this composer, which are still very numerous and am obliged to own myself unable, by their excellence, to account for the great reputation he acquired, and the numerous panegyrics bestowed on him by the greatest poets and musicians of his time. His temper and conversation must certainly have endeared him to his acquaintances and rendered them partial to the productions, and the praise of such writers as Milton and Waller is durable fame.

CHARLES BURNEY *History of Music* 1776

Lawes's younger brother, William, who met his death at the siege of Chester in 1645, is thus commemorated in that city

   Concord is conquor'd; in this urn there lies
   The master of great Music's mysteries;
   And in it is a riddle like the cause,
   Will Lawes was slain by those whose *Wills* are Lawes.

Long after all the many eulogies of Purcell written in the years immediately following his death comes this solitary poem, one of the most beautiful in the English language about a musician. It is almost music itself

Henry Purcell

The poet wishes well to the divine genius of Purcell and praises him that, whereas other musicians have given utterance to the moods of man's mind, he has, beyond that, uttered in notes the very make and species of man as created both in him and in all men generally.

Have fair fallen, O fair, fair have fallen, so dear
To me, so arch-especial a spirit as heaves in Henry Purcell,
An age is now since passed, since parted; with the reversal
Of the outward sentence low lays him, listed to a heresy, here.

Not mood in him nor meaning, proud fire or sacred fear,
Or love or pity or all that sweet notes not his might nursle:
It is the forgèd feature finds me; it is the rehearsal
Of own, of abrupt self there so thrusts on, so throngs the ear.

Let him oh! with his air of angels then lift me, lay me! only I'll
Have an eye to the sakes of him, quaint moonmarks, to his pelted
        plumage under
Wings: so some great stormfowl, whenever he has walked his while

The thunder-purple seabeach plumèd purple-of-thunder,
If a wuthering of his palmy snow-pinions scatter a colossal smile
Off him, but meaning motion fans fresh our wits with wonder.

GERARD MANLEY HOPKINS *Poems* 1918

Purcell died on the twenty-first day of November, 1695. There is a tradition that his death was occasioned by a cold which he caught in the night, waiting for admittance into his own house. It is said that he used to keep late hours, and that his wife had given orders to his servants not to let him in after midnight: unfortunately he came home heated with wine from the tavern at an hour later than that prescribed him, and through the inclemency of the air contracted a disorder of which he died. If this be true, it reflects but little honour on Madam Purcell . . .

SIR JOHN HAWKINS *History of the Science and Practice of Music* 1776

The Tomb of Scarlatti

Average depth of graves, four feet –
the illusion of allegro in our light
is hard: that Iberian heartlessness
is still with us but not such sweetness.
What miracles for the twentieth century
among castrati, melons, and the dribbling kings!
Average length of sonata, four minutes, with repeats.

I hate the idea of Spain, yet for Domenico
I'd round each corner with its urine smell,
tickle the garden fish with a martyr's bone,
sit in the shadow of a cancered priest.
So many slaps of black! The old dust jumps
for American recordings, keyboard clatters
like cruel dominoes – E major fills the afternoon.

Santo Norberto gone: cat stalks complacent
pigeons. The old gods swim for home.
What are the conversions? Scholars' rules
and lace handkerchiefs become duennas' breasts
leaning from all top windows. A tourist bus
is draped with moonlight while the sounding notes
go past like carloads of the glittering dead.

PETER PORTER *Preaching to the Converted* 1972

The Heiligenstadt Testament is surely one of the most tragic documents in the history of music. Written with evident care, and carefully preserved, it was not discovered until some twenty-five years later, when Beethoven died

For my brothers Carl and [Johann] Beethoven:

O my fellow men, who think or say that I am churlish, obstinate or misanthropic, what injustice you do me! You do not know the secret cause which makes me seem so to you. Ever since I was a child my heart and mind have been filled with tender feelings of goodwill towards humanity: to achieve great things has always been my desire. But you must know that for six years now I have been suffering from a grievous affliction, aggravated by the unskilful treatment of medical men, disappointed from year to year in the hope of relief and compelled at last to face the prospect of a chronic infirmity whose cure might take years – if indeed it was possible at all. I was born with a fiery, impulsive temperament, even susceptible to the diversions of society, yet at an early age I found myself forced to isolate myself from the world, to live in loneliness. If at times I tried to disregard my condition, it was only to be driven back more harshly still by the doubly painful experience of my defective hearing. Yet I could not bring myself to say to people, 'Speak louder – shout – for I am deaf!' Ah, how could I possibly proclaim myself deficient in the one sense which I ought to possess in greater perfection than anyone else, which I did once possess in the highest perfection, to a degree in which few of my fellow musicians know it or have ever known it? I cannot do it. Forgive me, then, if you see me draw back when I would so gladly mingle with you. My misfortune is doubly painful since it cannot but cause me to be misunderstood: for me there can be no relaxation in the company of friends and acquaintances, no refined conversation, no mutual exchange of ideas. I dare not venture into society more than absolute necessity requires: I must live alone, almost like an outcast. If I so much as approach other people I am overcome by burning terror lest the real nature of my condition should become known. Thus it has been during these last six months that I have spent here in the country. By advising me to spare my hearing as much as possible my doctor showed intelligence, and at the same time confirmed my own present instinct – even though I sometimes ran counter to it by yielding to my longing for companionship. But what humiliation I felt when someone standing beside me heard a flute in the distance *that I could not hear*, or a shepherd singing when I could not distinguish a sound. Experiences like this brought me to the brink of despair, and I was not far from putting an end to my life. Art alone held me back: ah, but it seemed impossible to leave the world before I had produced all that I knew myself capable of! And so I continued to endure this wretched existence – wretched indeed with a body so sensitive that any passing change can plunge me from one extreme of emotion to another. *Patience*, I am told, I must now choose for my guide, and I have done so. I hope that my resolution will remain steadfast to persevere until it shall please inexorable Fate to break the thread. Perhaps I shall get better, perhaps not. I am ready for what may come. I was forced to become a philosopher at 28: it is not easy – perhaps less easy for an artist than for anyone else. O Deity, thou who lookest down into my innermost soul, thou knowest that it is filled with love for mankind and the desire to do good. O fellow men, when one day you read these words, reflect that you did me wrong, and let any of you in affliction take comfort at finding one like himself who, in spite of every obstacle which Nature threw in his way, yet did all that lay in his power to gain admittance to the ranks of worthy artists and men. You my brothers Carl and [Johann], as soon as I am dead, if Dr Schmid be still living, request him in my name to describe my malady and attach this written document to his description so that, as far at least as is possible, the world may be reconciled to me after my death. At the same time I declare you two the heirs of my small fortune (if such it can be called); divide it fairly, agree together and help one another. Whatever injury you did me in the past, you know that it is long since forgiven. To you, my brother Carl, I give special thanks for the affection you have shown me of late. It is my wish that your life may be better, more free from care, than mine has been. Recommend *virtue* to your children, for that alone, not money, will make them happy. I speak from experience, for it was this that sustained me in times of misery, and to it, and to my art, I must give thanks that I did not end my life by suicide. Farewell, and love one another. I thank all my friends, especially *Prince Lichnowsky* and *Professor Schmidt*. I should like the instruments from Prince L to be preserved by one of you, but let there be no quarrel between you on their account. If it serves your purpose better, then sell them: how happy I shall be if, even in my grave, I can be of help to you still. So be it. With joy I hasten to meet death. If it comes before I have had the opportunity to develop all my abilities as an artist then, in spite of my cruel fate, it will come too soon and I shall probably wish it later. Even so, I shall be content, for will it not release me from a state of endless suffering? Come when thou wilt: I shall meet thee bravely. Farewell, and do not quite forget me when I am dead. I have deserved this of you, for in my lifetime I have often thought how to make you happy. Be so.

Ludwig van Beethoven.

Heiglnstadt [Heiligenstadt]
6 October 1802

. . . Thus I take leave of you, and indeed sadly. Yes, that fond hope, which I brought with me when I came here, that I might in some degree still be cured – that hope I must now abandon entirely. As the withered leaves of autumn that fall to the ground, so has my hope been blighted. I leave here almost as I came, and even that courage that often still inspired me in the beautiful days of summer has gone from me. O Providence, grant me still but one day of *pure joy*! It is so long now since I felt true joy in my heart. When, oh when, Divine Power, shall I once more feel it in the temple of Nature and of Man? Never? Oh, but no, that would be too hard.

If this had really been a last will and testament, the world would have been left without the last seven symphonies, the violin concerto, the 4th and 5th piano concertos, *Fidelio*, the *Missa Solemnis*, all the piano sonatas from the *Waldstein* onwards, and the last ten string quartets.

We read somewhere that, when Beethoven found on the last page of the newly copied score of *Fidelio* the traditional closing inscription 'Fine, by the help of God', he added below it the words 'Man, help yourself.' If it is not true it should be.

Obituary notices may often be accurate (and useful) in their facts, but tend on the whole to be unreliable in their judgements. Here, as an exception, is a nice example of intelligent, balanced and yet essentially sympathetic comment

There is a consensus of opinion in favour of Liszt as a player. His songs, too, have affected many musicians deeply; and though they are not generally familiar, their merit has not been at all emphatically questioned. His studies and transcriptions, if not wholly irreproachable in point of taste, shew an exhaustive knowledge of the pianoforte; and, unplayable as they are to people who attack a pianoforte with stiff wrists and clenched teeth, they are not dreaded by good pianists. The brilliancy and impetuous fantasy of his Hungarian Rhapsodies are irresistible, as Herr Richter has proved again and again at St James's Hall. But his oratorios and symphonic poems – especially the latter – have not yet won the place which he claimed for them. A man can hardly be so impressionable as Liszt was and yet be sturdy enough to be original. He could conduct Lohengrin like Wagner's other self, and could play Beethoven as if the sonatas were of his own moulding; but as an original composer he was like a child, delighting in noise, speed, and stirring modulation, and indulging in such irritating excesses and repetitions of them, that decorous concert-goers find his Infernos, his battles, and his Mazeppa rides first amusing, then rather scandalous, and finally quite unbearable. A pleasanter idea of the man can be derived from the many eulogies, some of them mere schoolgirl raptures, others balanced verdicts of great composers and critics, which, whether the symphonic poems live or die, will preserve a niche for him in the history of music as a man who loved his art, despised money, attracted everybody worth knowing in the nineteenth century, lived through the worst of it, and got away from it at last with his hands unstained.

BERNARD SHAW *Pall Mall Gazette* 2 August 1886

Hanslick's on Wagner is another memorable obituary, remarkable for its generosity and honesty towards a composer about whom the critic had never disguised his feelings

13 February 1883

The news of Richard Wagner's sudden death was a painful and shocking surprise. Although it was hardly to be assumed that the seventy-year-old man would further extend the proud series of his works or add to his fame, the disappearance of so extraordinary a personality is, and remains, a loss. Wherever he appeared there was immediate stimulation, excitement, and lively discussion, flowing out from an artistic center in ever-broadening waves to all branches of cultural activity. Wherever the divining rod of his acts or his will pointed, there bubbled forth some hitherto hidden problem. And if it is a hallmark of the path-breaking artist that he provokes questions of principle over and above the immediate aesthetic impression, then Wagner stands at the head of the moving forces of modern art. He shook the opera and all its associated theoretical and practical questions from a comfortable state of repose bordering on stagnation. We hope that the lull now inevitably setting in will not lead back to stagnation again.

When called away, not from spiritual death, but suddenly, from the full exercise of his powers, a man of such comprehensive effectiveness and unexampled success leaves behind him a gap deeply felt by friend and foe. Actually Wagner had no foes in the sense of absolute, one-sided enmity; I have never met a musician so obtuse, or so violently partisan, as to overlook his brilliant endowment and his astonishing art, or underestimate his enormous influence, or to deny the greatness and genius of his works, even granting personal antipathy. Wagner has been fought, but he has never been denied. Those who believe that, with the excogitated and obstinately executed methods of his last style, he has led opera into a treacherous byway are admiringly aware that he broke this path with his own strength and that he created a new genre, a new art. We lift our hats to its boldness and consistency, without, however, giving it our allegiance, and without a moment's infidelity to the 'old' art of Mozart, Beethoven, and Weber. The attempt to appraise Wagner's artistic-historical significance in general must be reserved for a later time. Today I wish only to set right the frequently misinterpreted conception of 'opposition,' and to state, once and for all, that there is no exasperated partisanship against Wagner but only against the Wagnerites. Even the latter may learn moderation – not today, to be sure, but in the near future.

What must console them is the fact of the master's enviably pleasant death. The saying of the Greek poet that the gods summon their favorites young is only half true. Even more fortunate are those who, like Wagner, achieve advanced years and high honors and then depart this life in good health, cheerfully, and without premonition. Yes, Wagner died a happy man. It was recently his privilege to bring his last great work to life in Bayreuth, to rejoice in its actual preparation, and to bask in the full sunlight of such a success as no other artist of any time or nation has enjoyed. I shall always remember him happily as I last saw him, on the balcony of his Festival Theater – which will soon be only a historic monument – rejoicing triumphantly in the all-conquering power of his will. And should one wish to remind us of his mortal weaknesses and passions, we can find no trace of them in our memory. We agree with Grillparzer that death 'is like a flash of lightning which transfigures that which it consumes.'

EDUARD HANSLICK Review 1883

'Sad, sad, sad, Wagner is dead!' wrote Verdi to Giulio Ricordi in February 1883. 'When I read the news yesterday I must tell you that I was overcome by grief.'

Here is Boito on Verdi's death, in a letter to Camille Bellaigue

Today is Easter Day, day of forgiveness; you must forgive me then. I used to spend this day with him at Genoa, every year; I arrived on Good Friday (he kept in his heart the great Christian festivals, Christmas and Easter); I stayed until Monday. The tranquil charm of that annual visit comes back to my mind, with the Maestro's conversation, the patriarchal table with the customary dishes, strictly according to ritual, the piercing sweetness of the air and of that great Palazzo Doria, of which he was the Doge.

This is the first time I have dared to write of him in a letter. You see that you must forgive me. I was the victim of a kind of partial *abulia*; my thoughts, in the form of true remorse, were with you almost every day. You write me such kind letters; I had read your beautiful words in *Le Temps*, so deeply moved and so nobly moving; my will was powerless to reply, for it would have been necessary to say something about this great loss, and I could not do it. I suffered over it; I was ill.

I threw myself into my work, as if into the sea, to save myself, to enter into another element, to reach I know not what shore or to be engulfed with my burden in exertions (pity me, my dear friend) too great for my limited prowess.

Verdi is dead; he has carried away with him an enormous measure of light and vital warmth. We had all basked in the sunshine of that Olympian old age.

He died magnificently, like a fighter, formidable and mute. The silence of death had fallen over him a week before he died.

Do you know the admirable bust by Gemito? M. Cain (the composer you know) has it in his house. That bust, made forty years ago, is the exact image of the Maestro, as he was on the fourth day before the end. With head bowed on his breast and knitted brows he looked downwards and seemed to weigh with his glance an unknown and formidable adversary and to calculate mentally the forces needed to oppose him.

His resistance was heroic. The breathing of his great chest sustained him for four days and three nights. On the fourth night the sound of his breathing still filled the room, but the fatigue . . . Poor Maestro, how brave and handsome he was, up to the last moment! No matter; the old reaper went off with his scythe well battered.

My dear friend, in the course of my life I have lost those I have idolized, and grief has outlasted resignation. But never have I experienced such a feeling of hatred against death, of contempt for that mysterious, blind, stupid, triumphant and craven power. It needed the death of this octogenarian to arouse those feelings in me.

He too hated it, for he was the most powerful expression of life that it is possible to imagine. He hated it as he hated laziness, enigmas and doubt.

Now all is over. He sleeps like a King of Spain in his Escurial, under a bronze slab that completely covers him. . . .

ARRIGO BOITO 1901

It is strange how the death of a composer affects the significance of his works. I remember the following incident, which I would like to quote here; it is very instructive. When the talented Russian composer, Vassili Kalinnikov, a slightly older contemporary of mine, died at the early age of thirty-four, he left no money whatever, as he had always been badly paid. His widow, who found herself in very straitened circumstances, asked me for a small loan so that she could erect a tombstone for him. She also brought with her some of Kalinnikov's musical remains, saying:

'It is useless to take them to a publisher. I know his prices.'

I took the compositions to the publisher Jurgenson, hoping he might buy one or the other of the pieces.

Without a word Jurgenson added up the prices I had quoted. They made a considerable sum, which was ten times larger than the loan for which I had been asked.

As he went to his safe and opened it, he remarked:

'Don't imagine that I pay this tremendous sum without a definite reason; I pay it because the death of the composer has multiplied the value of his works by ten.'

RACHMANINOFF *Recollections* 1934

Death comes to performing artists too, of course, though not always with the appalling suddenness of the occasion described by Sir Rudolf Bing, then general manager of the Metropolitan Opera, New York

It happened in Act II of our production of (appropriately) *La Forza del Destino*, with our all-star cast of Renata Tebaldi, Richard Tucker, Cesare Siepi, and Leonard Warren, who had only four nights before scored an immense success as Boccanegra. I was standing in the wings. Tucker and Warren had finished their duet, and Tucker had been carried offstage in the litter appropriate to a badly wounded soldier. He got off the litter and we stood whispering together while Warren worried about opening the 'Urna fatale', then did open it and launched into his paean to revenge. 'Gioia,' he sang, 'oh, gioia' – and then pitched forward like an oak felled by a woodsman's axe. To anyone near the stage, it was obvious that something very serious had happened. Schippers stopped the orchestra, and I ordered the curtain lowered while Tucker ran to Warren's side.

Warren's wife was in a nearby box with the family priest (born Jewish, Warren had converted to Catholicism and become extremely devout). They came running to the stage. I had someone call Mario Sereni, our cover baritone for the evening, and went out to join the throng, pushing my way through choristers who had surrounded the fallen man, many of them kneeling and praying. Our house doctor, Dr Adrian W. Zorgniotti, came rushing up from his seat, and began working to resuscitate a man who was in fact beyond help. I stepped before the curtain to assure the audience he was being treated, and that the performance would resume when Sereni arrived. Twenty minutes later Dr Zorgniotti, ashen, told me Warren was dead. His wife couldn't believe it; who could? Continuing the performance was, of course, unthinkable; I returned to the stage, in the fully lighted house, and asked the audience to rise 'in memory of one of our greatest performers'.

The theatre leaves no time for mourning. I was on the telephone the next day, engaging Anselmo Colzani to fill in for Warren in many of Warren's performances towards the end of the season and on tour.

But Warren's death was a terrible blow to the musical quality of our Italian wing . . . and his loss was felt for years throughout the schedule.

SIR RUDOLF BING 5,000 Nights at the Opera 1972

From high tragedy on stage to a pitiful execution for a ridiculous offence; here is a tale that has the pathos of a Wozzeck – perhaps some follower of Alban Berg will be inspired to compose a threnody for the victim.

The conductor Jules Rivière, sometime colleague of Gounod's friend Georgina Weldon, tells how he once had to witness the execution of a trombonist who had struck a bandmaster with his trombone

A deal of sympathy was expressed for the young fellow, who had been punished by the bandmaster, a German, for an imperfect rendering of a certain passage on his trombone, the punishment inflicted having been two days' confinement. This unjust and tyrannical treatment led the trombone player to commit the offence, for which he suffered death in the presence of all the troops of the garrison; the different regiments being drawn up in a large square on the Place d'Armes, in front of the citadel, twelve soldiers firing at the word of command, and sending their comrade into eternity. The preliminary was first gone through of the sentence being read over to him, and the buttons torn off his coat. I shall not forget the scene.

JULES RIVIÈRE My Musical Life and Recollections 1893

What next . . . ?

Uncertainty about where music is going, and about the quality of public understanding, is not a new preoccupation. Mozart clearly felt it

The golden mean of truth in all things is no longer either known or appreciated. In order to win applause one must write stuff which is so inane that a *fiacre* could sing it, or so unintelligible that it pleases precisely because no sensible man can understand it. This is not what I have been wanting to discuss with you; I should like to write a book on this, a short introduction to music, illustrated by examples but, I need hardly add, not under my own name.

MOZART Letter to his father 1782

Weber felt it too, as in this review of E. T. A. Hoffmann's opera *Undine* – though he clearly perceives the deep influence of the period of war through which he and his contemporaries have been living

Herein lies the great and profound secret of music, something that can be felt but cannot be expressed in words. The ebb, the flow and all the conflicting tides of anger, love and 'the pleasure that's all but pain' are here united, where Salamander and Undine mingle and embrace one another. In a word, what love is to human beings, music is both to the other arts and to human beings, for it is indeed love itself, the purest and most ethereal language, myriad-faced and containing all the colours of the rainbow in every mode of feeling, uniquely true, to be understood simultaneously by human beings of a thousand different emotional complexions. This veracity of music's language, in whatever unexpected form it may appear, is finally victorious in asserting its rights. The fates of all eras of musical and representational art prove this completely and on many occasions. For example, nothing could seem more improbable than Gluck's works at a time when all sensibilities were overwhelmed and unmanned by the flood of Italian music, with its powerful sensuous charm. At the present time the artistic errors that threaten us are of quite a different kind, though perhaps even more dangerous. The circumstances of life today have made it inevitable that the two extremes of death and pleasure rule our

lives. The horrors of war have depressed our spirits, and misery has
been all too common, so that relief has been sought in the coarsest and
most primitive forms in the arts. The theatre has become little more
than a peepshow in which the noble and satisfying excitement
associated with true artistic pleasure has been carefully avoided, and
in its stead we have been content with the titillations of trivial jokes
and melodies and dazzled by pointless stage spectacle. Accustomed in
everyday life to being astonished, nothing but astonishment will serve
us in the theatre. Following the gradual development of a passion or a
witty building-up of all the interests involved is considered exhausting, boring and – to the unobservant – unintelligible.

CARL MARIA VON WEBER Review 1817

Though the context is different, this is not so far in spirit from Delius in 1920 –
just after another horrific period of war, as it happens

The chief reason for the degeneration of present-day music lies in the
fact that people want to get physical sensations from music more than
anything else. Emotion is out of date and intellect a bore. Appreciation
of art which has been born of profound thought and intensity of
experience necessitates an intellectual effort too exhausting for most
people of the present day. They want to be amused; they would rather
feel music with their bodies than understand it through their emotions. It seems as though a tarantula has bitten them – hence the
dancing craze: Dixie, Dalcroze, Duncan and Diaghilev, they are all
manifestations of the same thing. In an age of neurasthenics, music,
like everything else, must be a stimulant, must be alcoholic, aphrodis-
iac, or it is no good. . . .

There is no longer any respect for music as such. It can only be
tolerated, it seems, as an accompaniment to something else, a dinner
or a dance or what not. An impresario, shrewd enough to see what the
public wants and to give it to them at the right time, comes along with
a resuscitation of the old Italian ballet from St Petersburg, proclaiming
a *new* form of art compared with which all past achievements are as
nothing. Led by the nose, the public and, worse still, many of the
young musicians flock around him, and the critics cannot find enough
adjectives of adulation for his shows.

A ballet is all very well in its proper place, as a pleasant after-dinner
entertainment; but we don't want ballets to everything, and to
proclaim the ballet as a form of great art, the art form of the future, in
fact, is sheer bunkum. But the English public seems to have an
insatiable appetite for ballets, and the demand for such works having

speedily exhausted the slender stock of living composers' ideas, the scores of long-dead musicians are pressed into service. No one is immune. Bach fugues are employed as exercises in muscular mathematics and Beethoven sonatas interpreted (!!!) by every hysterical, nymphomaniacal old woman who can gull the public into seeing 'a revival of the Greek spirit' or some other highfalutin vision in the writhings and contortions of her limbs.

What is the effect on young people who may perhaps hear some great work for the first time in such an environment? The music will inevitably become associated in their minds with hopping and prancing and jigging, and in the end they will themselves be unable to hear it without twitching and fidgeting.

There seems to be a very prevalent belief that any Tom, Dick or Harry has the right to tamper with a work of art, even to the extent of altering it beyond recognition and forcing it to serve a purpose its composer never dreamed of.

In this direction irresponsible 'editors,' 'adapters' and 'transcribers' are as much to blame as the dancing cranks. It is time a law was passed to keep good music from violation.

By all means become dancing dervishes if you want to, and dance in a delirious *cortège* right into the lunatic asylum; but don't try to justify your procedure in the name of art, nor degrade the works of great artists in doing so. Above all, don't spoil works of art for other people who may not want to dance in the same direction. We do *not* all go the same way home.

FREDERICK DELIUS in *The Sackbut* 1920

Delius was not the only one who objected to dancing. Filippo Tommaso Marinetti (1876–1944) was a leading light in the Futurist movement, which flourished in Italy before the First World War. The intention was to regenerate the arts in realistic terms – natural sounds and 'noise-makers' for music — but sometimes propaganda gave way to side-swipes

Futurist Circular Letter to Certain Cosmopolitan Friends who Arrange Tango Tea Parties and Parsifalize

A year ago, responding to a questionnaire, I denounced the debilitating poison of the tango. This epidemic swinging gradually invades the whole world. It threatens to corrupt all races by gelatinizing them. We must therefore inveigh with full force against the imbecility of this fad and turn back the sheepish current of snobbism.

The ponderous English and German tangos are mechanized lusts and spasms of people wearing formal attire who are unable to exteriorize their sensibilities, and plagiarize Parisian and Italian tangos. They are copulated mollusks, who stupidly alter, morphinize and pulverize the felinity and savagery of Argentina.

To possess a woman one does not rub against her but penetrates her! A knee between the buttocks? It should be mutual! You will say, this is barbarism! All right then, let us be barbarians! Down with the tango and its languid thrills! Do you believe that it is exciting to look into each other's mouth and ecstatically relish each other's teeth like a couple of hallucinating dentists? Do you find it amusing to uncork one another to get a spasm out of your partner without ever achieving it yourself, or manoeuvre the pointed toes of your shoes like a hypnotized cobbler? It is like Tristan and Isolde who delay their *frissons* to excite King Mark. It is a medicinal dropper of passion, a miniature of sexual anguish, a sugared pastry of desire, lust in open air, delirium tremens, hands and feet of alcoholics, coitus mimed for the cinema, a masturbation waltz! Fie on this skin diplomacy! Hail the savagery of brusque possession and the fury of muscular, exalting and fortifying dance! Tangos are slow and patient funeral processions of sex that is dead! In the name of health, force, will power and virility we spit on the tango and its superannuated enervations! . . .

If the tango is bad, *Parsifal* is worse because it inoculates an incurable neurasthenia with its floods and inundations of mystical lachrimosity. *Parsifal* is a systematic depreciation of life, a cooperative factory of gloom and desperation, an unmelodious discharge of squeamish stomachs, indigestion and heavy breath of virgins at forty, complaints of queasy and constipated old priests, sales in bulk and retail of remorse and elegant ennui for snobs. It is an insufficiency of blood, kidney weakness, hysteria, anaemia and chlorosis! It is a brutalization of man in ludicrous progressions of vanquished and wounded notes, snorting of drunken organs, wallowing in the vomit of bitter leitmotives, tears and false pearls of Mary Magdalene sitting in décolletage at Maxim's, polyphonic purulence of the wound of Amfortas, lachrymose somnolence of the Knights of the Holy Grail and preposterous satanism of Kundry. Away with all the obsolete offal.

Mesdames et Messieurs, Queens and Kings of Snobbism, you owe absolute obedience to us, the Futurists, the living innovators. Surrender to the enthusiastic putrefaction of the crowds [around] the corpse of Wagner, this innovator of fifty years ago, whose music, surpassed today by Debussy, by Strauss, and by our own great Futurist Pratella, no longer means anything. We will teach you to love the living, oh dear slaves and sheep of snobbism! And here is the most persuasive argument: It is no longer fashionable to love Wagner and

Parsifal, played everywhere, even in the provinces, or to give tango tea parties like all the good petits bourgeois. So quit the mollifying dances and rumbling organ sounds. We have something more elegant to offer you! Tango and *Parsifal* are no longer chic!

F. T. MARINETTI
Milan 11 January 1914

But Delius had, and still has, a point about 'editors', 'adapters' and 'transcribers'. The modern musical industry could not exist without them, and woe betide the 'serious' composer who crosses swords with them. Stravinsky's experience must serve as a terrible warning

In 1938 I received a request from the Disney office in America for permission to use *Le Sacre* in a cartoon film. The request was accompanied by a gentle warning that if permission were withheld the music would be used anyway. (*Le Sacre*, being 'Russian', was not copyrighted in the United States.) The owners of the film wished to show it abroad, however (i.e., in Berne copyright countries), and they therefore offered me $5,000, a sum I was obliged to accept (though, in fact, the percentages of a dozen esurient intermediaries quickly reduced it to a fraction of that). I saw the film with George Balanchine in a Hollywood studio at Christmas time 1939. I remember someone offering me a score and, when I said I had my own, the someone saying, 'But it is all changed'. It was indeed. The instrumentation had been improved by such stunts as having the horns play their glissandi an octave higher in the Danse de la Terre. The order of the pieces had been shuffled, and the most difficult of them eliminated – though this did not save the musical performance, which was execrable. I will say nothing about the visual complement as I do not wish to criticize an unresisting imbecility; I will say and repeat, however, that the musical point of view of the film sponsored a dangerous misunderstanding.*

*To the Editor of the *Saturday Review*
25 West 45th Street, New York, 36, N.Y.

Sir   4 February 1960

A letter printed in the *Saturday Review* for January 30th, 1960, quotes Mr Walt Disney as follows: 'When Stravinsky came to the studio . . . he was invited to conferences with (the) conductor . . . and (the) commentator . . . was shown the first roughed out drawings, said he was "excited" over the possibilities of the film . . . agreed to certain cuts and rearrangements and when shown the finished product emerged from the projection visibly moved . . . and we paid him $10,000 not $5,000.'
  In fact, my contract, signed and dated January 4, 1939, by my then New York attorney, states that the Walt Disney Enterprises paid the sum of $6,000 for the use of *Le Sacre du printemps* and that $1,000 of this fee was to be paid to the publisher for the rental

of the material. My *cachet*, gross, was, as I said, $5,000. This contract further states that the *Sacre* was to be recorded between March 25 and April 20, 1939. At this time I was in a tuberculosis sanatorium near Chamonix. I did not, indeed, could not have consulted with the musical director or commentator of the film and, in fact, I left the sanatorium only once in a period of several months and that was to conduct *Persephone* in the Maggio Fiorentino. The allegation that I visited the Disney studios on two separate occasions, once to see preliminary sketches and later to see the final film, is also false. I appeared there a single time only, as I wrote. I was greeted by Mr Disney, photographed with him, shown drawings and sketches of the already finished film and, finally, the film itself. I recall seeing a negative film of the *Sorcerer's Apprentice*, and I recall that I was amused by this and said so. That I could have expressed approbation over the treatment of my own music seems to me highly improbable – though, of course, I should hope I was polite. Perhaps Mr Disney's misunderstanding was like that of the composer who invited a friend of mine to hear the music of his new opera. When the composer had finished playing the first scene and the time had come for comment, all my friend could think of to say was, 'Then what happens?', whereupon the composer said, 'Oh, I am so glad you like it.'

IGOR STRAVINSKY
STRAVINSKY *Exposition and Developments*

In 1944 Stravinsky was commissioned by Billy Rose, of all people, to write a short ballet (later to be known as *Scènes de Ballet*) for inclusion in a Broadway revue entitled *The Seven Lively Arts*. The choreographer, Anton Dolin, wired the composer in Hollywood after the first night

BALLET GREAT SUCCESS STOP CAN THE PAS DE DEUX BE ORCHESTRATED WITH THE STRINGS CARRYING THE MELODY STOP THIS IS MOST IMPORTANT TO INSURE GREATER SUCCESS   DOLIN

The composer wired back

CONTENT WITH GREAT SUCCESS   STRAVINSKY

Here is another composer protecting his own (see p. 278)

(To be written in front of the orchestral score.)

May he be damned for evermore
Who tampers with Narcissus' score;
May he by poisonous snakes be bitten
Who writes more parts than what we've written.
We tried to make our music clear
For those who sing and those who hear,
Not lost and muddled up and drowned
In over-done orchestral sound;
So kindly leave the work alone
Or do it as we want it done.

SAMUEL BUTLER *Note-Books* 1912

The film industry is of course a whole world of its own, and one for which, by now, many excellent composers have written fine scores. Nevertheless it is surprising, to say the least, to find the name of Arnold Schoenberg cropping up in this connection.

Oscar Levant, pianist, composer, film, TV and radio personality, friend of George Gershwin, studied briefly with Schoenberg (also a friend of George Gershwin, incidentally: they used to play tennis together – there's another surprise) and knew the composer's difficult financial circumstances. The great film producer, Irving Thalberg, had *The Good Earth* in preparation. Schoenberg's name was suggested

It chanced then that the Columbia Broadcasting System was presenting a broadcast in Schoenberg's honor, of which a principal work was his early 'Verklärte Nacht.' Its romantic flavor and poetic character deeply impressed Thalberg, who thereafter sent an emissary to see Schoenberg, even though the music he might write now would have no possible resemblance to 'Verklärte Nacht.' The emissary found the composer indifferent to the idea and thereupon launched into a long recitation of the possibilities for music in the film, leading up to a dramatic exposition of its 'big scene.'

'Think of it!' he enthused. 'There's a terrific storm going on, the wheat field is swaying in the wind, and suddenly the earth begins to tremble. In the midst of the earthquake Oo-Lan gives birth to a baby. What an opportunity for music!'

'With so much going on,' said Schoenberg mildly, 'what do you need music for?'

OSCAR LEVANT A Smattering of Ignorance 1940

Not surprisingly, nothing came of it. Schoenberg's was hardly the temperament

One especially naïve young man took one of his problems to Schoenberg, hopeful of a quick, concise solution. He had been assigned to write some music for an airplane sequence and was not sure how he should go about it. He posed the problem to Schoenberg, who thought for a moment and then said,

'Airplane music? Just like music for big bees, only louder.'

OSCAR LEVANT ibid.

Some composers like to pick up ideas from the script and from the early days of production; others wait till they see the film in the projection room and go on from there

In the first class, I think particularly of Erich Wolfgang – for Mozart –
Korngold. This was exemplified during the production of *Midsummer
Night's Dream*, for which he had been hired to reorchestrate Mendelssohn's score and add some new material. As he entered the studio
yard one day on the way to his office a car drove up and James Cagney,
who played Bottom in the film, stepped out. It chanced that Cagney
and Korngold had not met previously, and the flunkey who was
guiding Korngold about thought this would be a favorable opportunity to bring the two together.

Korngold had no sooner been presented to Cagney than he stepped
back and said, 'Hold still, Mr Cagney. Hold still a minute.'

Then he rubbed his chin reflectively and began to hum a little.
Walking around to the other side, he continued the inspection and the
humming, meanwhile whistling contentedly under his breath.
Finally, when the image of Cagney had been securely captured in
musical terms, he thanked his subject and departed.

Cagney said he almost felt as if he should ask when to come in and
try on the theme for which Korngold had fitted him.

OSCAR LEVANT *ibid.*

Of all the mechanical developments that have affected the musical appreciation of this century, however, the gramophone, and now the ubiquitous hi-fi,
have the most to answer for. Here is Thomas Mann's classic description of that
wonderful, opulent domestic contrivance to which so many of our generation
owe their first, glittering experience of music

The excellent management, in its sleepless concern for the happiness
of its guests, had considered matters, there in the bowels of the earth,
had resolved, and acted. It acquired, at a cost which we need not go
into, but which must surely have been considerable, a new device for
the entertainment of the patients, and added it to those already
installed in the largest of the reception-rooms of House Berghof. Was
it some clever artifice, of the same nature as the stereopticon, the
kaleidoscope, or the cinematographic cylinder? Yes – and yet, again,
no, far from it. It was not an optical toy which the guests discovered
one evening in the salon, and greeted with applause, some of them
flinging their hands above their heads, others stooping over and
clapping in their laps. It was an acoustical instrument. Moreover, the
simple devices above-mentioned were not to be compared with it –
they were outclassed, outvalued, outshone. This was no childish
peep-show, like those of which all the guests were sick and tired, at
which no one ever looked after the first few weeks. It was an
overflowing cornucopia of artistic enjoyment, ranging from grave to
gay. It was a musical apparatus. It was a gramophone.

We are seriously concerned lest the term be understood in an unworthy, outworn sense, and ideas attached to it which are applicable only to the primitive form of the instrument we have in mind, never to the elegant product evolved by a tireless application of technical means to the Muses' own ends. My dear friends, we implore you to realize that the instrument we describe was not that paltry box with a handle to it, a disk and shaft atop and a shapeless brass funnel attached, which used to be set up on the table outside country inns, to gratify the ears of the rude with its nasal braying. This was a case finished in dull ebony, a little deeper than broad, attached by a cord to an electric switch in the wall, and standing chastely on its special table. With the antediluvian mechanism described above, it had nothing in common. You lifted the prettily bevelled lid, which was automatically supported by a brass rod attached on the inside, and there above a slightly depressed surface was the disk, covered with green cloth, with a nickelled rim, and nickelled peg upon which one fitted the hole in the centre of the hard-rubber record. At the right, in front, was a time-regulating device, with a dial and figures like a watch; at the left, the lever, which set the mechanism going or stopped it; and behind, also on the left, the hollow, curving, club-shaped, nickel-plated arm, with its flexible joints, carrying the flat round sound-box at the end, with a fitment into which the needle was screwed. If you opened the double doors at the front of the box, you saw a set of slanting shelves, rather like a blind, stained black like the case – and that was all.

'Newest model,' the Hofrat said. 'Latest triumph of art, my children; A-1, copper-bottomed, *superfinissimo*, nothing better on the market in this line of goods' – he managed to give the words the twang of an eager and ignorant salesman. 'This is not just a machine,' he went on, taking a needle out of one of the gay little metal boxes ranged on the table, and fitting it into the holder, 'it's a Stradivarius, a Guarneri; with a resonance, a vibration – *dernier raffinemang*, Polyhymnia patent, look here in the inside of the lid. German make, you know, we do them far and away better than anybody else. The truly musical, in modern, mechanical form, the German soul up to date. And here's the libretto,' he said, and gestured with his head toward a little case on the wall, filled with broad-backed albums. 'I turn it all over to you, it is yours. But take care of it; I commend it to the solicitude of the public. Shall we shoot it off once, just for fun?'

The patients implored him to do so. Behrens drew out a fat magic tome, turned over the heavy leaves, and chose a paper envelope, which showed a coloured title through a round hole on the front. He placed the record on the disk, set it in motion, waited until it was at full speed, and then carefully set the fine steel point upon the edge of the plate. There was a low, whetting sound. He let the lid sink, and at the same moment, from the open doors in front, from between the slats of the blind, or, rather, from the box as a whole, came a burst of music, with a hubbub of instruments, a lively, bustling, insistent melody: the first contagious bars of an Offenbach overture.

THOMAS MANN *The Magic Mountain* 1924

Music you say; it would be a good night for music. But I have music here in a box, shut up, like one of those bottled djinns in the *Arabian Nights*, and ready at a touch to break out of its prison. I make the necessary mechanical magic, and suddenly, by some miraculously appropriate coincidence (for I had selected the record in the dark, without knowing what music the machine would play), suddenly the introduction to the *Benedictus* in Beethoven's *Missa Solemnis* begins to trace its patterns on the moonless sky.

The *Benedictus*. Blessed and blessing, this music is in some sort the equivalent of the night, of the deep and living darkness, into which, now in a single jet, now in a fine interweaving of melodies, now in pulsing and almost solid clots of harmonious sound, it pours itself, stanchlessly pours itself, like time, like the rising and falling, falling trajectories of a life. It is the equivalent of the night in another mode of being, as an essence is the equivalent of the flowers, from which it is distilled.

There is, at least there sometimes seems to be, a certain blessedness lying at the heart of things, a mysterious blessedness, of whose existence occasional accidents or providences (for me, this night is one of them) make us obscurely, or it may be intensely but always fleetingly, alas, always only for a few brief moments aware. In the *Benedictus* Beethoven gives expression to this awareness of blessedness. His music is the equivalent of this Mediterranean night, or rather of the blessedness at the heart of the night, of the blessedness as it would be if it could be sifted clear of irrelevance and accident, refined and separated out into its quintessential purity.

'*Benedictus, benedictus . . .*' One after another the voices take up the theme propounded by the orchestra and lovingly mediated through a long and exquisite solo (for the blessedness reveals itself most often to the solitary spirit) by a single violin. '*Benedictus, benedictus . . .*' And then, suddenly, the music dies; the flying djinn has been rebottled. With a stupid insect-like insistence, a steel point rasps and rasps the silence.

ALDOUS HUXLEY *Music at Night* 1931

Silence

Once again the instruments
Rehearse their elaborate departure
And the eyes continue to stare ahead
When all excuse for pensiveness
Is gone, the record long unwound;
Only the miles-off surf of the speakers
Establishing its vacant musty
Presence: not worth listening to.

JOHN FULLER *Waiting for the Music* 1982

But these days the gramophone, and the radio, have ensured a ubiquity of musical experience that is by no means always to music's advantage

It is a terrible thought that never again will music require any exertion, except from a few professionals, composers and performers; that this handful of men and women will be able to supply the whole world with all the music that is needed. Now it has become preservable and transportable, music, particularly since the Second World War, has embarked on a truly ambitious career. It is on tap in every home, like gas, water and electricity. There is no corner where it cannot penetrate. This once delicate art has become stupendously obtrusive. One need only press a button for music to come running with mechanical servility. Workmen in factories cannot work without a loudspeaker droning out tune after tune (the BBC programme 'Music While You Work' used to reject tunes for being 'too good', liable to distract the men and women at their benches); people in bars and restaurants cannot drink or eat unless some secret device whispers music into their ears; housewives cannot cook or iron without the radio playing; in cars, coaches and planes music mixes chaotically with the noise of engines; on beaches, in fields and woods, boys and girls carry it in their transistors, like sandwiches . . .

ERNEST ROTH *The Business of Music* 1969

Dr Strabismus (Whom God Preserve) of Utrecht has been asked by
leading industrialists to carry out some experiments to discover the
effect of music on efficiency. There has long been a theory that people
would be happier if they sang or played at their work.

The Doctor visited a large factory yesterday where goloshes are
made and packed. He distributed violins to all the workers and told
them to play something. Those who were able to master the instrument, owing to previous knowledge of it, quickly became engrossed in
their own playing. Three sisters, who rendered Raff's 'Cavatina,'
failed to turn out a single golosh. On the other hand, those who, after
producing a few squeaks, abandoned the instrument, were distracted
by the din made by their neighbours, and turned out goloshes so large
or so small or so shapeless that their time was wasted.

The Doctor carried out his second experiment yesterday before the
Board of Industrial Psychology and Psychological Industry.

A number of pianofortes were installed in a jam-making factory, and
the workers were encouraged to play certain pieces as they worked. It
was found that the instruments quickly became smeared with jam,
and that, in consequence of this, the playing was not of a high class.

After the luncheon interval a pip-inserter and a jar-lid-screwer
essayed a duet. The black notes were clogged, and the attempt had to
be postponed, while the instrument was swilled down with warm
water.

The Doctor came to the conclusion that jam can be made just as well
without musical accompaniment. He next tried the effect of the
oratorio *Hiawatha* on door-hinge makers.

The Doctor visited a large door-hinge factory in the Midlands. In the
presence of experts from the Board of Industrial Psychology he carried
out an experiment to ascertain the effect of singing on the efficiency of
the workmen. The piece chosen was the oratorio *Hiawatha*.

The noise of the machines drowned the opening lines, but gradually
the employees warmed to the work, and set up such a bawling that the
machines were inaudible. In the excitement of the moment half-
completed hinges were passed as completed, and the overseers began
to jest and even to throw the hinges out of the windows.

The representative of a firm which had ordered 100,000 hinges
expressed the opinion that singing interfered with the work, and
when the experts examined the hinges they were compelled to admit
that they were a pretty poor lot. Some were large enough for a castle
door. Others wouldn't have fitted the doors of a dwarf's potting-shed.
The work was careless, unfinished, and slovenly. But all the workers
were happy.

Dr Strabismus (Whom God Preserve) of Utrecht was forced to abandon his fourth experiment in industrial psychology. He visited a glass-blowing establishment, in company with experts. The employees were asked to play the trombone every now and then, to cheer themselves up.

Some complained that they had no breath left after blowing glass. Others complained that, after playing the trombone, they found themselves blowing enormous and meaningless bulbs.

One lady glass-blower became confused in her blowing, and put such power into the making of a rather delicate rose-bowl that she blew a perfect rhomboid of a conservatory, went home with hiccoughs, was arrested by the police for 'advanced alcoholism,' and cried herself to sleep in the local gaol.

He next conducted an experiment to determine the effect of full orchestral performances of Wagner's music on shipbreaking.

He established the fact that under the stimulus of the noisier passages enormous ships were smashed to smithereens in a surprisingly short time. The inspiration of the music, lingering in excited brains, even led large numbers of workmen to visit other parts of the yards, and to destroy half-built liners, offices, public-houses, workshops, sheds, timber-yards, and coal-dumps.

When the music ended some lay down in the mud and screamed, others threw themselves into the water. Doctors were called, and recommended a month's holiday in the mountains, without music.

Per contra, under the effect of Offenbach's 'Barcarolle,' an experienced gang engaged on the new battle-cruiser, HMS *Intolerable*, turned out a tomfool gondola. Many were weeping softly as they finished their work.

The Doctor conducted a freak experiment to ascertain the effect of piccolo-playing in a brewery. Within an hour forty-three employees were caught in the act of filling their piccolos with beer. They pleaded lack of musical ability, but it was found that the sight of these unmusical men drinking from their piccolos demoralised all the others, so that they neglected their playing. The experiment was abandoned when the manager himself was discovered in a corner shaking cocktails in the largest piccolo in Europe.

J. B. MORTON *Gallimaufry* 1936

16 August 1940

As a result of a statistical survey conducted by the Parliamentary Secretary to the Ministry of Information of Great Britain, regarding the catalytic property of suitable music in wartime factory work, it is announced in London that the playing of music by Chopin and Rachmaninoff produces an increase of the munitions output from 6 to 12 per cent.

NICOLAS SLONIMSKY Music Since 1900

. . . Infinitely grotesque, we would all agree; indeed, we would insist that music is an art and, like any other art, mysterious. But mystery is out of fashion. We have, perhaps without realizing the deeper significance of the change, become accustomed to the most fantastic things, and can talk glibly about flying to the moon and beyond. Such a generation as ours does not easily accept a mystery, and so has lost the precious gift of wondering. When I was at school I used to think that the generation of Verdi had seen the most astonishing changes in everyday life. When Verdi was born, the few people who travelled at all did so by mail-coach at the speed at which Julius Caesar had travelled to Gaul nearly two thousand years earlier. When Verdi died, express trains were thundering along the permanent way at forty miles an hour, steamships crossing the oceans, telephones ringing in the offices of the more enterprising businessmen and postmen delivering telegrams. I thought it must have been wonderful to live while all this was still new and exciting.

Others thought so too. When, in 1843, the railways from Paris to Rouen and Orléans were inaugurated – and the *Flying Dutchman* first performed – that same Heinrich Heine (from whom, by the way, Richard Wagner had learnt the story of the Dutchman) wrote about 'the awe that possesses the thinking mind at the sight of such monstrous happenings', of the 'strong temptation of the unknown', of the 'new delights and new horrors awaiting us' and of the change such a 'providential' event would bring about. 'Our generation,' he concludes with slightly uneasy confidence, 'can be proud to have witnessed it.'

Today all this sounds rather naïve. Not Verdi's but my own hapless generation has lived through the most fundamental changes of all. Nothing since the very beginning of human history can compare with the advances of the last fifty years: with space flights, electronic microscopes and computers, antibiotics and deep-frozen foods. It is useless to speculate whether all this progress has been as salutary for the mind as it has for the body. There are some who would insist that man would be happier if he had never learnt to read and write, because it is there that the deliberate, calculated evil begins. But, though it all had to come, and we are justified in calling it a blessing, we have barely reached the fringe of the new era, of a new satisfaction and a new spiritual security, and are still left with the secret fear that one day frivolous curiosity may press a button and blast to dust this whole planet, and with it everything that thinks.

Compared with all such fateful changes, events in music are of almost total irrelevance. Indeed, how relevant *are* the arts in a world which has been divesting itself one by one of all its mysteries? Modern man has acquired a superstitious confidence in everything material. One can feel it oneself, when one is shot into the air in a jet plane at six hundred miles per hour and forgets that any one of thousands of screws and bolts may work loose and destroy the aircraft and everybody in it. There is much less confidence in the dreaming mind, in thought and inspiration for their own sakes – in the arts. From all the fantastic achievements of recent decades, one problem has arisen which was unknown to previous generations: the problem of leisure. Progress provides the working man in five days or less with every-thing material he needs in seven. What to do with those two or more days of leisure? Who could have thought that this might ever constitute a social and moral problem? One would think that today there is more to read, more to think, more to experience, than ever before; that the ceaseless spread of education ought to produce a multiplicity of interests which even our successfully prolonged life-spans with all their spare time could not satisfy. And yet man seems to have lost the taste for his own company. One summer's day on an Italian lake, when rain and thunderstorms kept us in the hotel lounge, I had a conversation with an American lady which was characteristic of the general mood. 'Do you play bridge?' she asked me. 'No,' I said, 'I don't seem to have time for it.' 'Do you play golf?' 'No,' I replied regretfully, 'this, too, requires more time than I have.' 'Do you paint?' she persisted. 'Unfortunately, I have no talent for painting.' She looked at me with concern. 'You'd better be careful or you'll become an introvert.'

ERNEST ROTH *The Business of Music* 1969

Perhaps the greatest problem of all is the change of perspective that mechanical music, scientific research and computerized musicology have imposed on the contemporary composer. Here is a view from New Zealand – though one with a universal application

The real problem for 20th century composers is not just one of coming to terms with new sounds and new techniques – it is, rather, that for the first time in history we are confronted with our total musical heritage. This has come about through new technology and the research of a growing army of musicologists. We composers are now faced with a musical continuum that has not only revolutionised its contemporary materials, but has also expanded enormously in breadth, geographically, and in depth, historically. We know, from a celebrated anecdote, of Mozart's delight at discovering a Bach motet. But I wonder whether Mozart, teeming with his own inspiration, would have had much time or inclination for the 45 large volumes of the Bach Gesellschaft Edition, and the collected works of other masters.

Under this new weight of history and global awareness, and this constant impact of new sounds and new theory, it may become more difficult for composers to realise their own identity. When travelling, I have been conscious of this as a problem for young American composers, though not for their European counterparts backed by strong traditions. Our own musical culture may tend to become passive, rather than be vital and creative. Is there a danger that we become involved in keeping well-informed, and have too little time and necessity for that creative brooding on facts of our own experience which might energise and give substance to whatever language we may formulate?

DOUGLAS LILBURN A Search for a Language 1985

Coda

In a garden shady this holy lady
With reverent cadence and subtle psalm,
Like a black swan as death came on
Poured forth her song in perfect calm:
And by ocean's margin this innocent virgin
Constructed an organ to enlarge her prayer,
And notes tremendous from her great engine
Thundered out on the Roman air.

Blonde Aphrodite rose up excited,
Moved to delight by the melody,
White as an orchid she rode quite naked
In an oyster shell on top of the sea;
At sounds so entrancing the angels dancing
Came out of their trance into time again,
And around the wicked in Hell's abysses
The huge flame flickered and eased their pain.

Blessed Cecilia, appear in visions
To all musicians, appear and inspire:
Translated Daughter, come down and startle
Composing mortals with immortal fire.

w. h. auden 'Anthem for St Cecilia's Day' 1940

One of the great problems in putting this book together has been the constant recurrence of pieces which, good, bad or marvellous, somehow wouldn't fit into the sequence which developed from page to page. So we have put them together, here, in a sort of quodlibet, hoping that they may make some illogical logic of their own.

First, our final piece of Virgil Thomson (of which the two preceding sections are on pages 13–15 and 81–3). Virgil still sits, we hope, in his New York apartment that is like a small museum commemorating the American invasion of the art world of Paris in the 1920s. In his nineties he gets to look more than ever like a Roman emperor, as genial a host as a guest, despite the occasional verbal cuff. His hearing is all to pieces these days, deficient and distorting music horribly, but that doesn't dampen his generous, wicked spirits.

His final piece is on a subject dear to his heart: The Ethical Content of Music

Just as we require of music, in order that it be acceptable as 'serious', not only that it move our hearts but also that it be interesting to the mind, there is yet a third qualification about which we are no less exigent. We insist that it be edifying. This demand is as old as time. . . .

Saint Clement of Alexandria was convinced that goodness is intrinsic to certain kinds of music and wickedness to others. He encouraged the faithful in the usage of diatonic melodies and regular meters, exhorted them to avoid 'chromatics and syncopation,' which he believed led to 'drunkenness and debauchery.' This belief is still widespread. Indeed, the proposition has never been disproved. And though Sebastian Bach employed both devices consistently and convincingly (at least to posterity, though his congregation did complain) in the praise of God, and though Beethoven employed them no less to celebrate the brotherhood of man, the fact remains that when any composer wishes to depict heaven in contrast to hell or the serenities of virtue versus the excitements of sin, he is virtually obliged to use for the one a plainer, stiffer melodic and rhythmical vocabulary than for the other.

Olivier Messiaen has devoted his whole musical career to the purging, so to speak, or conversion to devotional uses, of all the most dangerous musical devices. The augmented fourth (or *diabolus in musica*), the major sixth, the false relation (or use of contradictory chromatics in two voices), the exaggerated employment of chromatics in melody and harmony, the ornamental dissonance, the integral dissonance, the highest elaborations of syncopated and other broken rhythms, and an almost sinfully coloristic orchestration are the very substance of his musical style, though piety is certainly its subject. And yet even he is obliged, for the depiction of evil, to go farther in the same direction and to insert additional violations of custom and of symmetry. I suspect, indeed, that it is not so much the employment in music of all the known picturesque effects that is valuable for suggesting the dark forces as it is a certain absence of symmetry in their employment. There is no reason why the music of the higher spheres should not be represented by the higher complexities and that of man's lower tendencies by all that is banal, bromidic, and puny, though so far no major composer has, to my knowledge, essayed to represent beatitude by interest and fantasy, in contrast to a damnation (as in Sartre's *No Exit*) of boredom by monotony. . . .

A major problem of our time is the concert symphony. The court guest of Haydn's and Mozart's day was less exigent than we are about moral impressiveness. What he liked was liberty. The nineteenth-century music lover, a bourgeois, loved literary, nationalistic, and travelogue content. In our time many composers have endeavored to satisfy the public's taste for news commentary by using current events and international relations as a subject of musical reflection, but so far the results have not been very satisfactory. No contemporary composer has yet matched Beethoven's mastery of the editorial vein, though they can draw circles around him at literary and exotic evocation. And though a great deal of the supposed editorial content in Beethoven is an invention of later times (that which associated his Fifth Symphony, for instance, with the ultimate victory of our side in the last war), it is perfectly certain that his 'Battle of Vittoria' does represent a comment on a news event (over and above its delightful straight reporting) and that his Third (or 'Heroic') Symphony is the ancestor of the modern editorial symphony.

But if Beethoven invented the editorial symphony, he also furnished, in my opinion, the earliest precedent for its misuse. That precedent is the final movement of his Fifth Symphony. In this piece, I am convinced after much reflection, the form is determined not by any inner necessity or logic derived from its musical material, nor yet from any expressive necessity that grows out of the preceding movements. I think it is a skillful piece of pure theater, a playing upon audience psychology that has for its final effect, along with the expression of some perfectly real content, the provoking of applause for its own sake. If I am right, here is the first successful precedent and model (the

finale of Brahms's First Symphony being the second) for that application to symphonic composition of the demagogic devices that are
characteristic of so much symphonic music in our time. . . .

The symphony, after all, is a romantic form. It is subjective and must
therefore be sincere. And though any man can have sincere sentiments about a political matter, I have yet to hear a political symphony,
excepting Beethoven's Third, that convinced me that the sentiments
expressed were entirely spontaneous. There is a hortatory tone about
all such work nowadays that is unbecoming to a form with so grand a
history of deeply personal expression. Perhaps the political symphony
is eloquent only when inspired by protest or revolt. Perhaps, too, the
political passions of our time are less grandiose than we like to think.
Certainly they are less impressive than the vast variety of human
suffering that has been provoked by their translation into political,
economic, and military action.

. . . On the whole, modern composers have done better work when
they have treated history, travel, anthropology, autobiography, sex,
and abnormal psychology than they have done with current events.
Simple patriotism they handle well, too. Even religion they can be
convincing about, though few of them are pious men. Their political
ideas, however sound from a voting point of view, have not yet
proved adequate for the graver responsibilities involved in concert
exposition.

April 27, 1947

VIRGIL THOMSON 1947 *The Art of Judging Music*

Handel said to Lord Kinnoull, after the first London performance of *Messiah*: 'I
should be sorry, my Lord, if I have only succeeded in entertaining them; I
wished to make them better'

Grandest number in the whole opera, Goulding said.

It is, Bloom said.

Numbers it is. All music when you come to think. Two multiplied by two divided by half is twice one. Vibrations: chords those are. One plus two plus six is seven. Do anything you like with figure juggling. Always find out the equal to that, symmetry under a cemetery wall. He doesn't see my mourning. Callous: all for his own gut. Musemathematics. And you think you're listening to the etherial. But suppose you said it like: Martha seven times nine minus x is thirtyfive thousand. Fall quite flat. It's on account of the sounds it is.

Instance he's playing now. Improvising. Might be what you like till you hear the words. Want to listen sharp. Hard. Begin all right: then hear chords a bit off: feel lost a bit. In and out of sacks over barrels, through wire fences, obstacle race. Time makes the tune. Question of mood you're in. Still always nice to hear. Except scales up and down, girls learning. Two together nextdoor neighbours. Ought to invent dummy pianos for that. *Blumenlied* I bought for her. The name. Playing it slow, a girl, night I came home, the girl. Door of the stables near Cecilia street. Milly no taste. Queer because we both I mean.

JAMES JOYCE Ulysses 1922

Shaw once more, tried beyond endurance by the academic 'analyses' contained in the programme books of his day, giving his own analysis of Hamlet's soliloquy on suicide in the same style

'Shakespear, dispensing with the customary exordium, announces his subject at once in the infinitive, in which mood it is presently repeated after a short connecting passage in which, brief as it is, we recognize the alternative and negative forms on which so much of the significance of repetition depends. Here we reach a colon; and a pointed pository phrase, in which the accent falls decisively on the relative pronoun, brings us to the first full stop.'

I break off here, because, to confess the truth, my grammar is giving out. But I want to know whether it is just that a literary critic should be forbidden to make his living in this way on pain of being interviewed by two doctors and a magistrate, and haled off to Bedlam forthwith; whilst the more a musical critic does it, the deeper the veneration he inspires.

BERNARD SHAW 1893 Music in London

Most of the literary works with which we are acquainted fall into one of two classes, those we have no desire to read a second time – sometimes, we were never able to finish them – and those we are always happy to reread. There are a few, however, which belong to a third class; we do not feel like reading one of them very often but, when we are in the appropriate mood, it is the only work we feel like reading. Nothing else, however good or great, will do instead. . . .

In trying to analyse why this should be so, I find helpful a distinction which, so far as I have been able to discover, can only be made in the English language, the distinction between saying, 'So-and-so or such-and-such is *boring*,' and saying, 'So-and-so or such-and-such is a *bore*.'

In English, I believe, the adjective expresses a subjective judgment; *boring* always means *boring-to-me*. For example, if I am in the company of golf enthusiasts, I find their conversation boring but they find it fascinating. The noun, on the other hand, claims to be an objective, universally valid statement; *X is a bore* is either true or false.

Applied to works of art or to artists, the distinction makes four judgments possible.

1 Not (or seldom) boring but a bore. *Examples*: The last quartets of Beethoven, the Sistine frescoes of Michelangelo, the novels of Dostoevsky.
2 Sometimes boring but not a bore. Verdi, Degas, Shakespeare.
3 Not boring and not a bore. Rossini, the drawings of Thurber, P. G. Wodehouse.
4 Boring and a bore. Work to which one cannot attend. It would be rude to give names.

Perhaps the principle of the distinction can be made clearer by the following definitions:

A   The absolutely boring but absolutely not a bore: the time of day.
B   The absolutely not boring but absolute bore: God.

w. h. auden *The Dyer's Hand* 1962

This thought-provoking proposition has an interesting little pendant in a later essay in the same volume

The quality common to all the great operatic roles, e.g., Don Giovanni, Norma, Lucia, Tristan, Isolde, Brünnhilde, is that each of them is a passionate and wilful state of being. In real life they would all be bores, even Don Giovanni.

W. H. AUDEN *ibid.*

Homage to Gaetano Donizetti

There was a sugar farmer's son (hyperthyroid)
I knew who was just like Nemorino,
And a girl in the Everest Milk Bar
Whose tits rubbed the cold of the ice-cream churn
As she reached down with her cheating scoop –
You saw more if you asked for strawberry –
She had a cold Christ hung over that defile
Crucified in silver, his apotheosis
In dry ice fumes. She was just like bel'Adina,
All the magic in the world wouldn't get
Your hand down her front unless she'd heard
Your rich uncle had just died.
Transistors behind her played Pat Boone,
But only to make a money music
In the till. Dear Master, what they say
About your big guitar is academic prejudice.
The truth is Dr Dulcamara's got
The Times Music Critic's job; the rustici
Are cooking on Sicilian gas, Venetian composers
Are setting Goethe to gongs and spiels and phones,
Teutons still come south to add a little
Cantilena to their klangschönheit
(Not to mention the boys of Naples), and those apostles,
The Twelve Notes, are at work on their Acts
To beautify our arrogance. Why should you care
That your audience are stuffed shirts if you know
That half at least have paid up for their seats.

PETER PORTER *Poems Ancient and Modern* 1964

Everyone suddenly burst out singing;
And I was filled with such delight
As prisoned birds must find in freedom,
Winging wildly across the white
Orchards and dark-green fields; on – on – and out of sight.

Everyone's voice was suddenly lifted;
And beauty came like the setting sun:
My heart was shaken with tears; and horror
Drifted away . . . O, but Everyone
Was a bird; and the song was wordless; the singing
will never be done.

                      SIEGFRIED SASSOON from *Picture Show* 1919

The morning stars sang together, and all the sons of God shouted
for joy.

                                                      JOB XXXVIII 7

A last glimpse of Rossini: the dedication of the *Petite Messe Solennelle*, finished
when he was seventy-two years old

Petite Messe Solennelle for four voices with accompaniment for 2 pianos
and harmonium, composed during my stay in the country at Passy,

– Twelve singers of three sexes, Men, Women and Castratos, are all
that is needed for its performance: that is, eight for the Chorus, four
for the Solos, total twelve Cherubim in all.

– Forgive me, God, the comparison that follows. Twelve is also the
number of the Apostles in the celebrated *coup de machoire* painted by
Leonardo, known as The Last Supper, – and who would believe it,
even among your disciples there are some who sing false notes!! Lord,
set your mind at rest; I swear that there will be no Judas at my Supper,
and that mine will sing truly, *con amore*, both your praises and this little
composition which is, alas, the last mortal sin of my old age.

– Passy, 1863.

And there is a note at the very end of the score

Dear God – here it is, finished, this poor little Mass. Is this really *de la musique sacrée* that I have written, or simply *de la sacrée musique*? I was born for *opera buffa*, as you well know! Little science, some heart, that's all there is to it. Be blessed, then, and grant me a place in Paradise.

– G. ROSSINI
Passy 1863

From the heart   –   May it go again   –   *to* the heart
BEETHOVEN on the manuscript score of the *Missa Solemnis* 1824

And a last glimpse of Berlioz – for both of us the ultimate and perfect romantic

If I were rich, very rich, I would go to Mehemet-Ali, or the Sultan, or whoever it may be, and I would say:
'Highness, sell me the island of Tenedos, sell me Cape Sigeium and the Simoïs, and the Scamander *et campos ubi Troja fuit*. Don't be alarmed – it has nothing to do with war or commerce or your operations on the Hellespont; it's a matter of music – but that needn't concern you. . . .'
   Once I had become master of those places consecrated by the Muse of antiquity, of those hills, those woods where flowed the blood of Hector and the tears of Andromache, I would fit out a vessel and embark a great orchestra, and set sail for Troy. And when I arrived in that sublime country I would create a place of solitude. No more Italian amateurs, no English tourists. . . . I would build a temple of sound at the foot of Mount Ida, and there, one evening, my royal orchestra should recite that other poem by the king of musicians, the *Eroica* Symphony of Beethoven.

HECTOR BERLIOZ Feuilleton *c.* 1830

At a Solemn Musick

Blest pair of *Sirens*, pledges of Heav'ns joy,
Sphear-born harmonious Sisters, Voice, and Vers,
Wed your divine sounds, and mixt power employ
Dead things with inbreath'd sense able to pierce,
And to our high-rais'd phantasie present,
That undisturbèd Song of pure content,
Ay sung before the saphire-colour'd throne
To him that sits theron
With Saintly shout, and solemn Jubily,
Where the bright Seraphim in burning row
Their loud up-lifted Angel trumpets blow,
And the Cherubick host in thousand quires
Touch their immortal Harps of golden wires,
With those just Spirits that wear victorious Palms,
Hymns devout and holy Psalms
Singing everlastingly;
That we on Earth with undiscording voice
May rightly answer that melodious noise;
As once we did, till disproportion'd sin
Jarr'd against natures chime, and with harsh din
Broke the fair musick that all creatures made
To their great Lord, whose love their motion sway'd
In perfect Diapason, whilst they stood
In first obedience, and their state of good.
O may we soon again renew that Song,
And keep in tune with Heav'n, till God ere long
To his celestial consort us unite,
To live with him, and sing in endles morn of light.

JOHN MILTON 1645

We are the music-makers,
　And we are the dreamers of dreams,
Wandering by lone sea-breakers,
　And sitting by desolate streams;
World-losers and world-forsakers,
　On whom the pale moon gleams:
Yet we are the movers and shakers
　Of the world for ever, it seems.

With wonderful deathless ditties
We build up the world's great cities,
　And out of a fabulous story
　We fashion an empire's glory:
One man with a dream, at pleasure,
　Shall go forth and conquer a crown;
And three with a new song's measure
　Can trample an empire down.

We, in the ages lying
　In the buried past of the earth,
Built Nineveh with our sighing,
　And Babel itself with our mirth;
And o'erthrew them with prophesying
　To the old of the new world's worth;
For each age is a dream that is dying,
　Or one that is coming to birth.

ARTHUR O'SHAUGHNESSY 'Ode' 1874

Heard melodies are sweet, but those unheard
  Are sweeter; therefore, ye soft pipes, play on;
Not to the sensual ear, but, more endear'd,
  Pipe to the spirit ditties of no tone. . . .

KEATS Ode on a Grecian Urn 1820

There is always music somewhere just behind Keats's verse, but it's rarely that he lets it come into the foreground, and then only fleetingly

Adieu! adieu! thy plaintive anthem fades
  Past the near meadows, over the still stream,
    Up the hill-side; now 'tis buried deep
      In the next valley-glades:
Was it a vision, or a waking dream?
  Fled is that music: – Do I wake or sleep?

KEATS Ode to a Nightingale 1820

Where gripinge grefes the hart would wounde
  And dolefulle dumps the mynde oppresse,
There musicke with her silver sound
  With spede is wont to send redresse.

RICHARD EDWARDS Paradyse of Dainty Devises 1576

There's sure no passion in the human soul
But finds its food in music

GEORGE LILLO Fatal Curiosity 1736

Now, divine air! now is his soul ravish'd! – Is it not strange that sheeps' guts should hale souls out of men's bodies?

SHAKESPEARE Much Ado About Nothing 1600

This is the news: two sounds
At a guarded melodious distance
Follow each other wherever
Either chooses to go.

And all our lives we are
Waiting for the music,
Waiting, waiting for the music.

Scanning the instructions,
Hand reaching for hand.

Waiting for the music.

JOHN FULLER *Waiting for the Music* 1982

Music is well said to be the speech of angels.

THOMAS CARLYLE 'The Opera' 1838

Music, the greatest good that mortals know,
And all of heaven we have below.

JOSEPH ADDISON 'Song for Saint Cecilia's Day' 1694

If I were to begin life again, I would devote it to music. It is the only
cheap and unpunished rapture on earth.

SYDNEY SMITH Letter 1844

Musick is the thing of the world that I love most.

SAMUEL PEPYS *Diary* 30 July 1666

Sources and acknowledgements

In the following list, where copyright still applies, it is held by the publisher unless otherwise indicated. In all cases our grateful thanks are extended to the publisher, or to any person mentioned in this connection, for permission to include extracts from copyright works; if, by oversight, or misinformation, or inability to obtain information, we have omitted any name from this list we apologize and will, of course, remedy the situation in any future edition of this work.

Ade, George quoted in Muir, Frank, *The Frank Muir Book*, q.v.
Addison, Joseph, in *The Spectator*, 3 April 1711
– *Ode*, 1712
– 'Song for Saint Cecilia's Day' in *Miscellaneous Poems*, 1694
Agate, James, *Ego 8*, Harrap, London, 1946
Ailred, *see* Rievaulx, Abbot of
Amiel, Henri-Frédéric, *Fragments d'un journal intime*, Geneva, 1883, trans. anon
Amis, Kingsley, *Lucky Jim*, Gollancz, London, 1954; (USA) Doubleday, a division of Bantam, Doubleday, Dell Publishing Group, Inc.
Anderson, Emily, *The Letters of Mozart and his Family*, 2nd edn, Macmillan, London, 1966
Anon, after Tennyson, quoted in Brett, Simon, *The Faber Book of Parodies*, q.v.
Auden, W. H.
– *The Dyer's Hand*, Faber & Faber, London, 1963
– 'Anthem for St Cecilia's Day' in *Collected Poems*, Faber & Faber, London, 1976
– 'The Composer', *ibid*
  All items (USA) Random House, New York
Augustine, St, *Confessions*, c. 400
Austen Jane, *Pride and Prejudice*, 1813

Bach, C. P. E., letter to J. N. Forkel, quoted in David, Hans T., and Mendel, Arthur, *The Bach Reader*, q.v.
– letter to J. J. Eschenburg, in Plamenac, Dragan, 'New light on the last years of Carl Philipp Emanuel Bach', q.v.
Bach, J. S. quoted by J. F. Köhler in David, Hans T., and Mendel, Arthur, *The Bach Reader*, q.v.
The Bangkok Post, concert review by Kenneth Langbell
Barbellion, W. N. P., *Journal of a Disappointed Man*, Chatto & Windus, London, 1919
Baring, Maurice, 'C', Heinemann, London, 1924
Barnefield, Richard, *Poems: In divers humors*, 1598
Barrington, The Hon. Daines, 'Account of a Very Remarkable Young Musician' in *Philosophical Transactions of the Royal Society*, 1771, reprinted in Barrington's *Miscellanies of Various Subjects*, London, 1781
Barzun, Jacques, *The Pleasures of Music*, Michael Joseph, London, 1952
Baudelaire, Charles, 'Richard Wagner et Tannhäuser à Paris', in *La Revue européenne*, Paris, 1861, quoted in Blom, Eric, *The Music Lover's Miscellany*, q.v.
Beaumarchais, Pierre-Augustin Caron de, *Le Mariage de Figaro*, 1784

Beerbohm, Max, *Zuleika Dobson*, Heinemann, London, 1911
Beethoven, Ludwig van, 'Heiligenstadt Testament', trans. Hanns Hammelmann and
	MR
Bennett, Arnold, *The Roll-Call*, Hutchinson, London, 1918
[Bentley,] E[dmund] Clerihew, *Biography for Beginners*, T. Werner Laurie, London,
	1905 (By courtesy of Messrs. Curtis Brown)
Berlioz, Hector, *Mémoires*, Paris, 1870, trans. and ed. David Cairns, Gollancz,
	London, 1969; (USA) Doubleday
– trans. Katharine F. Boult, *The Life of Hector Berlioz as written by himself in his Letters
	and Memoirs*, Everyman, Dent, London, 1870
– letter, 12 August 1856, in *Briefe von Hector Berlioz an die Fürstin Carolyne Sayn-
	Wittgenstein*, ed. La Mara, Breitkopf & Härtel, Leipzig, 1903, trans. MR
– feuilleton, *c*. 1830, quoted in Boschot, Adolphe, *Le Crépuscule d'un romantique, H.B.,
	1842–1869*, Plon, Paris, 1913, trans. MR
Bertani, Prospero, *see* Verdi, Giuseppe
Bing, Sir Rudolf, *5,000 Nights at the Opera*, Hamish Hamilton, London, 1972; (USA)
	International Creative Management
Bizet, Georges, *Lettres*, ed. Louis Ganderax, Calmann-Levy, Paris, 1908
Blom, Eric, *The Music Lover's Miscellany*, Gollancz, London, 1935
Boito, Arrigo, letter to Camille Bellaigue, 1901, quoted in Walker, Frank, *The Man
	Verdi*, q.v.
Boswell, James, *Journal of a Tour to the Hebrides*, London, 1785
Bowra, Maurice, *Memories 1898–1939*, Weidenfeld & Nicolson, London, 1966
Brailsford, H. N., *Adventures in Prose*, Herbert & Daniel, London, 1911
Brett, Simon, ed. *The Faber Book of Parodies*, Faber & Faber, London, 1984
Breuning, Gerhard von, *Aus dem Schwarzspanierhause*, 1874, quoted in Sonneck,
	O. G., *Beethoven: Impressions of Contemporaries*, q.v.
Brewer's Dictionary of Phrase and Fable, revised edn, Cassell, London, 1970
Britten, Benjamin, letter, in *Michael Tippett, A Symposium*, q.v. (By courtesy of the
	executors of the Britten Estate)
Brodsky, Anna Lvovna, *Recollections of a Russian Home*, Sherratt & Hughes,
	Manchester, 1904, quoted in Norris, Gerald, *Stanford, The Cambridge Jubilee and
	Tchaikovsky*, q.v.
Brown, T. E., 'The Organist in Heaven', 1876, from *The Collected Poems of T.E.B.*,
	Macmillan, London, 1900
Browne, Sir Thomas, *Religio Medici*, 1643
Browning, Robert, *Abt Vogler*, 1864
– *A Toccata of Galuppi's*, 1855
Bunyan, John, *The Pilgrim's Progress*, 1684
Burney, Charles, *An Account of the Musical Performances in Westminster Abbey and the
	Pantheon . . . in Commemoration of Handel*, London, 1785
– *The Present State of Music in France and Italy*, London, 1771, 2nd edn 1773
– *The Present State of Music in Germany, the Netherlands and the United Provinces*,
	London, 1773 (New edn of both vols: Percy Scholes, *Dr. Burney's Musical Tours in
	Europe*, Oxford University Press, 1959)
– *History of Music*, London, 1776–1789
Busoni, Ferruccio, *Letters to his wife*, trans. Rosamund Ley, Edward Arnold, London,
	1935
– 'Mozart-Aphorismen' in *Lokal-Anzeiger*, Berlin, 1906, trans. JA & MR
Butler, Samuel (1613–80), *Characters*, quoted in Blom, Eric, *The Music Lover's
	Miscellany*, q.v.

Butler, Samuel, *Note-Books*, ed. Henry Festing Jones, A. C. Fifield, London, 1912
– *Narcissus*, 1888
Byrd, William, *Psalmes, Sonets, & songs of Sadnes and Pietie*, 1588
Byron, George Gordon, Lord, letter from Venice, 3 March, 1818, in *Collected Letters*, ed. L. A. Marchand, London, 1973–81

Calzabigi, Ranieri de', letter to Count Kaunitz, *Musikologie*, Praha-Brno, 1938, trans. Hanns Hammelmann & MR in 'New Light on Calzabigi and Gluck' in *The Musical Times*, vol. 110, 1969
Carroll, Lewis, *Alice's Adventures in Wonderland*, Macmillan, London, 1865
Castiglione, Baldassare, *Libro del Cortigiano*, 1528, trans. Sir Thomas Hoby, *The Book of the Courtier*, 1561
Carlyle, Thomas, 'The Opera' in *Critical and Miscellaneous Essays*, Boston, 1838
Cellamare, Daniele, *Umberto Giordano, La Vita e Le Opere*, Garzanti, Milano, 1949, quoted in Conati, Marcello, *Interviews and Encounters with Verdi*, q.v.
Checchi, Eugenio, *Giuseppe Verdi, Il Genio e le opere*, Florence, 1901, quoted in Conati, Marcello, *Interviews and Encounters with Verdi*, q.v.
Chesterton, G. K., 'The Song against Songs' in *The Flying Inn*, Methuen, London, 1914
Chopin, Frédéric, quoted by Ravel in *Le Courier Musical*, January 1910
– *Correspondance de F.C.*, ed. Bronislas Edouard Sydow, Richard-Masse, La Revue Musicale, Paris, 1981, trans. MR
Chotzinoff, Samuel, *Toscanini, an Intimate Portrait*, Knopf, New York, 1956
Closson, Ernest, 'Edvard Grieg et la musique scandinave' in *Le Guide musicale*, Brussells & Paris, 1892, quoted in Jacobs, Arthur, *Music Lover's Anthology*, q.v.
Coffey, Lisa, article in Las Vegas newspaper, 23 March 1983
Coleridge, Samuel Taylor, *Table Talk* (5 October 1830)
– verse quoted in Norwich, John Julius, *Christmas Crackers*, Penguin, London, 1982
Collier, Jeremy, *A Short View of the Immorality and Profaneness of the English Stage*, 1698
Conan Doyle, Arthur, 'The Red-Headed League' in *The Adventures of Sherlock Holmes*, London, 1892
Conati, Marcello, *Interviews and Encounters with Verdi*, Gollancz, London, 1984
Copland, Aaron,
– *What to Listen for in Music*, McGraw-Hill, New York, 1939
– *Music and Imagination*, Harvard University Press, Cambridge, Mass., 1952 (By courtesy of the President and Fellows © 1952, and the author © 1980)
– *Copland on Music*, Doubleday & Co., New York, 1960
Cowley, Abraham, 'Davideis', 1656
Crowest, F. J., *Musicians' Wit, Humour, & Anecdote*, Walter Scott Publishing Co. Ltd., London & Newcastle-on-Tyne, 1902
Culshaw, John, *Putting the Record Straight*, Secker & Warburg, London, 1981
Czerny, Carl, *Erinnerungen aus meinem Leben*, 1842, quoted in Sonneck, O. G., *Beethoven: Impressions of Contemporaries*, q.v.

Da Ponte, Lorenzo, *Memorie di Lorenzo da Ponte, da Ceneda: scritte da esso*, New York, 1823–27, trans. L. A. Sheppard, *Memoirs of Lorenzo da Ponte*, Routledge, London, 1929
David, Hans T., and Mendel, Arthur, *The Bach Reader*, Dent, London, 1946
de Brosses, Charles, *Lettres familières écrites d'Italie en 1739 et 1740*
Debussy, Claude, *Correspondance de Claude Debussy et Pierre Louÿs*, ed. Henri Borgeaud, José Corti, Paris, 1945, trans. MR

– *Monsieur Croche Antidilettante*, Paris, 1921, trans. anon, *Monsieur Croche the Dilettante Hater*, Noel Douglas, London, 1927
– *Lettres à son Editeur*, ed. Jacques Durand, Durand, Paris, 1927
– quoted by Prod'homme, J. G., q.v.
– quoted in Emmanuel, Maurice, *Pelléas et Mélisande de Debussy*, q.v.
de la Mare, Walter, 'Song of Shadows', from *Peacock Pie*, Faber & Faber, London, 1913
Delius, Frederick, 'At the Crossroads', in *The Sackbut*, vol. I, 1920 (By courtesy of the Delius Trust)
Del Mar, Norman, *Richard Strauss – A Critical Commentary on his Life and Works*, Barrie & Rockliff, London, 1962
Demuth, Norman, *An Anthology of Musical Criticism*, Eyre & Spottiswoode, London, 1947
de Quincey, Thomas, *The English Mail-Coach*, 1849
Devonshire and Cornwall Notes and Queries, vol. X, quoted in Blom, Eric, *The Music Lover's Miscellany*, q.v.
Dickens, Charles, *David Copperfield*, Chapman & Hall, London, 1850
– *Sketches by Boz*, Chapman & Hall, London, 1836
Dies, A. C., *Biographische Nachrichten von Joseph Haydn*, 1810, quoted in Jacobs, Arthur, *Music Lover's Anthology*, q.v.
D'Indy, Vincent, *César Franck*, Paris, 1906, trans. Rosa Newmarch, John Lane, London, 1910
Dorati, Antal, *Notes of Seven Decades*, Hodder & Stoughton, London, 1979
Dryden, John, 'Song for St Cecilia's Day', in *Miscellaneous Poems*, 1694
– Dedication of *King Arthur*, 1691
Duncan, Ronald, *Working with Britten*, The Rebel Press, Bideford, 1981 (By courtesy of the Ronald Duncan Literary Fund)

Edwards, Richard, *Paradyse of Dainty Devises*, 1576
Emmanuel, Maurice, *Pelléas et Mélisande de Debussy*, Paris, 1933, trans. MR
The English Hymnal, Oxford, 1906: J. Keble, 'The voice that breathed o'er Eden'

Fétis, François-Joseph, *Notice sur Nicolo Paganini*, Paris, 1851, quoted in Jacobs, Arthur, *Music Lover's Anthology*, q.v.
Finck, H. T., *Grieg and his Music*, John Lane, London/New York, 1909
Flaubert, Gustave, *Madame Bovary*, 1857, trans. Alan Russell, Penguin, London, 1950
Förster-Nietzsche, Elizabeth, *The Nietzsche–Wagner Correspondence*, trans. Caroline V. Kerr, Duckworth, London, 1922
Forkel, J. N., *Über Johann Sebastian Bachs Leben, Kunst und Kunstwerke*, Leipzig, 1802, trans. Mr Stephenson, *Life of John Sebastian Bach*, T. Boosey, London, 1820
Forster, E. M., *Where Angels Fear to Tread*, Edward Arnold, London, 1905; (USA) © 1920 Alfred A. Knopf, Inc. and renewed 1948 by Edward Morgan Forster
– *Howard's End*, Edward Arnold, London, 1910; (USA) © E. M. Forster.
Both items reprinted by permission of Alfred A. Knopf, Inc.
Forzano, Giovacchino, *Come li ho conosciuti*, Edizione Radio Italiana, Torino, 1957, trans. MR
Fuller, John, *Waiting for the Music*, Salamander Press, 1982

Gal, Hans, *The Musician's World*, Thames & Hudson, London, 1965
Gaskell, Mrs, *Cranford*, 1853

Gerbier, Balthazar, letter, quoted in Blom, Eric, *The Music Lover's Miscellany*, q.v.

Gesner, Johann Matthias, *Institutio oratoria*, 1738, quoted in David, Hans T., and Mendel, Arthur, *The Bach Reader*, q.v.

Gibbons, Orlando, *The First Set of Madrigals and Motetts*, London, 1612, preface
– *ibid*, 'The silver Swan' (anon)

Giordano, Umberto, letter, 1896, in Cellamare, D., *Umberto Giordano, La Vita e le opere*, q.v.

Goethe, Johann Wolfgang von, in Eckermann, Johann Peter, *Gespräche mit Goethe in den letzten Jahren seines Lebens*, Leipzig, 1836–48

Goldbeck, Frederick, *The Perfect Conductor*, Dennis Dobson, London, 1960

Goldsmith, Oliver, 'Beau Tibbs at Vauxhall' in *The Citizen of the World*, 1762

Gorky, Maxim, *Days with Lenin*, Martin Lawrence, New York & London, 1933

Graf, Max, *Composer and Critic*, Chapman & Hall, London, 1947

Graham, Virginia, *Consider the Years*, Cape, London, 1946 (By courtesy of Mrs Thesiger)

Greenwich Old Church, *see* Tallis, Thomas

Grétry, André-Ernest-Modeste, *Mémoires, ou Essais sur la musique*, Paris, 1789

Grieg, Edvard, quoted in Finck, H. T., *Grieg and his Music*, q.v.

Grierson, Edward, *Storm Bird: The Strange Life of Georgina Weldon*, Chatto & Windus, London, 1959 (By courtesy of the author's Estate)

Griesinger, Georg August, *Biographische Notizen über Joseph Haydn*, 1809, quoted in Morgenstern, Sam, *Composers on Music*, q.v.

Grillparzer, Franz, *Diary*, 1809, quoted in Blom, Eric, *The Music Lover's Miscellany*, q.v.

Grove's Dictionary of Music and Musicians, Macmillan, London, 1st edn. 1878
– 5th edn, 1954

Hammelmann, Hanns, and Osers, Ewald, *The Correspondence between Richard Strauss and Hugo von Hofmannsthal*, Collins, London, 1961

Hanslick, Eduard, *Von Musikalisch-Schönen*, Leipzig, 1854
– *Vienna's Golden Years of Music 1850–1900*, trans. & ed. Henry Pleasants III, Gollancz, London, 1951 (By kind permission of Henry Pleasants); (USA) Dover Publications 1988

Harding, James, *Saint-Saëns and his Circle*, Chapman & Hall, London, 1965

Harding, Rosamond E. M., *The Piano-Forte: its History traced to the Great Exhibition of 1851*, Cambridge University Press, 1933

Hardy, Thomas, *Under the Greenwood Tree*, Macmillan, London, 1872
– 'A Few Crusted Characters' in *Life's Little Ironies*, Macmillan, London, 1894
– *Moments of Vision and other Miscellaneous Verses*, Macmillan, London, 1917

The Harmonicon, January 1824, article by Edward Schultz

Hartford, Robert, *Bayreuth: The Early Years*, Gollancz, London, 1980

Hawkins, Sir John, *History of the Science and Practice of Music*, London, 1776

Heine, Heinrich, *Letters on the French Stage*, Berlin, 1837, quoted in Graf, Max, *Composer and Critic*, q.v.
– on Paganini, quoted in Pulver, Jeffrey, *Paganini*, q.v.

Henschel, George, *Personal Recollections of Johannes Brahms*, Boston (Mass.), 1907, quoted in Norris, Gerald, *Stanford, the Cambridge Jubilee and Tchaikovsky*, q.v.

Herbert, George, *Jacula Prudentum, or Outlandish Proverbs, Sentences, &c*, 1640

Herrick, Robert, 'To Musick', in *Hesperides*, 1648

Hiller, Ferdinand, 'Hector Berlioz' in *Westermanns Monatshefte*, 45. Band, Braunschweig, 1879, quoted in Zoff, Otto, *Great Composers*, q.v.

Hoffmann, E. T. A., *Kreisleriana*, 1814, quoted in Graf, Max, *Composer and Critic*, q.v.
– article, n.d., *ibid*
Hofmannsthal, Hugo von, letters 1911, 1916, in Hammelmann, Hanns, and Osers, Ewald, *The Correspondence between Richard Strauss and Hugo von Hofmannsthal*, q.v.
Hogwood, Christopher, *Music at Court*, Folio Society, London, 1977
Holst, Gustav, *Letters to W.G. Whittaker*, ed. M. Short, Glasgow, 1974
Holst, Imogen, *Conducting a Choir – A Guide for Amateurs*, Oxford University Press, 1973
Hopkins, Gerard Manley, *Poems*, Oxford University Press, 1918
Horace, *Satires*, c. 30 B.C.
Housman, A. E., from a letter to his stepmother, c. 1897, quoted in Laurence Housman, *A.E.H.*, Cape, London, 1937; by permission of the Society of Authors as the literary representative of the Estate of A. E. Housman
Huxley, Aldous, *Antic Hay*, Chatto and Windus, London, 1923 (By kind permission of Mrs Laura Huxley)
– *Music at Night & Vulgarity in Literature*, Chatto & Windus, London, 1931 (By kind permission of Mrs Laura Huxley)

Jacobs, Arthur, *Music Lover's Anthology*, Winchester Publications, London, 1948
Jahn, Otto, *W.A. Mozart*, Leipzig, 1856, trans. Pauline Townsend, *Life of Mozart*, Novello Ewer, London, 1882
James, Henry, letter, 1895, quoted in Blom, Eric, *The Music Lover's Miscellany*, q.v.
Jennens, Charles, letter, 1738, quoted in Deutsch, A. E., *Handel. A Documentary Biography*, Collins, London, 1954
Johnson, Samuel, *Lives of the Poets*, 1779–81
Jonson, Ben, *The Poetaster*, 1602
Joyce, James, *Ulysses*, Paris, 1922; John Lane, London, 1936; by permission of the Society of Authors as the literary representative of the Estate of James Joyce

Keats, John, 'Ode on a Grecian Urn', from *Lamia, Isabella . . . and other poems*, 1820
– 'Ode to a Nightingale', *ibid*
Kelly, Michael, *Reminiscences of Michael Kelly*, Henry Colburn, London, 1826
Kennedy, Michael, *Britten*, Master Musicians, Dent, London, 1981
Kington, Miles, *Moreover, too . . .*, Penguin, London, 1985
Kinscella, Hazel G., article in *Musical America*, 25 May 1933
Klemperer, Otto, *Erinnerungen an Gustav Mahler*, Zurich, 1960, trans. J. Maxwell Brownjohn, 'Memories of Gustav Mahler' in *Minor Recollections*, Dennis Dobson, London, 1964 (By kind permission of Lotte Klemperer)
Köhler, J. F., *Historia Scholarum Lipsiensium*, 1776, quoted in David, Hans T., and Mendel, Arthur, *The Bach Reader*, q.v.

Lamb, Charles, 'A Chapter on Ears', in *The Essays of Elia*, London, 1823
– 'Poem addressed to William Ayrton', in *The Poetical Works of Charles Lamb*, Edward Moxon, London, 1836
Lambert, Constant, article in *The Sunday Referee*, quoted in Shead, Richard, *Constant Lambert*, q.v.
Lang, Paul Henry, *Music in Western Civilization*, Dent, London, 1942
Langbell, Kenneth, review in the *Bangkok Post*, q.v.
Lawrence, D. H., 'Piano' in *New Poems*, Martin Secker, London, 1918; (USA) printed in *The Complete Poems of D. H. Lawrence*, collected and edited by Vivian de Sola Pinto and F. Warren Roberts © 1964, 1971 by Angelo Ravagli and C. M.

Weekley, executors of the Estate of Frieda Lawrence Ravagli. All rights reserved. Reprinted by permission of Viking Penguin, a division of Penguin Books USA Inc.
– letter to Louie Burrows, 1 April 1911,
Lear, Edward, *Letters of Edward Lear*, ed. Lady Strachey, Fisher Unwin, London, 1907
Legge, Walter, *see* Schwarzkopf, Elisabeth
Lenin, quoted by Gorky, Maxim, q.v.
Levant, Oscar, *A Smattering of Ignorance*, Garden City Publishing Co., New York, 1940 (By kind permission of Mrs June Levant)
Levin, Bernard, *Conducted Tour*, Cape, London, 1981; by permission of Curtis Brown
[?Lichtental, Peter], 'Frühlingsopern u.s.w. in Italien' (Forsetzung) in *Allgemeine musikalische Zeitung*, 24 September 1845, quoted in Conati, Marcello, *Interviews and Encounters with Verdi*, q.v.
Lilburn, Douglas, *A Search for Language*, Alexander Turnbull Library Endowment Trust, Wellington N.Z., 1985
Lillo, George, *Fatal Curiosity*, 1736
Liszt, Franz, *Chopin*, Paris, 1852, rev. edn. Leipzig, 1879, quoted in Jacobs, Arthur, *Music Lover's Anthology*, q.v.
– letter, 5 November 1853, in *Franz Liszts Briefe*, ed. La Mara, Leipzig, 1893, trans. Constance Bache, *Letters of Franz Liszt*, H. Grevel, London, 1894
Lochner, Louis, *Fritz Kreisler*, Rockliff, London, 1951
Louÿs, Pierre, letter, 1899, *see* Debussy, Claude
Lyttelton, George, *The Lyttelton Hart-Davis Letters*, Vol. 2, John Murray, London, 1979

Mace, Thomas, *Musick's Monument: or, a Remembreancer of the Best Practical Musick, both Divine, and Civil, that has ever been known, to have been in the World*, 1676
Mainwaring, John, *Memoirs of the Life of the late George Frederic Handel*, London, 1760
Mann, Thomas, *Doctor Faustus*, 1947, trans. H. T. Lowe-Porter, Secker & Warburg, London, 1949
– *The Blood of the Walsungs*, 1905, trans. H. T. Lowe-Porter, Secker & Warburg, London, 1961
– *Der Zauberberg*, Berlin, 1924, trans. H. T. Lowe-Porter as *The Magic Mountain*, Martin Secker, London, 1927
Manufacturer's description, 1851, quoted in Harding, Rosamund E. M., *The Piano-Forte*, q.v.
Marinetti, F. T., 'Futurist Circular Letter', trans. and quoted in Slonimsky, Nicolas, *Music Since 1900*, q.v.
Marx, A. B., article in *Berliner allgemeine musikalische Zeitung*, 1829, quoted in Graf, Max, *Composer and Critic*, q.v.
Melvil, Sir James, *Memoirs*, London (posthumously), 1683
Mendelsohn, Eric, *Letters of an Architect*, ed. Oskar Beyer, Abelard Schumann, London, 1967 (By kind permission of Esther Mendelsohn Josephs)
Mendelssohn-Bartholdy, Felix, letter, 1831, in *Letters from Italy and Switzerland*, trans. Lady Wallace, Longman, Green, Longman and Roberts, London, 1862
– letter, 14 July 1836, in *Letters . . . from 1833 to 1847*, trans. Lady Wallace, Longman, Green, Longman, Roberts & Green, London, 1863
Meng-tzu, 300 B.C.
Menuhin, Yehudi, *Unfinished Journey*, Macdonald & Jane's, London, 1976 (By kind permission of Sir Yehudi Menuhin)
Meredith, George, *Sandra Belloni*, Chapman & Hall, London, 1889
Michael Tippett, A Symposium on his 60th Birthday, ed. Ian Kemp, Faber & Faber, London, 1965

Milton, John, 'Il Penseroso', 1632
- 'To Mr H. Lawes, on his Aires', 1648
- 'At a Solemn Music', 1645
Mitford, Nancy, *The Pursuit of Love*, Hamish Hamilton, London, 1945; by permission of the Peters Fraser and Dunlop Group Ltd.
Monaldi, Gino, *Verdi nella vita e nell' arte*, Ricordi, Milano, nd, quoted in Conati, Marcello, *Interviews and Encounters with Verdi*, q.v.
Monteverdi, Claudio, letter to Alessandro Striggio, 19 December 1616, in Malipiero, G. F., *Claudio Monteverdi*, Milan, 1929, trans. MR
Moore, George, *Memoirs of my dead life*, Heinemann, London, 1906
Morley, Thomas, *A Plaine and Easie Introduction to Practicall Musicke*, London, 1597
Morgenstern, Sam, *Composers on Music*, Pantheon, New York, 1956
Morton, J. B., ['Beachcomber'], *By The Way*, Sheed & Ward, London, 1932
- *A Diet of Thistles*, Cape, London, 1938
- *Gallimaufry*, Cape, London, 1936
  (All by courtesy of the Peters Fraser and Dunlop Group Ltd)
Moscheles, Charlotte, *Aus Moscheles Leben*, Leipzig, 1872 (English version by A. D. Coleridge, *Life of Moscheles*, London, 1873)
Mozart, Wolfgang Amadeus, and Leopold, letters, all trans. in Anderson, Emily, *The Letters of Mozart and his Family*, q.v.
Münchner Volksbote, 1865, quoted in Blom, Eric, *The Music Lover's Miscellany*, q.v.
Muir, Frank, *The Frank Muir Book*, Heinemann, London, 1976
Musical World, The, article on Liszt, 1841, quoted in Blom, Eric, *The Music Lover's Miscellany*, q.v.

Newton, Ivor, *At the Piano*, Hamish Hamilton, London, 1966
Newman, Ernest, *Wagner as Man and Artist*, Dent, London, 1914
Niecks, Frederick, *Frederick Chopin as a Man and Musician*, Novello, Ewer & Co., London, 1888
Nietzsche, Friedrich, *Nietzsche contra Wagner*, Berlin, 1888, quoted in Barzun, Jacques, *The Pleasures of Music*, q.v.
Norris, Gerald, *Stanford, the Cambridge Jubilee and Tchaikovsky*, David & Charles, London, 1980
North, The Hon. Roger, *The Musicall Grammarian*, 1728, unpublished at his death; extracts ed. John Wilson in *Roger North on Music*, Novello, London, 1959

Oakes, Philip, *From Middle England – a Memory of the 1930s and 1940s*, Penguin, London, 1980
O'Shaughnessy, Arthur, 'Ode', 1874

Parker, John Rowe, *A Musical Biography*, 1824, reprinted by Detroit Reprints in Music Information Coordinators, Detroit, 1975
Parsley, Osbert, memorial to, in Norwich Cathedral
Pater, Walter, 'The School of Giorgione', in *The Renaissance*, 1873
Peacham, Henry, *The Compleat Gentleman*, 1622
Pepys, Samuel, *Diary*, 1825, (modern ed., R. Latham & W. Matthews, Bell & Hyman, London, 1970–83)
Pitoëff, Liudmilla, *Souvenirs Intimes*, 1945, trans. and paraphrased in Stravinsky, Vera, and Craft, Robert, *Stravinsky in Pictures and Documents*, q.v.
Plamenac, Dragan, 'New light on the last years of Carl Philipp Emanuel Bach', in *The Musical Quarterly*, XXXV, October 1949

Plato, *The Republic*, c. 400 B.C. (quotes Socrates quoting Damon of Athens)
Po Chü-i, 'The Old Lute', *see* Waley, Arthur
Poe, Edgar Allan, *Israfel*, 1836
Pope, Alexander, 'On Mrs Tofts', from *The Poems, Epistles and Satires of Alexander Pope*, Dent, Everyman, London n.d.
– *Essay on Criticism*, 1711, *ibid*
Porter, Peter, 'Poems for Music' No. 3, in *A Porter Folio*, Oxford, 1969
– *The Cost of Seriousness*, Oxford, 1978
– *Poems Ancient and Modern*, Oxford, 1964
– *Preaching to the Converted*, Oxford, 1972
Praetorius, Michael, *Syntagma Musicum*, 1619, quoted in Blom, Eric, *The Music Lover's Miscellany*, q.v.
Prod'homme, J. G., 'Claude Achille Debussy', in *The Musical Quarterly*, vol. IV No. 4, October 1918
Pulver, Jeffrey, *Paganini*, Herbert Joseph, London, 1936
Purcell, Henry, Dedication of *Dioclesian*, 1690
– Epitaph in Westminster Abbey, 1695
Pushkin, Alexander, *Mozart and Salieri*, trans. Antony Wood, Angel Books, revised edn, London, 1987 (By kind permission of Antony Wood)

Rachmaninoff, Sergei, quoted in Riesemann, Oskar von, *Rachmaninoff's Recollections*, Macmillan, New York, 1934
Rameau, Jean-Philippe, *Le nouveau système de musique théorique*, Paris, 1726
Raverat, Gwen, *Period Piece*, Faber & Faber, London, 1952; (USA) W. W. Norton Inc.
Reich, Nancy B., *Clara Schumann*, Gollancz, London, 1985
Reichardt, J. F., article, quoted in Graf, Max, *Composer and Critic*, q.v.
Reynolds, Gordon, *Organo Pleno*, Novello, London, 1970
Ries, Ferdinand, in Wegeler, Franz Gerhard, & Ries, Ferdinand, *Biographischen Notizen über L. von Beethoven*, 1838, quoted in Sonneck, O. G., *Beethoven: Impressions of Contemporaries*, q.v.
Rievaulx, Ailred Abbot of, *Speculum Charitatis*, 12th century, trans. William Prynne (1600–1669)
Rilke, Rainer Maria, 'To Music' in *Poems 1906–1926*, trans. J. B. Leishman, Penguin Books, London, 1964
Rimsky-Korsakov, N. A., *My Musical Life*, trans. J. A. Joffe, Secker & Warburg, London, 1924
Rivière, Jules, *My Musical Life and Recollections*, 1893, quoted in Norris, Gerald, *Stanford, The Cambridge Jubilee and Tchaikovsky*, q.v.
Rockstro, W. S., *The Life of George Frederick Handel*, London, 1883
Röckl, Sebastian, *Ludwig II und Richard Wagner*, Munich, 1903, quoted in Newman, Ernest, *Wagner as Man and Artist*, q.v.
Rolland, Romain, *Cahiers Romain Rolland*, 3, 'Richard Strauss et R. R.', Albin Michel, Paris, 1951, trans. Kensington Davison
Roosevelt, President F. D., quoted in *Reader's Digest*, 1938
Roth, Ernest, *The Business of Music*, Cassell, London, 1969
Rosen, Charles, review of *The New Grove* in *New York Review of Books*, 28 May 1981
Rossini, Gioacchino,
– two letters in *Lettere di G. R. raccolte e annotate a cura di G. Mazzatinti & F. & G. Manis*, Firenze, 1902, trans. MR
– *Petite Messe Solennelle*, 1863, dedication, trans. MR

– on Paganini, quoted in Pulver, Jeffrey, *Paganini*, q.v.
– reported in a letter to Ignaz Moscheles, q. v.
Rostropovich, Mstislav, quoted in *The Gramophone*, September 1986
Rubinstein, Arthur, *My Many Years*, Cape, London, 1980
Ruskin, John, letter, 1882, quoted in Blom, Eric, *The Music Lover's Miscellany*, q.v.

Sainsbury, John S., *A Dictionary of Musicians from the Earliest Times*, original ed.
    London, 1825, reprinted Da Capo Press, New York, 1966
Saint-Evrémond, Charles de Saint-Denis, letter to the Duke of Buckingham, 1678
Saint-Saëns, Camille, letter to C. Bellaigue, quoted in Morgenstern, Sam, *Composers on Music*, q.v.
Sand, George, *Histoire de ma vie*, 1854, quoted in Gal, Hans, *The Musician's World*, q.v.
– *ibid*, quoted in Niecks, Frederick, *Frederick Chopin as a Man and Musician*, q.v.
Sandoval, Prudencio de, quoted in Burney, Charles, *History of Music*, q.v.
Sassoon, Siegfried, 'Concert-interpretation' from *Satirical Poems*, Heinemann,
    London, 1926
– *Picture Show*, privately printed, Cambridge, 1919
    (Both by kind permission of George Sassoon); (USA) from the *Collected Poems* by
    Siegfried Sassoon © 1918, 1920 by E. P. Dutton & Co., 1936, 1946, 1947, 1948 by
    Siegfried Sassoon. All rights reserved. Reprinted by permission of Viking Penguin,
    a division of Penguin Books USA, Inc.
Schachtner, J. A., letter to Maria Anna von Berchtold zu Sonnenburg, 24 April 1792,
    quoted in Deutsch, Otto Erich, *Mozart, A Documentary Biography*, A. & C. Black,
    London, 1965
Schindler, Anton, *Biographie von Ludwig van Beethoven*, 2nd edn. Münster, 1860,
    quoted in Sonneck, O. G., *Beethoven: Impressions of Contemporaries*, q.v.
Schoenberg, Arnold, *Style and Idea*, Williams & Norgate, London, 1951
Scholes, Percy, *The Oxford Companion to Music*, 4th edn, Oxford University Press, 1942
Schubert, Franz (namesake), letter, 1817, trans. MR
Schulz, Edward, article in *The Harmonicon*, q.v.
Schumann, Clara, diaries, quoted in Reich, Nancy B., *Clara Schumann*, q.v.
Schumann, Robert, articles in the *Allgemeine musikalische Zeitung*, quoted in Graf,
    Max, *Composer and Critic*, q.v.
Schwarzkopf, Elisabeth, *On and Off the Record – A Memoir of Walter Legge*, Faber &
    Faber, London, 1982 (By kind permission of the author); (USA) by permission of
    Charles Scribner's Sons, an imprint of Macmillan Publishing Company © 1982
    Musical Adviser Establishment
Selden, John, *Table-Talk*, 1689
Seu-ma-tsen, quoted in Stravinsky, Igor, *The Poetics of Music*, q.v.
Shakespeare, William
– *Twelfth Night*, 1623
– *The Merchant of Venice*, 1600
– *Richard II*, 1597
– *Much Ado About Nothing*, 1600
Shaw, George Bernard, review, 23 January 1889, in *London Music in 1888–9 as heard by
    Corno di Bassetto*, Constable, London, 1937
– on brandy, in *Man and Superman*, Constable, London, 1903
– on Liszt, in the *Pall Mall Gazette*, 2 August 1886
– *Music in London 1890–94*, vols. I–III, Constable, London, 1932
    (All reprinted by permission of the Society of Authors on behalf of the Bernard
    Shaw Estate)

– letter to *The Times*, 3 July 1905, reprinted in *How to Become a Musical Critic*, ed. Dan H. Laurence, Rupert Hart-Davies, London, 1960

Shead, Richard, *Constant Lambert*, Simon Publications, London, 1973

Sitwell, Osbert, *Great Morning*, Macmillan, London, 1948

Slonimsky, Nicolas, *Music Since 1900*, 4th ed. Cassell, London, 1971

Smith, Logan Pearsall, 'The Concerto' in *More Trivia*, Constable, London, 1921

Smith, Sydney, August 1844, letter to the Countess of Carlisle

Smollett, Tobias, *Humphrey Clinker*, 1771

Smyth, Ethel, *Impressions that Remained*, Longmans, Green, London, 1919

Sonneck, O. G., *Beethoven: Impressions of Contemporaries*, G. Schirmer, New York, 1927

Southerne, Thomas, *The Maid's Last Prayer*, 1693

Specht, Richard, *Johannes Brahms*, trans. Eric Blom, Dent, London, 1930

Speyer, Edward, *My Life and Friends*, Cobden Sanderson, London, 1937

Spohr, Louis, *Selbstbiographie*, 1860–61, trans. anon., *Autobiography*, Longman, Green, Longman, Roberts & Green, London, 1865

Stanford, Charles Villiers, *Pages from an Unwritten Diary*, Edward Arnold, London, 1914

– *Studies and Memories*, Archibald Constable, London, 1908

Steele, Richard, letter in *The Spectator*, 25 October 1711

Stendhal, *Vie de Rossini*, 1824, trans. R. N. Coe, *Life of Rossini*, Calder, London, 1956

Strauss, Richard, quoted in Rolland, Romain, *Cahier's Romain Rolland*, 3, q.v.

– *Betrachtungen und Erinnerungen*, Atlantis, Zurich, 1949 trans. L. J. Lawrence, *Recollections and Reflections*, Boosey & Hawkes, London, 1953

Stravinsky, Igor, *Chroniques de ma vie*, Paris, 1935, trans. as *An Autobiography*, Simon & Schuster, New York, 1936

– *Poétique musicale*, Cambridge, Mass., 1942, trans. A. Knodel & Ingolf Dahl as *The Poetics of Music*, Oxford & London, 1947

Stravinsky, Igor, and Craft, Robert, *Conversations with Igor Stravinsky*, Faber & Faber, London, 1959

– *Expositions and Developments*, Faber & Faber, London, 1962;
Both (USA) by permission of the University of California © 1959, 1960, 1961, 1962 Igor Stravinsky

Stravinsky, Vera, and Craft, Robert, *Stravinsky in Pictures and Documents*, Hutchinson, London, 1979

Sullivan, J. W. N., *Beethoven: his Spiritual Development*, Cape, London, 1927

Tallis, Thomas, epitaph in Greenwich Old Church (destroyed about 1720) quoted in Jacobs, Arthur, *Music Lover's Anthology*, q.v.

Taylor, John, *Records of my Life*, London, 1832

Tchaikovsky, Modeste, *The Life and Letters of Peter Ilich Tchaikovsky*, trans. and ed. Rosa Newmarch, John Lane, Bodley Head, London, 1906

Tchaikovsky, Peter Ilich, letter to Nadezhda von Meck, 2 February 1878, version revised MR

– *Diaries*, Moscow, 1923 (English version by W. Lakond, Norton, New York, 1945)

Tennyson, Alfred, Lord, 'The Brook', *Enoch Arden and other Poems*, 1864

Thomson, Virgil, *The Art of Judging Music*, Knopf, New York, 1948 (By kind permission of the author)

Tolstoy, Leo, *The Kreutzer Sonata*, Moscow, 1889, trans. Aylmer Maude, Humphrey Milford, London, 1924

Turgenev, Ivan, *A House of Gentlefolk*, Moscow, 1859, trans. Constance Garnett, Heinemann, London, 1894–99

– *On the Eve*, 1859, trans. Gilbert Gardiner, Penguin, London, 1950

Twain, Mark, 'At the Shrine of St Wagner' in *New York Sun*, 1891
– quoted in Hogwood, Christopher, *Music at Court*, q.v.

Verdi, Giuseppe, letter, 21 January 1852, quoted in Walker, Frank, *The Man Verdi*, q.v.
– letter, quoted in Graf, Max, *Composer and Critic*, q.v.
– letter to Salvatore Cammarano, 23 November 1848, from *I Copialettere di Giuseppe Verdi*, ed. G. Cesari & A. Luzio, Milan, 1913, trans. MR
– quoted in Cellamare, Daniele, *Umberto Giordano*, q.v.
– correspondence with Prospero Bertani, quoted in Pougin, Arthur, *Verdi, histoire anecdotique de sa vie et de ses oeuvres*, Paris, 1886, trans. J. E. Matthew, Grevel, London, 1887
Villard-Gilles, Jean, 'Souvenirs du Diable' in *Homage à C. F. Ramuz*, quoted in White, E. W., *Stravinsky, The Composer and his Works*, q.v.

Wagner, Richard
– two letters to Robert von Hornstein, 1861, quoted in Newman, Ernest, *Wagner as Man and Artist*, q.v.
– *The Bayreuth Letters of Richard Wagner*, trans. and ed. Caroline V. Kerr, Nisbet, London, nd [1912]
– *Über das Dirigieren*, 1869, trans. William Ashton Ellis, 'About Conducting', in *Richard Wagner's Prose Works*, vol. IV, Kegan Paul, Trench, Trübner, London, 1912
Waley, Arthur, *Chinese Poems*, George Allen & Unwin, London, 1946
Walker, Frank, 'Francesco Durante' in *Grove's Dictionary*, 5th edn, q.v.
– *The Man Verdi*, Dent, London, 1962
Walpole, Horace, letter to Richard West, 1739, quoted in Blom, Eric, *The Music Lover's Miscellany*, q.v.
Walton, Izaak, *The Life of Mr. George Herbert*, 1675
Warrack, Guy, *Sherlock Holmes and Music*, Faber & Faber, London, 1947
Watts, Isaac, *Hymns*, 1707
Weber, Carl Maria von, review, 1817, in *Sämtliche Schriften*, Berlin, 1908, trans. Martin Cooper, in *Carl Maria von Weber, Writings on Music*, ed. J. Warrack, Cambridge, 1981
Wechsberg, Joseph, *Looking for a Bluebird*, Michael Joseph, London, 1946
White, E. W., *Stravinsky, A Critical Survey*, John Lehmann, London, 1947
– *Stravinsky, The Composer and his Works*, Faber & Faber, London, 1966
Wille, Eliza, *Fünfzehn Briefe von Richard Wagner. Nebst Erinnerungen von Eliza Wille*, Berlin, 1894, quoted in Zoff, Otto, *Great Composers*, q.v.
Windebank, Sir Francis, letter, quoted in Blom, Eric, *The Music Lover's Miscellany*, q.v.
Wodehouse, P. G., *Jeeves and the Song of Songs*, from *Very Good Jeeves!* Herbert Jenkins, London, 1930; by permission of A. P. Watt Ltd on behalf of The Trustees of the Wodehouse Trust no. 3; (British Commonwealth and Canada) Century Hutchinson
Wordsworth, William, 'The Solitary Reaper', from *A Tour in Scotland*, 1803
Wyndham Lewis, D. B., and Lee, Charles, *The Stuffed Owl*, Dent, London, 1930

Zoff, Otto, *Great Composers*, Dutton, New York, 1951; translations by Phoebe Rogoff Cave

Index